Juvenile Offending

Crime and Punishment: Critical Essays in Legal Philosophy
Series Editor: Thom Brooks

Titles in the Series:

Retribution
Thom Brooks

Deterrence
Thom Brooks

Shame Punishment
Thom Brooks

Juvenile Offending
Thom Brooks

Sentencing
Thom Brooks

Juvenile Offending

Edited by

Thom Brooks

University of Durham, UK

ASHGATE

Published by
Ashgate Publishing Limited
Wey Court East
Union Road
Farnham
Surrey GU9 7PT
England

Ashgate Publishing Company
110 Cherry Street
Suite 3-1
Burlington, VT 05401-3818
USA

www.ashgate.com

British Library Cataloguing in Publication Data.
A catalogue record for this book is available from the British Library.

The Library of Congress has cataloged the printed edition as follows: 2013949704

ISBN 9781409451235

MIX
Paper from responsible sources
FSC www.fsc.org FSC® C013985

Printed in the United Kingdom by Henry Ling Limited,
at the Dorset Press, Dorchester, DT1 1HD

Contents

PART IV YOUTH OFFENDERS AND RESTORATIVE JUSTICE

Acknowledgements

Ashgate would like to thank our researchers and the contributing authors who provided copies, along with the following for their permission to reprint copyright material.

James M. Frabutt, Kristen L. Di Luca and Kelly N. Graves for the essay: James M. Frabutt, Kristen L. Di Luca and Kelly N. Graves (2008), 'Envisioning a Juvenile Justice System That Supports Positive Youth Development', *Notre Dame Journal of Law, Ethics and Public Policy*, **22**, pp. 107–25.

John Wiley and Sons for the essay: David O'Mahony and Jonathan Doak (2004), 'Restorative Justice – Is More Better? The Experience of Police-led Restorative Cautioning Pilots in Northern Ireland', *Howard Journal of Criminal Justice*, **43**, pp. 484–505. Copyright © 2004 Blackwell Publishing Ltd.

Nottingham Trent University for the essay: David O'Mahony (2012), 'Restorative Justice and Youth Justice in England and Wales: One Step Forward, Two Steps Back', *Nottingham Law Journal*, **21**, pp. 86–106.

Oxford University Press for the essay: Tali Gal and Shomron Moyal (2011), 'Juvenile Victims in Restorative Justice: Findings from the Reintegrative Shaming Experiments', *British Journal of Criminology*, **51**, pp. 1014–34. Copyright © 2011 Tali Gal and Shomron Moyal. Reprinted by permission of Oxford University Press.

Queen's Law Journal for the essay: Carla Cesaroni and Nicholas Bala (2008), 'Deterrence as a Principle of Youth Sentencing: No Effect on Youth, but a Significant Effect on Judges', *Queen's Law Journal*, **34**, pp. 447–81.

Rutgers Law Review for the essay: Alison Powers (2009), 'Cruel and Unusual Punishment: Mandatory Sentencing of Juveniles Tried as Adults without the Possibility of Youth as a Mitigating Factor', *Rutgers Law Review*, **62**, pp. 241–68.

SAGE Publications for the essays: Shawn D. Bushway and Anne Morrison Piehl (2007), 'The Inextricable Link between Age and Criminal History in Sentencing', *Crime and Delinquency*, **53**, pp. 156–83. Copyright © 2007 SAGE Publications. Reprinted by permission of SAGE Publications; Jo Phoenix (2010), 'Pre-Sentence Reports, Magisterial Discourse and Agency in the Youth Courts in England and Wales', *Punishment and Society*, **12**, pp. 348–66. Copyright © 2010 Jo Phoenix. Reprinted by permission of SAGE Publications.

Taylor and Francis Books UK for the essays: Stephen Case and Kevin Haines (2009), 'Hunting for the Universal Risk Factor', in *Understanding Youth Offending: Risk Factor Research, Policy and Practice*, Cullompton: Willan, pp. 192–255. Copyright © 2009 Stephen Case and Kevin Haines; Monica Barry (2006), 'Power and Powerlessness in Transition', in *Youth*

Publisher's Note

The material in this volume has been reproduced using the facsimile method. This means we can retain the original pagination to facilitate easy and correct citation of the original essays. It also explains the variety of typefaces, page layouts and numbering.

Series Preface

Crime and punishment grip the imagination and concerns of both the public and policymakers raising several serious challenges. Can punishment be justified? If so, then what purpose (or purposes) does it have? Which practices best cohere with this purpose(s)? These and many other questions are addressed with rigour and insight in this new book series.

Crime and Punishment: Critical Essays in Legal Philosophy comprises an authoritative and comprehensive set of five volumes reprinting the most influential essays by leading international figures engaged in this field. Each volume is organized thematically with a general introduction to provide an accessible launching pad to the latest research.

The first volume is on *Retribution.* This approach to punishment is widely held to be the oldest such view. Retributivists traditionally claim that punishment must be deserved and proportionate to what is deserved. This volume of essays covers several topics, including desert, proportionality, retributivist emotions, capital punishment and mercy. The second volume is a collection of essays about what is often regarded as the second oldest theory of punishment: *Deterrence.* This is the idea that punishment is justified by its effectiveness at deterring potential future offenders from committing crime. Topics covered include deterrence and crime reduction, incapacitation and the death penalty.

The next two volumes focus on particular issues. The third volume examines the latest research into *Shame Punishment.* Shame punishments are understood in multiple ways, such as an attempt to improve crime reduction through deterrence or as an effort at moral education. This volume covers topics such as shame and desert, shaming and dignity, shame and deterrence, and shame and restorative justice. The fourth volume is *Juvenile Offending* and it considers whether we should punish offenders differently because of their age as well as how this might be best achieved. Topics included are risk factors, the justification of punishing youth differently from adults and restorative justice for juvenile offenders.

The final fifth volume is about punishment as imprisonment: *Sentencing.* This volume examines sentencing in theory and practice, the Model Penal Code and use of sentencing guidelines, punitive restoration and the unified theory of punishment and alternatives to sentencing.

This *Crime and Punishment: Critical Essays in Legal Philosophy* book series covers exciting and innovative contemporary work by the leading international figures in the field today writing on retribution, deterrence, shame punishment, youth offending and sentencing. Each essay has been carefully selected for inclusion to ensure the seminal work available in English is brought together in one series for easy reference by students, practitioners, scholars and the general public.

THOM BROOKS
Series Editor
Reader in Law, Durham Law School, Durham University

Introduction

Introduction

Juvenile offending has attracted increasing attention. Interestingly, the idea of the juvenile offender is relatively recent even if underage criminals have existed since time immemorial. This is because to be a 'juvenile' or 'youth' offender that person must be under a certain age, such as 18 years old. This would require some means of confirming the age of offenders and adequate birth records making this possible. The compulsory registration of births was not introduced until 1836 and so it was not until the 1850s that birth certificates were generally available for the purpose of determining whether someone qualified as a 'juvenile' (Brooks, Chapter 3, p. 97).

There has been greater attention to juvenile offenders today with the recognition that many of the youth offenders of today become the adult offenders of tomorrow: tackling juvenile offending has become a key part of crime reduction strategies. Getting juvenile justice right is important both now and in the future. But how? Youth offenders have different needs and share perspectives that are often at odds with adults. What are these differences? Should we treat some offenders differently from others because of their age? What effects and policy changes should we recommend? This book brings together the leading work on juvenile offending from the dominant international figures in the field. Juvenile offending is examined from various critical perspectives, including the identification of risk factors, issues surrounding the sentencing of juvenile offenders and their punishment more generally, and the relevance of restorative justice.

This introduction will consider each of these topics with primary reference to the important contributions to our thinking about juvenile offending carefully selected for inclusion in this collection. This survey of leading work will highlight the key debates and issues pertaining to contemporary research about juvenile offending.

Youth Offending and Risk Factors

What are the risk factors for youth offending? If we are able to best identify these factors, then it might make efforts to tackle youth offending more effective. Stephen Case and Kevin Haines (Chapter 1) examine what, if any, factors might serve as *the* universal risk factor in a critical survey of cross-national research (or what they abbreviate as 'RFR': 'Risk Factor Research'). One approach is to consider factors that might be *predictive* of future offending relating to family, school, neighbourhood and community, peer group and individual issues (such as hyperactivity and low attainment). Another approach is to focus on causal risk factors (or 'mechanisms') categorized as the individual (for example, cognitive impairment, distorted social information), the psychosocial (for example, abusive childhood, unemployment) and the societywide (for example, exposure to film violence, truancy).

Ultimately, Case and Haines are doubtful there is any universal risk factor for youth offending. This argument is based upon the wide diversity they claim exists in the prevalent research. There is sufficient disunity, in their view, to warrant scepticism that any single or shared set of factors holds true. Instead, our focus should be more precise and recognize that risk factors may vary widely across different communities and states.

This perspective is challenged by Monica Barry (Chapter 2). She argues there is a distinctive starting point concerning the idea of *recognition* that has importance. Barry notes that 'youth' occupy a developmental stage between childhood and adulthood. Children are those persons who lack any legal responsibilities and adults are those that possess full legal responsibilities, all things considered. Youth are in the space between these legal extremes. Barry argues that the key is focusing not on chronological age, but youth as a developmental stage where problems in this transition may often translate into risk factors for criminal offending. Broadly speaking, juveniles struggle to some degree for recognition in their transition to adulthood. Juveniles might be understood as 'transitional beings' normally lacking permanent obligations or expectations beyond their immediate coterie of friends and family (p. 87). Youth seek recognition as a source of affirmation that helps them steer the choppy waters of transition. If we want to tackle juvenile offending, then we must examine this source closely. There is a real need to get this right, too. Barry notes that offending is to some degree the province of the young: much crime is committed by youth and persons active in criminal activity since their youth often tapering off as they age. So improving crime reduction efforts in relation to youth offenders is not simply a matter of reducing offending by juveniles, but perhaps offending by all.

This model is developed further by Thom Brooks (Chapter 3) who offers a universal risk factor for youth and adults alike. Lists of risk factors lack any obvious normative coherence. Researchers identify risk factors such as low attainment or unemployment and then recommend policy-makers focus on improving attainment and employability to reduce offending. And this can have beneficial effects and so the cycle continues. But it is often pointed out that there seems something odd about this. For example, many communities (at least in Britain) struggled during the Second World War, but yet criminal offending was not considered to be the problem it is today where British society is more affluent. Perhaps risk factors change over time, but are they mere signs that pop in and out of criminological existence like quarks? Or is there a richer, more normative coherence that can be given to risk factors to help explain and justify why some and not others might help inform how we tackle offending?

Brooks (see also Brooks, forthcoming) argues that *stakeholding* is a key concept that does this explanatory work. It is not merely that a person has risk factors such as financial insecurity, housing insecurity, unemployment and other factors (often interlinked) that explains why he or she may be at some real risk of future offending. Instead, it is a question of whether or not individuals see themselves as having a stake in society. The hypothesis by Brooks is that the more likely individuals are to see themselves as having a stake – or seeing themselves as 'stakeholders' – the less likely they will be to engage in unlawful activity. What explains this is to see oneself as a stakeholder is to have the judgement that it is more desirable to work within the current system than not. Persons who lack risk factors are individuals who have mortgages, pursue careers and possess pensions: they are people who have a stake in the society and much to lose (and not only materially) by engaging in criminality.

This idea of stakeholding is a development of Hegel's theory of the rabble.[1] For Hegel, the rabble posed a significant challenge for modern society. The rabble is often the most poor, but they can also be found among the most wealthy. The core factor is not material wealth, but their mind-set. For Hegel, the problem of the rabble for modern society is that they are a group that fail to see the political community as a home: the state and its laws are like an other to them and alien. Of course, it is necessary that the society be a place worth living in and this requires that various needs and concerns are satisfied. Nonetheless, stakeholding is about a belief that the state is a place more worth working within than without where I, the individual, believe I have a stake in its future. We might reduce the risk factors, but not address the true, substantive feature behind most offending. The remaining challenge is that it may be far easier to make policies that address individual risk factors than it is to change hearts and minds. But it is the latter that might yield the biggest prize.

Punishment and Juvenile Offenders

Should juvenile offenders be punished *differently* from adult offenders? The traditional answer is 'yes' and favours rehabilitation over retribution. The argument is that youth are less responsible for their crimes because of their age and so they should not be treated as fully autonomous adults. Juveniles are in transition to adulthood and most likely to benefit from reformative intervention. Or so it is thought. One implication is that youth and adults are treated very differently despite committing the same types of offences. If like cases should be treated alike, then juvenile offenders may raise serious concerns about equal treatment.

Brooks argues that our traditional ways of thinking about juvenile offenders require serious reform. One reason is that most theories of punishment have real problems with youth justice. For example, deterrence proponents argue that punishment is justified where it deters future offenders. The state issues a threat to the general public and this can and should be designed so this helps potential future offenders reconsider their actions and desist from crime. The problem is that this assumes a one-size-fits-all model of penal deterrence. Even if deterrence were possible and measurable, threats are known to have very different effects on youth and adults. Furthermore, deterrence proponents might only create public confusion if different kinds of threats are attached to the same types of offences.

Retribution also runs into difficulties. Retributivists argue that punishment must be deserved and proportionate to what is deserved. Retributivist desert is determined in relation to the moral responsibility an offender has for some evil. So perhaps juvenile offenders should be punished less severely than many adults because youth may lack full autonomy, but likewise so might many adults. It is unclear if and how retributivists might account for youth justice and the distinctive needs of youth offenders.

Brooks (2012) defends a 'unified' theory of punishment. The unified theory brings together multiple penal purposes in a single, coherent sentencing framework. The criminal law is understood as one (and not the only) effort to secure and protect our rights. Crimes are not mere illegality, but violations of rights of self and others. Punishment is a response to crime that aims at the restoration of rights through ensuring their security and future maintenance. Some violations of rights are more problematic than others because some are more central

---

1 See Brooks (forthcoming) on Hegel's political philosophy more generally.

than others or because other rights are dependent upon them. We punish murder more than theft because murder is a violation of a more important right or set of rights as judged by that community. The unified theory of punishment can justify roles for desert, penal proportionality, deterrence, rehabilitation and restoration among other penal principles in a coherent framework where we punish crimes as rights violations to the degree necessary to protect and maintain the rights infringed.

One model of the unified theory of punishment in practice is *punitive restoration.* Standard use of restorative justice as an alternative to trial and punishment is that victims and offenders meet with a trained facilitator who helps foster a constructive dialogue leading to a contract to be agreed by the offender that is punishment tailored to his needs. These contracts typically require offenders to undertake drug and alcohol treatment, community service and the reparative payment to the offender in addition to an apology. Restorative justice has been shown to lead to improvements in crime reduction rates, greater satisfaction rates for offenders and victims alike, and all at significant savings in costs. One limitation with restorative justice is that it is normally reserved for minor offences by minors. Punitive restoration expands the range of penal possibilities to include short imprisonment (and, hence, include a more punitive element than traditional restorative accounts) and mandates the use of restorative conferencing where members of the public participate in the discussion also (see Brooks, forthcoming).

The unified theory of punishment is a context-sensitive approach. This is because any punishment must help secure and maintain the rights violated by a crime. Punishment must be tailored to offenders to enable the restoration and protection of rights for all. This framework offers us a penal theory that can account for differences in offenders. For example, the protection of rights will require variations in our response to offending best designed to reduce future offending to protect rights.

Juvenile Offending and Sentencing

This part examines research on the sentencing of juvenile offenders. Shawn D. Bushway and Anne Morrison Piehl (Chapter 4) focus on the link between age and sentencing. They argue that the age of an offender is an important variable in sentencing policy regularly overlooked. Age has importance because sentencing laws often specify greater punishment for reoffenders and older individuals are more likely than younger individuals to have a criminal history because of their ages. The problem is that people are not treated alike: offenders performing the same crime may be treated differently because of variance in their ages.

Of course, whether or not this is problematic will depend to some degree on which penal theory is endorsed. For example, a retributivist who believes criminals should be punished when deserved to the degree deserved would find this a problem. Retributivists have traditionally argued against noting past offences in sentencing because these are factors separate from the present offence (and for which just deserts may have been paid). However, a proponent of deterrence might argue that older criminals who continue to reoffend might be treated differently (and more harshly) than younger offenders, but this is warranted by the need to act further to secure macro-deterrence (or 'general' deterrence). Or a proponent of rehabilitation might argue that older offenders require different and greater treatment because more must be done to ensure their rehabilitation.

Carla Cesaroni and Nicholas Bala (Chapter 5) examine the use of deterrence as a rationale for youth offenders. They reveal several interesting facts in their study of youth sentencing in Canada. The first is that the severity of punishment for crimes committed by youths has relatively minor effects. This is because youth are less likely to consider likelihood of apprehension and possible consequences for their actions. A second fact they uncover is that the views held by judges about deterrence were more likely to influence sentences than the nature of the offence. Cesaroni and Bala note that deterrence is traditionally not associated with youth offenders: juveniles are often thought not to be fully autonomous and so cost–benefit analysis, such as assumed by deterrence models, are considered inapplicable. This is further supported by the fact deterrence may have little effect in shaping youth behaviour. Deterrence has not been a principle for youth sentencing before and ought not to be incorporated in any new sentencing guidelines.

James M. Frabutt, Kristen L. Di Luca and Kelly N. Graves (Chapter 6) examine the US juvenile justice system arguing that it requires urgent reforms. They call for a more robust approach consisting of a wider focus and commitment to treatment, rehabilitation and, ultimately, restoration with special attention paid to mental health issues. Frabutt and colleagues also argue for improvements with the transition process from incarceration to community, a critical time to secure future desistance. Community-based programmes should become more evidence-based and cost-effective.

Alison Powers (Chapter 7) considers the issue of trials and punishments for juveniles treated as adults. Many jurisdictions permit juveniles to be tried as if they are adults in limited circumstances. These exceptions often include particularly violent crimes, such as murder and/or offences undertaken using guns. It is a curiosity that juveniles may, in exceptional circumstances, be tried and sentenced as if an adult only for the most violent crimes and never others. If it is possible for a juvenile to show sufficient responsibility, then why not for more crimes? The implication here is that what is doing the work is not the presence (or absence) of personal responsibility, but rather a reaction to the violent conduct. (Note that a unified theory of punishment discussed above can address this problem: if our focus is on the protection of rights, then this might justify exceptional measures in special cases where these measures are necessary for securing the protection of rights.)

It is a further curiosity that juveniles are then unable to include their being underage as a mitigating factor if sentenced. If tried as an adult, then they are to be sentenced as if adults and so other factors, such as their not being an adult, cannot figure. Powers argues this is a clear mistake that should be corrected.

Jo Phoenix (Chapter 8) interviewed Youth Court magistrates to determine which strategies concerning risk governance had an effect on their decision-making. She exposes the complex relationship between the agency of magistrates in making decisions in individual cases and the more general youth justice policies focusing on risk management. Phoenix argues that, contrary to what we might expect, magisterial decision-making is framed by the claims of magistrates that they are 'knowing outsiders' (and not expert assessors of risk) able to provide objective judgements about risk assessment from the evidence uncovered in cases before them and their own life experiences.

Youth Offenders and Restorative Justice

One invaluable approach to addressing youth offending is restorative justice. This approach is broadly an alternative to traditional sentencing. Instead of subjecting offenders to a formal trial and the possibility of hard treatment, restorative justice is about constructive dialogue between victims and offenders to promote restorative healing. Offenders receive punishment more targeted to their needs, such as drug and alcohol treatment and cognitive behavioural therapy, normally held in tandem with a community sentence and a requirement to pay some means or reparation to victims all to be agreed by the offender in a restorative contract. It has been found that restorative justice can bring about improved crime reduction at significantly lower costs.

Restorative justice has been primarily used for youth offenders. One reason is that the traditional rehabilitative focus with youth punishment makes these offenders more palatable for restorative outcomes. A second reason is that restorative justice is most often an option for offenders who have no previous convictions and have committed relatively minor offences which suits youth offenders well.

David O'Mahony and Jonathan Doak (Chapter 9) examine restorative justice schemes in Northern Ireland. The schemes introduced new police-led restorative cautioning pilots. While they offer some advantages over traditional cautioning schemes, O'Mahoney and Doak argue there remains more work to be done. One problem was 'net-widening' whereby some offenders appear to have been brought into the scheme unnecessarily. A second problem was that significant resources were required to ensure victims participated. They argue that the greater use of restorative justice for youth offenders is to be encouraged, but it must be better designed to secure restorative outcomes.

Tali Gal and Shomrom Moyal (Chapter 10) argue that restorative justice is to be welcomed as a more popular alternative to the court for both victims and offenders. But one problem they uncover is that juvenile victims were more likely to be satisfied with the court than the restorative conference setting. Gal and Moyal claim that restorative practices must provide better protections against adult domination of proceedings and insensitivity to the needs of youth victims. Restorative justice can flourish, but more care must be exhibited in its implementation.

This book concludes with David O'Mahony's (Chapter 11) examination of the emergence and impact of restorative justice practices on juvenile justice in England and Wales in a critical survey of real significance. O'Mahoney notes the major inroads restorative justice has made in cases of low-level offending and first-time offenders and identifies ways in which restorative justice has become incorporated by other jurisdictions as part of a mainstream approach to sentencing.

Conclusion

Juvenile offending is a problem that raises distinctive challenges to tackling adult offenders and these challenges can have long-standing effects: the youth offenders of today are often the adult offenders of tomorrow. But what is a juvenile? Why should juveniles be treated differently than adults? If they should be treated differently, then how should this take shape in practice? These and other questions remain hotly contested. This collection brings together the leading critical work on juvenile offending. These essays seek to deepen our collective understanding of this important subject-matter pertaining to punishment to shed greater light on future possibilities about how we might improve our comprehension of and ability to address juvenile offending.

References

Brooks, Thom (2012), 'Unified Theory', in *Punishment.* New York: Routledge, pp. 123–48. Also in *Sentencing*, ed. Thom Brooks, Farnham: Ashgate, 2014, pp. 417–48.

Brooks, Thom (forthcoming), 'Stakeholder Sentencing', in J.V. Roberts and J. Ryberg (eds), *Popular Punishment: On the Normative Significance of Public Opinion for Penal Theory*, Oxford: Oxford University Press. Also in *Sentencing*, ed. Thom Brooks, Farnham: Ashgate, 2014, pp. 449–465.

Part I
Youth Offending and Risk Factors

[1]

Hunting for the universal risk factor

Stephen Case and Kevin Haines

RFR in England and Wales has been limited in its attempts to progress understandings of the aetiology of offending and to inform preventative and ameliorative policy and practice due to a group of common, unresolved methodological paradoxes. Typically, definitive and simplistic conclusions have been drawn regarding the existence and nature of risk and the nature of its relationship with offending or antisocial behaviour, founded on methodologies and analyses too restricted to have supported such conclusions. Researchers conducting longitudinal and cross-sectional RFR have tended to convert potentially complex risk and protection information into quantifiable factors (in the case of protective factors, often simply dichotomised in relation to risk) which have been measured in relation to a generalised period of time (e.g. current life, the last 12 months, a specific developmental stage) and aggregated across large, homogenised samples of young people. This over-simplification and subsequent between-groups analysis has been preferred to measuring the onset and influence of risk relative to different forms of offending behaviour or by subjecting the data to analysis at the level of the individual young person. The body of factors measured have been labelled 'risk and protective factors' despite uncertainty about their temporal precedence over, or the nature and direction of their relationship with, offending and desistance. The factors created and analysed have reflected the psychosocial biases of the developmental strand of RFR and have largely overlooked socio-structural influences and constructivist explanations of risk and protection. This has resulted in a self-perpetuating artefact RFR literature seemingly intent on replicating a narrow group of psychosocial risk factors that are unrepresentative of the scope and complexity of risk influence or the characteristics and behaviours of the groups from which they have emanated. In contrast to the simplistic and practical (yet methodologically-flawed) artefact-based RFR, constructivist explanations of risk (e.g. the pathways approach) have appeared unconstructive, ethereal, impractical (although possibly more 'real') and unappealing to policy makers and practitioners seeking clear, simplistic and achievable solutions to youth offending. Thus RFR in England and Wales remains dominated by developmentalism and 'artefactualism'.

It is necessary, therefore, to look further afield towards the rapidly expanding corpus of international RFR to evaluate the extent to which the methodological limitations and biases demonstrated in England and Wales have been addressed and resolved, or simply exacerbated and further entrenched within RFR across the globe.

A series of theoretical and methodological questions must be asked of the most mainstream and widely-cited international RFR studies conducted by researchers with the highest profiles and reputations in the RFR field; questions which reflect those employed to evaluate the achievements of RFR studies in England and Wales:

- What has been the theoretical basis of the main studies and has this been compatible with the research design employed?
- How have data been collected and analysed, and what conclusions have been made regarding the prevalence, extent and nature of relationships between risk factors and offending by young people?
- Have these conclusions been justified/legitimised by the methodologies employed, the quality of the data and the nature of the analyses?
- Have the designs of RFR studies across the globe offered a sensitive, flexible and valid method of evolving RFR and our understanding of the concept of risk and risk factors?

Farrington (2000, 2007) claims that there has been a 'globalisation' of risk factor knowledge which has proliferated and facilitated cross-fertilisation between academics, policy-makers and practitioners from many different countries, such that RFR has become a prominent, if not the dominant, approach to explaining and preventing youth offending in, for example, England and Wales, Scotland, the US, Canada and New Zealand. An overarching question that must be addressed in this chapter, therefore, is to what extent this globalisation has relied on a theoretical, methodological, analytical and interpretive uniformity in order to identify the factor(s) that underpin offending by young people in all countries and that would provide a 'unified explanatory edifice' (D. Smith 2006) for youth offending. Has there been, as Case (2007) suggests, a tangible quest amongst risk factor researchers in the Western world to hunt down the 'holy grail' of the globalised, *universal* risk factor?

The pervasive influence and theoretical hegemony of developmental understandings of risk at the global level has been exemplified in two large scale reviews of international RFR: *Understanding and Preventing Youth Crime* (Farrington 1996) and *Antisocial Behaviour by Young People* (Rutter *et al.* 1998). Each of these ostensibly 'extensive' and 'comprehensive' reviews has privileged developmental studies of quantified psychosocial risk factors measured in childhood and allegedly predictive of later offending. These artefactual and psychosocial biases have emerged, in part, from the limited availability of alternative forms of RFR from which to select (creating an unavoidable selection bias), but they have also been a product of the developmental, psychological preferences of the authors.

Understanding and Preventing Youth Crime

The *Understanding and Preventing Youth Crime* review of empirical RFR in the Western world, conducted for the Joseph Rowntree Foundation in the UK by David Farrington, presented 'knowledge about the development, causes and prevention of youthful offending' (Farrington 1996: 46). The review was focused on what Farrington himself perceived to be the most 'methodologically adequate' RFR studies, which typically were those that utilised prospective longitudinal designs (particularly studies using several data sources, such as child, parent, teacher and peers). Farrington's methodological choices were made to enable him to explore a developmental view of the influence of childhood risk factors on future offending, on the basis of the assumption that 'there is no shortage of risk factors that significantly predict offending and antisocial behaviour' (Farrington 1996: 7).

Although Farrington defined a risk factor as that which predicts an increased (statistical) likelihood of later offending, he did not clarify whether longitudinal studies were chosen for review on the basis of an empirical demonstration of the predictive influence of risk factors. He did state, however, that the (static) variables of gender and ethnicity would not be reviewed 'because such factors have no practical implications for prevention' as they cannot be changed (Farrington 1996: 7). Cross-sectional studies were also excluded from the review on the basis that they were less able than longitudinal designs to measure the development of risk and protective factors over time and were more prone to 'mistaken assessments' that could not be resolved at a later stage in the study through repeated contacts that 'help to maximise validity' (Farrington 1996: 7). However, no other details were provided in the report regarding how many studies were reviewed, how they were chosen (e.g. what other criteria were used to assess a study to be 'methodologically adequate') and how different risk factors and offending had been defined, measured and analysed in each study (e.g. whether the methodologies and analyses were internally robust and externally comparable).

Understanding and Preventing Youth Crime findings and conclusions

Despite an absence of methodological and analytical detail, Farrington concluded that the most commonly-identified risk factors in his review were *predictive* of future offending and could be grouped into five domains:

- *Family* – prenatal and perinatal factors (e.g. teenage motherhood), poor parental supervision and discipline, low social economic status, parental conflict and separation.
- *School* – negative school influences (e.g. bullying), academic underachievement.
- *Neighbourhood/Community* – negative community influences (e.g. neighbourhood disorganisation, household overcrowding, physical deterioration of neighbourhood).
- *Peer group* – association with delinquent friends.
- *Individual* – personality (impulsivity, hyperactivity, restlessness), low intelligence and attainment.

(see Farrington 1996)

The review concluded that British longitudinal studies of delinquency had produced findings that were consistent with methodologically-comparable studies in North America (e.g. McCord 1979), Scandinavia (e.g. Pulkkinen 1988) and New Zealand (e.g. Moffitt and Silva 1988), as well as with British cross-sectional surveys (e.g. Hagell and Newburn 1994; Graham and Bowling 1995). However, Farrington qualified his conclusions by cautioning that the risk-factor–offending relationship remained only partially understood because:

> identifying which risk factors are causal and which are merely predictive or symptomatic of an underlying antisocial personality can be problematic . . . a further problem is that most risk factors tend to coincide and be interrelated. (Farrington 1996: 26)

Understanding and Preventing Youth Crime as RFR

The Understanding and Preventing Youth Crime review consolidated the growing internationalisation of RFR by identifying a series of ostensibly globally-applicable and universally-replicated risk factors for youth offending. This widespread replication of risk factors through studies with allegedly robust methodologies (e.g. multiple data sources, large community samples, prospective longitudinal designs) was an apparent validation of the risk factors that had been identified in developmental and ecological RFR since the early work of the Gluecks.

However, Farrington provided insufficient detail in his review to substantiate or enable a full evaluation of many of his conclusions regarding the universalism of risk factors. For example, little detail was provided regarding:

- the choice of studies to review;
- how the methodological robustness of these studies was analysed and evaluated;
- whether studies measured the temporal relationship between factors and offending;
- whether measurement of temporality was robust enough to substantiate conclusions regarding the predictive nature of risk factors;
- to what extent the replicability of findings across different studies, samples and countries indicated a comparability and universalism in the definitions of risk and protection, definitions of offending employed (indeed, whether offending was the target behaviour at all or whether measures of 'antisocial behaviour' or 'delinquency' were used) and the nature of the risk-factor–offending relationship.

Differences and ambiguities in any of the above areas must seriously limit the validity and reliability of any conclusions that certain risk factors have been universally-replicated and that they influence youth offending in an equivalent manner across the globe.

There were further omissions and biases that raise issues as to the validity of the conclusions drawn and the comprehensiveness of the review itself. For example, the range of factors investigated was limited by the psychosocial and developmental focus of much RFR to that point. Consequently, whilst psychosocial risk factors in the family, school, peer group and the community (an emerging focus within ecological RFR at that time) received comprehensive coverage, the impact of socio-political, legal, socio-structural, economic, historical and cultural factors and contexts, all of which were likely to vary greatly across different countries, were crucially neglected by the review. This is not to say, necessarily, that the psychosocial risk factors identified were not predictive of offending in different countries for different samples of young people, but rather that their influence may have been mitigated, moderated or usurped by the presence and analysis of these other neglected factors.

An important omission in the review was the failure to consider research that suggests the possibility that risk and protection operate as mechanisms and processes (as opposed to deterministic factors) with complex relationships to offending in different contexts at different times for different groups of young people. Farrington (1996) presented risk in a psychosocial reductionist manner and as a developmental concept (reflected in the studies reviewed), thus oversimplifying the nature of risk and the risk–offending relationship. The result was an over-generalised, mechanical representation of how risk and offending interrelate, with limited actual understanding of, or ability to explain, *how* risk and risk factors may encourage offending behaviour.

Farrington's confident conclusions that predictive risk factors have been globally-replicated gave rise to similarly confident recommendations for appropriate preventative interventions, notably based on the CtC programme (Farrington 1996). However, these recommendations animate and exacerbate the existing methodological weaknesses of the review and the studies within it. If factors prevalent at age eight years are causal or predictive of later offending then there is a logic to preventative interventions conducted with young people when they are eight years old. CtC, however, is a social development programme implemented in the teenage years and the logic of targeting causal or predictive factors prevalent at age eight years when the young person is, say, 14 years old, no longer has credibility. Thus, a generalised, biased and partial understanding of the risk–offending relationship inevitably promoted a similarly-flawed and unsubstantiated 'understanding' of how risk-focused interventions could prevent offending.

The studies highlighted in Farrington's review appear, therefore, to have been too restricted to allow a comprehensive review of RFR. The studies reviewed reflected a selection bias (which may have been due, in part, to Farrington's own developmental, psychosocial leanings) that precipitated an oversimplification of the nature and extent of risk factor influence and produced definitive conclusions that were only partially informed and over-generalised. Further to the alleged global predictive validity of the 'risk factors' identified in the review, there was insufficient information provided of the methodologies and analyses employed to identify risk factors to enable an assessment of whether the relationship between factors and offending had been adequately explored in each study. For example, it was unclear whether issues of temporality had been fully addressed in each study in a comparable manner. There was also a lack of sensitivity as to whether risk factors had been explored relative to age, gender or ethnicity. The homogenisation of samples and aggregation of data across groups of young people in different studies meant that the replicated risk factors were identified on the basis of 'group' analysis which is inherently less sensitive and accurate than within-individual analysis and not necessarily representative of/applicable to any specific individual participating in the studies reviewed. Similarly, there was no concession that the general, homogenised categories of 'offending' against which risk factors were measured in each study could have been too broad and insensitive to fully capture the essence of the risk-factor–offending relationship, particularly as risk factors may vary according to, *inter alia*, the nature of offending (e.g. active versus lifetime, property versus violent, first-time versus persistent), its frequency, seriousness and duration. Neither was there any discussion that definitions of offending can vary greatly across different countries, which questions the validity of any conclusions regarding replicable risk factors because the same risk factors may actually be linked to different measures of offending behaviour (see also O'Mahony 2008). Overall, Understanding and Preventing Youth Crime has promoted developmental and deterministic, globalised conceptions of risk that are, in fact, partial and unsubstantiated by the evidence.

Antisocial Behaviour by Young People

Funded by the UK government's Department of Health, Michael Rutter and colleagues conducted a review of empirical studies across the Western world that examined the relationship between risk factors and youth antisocial behaviour. The review, published as *Antisocial Behaviour by Young People* (Rutter *et al.* 1998), updated and extended a similar review conducted 15 years previously (Rutter and Giller 1983) on the basis that, since the original review 'there has been a substantial increase in empirically based knowledge on the nature of delinquency, its causes, factors that influence its perpetuation into adult life, and its prevention and treatment' (Rutter *et al.* 1998: 2). Antisocial behaviour was the behavioural measure preferred over delinquency/offending because it was seen as crucial to investigate behaviour that was problematic, yet which could lie 'outside the realm of the law' (Rutter *et al.* 1998: 1).

The Antisocial Behaviour by Young People methodology

The Antisocial Behaviour by Young People review incorporated large scale prospective longitudinal studies conducted across the Western world, on the basis that this form of RFR represented 'the most useful research' according to a set of methodological criteria that were perceived to increase the reliability, validity and comprehensiveness of the data collected and the analysis conducted. Studies were selected if they:

- used *prospective longitudinal designs*, which were considered necessary to study causaility;
- accessed *large samples* of the general population of young people throughout childhood, adolescence and early adulthood;
- accessed 'young people' aged 10–19 years;
- collected data from *multiple sources* in order to account for biases and to enable the triangulation and validation of findings and conclusions across different sources;

- attempted to *measure causality* on at least one of five criteria: individual differences in liability to engage in antisocial behaviour, the translation of that liability into the actual committing of illegal acts, differences over time or between places in the overall levels of crime, situational variations in delinquent activities and persistence or nonpersistence of antisocial behaviour as individuals grow older.

(see Rutter *et al.* 1998: 15)

The Antisocial Behaviour by Young People findings and conclusions

Rutter *et al.* separated the risk factors they identified into risk *mechanisms* ('causal' risk factors) and risk *indicators* (factors associated indirectly with the causal process). These risk mechanisms and indicators were placed into three distinct categories: *individual, psychosocial* and *societywide* and reported by Rutter *et al.* (1998) as follows:

- *Individual* – the factors of cognitive impairment, temperament (impulsivity, sensation seeking, lack of control, aggression) and distorted social information processing were all identified as risk mechanisms. Genetics was found to function as both a risk mechanism and risk indicator. Hyperactivity was considered to be a risk indicator, most likely to be associated with poor social functioning.
- *Psychosocial* – risk mechanisms included poor parenting (coercive or hostile, abusive or neglectful, ineffective, poor supervision), association with delinquent peers (supporting the hypothesis that 'birds of a feather flock together') and unemployment. Risk indicators in the psychosocial domain were family structure (teenage parenthood, large family, broken home) and family poverty and social disadvantage, both of which were linked to the risk mechanism of poor parenting.
- *Societywide* – the risk mechanisms of mass media (e.g. exposure to TV or film violence) and gender were identified, but found to have a limited evidence base. School factors (truancy, school ethos, teacher behaviour, clear management, make-up of pupil body) were also identified as risk mechanisms, but it was concluded that they were, as yet, under-researched and that there was insufficient understanding of exactly how they operated on antisocial behaviour. Ethnicity was highlighted as a factor more likely to be a risk indicator (linked to the risk mechanisms of poor living conditions and unemployment). Area differences (e.g. the architecture of the area) was considered to be a potential risk indicator linked to the risk mechanisms of style of policing and population make-up in different areas.

Rutter *et al.* concluded that individual risk factors were the most common form of risk mechanisms for antisocial behaviour, particularly for young people who persistently offend across their life course. The authors further concluded from the international literature (with particular reference to the work of the Gluecks and the follow-up study of Sampson and Laub (1993) – see Chapter 2 for a fuller discussion of this research) that risk mechanisms can serve as pre-existing dispositions towards antisocial behaviour by interacting with life experiences in a cyclical and cumulative way. Whilst this hypothesis illuminates the potentially criminogenic interaction between risk factors and life events, it was suggested that it also allows for the possibility of young people escaping/breaking out of (i.e. desisting from) patterns of antisocial behaviour at key turning points in their life.

Rutter *et al.* (1998) claimed that they had been able to consider a 'wide range of possible influences' on antisocial behaviour, from wider society to 'personal social contexts' (such as family, school, peers) to the individual. They also asserted that the 'systematic epidemiological testing of causal hypotheses' reviewed in their book was highly instructive in its ability to examine within-individual changes in risk factors over time (see also Farrington 2007), particularly if the individual's prior behaviour and social circumstances were taken into account at the same time. With regard to the studies' attempts to measure causality using any of the five causal dimensions, Rutter *et al.* suggested that 'what works in one of these categories may not be a factor in another ... (because) causal processes are neither simple nor unidirectional' (Rutter *et al.* 1998: 378). They concluded their report by claiming that the development of a multi-disciplinary international community of risk factor researchers has contributed to the more effective dissemination of risk-focused methods, more robust analyses and stronger conclusions as to the influence of different risk factors for antisocial behaviour by young people.

Antisocial Behaviour by Young People as RFR

Like Understanding and Preventing Youth Crime before it, the Antisocial Behaviour by Young People review made a significant contribution to the internationalisation and globalisation of RFR through its confident claims that universal risk factors had been identified and replicated in international RFR and that these factors were globally applicable across countries, samples and contexts. The review took a less simplistic approach to examining the causal influence of factors in comparison to other RFR reviews, particularly through the use of five distinct causal hypotheses as criteria for inclusion of studies in the review and by making the analytical distinction between risk mechanisms and risk indicators. Unlike much of the dominant RFR literature, the review did not rely entirely on a psychosocial focus (although this did dominate), instead including limited coverage of neglected areas of risk influence such as life events and socio-structural factors (which were labelled 'societywide' factors). However, the authors acknowledged the psychosocial bias to the studies available for selection, noting that 'this is where much recent research has been concentrated' (Rutter *et al.* 1998: 379). Rutter and colleagues, however, drew heavily on the developmental RFR of Farrington, citing over 40 of his publications at length during the course of the review and making reference to many of the studies reviewed in *Understanding and Preventing Youth Crime*.

Due to the inherent limitations and biases of much of the RFR evidence reviewed, the legitimacy of the confident and broad conclusions made by Rutter and his colleagues is debatable. Although the concept of a risk factor was less simplistic than in previous studies due to the focus on imputed risk mechanisms that could explain the causal influence of risk on offending, the studies reviewed made only limited attempts (if at all) to evidence this putative causal influence in favour of imputing causal processes and concluding causation on the basis of post-hoc statistical manipulations. Furthermore, it is frequently unclear in the book as to which studies reviewed actually attempted to measure exposure to risk relative to the onset and development of antisocial behaviour, so the existence of temporal precedence and the consequent predictive and causal influence of risk factors are difficult to evaluate from the information presented.

Rutter *et al.* (1998) acknowledged their conscious decision to exclude qualitative, ethnographic studies from the review (as these apparently rendered the measurement of risk mechanisms problematic). However, this exclusion ultimately resulted in a focus on survey-based RFR that had been underpinned by the reductionist factorisation of risk and that had ignored constructivist explanations of how risk influences offending. The restricted scope of their review, therefore, not only limited the range of possible conclusions, but it was based on research which itself was limited in scope and which had a tendency towards over-simplified and over-exaggerated claims.

Perhaps most debilitating to the validity of the conclusions of universality in *Antisocial Behaviour by Young People* was the lack of critique of, and reflection on, potential cross-cultural differences in the definition of antisocial behaviour, which is a notoriously ambiguous, subjective and dynamic measure (perhaps even more so than its counterpart 'offending'). Unacknowledged disparities in definitions of this core behaviour between the countries and studies in the review render valid comparisons difficult and could illegitimate the definitiveness of any conclusions drawn regarding replicable, universal risk factors.

Any conclusions of causality (let alone universal causality), simply cannot be unequivocal in the face of the limitations of the Rutter *et al.* review and the studies included in the review. Even if common 'global' risk factors for antisocial behaviour could be identified (and this is highly doubtful given differences in definitions, measurement, factorisation and analysis used across the various studies), the nature of the relationship of these risk factors and antisocial behaviour is far from universally established or clear. Despite claims to have identified 'findings that do generalize across samples and across social contexts' (Ruttter *et al.* 1998: 13), replication of lists of factors across the studies does not necessarily indicate that risk factors were operating in an equivalent, comparable fashion (e.g. functioning as 'risk' factors for antisocial behaviour) for different groups in different countries, particularly when the disparate definitions of antisocial behaviour across studies, contexts and the cultures are considered.

Globally flawed?

The Farrington and Rutter *et al.* reviews have represented international RFR and offered a series of positive conclusions about the methodologies employed and the utility of the data for developing understandings of the extent and nature of risk factors and their relationships with offending and antisocial behaviour. Most notably amongst these conclusions has been support for putative globally applicable, universal risk factors, which have been viewed as the products of comparative (ostensibly comparable) methodologies and replicated findings across different groups of young people in different contexts and countries. Whether such far-reaching conclusions have been (or could ever be) justified by the methodological and analytical quality of the studies included in these reviews is questionable. This is of enormous concern, as the support for the universal risk factor as a measurable, feasible, practical concept that has been engendered by these reviews has rapidly accelerated the popularity and application of (artefactual, developmental) RFR across the globe. It is entirely possible, therefore, that such widespread support for globalised RFR amongst researchers, politicians, policy makers and practitioners has been grounded in developmentally-biased, methodologically-dubious and incomparable studies that have dramatically over-inflated their collective conclusions beyond the scope and potential of their data and analysis.

The review of both longitudinal and cross-sectional RFR in England and Wales conducted in this book (see Chapters 3 and 4) has reached conclusions which are seriously at odds with the conclusions of the Farrington and Rutter *et al.* reviews. Attention now turns to evaluating some of the most notable RFR studies (such as those utilised by Farrington and Rutter *et al.*) from around the world to further explore the validity of the concept of a universal risk factor.

The International Self-Reported Delinquency study: standardised RFR and universal risk factors

The cross-sectional ISRD study was founded in 1990 by the Dutch Ministry of Justice, under the direction of Josine Junger-Tas. The study's main aim was to examine 'cross-national variability in patterns of correlates of self-reported delinquent behaviour' (Junger-Tas *et al.* 2003: 11). The authors emphasised that this aim could be most effectively achieved by using a standardised methodology (e.g. a common measuring instrument) to enable 'valid international comparisons' (Junger-Tas *et al.* 2003: 3).

In order to address the aim of making international comparisons between the correlates of delinquency, a working group of researchers from 13 participant countries was established to devise a standardised questionnaire. This working group was comprised from six government-linked centres (in the Netherlands, England and Wales, Finland, Northern Ireland, Portugal and New Zealand) and seven universities (in Belgium, Germany, Spain, Italy, Greece, Switzerland and the US). The ISRD-1 instrument contained questions regarding delinquency, social reactions to the young person's delinquency, socio-demographic variables relating to the young person and 'a small number' of theoretical variables relating to the central features of Social Control Theory – attachment to, commitment to, involvement in, and belief in, the formal and informal institutions of social control, particularly the family and school (see Hirschi 1969). Social Control Theory was chosen as the explanatory basis for the first ISRD (ISRD-1) because the theory was considered to have a 'universal character' and a robust empirical base in a 'great number of countries' (Junger-Tas *et al.* 2003). The research team 'hypothesized that the way these bonding variables operate would be similar across countries' (Junger-Tas *et al.* 2003: 9) – comparable to the concept of the universal risk factor. However, details regarding what informed the selection of the individual constructs used in the questionnaire have not been forthcoming.

ISRD-1 has been followed up by ISRD-2, a study based on a similar but expanded questionnaire and an extended number of (mainly European) countries – 33 in total. Only the methodology and results from ISRD-1 will be discussed here as the results from ISRD-2 (which commenced 2003–2005) were not available at the time of writing.

The ISRD-1 methodology

From 1991–1992, the ISRD-1 accessed five *national* and six *city-based* multistage, random samples of 14–21 year olds. The target age range was chosen by the working group to reflect what they considered to be the mean age of onset of youth offending (14 years old) and also to include younger adults in the sample (up to 21 years of age) who may have desisted from offending. The national samples were drawn from the Netherlands, Spain, Switzerland, Portugal and finally England and Wales (where a non-multistage, random sample was taken) and six city samples were taken from Germany (Mannheim), Northern Ireland (Belfast), Italy (Sienna, Genoa and Messina), Finland (Helsinki), Belgium (Liege) and the US (Omaha). The New Zealand city sample (Dunedin) was excluded as it was a longitudinal cohort sample using a modified survey instrument (see later in this chapter for further discussion of the Dunedin Study), whilst the Greek study was excluded because precise sampling details were not provided.

Delinquency amongst sample members was measured using a bespoke self-reported inventory of acts that were agreed by the working group to represent offences in the countries participating in the ISRD-1. Young people were asked whether they had ever committed any of the offences (*lifetime* prevalence). If they responded 'yes', they were asked if this offending had occurred in the last year (*current* prevalence) and how many times it had occurred (*frequency*). Young people were considered to be offenders if they self-reported having committed at least one of the offences on the inventory. A sub-measure of *serious* delinquency consisted of acts judged by the working group to indicate serious offences – theft, car theft, robbery, burglary, extortion, beating someone up, injuring with a weapon and selling drugs.

The correlates of delinquency were assessed in two main domains:

- *Socio-demographic variables* – gender, age, family composition, socio-economic status, education level, school attendance, leisure activities;
- *Social control constructs* – parental supervision, relationship with parents, attachment to school, commitment to school, academic achievement, relationship with peers.

(Junger-Tas *et al.* 2003: 22)

Questionnaire variables/constructs were measured using a mixture of yes/no and (more often) Likert-scale response formats. For example, the construct 'parental supervision' required young people to indicate their strength of agreement with two statements ('parents know with whom you are' and 'parents know where you are') on a dichotomous yes/no response scale. In contrast, 'relationship with parents' was assessed with the statement 'get along with mother/father' and a three-point Likert scale for responses ('well', 'quite well', 'not very well at all').

The ISRD-1 was designed to test 'cross-national variability in patterns of correlates of self-reported delinquency [which] may be socio-demographic in nature, or related to school, family, leisure, or peers' (Junger-Tas *et al.* 2004: 28). However the authors noted 'several drawbacks' in making direct statistical comparisons between the results from each participating country, particularly that:

> the cultural, social, economic and political differences among the 11 individual countries are too many to enumerate, which makes interpretation of international differences in delinquency in terms of macro-level variables problematic. (Junger-Tas *et al.* 2003: 28)

Consequently, the authors decided to adopt what they termed a 'middle course strategy' of grouping the countries and cities into three regionalised clusters to reflect similarities in macro-level cultural, political and socio-economic characteristics (precise details of which were not provided). These clusters were:

- *Anglo-American* – England and Wales, Northern Ireland (Belfast), US (Omaha).
- *North West European* – Netherlands, Switzerland, Finland (Helsinki), Germany (Mannheim), Belgium (Liege).
- *Southern European* – Spain, Portugal, Italy (Sienna, Genoa, Messina).

The ISRD-1 findings and conclusions

For ease of presentation, the statistically significant relationships between social control constructs and delinquency at the levels of region and gender that were identified by the study team (Junger-Tas *et al.* 2003) have been set out in a table below. Statistical links between socio-demographic variables (other than gender) and delinquency were marginalised in the study analyses, presumably (although this is not explicitly discussed in a report) because their static nature offered less explanatory utility in comparison to social control constructs.

Table 5.1 demonstrates the replicability found within- and between-regions in the ISRD-1 in terms of statistical correlations between social control constructs and different measures of delinquency. For example, the school-based constructs of 'attachment to school' ('like school') and 'truancy in the last year', along with the family-based construct 'get along with mother' were statistically related to delinquency for both males and females across each of the three regions, whilst 'get along with father' was correlated with general delinquency for all groups apart from Anglo-American females. By way of another example, in the family domain, 'parents know where you are' was correlated with general delinquency for both genders throughout the Anglo-American and North West Europe regions and was correlated with serious delinquency for males in these regions and for males in South Europe. Other constructs were not replicated as widely across the regions but demonstrated replicability within specific regions (each of which were composed of samples from a least three countries) and for specific groups (e.g. 'going out with family' was correlated with serious delinquency by Anglo-American males and general delinquency by North West European females).

Table 5.1 The relationship between social control constructs and delinquency

	Anglo-American		North West Europe		South Europe	
FAMILY	M	F	M	F	M	F
Get along with father	X		XO	XO	X	X
Get along with mother	X	XX	O	X	X	X
Going out with family	O			X		
Parents know where you are	XO	X	XO	X	O	
Parents know with whom you are	XO	X	XO			
SCHOOL						
Like school	X	X	X	X	X	X
Work hard at school	X					
Held back	X					
Truancy in last year	X	X	X	X	X	X

M = male, F = female.
X = statistically correlated with general offending, O = statistically correlated with serious offending.

The authors acknowledged that 'comparisons between countries and country clusters are rather crude. This means that we cannot in all fairness make well founded and explicit policy recommendations' (Junger-Tas *et al.* 2003: 143). However, notwithstanding this, Junger-Tas *et al.* saw fit to 'speculate' about the methodological and policy implications of their work, namely that:

- all family control variables in the study show a clear decline with age (n.b. a conclusion relating to the reported levels of each variable rather than their age-specific relationship with delinquency);
- in all countries there was tighter control on females than males;
- the social control variables selected had a strong association with delinquency;

(see Junger-Tas *et al.* 2003)

Junger-Tas *et al.* (2003) concluded that social control constructs had been replicated across the participating countries and, therefore, could be considered to be universally-applicable correlates with delinquency:

> It seems clear that biological, cultural, socialization and environmental factors all play a role in the prediction of delinquent behaviour. (Junger-Tas *et al.* 2003: 368)

However, the authors qualified their generalised conclusions by acknowledging that further work was needed to explore the cross-national applicability of social control constructs in relation to specific contexts and cultural settings.

The ISRD-1 as RFR

In the foreword to *Delinquency in an International Perspective*, the full report of ISRD-1, David Farrington heralded the ISRD-1 as 'a unique, highly significant and path-breaking research project', insisting that 'the authors should be commended for their heroic attempts to compare both individual countries and groups of countries' (Farrington, in Junger-Tas *et al.* 2003: ix). For their part, the authors have maintained that the project's central component, namely the *standardisation* of delinquency measures and social control constructs across different countries, has been 'quite viable' and offered a 'huge advantage of assuring comparability across varying samples and contexts' (Junger-Tas *et al.* 2003: 145).

Meanwhile, the authors have acknowledged that their cross-national comparisons were 'rather crude' and did not facilitate 'well-rounded and explicit policy recommendations' (Junger-Tas *et al.* 2003: 143). They drew particular attention to discrepancies in the sampling techniques and sample compositions in the participant countries, which resulted in 'varying claims to representativeness' and variations in core questionnaire content between countries. However, despite these caveats and the tentativeness of some of the ISRD-1 conclusions the study is problematic in a number of important respects.

A cross-national, comparative study of 'risk' correlates with offending that ignores or marginalises potential socio-economic, cultural, political and legal differences between- and within-countries can only, at best, present a partial picture. Despite such macro-level differences being viewed as 'enumerable' at a between-country level, there was no discussion of their potential influence within-countries (e.g. between different localities spread across the national samples), their capacity to change over very short periods (e.g. due to significant socio-economic or political changes in a given country) or, perhaps most importantly, the relative influence of these macro-level factors on the social control constructs at different times in different places on different groups of young people.

In the ISRD-1, the reliability of cross-national comparisons appeared to rest on the aggregation of social control data and its relationship with delinquency across the target age range, across genders, across cities, across countries and even across multiple countries within the three regions analysed. This aggregation involved an homogenisation of the demographic make-up and responses obtained from regions, nations, cities, age groups and genders, each of which were potentially broad categories containing disparate individuals. The aggregation and homogenisation employed may, therefore, have resulted in the overgeneralisation and desensitisation of findings and conclusions to the point that they do not represent any actual relationship between a given construct and delinquency beyond one that has been statistically-manufactured.

There are also concerns in ISRD-1 about the chosen measure of delinquency. Table 5.1 (above) shows the statistically significant relationships between a range of factors and delinquency (indicated by X) – where delinquency was measured by one (or more) positive responses to the self report inventory. This is a particularly blunt measure of delinquency and one which is highly likely to produce a larger number and range of positive statistical associations than a more refined notion of a delinquent. Thus, when a slightly more stringent definition of delinquency is employed (serious offending, O in Table 5.1), the statistical correlations between factors and offending drop away. It must be said that even the measure of serious offending is not very sharp as it may include just one 'serious' offence and not be indicative of a young person with a delinquent lifestyle. ISRD-1, therefore, has poorly operationalised its measure of delinquency and seriously over-estimated the reported links between a range of factors and offending.

Finally, whilst the ISRD-1 authors were generally careful to point out that their study could not address issues of causality but was concerned to explore a range of cross-national correlates with delinquency, they did conclude that a range of factors all play a part in *predicting* delinquency. Whilst this might have been simply a 'slip of the pen' it is a serious error and one which is reflected much more widely in a cross-sectional RFR literature which is given to misrepresentation.

The ISRD-1 researchers should be congratulated for their attempts to conduct a single international research project, but their methodology and analysis do not sustain any claim to have identified cross-national patterns of correlates of self-reported delinquent behaviour.

The Causes and Correlates Studies: universalised risk across the US

The Office of Juvenile Justice and Delinquency Prevention in the US began the Causes and Correlates *studies* in 1986. The overarching aim of the project was 'to improve the understanding of serious delinquency, violence, and drug use by examining how youth develop within the context of family, school, peers, and community' (Browning *et al.* 1999: 1). The project has consisted of three prospective longitudinal studies: the Rochester Youth Development Study (Thornberry 1994; Thornberry *et al.* 2003), the Denver Youth Survey (Huizinga and Espiritu 1999; Huizinga *et al.* 2003) and the Pittsburgh Youth Study (Loeber and Hay 1997; Loeber *et al.* 2003). From the outset, all three projects were designed to investigate the causes, correlates and consequences of delinquent behaviour, especially serious and chronic delinquency. Since their inception, the partner studies have each expanded to incorporate the investigation of additional and associated issues of concern, including the antecedents of both prosocial and antisocial behaviour, teenage parenthood, transitions into adulthood and patterns of work (see Thornberry and Krohn 2003).

A central feature of the Causes and Correlates *studies* has been the use of a 'similar research design' to aid comparability between the studies (Browning *et al.* 1999) and, as a consequence, to identify risk factors that could be generalised (universalised) across the studies. To this end, the three research teams initially worked together closely to develop a set of core measures, including a shared inventory of self-reported delinquent behaviour (adapted from the National Youth Survey Self-Reported Delinquency Scale, Elliott *et al.* 1985) and risk-focused questions relating to demographic characteristics, drug use, involvement with the juvenile justice system, family and educational experiences, peer relationships, community characteristics and attitudes and values.

The Rochester Youth Development Study

Led by Terence Thornberry, the Rochester Youth Development Study (RYDS) began in 1988 with the aim 'to investigate the causes and consequences of adolescent delinquency, with a particular focus on serious, chronic offenders' (Thornberry *et al.* 2003: 11), although this original aim has subsequently 'expanded into a broader investigation of both prosocial and antisocial development across the life course' (Thornberry *et al.* 2003: 11). The RYDS has been theoretically-underpinned by Interactional Theory (Thornberry 1987) and Social Network Theory (Krohn 1986):

- *Interactional Theory* – according to Thornberry, risk factors and offending function within a relationship of reciprocal causal influence (which varies at different developmental stages and for young people with varying levels of structural disadvantage) and weak social controls, especially attachment to family, commitment to school and association with delinquent peer groups (similar to the Social Development Model's fusion of social control, differential association and social learning – see Catalano and Hawkins 1996) – hence the link to ...

- *Social Network Theory* – Krohn suggests that delinquency occurs when the individual becomes 'enmeshed' in networks that promote antisocial behaviour, particularly if these networks (e.g. peer groups) are multiple, overlapping, dense, stable and contain members demonstrating equivalent antisocial attitudes and behaviours (Krohn 1986).

The RYDS methodology

Due to the intended focus on serious delinquency, the RYDS research team decided to sample only young people perceived to be at 'high risk' of demonstrating this behaviour. The team chose to sample only young people from public (i.e. non-selective) schools in Rochester (New York) and only those in the seventh and eighth grades (aged 12–14 years old – widely considered to be the peak age of offending onset). From this sampling frame, males were 'over-sampled' to constitute 75 per cent of the final sample and similar oversampling took place in areas of Rochester with the highest arrest rates – the assumption being that males in these areas are the group most likely to commit serious delinquency.

The RYDS team conducted interviews on a biannual basis from 1988–1992 and on an annual basis from 1994–1997 with 1,000 boys and girls who were aged 13–14 years old when the study commenced. Biannual and annual interviews over the same periods were also conducted with parents/carers of the sample members.

Delinquency in its active form (i.e. committed currently or recently) was measured using an inventory of 36 delinquent acts derived from the National Youth Survey's Self-Reported Delinquency Scale (Elliott *et al.* 1985), the shared measure of delinquency within the Causes and Correlates studies). Responses were subsequently categorised into *general offending* (e.g. status offences, vandalism, minor property crimes), *serious property offending* (e.g. burglary, arson) and *serious violent offending* (e.g. attacking someone with a weapon, throwing rocks or bottles at someone). The self-reported delinquency data was supplemented by official records of arrests obtained from the Rochester Police Department (youth offending data) and the New York State Division of Criminal Justice Services (adult offending data).

Interviews with both young people and parents/carers focused on the 'wide range of environmental, social, and psychological forces' (Thornberry *et al.* 2003: 18) that allegedly contribute to delinquency and substance use. The environmental, social and psychological forces measured were grouped into six categories:

- *Family* – socio-demographic characteristics, parent-child relations, attachment to parents, maltreatment parental stressors;
- *School* – commitment to school, academic achievement;
- *Area characteristics;*
- *Peer group relationships* (e.g. association with delinquent peers);
- *Social networks;* and
- *Individual characteristics* (e.g. beliefs).

(Thornberry *et al.* 2003: 18)

A structured interview schedule collected data on different elements of risk, with over half of the items measured derived from the core measures agreed by the Causes and Correlates partners at the outset of the study, including:

- *Child Behaviour Checklist* – a 112 item questionnaire measuring problem behaviours such as anxiety, depression, oppositional behaviour and hyperactivity, using a three point response scale of 'not true', 'somewhat or sometimes true' and 'very true or often true';
- *Revised Diagnostic Interview Schedule for Children* – a measure of the child's psychopathology;
- *Attitude Towards Delinquent Behaviour Scale* – a 15 item measure of attitudes towards delinquency, antisocial behaviour and substitutes;
- *Child's Relationship with Parents/Siblings Scale* – 30 items measuring the boys' perceptions of their relationship with their mother and father;
- *Positive Parenting Scale* – measuring boy's perceptions of positive parental responses to their behaviour;
- *Peer Delinquency Scale* – a 15 item measure of the proportion of boys' peers engaged in delinquency.

(Loeber *et al.* 1998)

In each scale, the environmental and psychosocial forces were converted to a numeric variable (i.e. factorised). For example, on the Child's Relationship with Parents/Siblings Scale, 'attachment to parents' was a composite of 11 statements measuring how often ('never', 'seldom', 'sometimes', 'often') young people felt that they got along well with, respected and enjoyed being with their parents, felt anger, violence, trust or pride towards their parents and felt that their parents lacked understanding, were too demanding and interfered with their activities (Thornberry *et al.* 1991: 34).

At the time of writing, 12 waves of interview data had been collected – up until the sample members were aged 22 years. Data from the interviews has been supplemented with official data from school (e.g. truancy and exclusion data), police (e.g. arrest records), probation departments, family court and social services.

At a general analytical level, the researchers 'tried to examine the various conceptual premises that underlie interactional and network theories . . . for example . . . bidirectional causal influence, developmental changes in causal effects, and how family and peer networks coincide to produce delinquency and drug use' (Thornberry *et al.* 2003: 20). Two forms of bidirectional/reciprocal relationship between risk and delinquency were outlined prior to analysis (Thornberry *et al.* 1991):

- *Instantaneous/contemporaneous* 'causal links' between factors and offending at the same point in time;
- *Lagged/cross-lagged* mutual causal relationships that develop over time.

Due to the potential for 'multicollinearity' between the two models (i.e. they may be measuring the same factors and relationships) and the inability of the instantaneous model to examine the 'temporal and causal ordering' of factors and delinquency (Thornberry *et al.* 1991: 20), only the lagged model has been explored. To do so, the RYDS has measured risk factors and delinquency contemporaneously at each data collection stage/wave, but analysed the relationship between the two sets of variables across data collection waves, typically analysing measures of risk taken at time A (e.g. wave one) against changes in levels of delinquency between time A and time B (e.g. wave two).

The RYDS findings and conclusions

Following analysis of the interview data, the researchers hypothesised an influence on delinquency of the following environmental, social and psychological 'forces':

- *Family* – parental perceptions of low attachment to their child and the young person having a negative perception of involvement with and control by their parents were exacerbated (statistically) by the exogenous factors of economic hardship and single-parent family structure (Smith and Krohn 1995).
- *School* – low commitment to school and low academic achievement were statistically-correlated with an increased likelihood of self-reporting delinquency, whilst high levels of commitment to school and high academic achievement correlated with non-delinquency (Thornberry *et al.* 1991; Thornberry and Krohn 2003).
- *Neighbourhood* – living in a disadvantaged neighbourhood exerted an indirect statistical effect on delinquency by being linked to an increased likelihood of reporting exposure to negative socio-structural and neighbourhood factors such as economic hardship and lack of social support. These factors were then statistically-linked to low levels of attachment to parents, parent-child involvement and parental control over their child (Thornberry *et al.* 2003).
- *Peers* – gang membership was strongly associated with delinquency, whilst association with delinquent peers had an indirect statistical effect on delinquency through the reinforcing effects of the peer network. In turn, delinquent behaviour was linked to the increased likelihood, frequency and intensity of associations with delinquent peers (Thornberry *et al.* 1994).

- *Individual* – positive beliefs about drug use were associated with an increased probability of young people reporting delinquency.

The RYDS authors have interpreted their findings as offering support for the existence of the 'bidirectional causal influences [and] developmental changes in causal effects' that their theoretical model predicted (Thornberry *et al.* 2003). For example, Thornberry *et al.* (2003) have concluded that:

- the child's individual characteristics and the parent's inept parenting style are likely to become causally interwoven. Bidirectional, reciprocal influences (positive correlations) between the child's temperamental qualities and the parent's child management style can be observed as early as toddlerhood;
- neighbourhood characteristics affected delinquency indirectly, for example, through the impact of poverty and social disadvantage on risk factors such as parental supervision, attitudes to parents, association with delinquent peer groups and social isolation;
- association with delinquent peers indirectly affected delinquency through the 'reinforcing environment' of the peer network. In turn, delinquency increases associations with delinquent peers;
- isolation in deviant peer networks, coercive behavioural styles and academic failure, all influenced in part by earlier antisocial behaviour, lead to continuing involvement in delinquency during adolescence.

The RYDS as RFR

The RYDS has been ostensibly better able to address the nature of the relationship between risk and delinquency than previous examples of RFR due to its explicit focus on the temporal ordering of the two measured variables. However, there is a possibility that the temporal precedence of factors over delinquency has been imputed rather than empirically demonstrated. Just because the measurement of risk pre-dated the measurement of delinquency and thus allowed the interpretation of a time-lagged (predictive) relationship between the two, this does not necessarily mean that the two variables were causally related. It could be, for example, that delinquency actually occurred beforehand or concurrently, but simply was not measured, self-reported or officially recorded at that time. Of course, the multi-method approach and lagged model analysis minimises the potential influence of such confounding variables. However, even if the data collected was accurate, the conclusion of a predictive relationship may not be a true reflection of reality. Any measured relationships between risk at point A and (changes in) delinquency at point B may have been entirely statistical (artefactual), rather than existing in any real sense. It is equally likely that changes in delinquency between measurement time A and B are not attributable to the presence of particular risk factors in the intervening period. That is not to say that risk factors cannot influence delinquency causally, but such conclusions should not even be considered without further exploration of potential explanations of this causal influence, the precise temporal episodes of exposure to, or onset of, risk and offending and more detailed investigation of the purported processes of behavioural changes fostered by exposure to risk. With this in mind, the extent to which the risk factors identified as predating offending could be definitively concluded to be *causes* was overestimated by the study, which of course affects (reduces) the capacity to identify bidirectional causal influences. There is a significant sense that the results were interpreted selectively to fit Thornberry's original theoretical framework and that alternative explanations of the findings have not been explored.

Even if it were assumed that issues of temporality and causality were settled and agreed, would the conclusions of the RYDS stand up to scrutiny? The answer is undoubtedly no, for a series of cogent methodological reasons. For one thing, even if the risk constructs measured in the RYDS could be uncritically accepted as having a causal influence, their factorisation deprived the researchers of any qualitative depth and detail with which to explore the nature and operation of this causality as a mechanism, process or explanation. The crudity and reductionism of the risk measures were compounded by their aggregation across a single broad group of young people, with no sensitivity to potential individual differences and a disregard for within-individual analysis, which could better support explanations of individual behavioural change based on exposure to risk. The RYDS conclusions, already underpinned by uncritical reductionism and broad-brush generalisations, were further undermined by the developmental and psychosocial biases of the data collection instruments; partialities that seriously question the explanatory scope and breadth of the factors measured and the conclusions drawn.

The Denver Youth Survey

The prospective longitudinal Denver Youth Survey (DYS) aimed 'to identify social conditions, personal characteristics, and developmental patterns that are linked to sustained involvement in delinquency and drug use [particularly] risk and protective factors that may initiate, sustain, terminate, or, perhaps more importantly, prevent delinquency and problem drug use across the lifespan' (Huizinga *et al.* 2003: 47). The DYS research team, under the supervision of David Huizinga, stated that their study was based on an integrated theoretical model that synthesised strain, social control and social learning perspectives (see also Elliott *et al.* 1985) and that this model has been expanded to account for the effects of 'neighbourhood social disorganisation, biological history including perinatal events, childhood experience and socialisation, personality and mental health, formal and informal secondary (external) controls, and rational choice' (Huizinga *et al.* 2003: 49).

The DYS methodology

In order to assess young people considered to pose the highest risk of carrying out the target behaviours (delinquency and drug use), the research team sampled randomly from households in 'high risk neighbourhoods' in the target area, Denver. Neighbourhoods were chosen as high risk if their official crime rate was in the top third across Denver and if they had accompanying population and housing characteristics considered to be criminogenic such as a high proportion of ethnic minorities and low socio-economic status amongst residents.

The DYS team conducted annual interviews (from 1988–1992 and from 1995–1999) with 1,527 boys and girls who were aged either seven, nine, 11, 13 or 15 years old when the study began. Young people in the seven and nine year old groups were re-interviewed in 2003 when they were aged approximately 22 years.

Delinquency over the past year and the age of onset were measured using a Self-Reported Delinquency Scale: an inventory of *serious property offences* (e.g. robbery, burglary, car theft, arson), *serious violent offences* (e.g. serious assault, gang fights) and *minor offences* (e.g. public disorder, theft under five dollars, minor property crime). For younger children (aged seven and nine years), the Self-Reported Antisocial Behaviour Scale was used, wherein age-inappropriate acts such as joyriding were removed from the Self-Reported Delinquency Scale. Drug use and the age at which it began (onset) were recorded in relation to alcohol, marijuana and 'hard' drugs.

The interview foci were located in the biopsychosocial risk domains of family (parenting, attachment, marital discord, domestic violence, parental criminality), neighbourhood social characteristics (including family integration and support within the neighbourhood), school (involvement in education, educational strain) involvement in activities (community, religious, work, peer group delinquency), personal and psychological characteristics (of the young person and their parents) and medical history. Each factor was a composite of several sub statements with which young people had to indicate their strength of agreement ('never, seldom, sometimes, often'). For example, 'positive parenting' was measured as:

> When you do something your parents approve of how often do they – 'give you a wink or a smile?', 'say something nice about it?', 'give you a hug?', 'give you a reward?', 'mention it to someone else?' (Huizinga *et al.* 1991: 106)

Multivariate regression analysis examined statistical relationships between the psychosocial factors measured in the interviews and delinquency measured at a later date. The factors linked to delinquency/non-delinquency were viewed as 'risk' factors and were also labelled 'explanatory' and 'causal' variables. Subsequently, cluster analysis was conducted to identify the risk factors that were particular to delinquents in two distinct developmental groups: childhood (aged seven to nine years) and youth (aged 11–15 years). The intention was to identify multiple aetiological (causal) pathways ('personal typologies' of risk) into delinquency rather than to uncritically assume that the same constellation of risk factors was responsible for delinquency in all young people. Huizinga and colleagues were clear that their 'orientation is not atheoretical. Our search is structured in data reflecting a general developmental model' (Huizinga *et al.* 1991: 86).

The DYS findings and conclusions

The key risk factors for delinquency in the DYS were identified (using multivariate statistical analysis) as:

- *Family* – criminality of family members, parental drug use and the family claiming welfare benefits were all statistically-associated with self-reported delinquency by males. Multiple changes to family structure was considered to be a risk factor for both males and females. Parental monitoring, home curfew rules, having a stable two-parent family and high levels of parental discipline were linked to non-delinquency by males and females.

- *School* – academic achievement, being in an age-appropriate school grade and graduating from high school were all hypothesised to increase resilience to and protect against delinquency due to their statistical relationship (association) with self-reported non-offending. Low academic achievement was associated with an increased likelihood of reporting delinquency (Huizinga *et al.* 2003).

- *Neighbourhood* – living in a disadvantaged neighbourhood was theorised to exert an indirect (statistical) influence on delinquency through its significant statistical relationship with socio-structural and neighbourhood factors, which themselves were linked to lower levels of attachment to parents, parent–child involvement and parental control over their child (Thornberry *et al.* 2003). Neighbourhood social control, social bonding and normative consensus on values and behaviour were found to mediate the effects of neighbourhood social disorganisation (poverty, mobility, single parent families, ethnic diversity) on delinquency (Huizinga *et al.* 2003).

- *Individual* – psychological problems (low self-esteem, social isolation, positive attitudes to delinquency, low guilt, lack of perceived opportunities in the future) were statistically-associated with self-reported delinquency. In contrast, high self-esteem and high self-efficacy were statistically-related to reports of non-delinquency (Huizinga 1997).
- *Individual delinquent typologies* – Huizinga *et al.* concluded that 'there is typological diversity among the child and youth samples in etiological or explanatory variables' (Huizinga *et al.* 2003: 75). In both the child and youth samples, having a more positive home life and a prosocial orientation were significantly more likely amongst *non-delinquents* compared to *low-level* or *high-level* delinquents. In contrast, the delinquent groups identified were more likely than non-delinquents to have pro-delinquent attitudes and beliefs, to have delinquent friends and to be impulsive/hyperactive (Huizinga *et al.* 1991). When the developmental typologies were explored for gender differences, Huizinga *et al.* (1991) discovered that delinquent personality, weak prosocial beliefs and the use of neutralisation techniques (making excuses for delinquency) were stronger influences on delinquency for males, especially in mid-adolescence and young adulthood, compared to females at the same developmental stage. The most important predictors of delinquency across both genders and all developmental stages were association with delinquent peers and psychological problems in adolescence.

The authors concluded that the integrated theoretical model that underpinned the data collected had enabled them to identify 'typological diversity . . . in etiological or explanatory variables', multiple 'etiological pathways' to delinquency and different developmental sequences related to the onset and maintenance of, as well as desistance from, delinquency (Huizinga *et al.* 2003: 75). The main conclusions from the DYS have been that there is not one specific 'constellation of variables' that produces delinquency at all times within all individuals and that much greater attention should be paid to the asserted 'typological diversity' in risk factor influence – with the implication that the integrated theory that underpinned the study would be the ideal explanatory device for this purpose in future studies.

The DYS as RFR

The DYS conclusion of multiple 'etiological pathways' adds a layer of complexity and sensitivity to the traditionally over-generalised and universalised conclusions of RFR. The definitiveness of this innovative aetiological conclusion is not, however, fully substantiated by the evidence from the study. The causal influence of risk factors assumed by the notion of 'etiological pathways' has been premised on crude, desensitised, factorised measures of risk, aggregation of data across homogenised developmental groups (with little detailed consideration of age or gender differences) and a presumed control over the measurement of variables in the real world. There has, for example, been very limited analysis of the relative influence of different risk factors (or groups of risk factors) for specific age groups (as opposed to the broad child and youth age groups) and for different forms of delinquency in the DYS. Moreover, the conclusion that risk factors operate in dynamic 'pathways' and pre-date delinquency has been implicated from the repeated measurement of statistical associations, not causal relationships, and the assumption that risk has temporal precedence over delinquency, despite measures of each being taken concurrently (risk measured in current life, delinquency in measured over the past year), with no exploration of the precise timing of exposure to either. Unlike the RYDS, the DYS has attempted to address the explanatory influence of risk through measuring the age of onset of delinquency. However, devoid of an equivalent measure of the *onset* of risk, temporality has been dependent on the measurement period rather than actual exposure to risk relevant to delinquent behaviour. However, even if it could be established that the onset of a risk factor predates the onset of delinquency, this does not necessarily imply any explanatory/causal relationship between the two at that point in time (although this relationship could have existed at that time or at some point in the past or subsequently). In this case, once again, risk factor researchers have been restricted to explanation based on statistical measurement rather than a developed understanding of how risk explains delinquency at a specific point in time or over a given period.

The Pittsburgh Youth Study

Managed by Rolf Loeber, the Pittsburgh Youth Study stated the key aims 'to investigate and describe developmental pathways to serious delinquency ... [and] the risk and protective factors that influence the development of serious offending' (Loeber *et al.* 2003: 94). The Pittsburgh Youth Study (PYS) set out to address the 'adevelopmental' nature of most theories of youth offending (citing the Social Development Model and the work of Farrington as notable exceptions) by expanding on developmental criminology with a broader and more detailed account of the 'causal processes' that underpin the development of offending from childhood into adulthood (Loeber *et al.* 2003). In particular, the authors noted the paucity of RFR focused on preadolescent samples, such that 'it is often impossible to gauge whether the measured onset of delinquent acts (e.g. in the previous year) was truly an onset or a mere repetition of earlier behaviour' (Loeber *et al.* 2003: 93).

The Pittsburgh Youth Study methodology

In order to access young people considered most at 'at risk' of committing serious offences, the PYS team drew a random sample of 1,517 'preadolescent' boys from public schools in inner-city Pittsburgh. Sample members were aged 5–6, 8–9 or 11–12 years old when the study began. From 1992 onward, annual interviews were conducted with the youngest sample (five and six year olds) and oldest sample (11–12 year olds). At each interview stage, parents/carers of the sample members were interviewed. The middle age group (those aged eight and nine years old when the study began) were re-interviewed when they were aged 22 years.

The interviews at each successive administration utilised a range of quantitative behavioural scales and questionnaires, many of which were shared measures across the causes and correlate partnership (e.g. Positive Parenting Scale, Peer Delinquency Scale – see Loeber *et al.* 1998) to obtain data from sample members. The PYS is notable, therefore, for the way in which it has utilised pre-existing validated research instruments for data collection although this does not signify a move away from the established concerns of developmental risk factor researchers concerning the domains where risk is held to originate:

- the individual (impulsivity, guilt, intelligence and IQ, personality, attitudes);
- family (interactions with parents, parental discipline, parental anxiety and depression, communication with parents, family transitions – including; divorce, parental separation, relationship with parents);
- school (e.g. academic achievement); and
- socio-economic status (neighbourhood status, welfare dependency, living in a disadvantaged neighbourhood, broken homes, unemployment, low level of education).

Loeber *et al.* considered that each of these domains contained and constituted potential 'risk factors' that represented the 'causes or correlates of delinquency' (2003: 108). Each potential risk factor was a 'construct' or composite of several sub-factors derived from ratings scales and Likert-scale responses. For example, the construct of 'parental discipline' was a composite of non-persistent discipline, counter-control, physical punishment and parents disagreeing on discipline. The construct relating to 'friends' was a composite of having few friends, having bad friends and having poor relationships with peers (Loeber *et al.* 1998).

Official delinquency was measured using official court records. Self-reported delinquency and drug use were measured with a 33 item Self-Reported Antisocial Behaviour Scale (Loeber *et al.* 1989) for the youngest and middle samples and the Self-Reported Delinquency Scale and 16 item Substance Use Scale (Elliott *et al.* 1985) for the older sample. A sub-measure of *serious delinquency* was taken that consisted of car theft, breaking and entering, strong-arming, attacking to seriously hurt or kill and forced sex. On the self-reported delinquency questionnaire, young people were asked to indicate if they had ever committed any of the delinquent acts listed and, if so, at what age they had committed them the first time (the onset of delinquency).

So-called 'explanatory factors for delinquency' (Loeber *et al.* 1998: 97) in each age range were identified using logistic regression analysis to measure the statistical relationship between factors and dichotomised measures of general and serious delinquency in concurrent (rather than time-lagged) measurement periods. The research team acknowledged the limitation of this analytical procedure in passing when admitting that 'we will often refer to "predictors", while realising that analyses are essentially correlational' (Loeber *et al.* 1998: 97).

The Pittsburgh Youth Study findings and conclusions

At each wave of data collection, the correlation between different risk factors and delinquency was assessed for each of the age-related samples in order to develop a profile of which correlations increased and decreased with age. The risk factors that were statistically-associated with self-reported juvenile delinquency in the PYS samples were:

- *Family* – in the youngest and middle samples, low socioeconomic status of the family, living in a small house, father's unemployment, having a poorly-educated mother, coming from a broken home, high levels of maternal stress, substance use problems, anxiety/depression were associated with early onset and serious delinquency, as were unhappy parents (youngest sample only) and parental anxiety/depression (middle sample only) (Farrington and Loeber 1999). Poor parental supervision was the family-based 'risk' factor linked most strongly to an increased likelihood of reported delinquency by boys in each of the three samples (Loeber *et al.* 1998).
- *School* – in each age group, low academic achievement was statistically linked to self-reported delinquency, whereas high academic achievement was associated with reports of non-delinquency.
- *Neighbourhood* – across all three samples, living in a disadvantaged neighbourhood (measured using census variables) was correlated with an increased likelihood of reporting exposure to the family-based factors of low socioeconomic status and poor parental supervision (Stouthamer-Loeber *et al.* 2002).
- *Individual* – cognitive and behavioural impulsivity and high ADHD (youngest and middle samples) and depressive mood (boys in the youngest and oldest samples) were all linked to delinquency (Loeber *et*

al. 1998). Certain individual factors were hypothesised as having an indirect effect on delinquency through their statistical relationship with other risk factors. For example, it was hypothesised that low IQ could be linked to feelings of frustration, failure and humiliation at school, which were themselves statistically-linked to alienating experiences, a factor with a significant statistical relationship to delinquency (Lynam 1993). Conversely, it was speculated that students with high IQ may experience better relationships with teachers and enjoy the rewards of education above those offered by delinquent behaviour.

- *Protective factors* – high accountability, trustworthiness, ability to feel guilt, motivation at school and living in a non-disadvantaged neighbourhood all reduced the statistical probability of the PYS sample members reporting delinquency (Stouthamer-Loeber *et al.* 2002).
- *Age-group factors* – school problem behaviours, deviant peers and positive attitudes to deviancy were more predictive of delinquency as young people got older. In contrast, physical aggression and social withdrawal decreased in their ability to predict delinquency as young people aged.

Loeber *et al.* (2003) hypothesised that individual risk factors dominated the causal processes that lead to early onset offending (an original focus of their study) and that 'from childhood to adolescence, children are introduced to factors in their peer group and neighbourhood, which for most did not exist in their early childhood' (Loeber *et al.* 2003: 120). They went on to conclude that psychosocial factors (in the family, school and neighbourhood domains) were primarily responsible for late onset offending. On the basis of the PYS results, Loeber *et al.* concluded that:

> offending by most juveniles results from forces within the individual and forces in the individual's social environment (parents, siblings, and peers) in different social contexts (family home, school, neighbourhood). (Loeber *et al.* 2003: 129)

The PYS researchers claimed to have addressed the 'adevelopmental' nature of many theories of delinquency by focusing on operationalising and investigating the main developmental elements of youth offending (Loeber *et al.* 2003). The research team has stressed that unlike most theories that have emerged from RFR, which have focused on correlations between risk factors and offending, they have been able to produce information about the 'causes' that differentiate young people who escalate into serious offending (Loeber *et al.* 1998). The research team has further claimed to have contributed:

> empirical knowledge . . . based on the life course of individuals rather than the usually weak relationships between variables, while recognising that knowledge about relationships between variables can inform knowledge about types of individuals. (Loeber *et al.* 2003: 130)

Theoretically, the key conclusion from the PYS (reflecting a key conclusion of the entire Causes and Correlates project) has been that similar risk factors affect all young people, but that the causal influence of these factors is different at different ages. The claims and conclusions of Loeber and colleagues, however, do not stand up to critical scrutiny.

The Pittsburgh Youth Study as RFR

Certainly, when compared to the single age group studied in the RYDS and the aggregated age group data of the DYS, the accelerated longitudinal design of the PYS (analysing factors related to delinquency for different age groups over the same time period) had more potential to explore the different causal processes for different elements of the delinquent career (onset, escalation, desistance) and for young people at different developmental stages; which could have offered a first tentative step towards specific theories of the developmental pathways into delinquency (as claimed by Loeber *et al.* 2003). However, despite this potential advantage in analytical complexity and sensitivity over its Causes and Correlates partner studies, the PYS has produced definitive conclusions regarding the causality of risk factors that are invalidated by the partial and methodologically-crude understanding of the risk-delinquency relationship provided in this study. As in the other Causes and Correlates studies, the measurement of risk and the risk-delinquency relationship has been over-simplified in the PYS by the factorisation of standardised risk constructs and further reduced by the psychosocial bias within these standardised measures. There has been an equivalent uncritical imputation of (and consequent failure to reflect upon the detrimental impact of) the lack of methodological control over the variables measured, the aggregation of risk factor data across a broad and inappropriately homogenised age groups (thus ignoring individual differences) and the consequent absence of within-group, within-individual analyses. Although analysis of temporal ordering has been attempted, it has relied on measuring the onset of delinquency without an accompanying measure of the onset of risk, which even in itself would be insufficient to evidence a relationship between risk and delinquency without a robust explanation of the processes by which risk can influence delinquency.

Perhaps most damningly, however, the authors imputed the developmental influence of risk by comparing their results for different ages across the sequential administrations of their questionnaires. However, such developmental conclusions are misplaced as the authors have reduced their longitudinal design (and the potential to carry out powerful within-individual analysis) to a simple repeat cross-sectional study by choosing to only analyse the relationships between variables collected in the same annual sweep. It is difficult to understand or explain why the authors did this, but it means, of course, that they cannot say anything definitive about causality. The results and conclusions, therefore, reported by Loeber *et al.* above, are simply not sustained by the analysis they employed and should be regarded as spurious.

The Causes and Correlates studies revisited

The triumvirate of Causes and Correlates studies has attempted to develop multiple theories of serious delinquency by identifying so-called explanatory, causal risk factors and pathways that are shared by young people across different cities in the US, with the resultant imputation that these factors are universally-applicable. Do these collective, replicated findings, therefore, take RFR forward? The Causes and Correlates project has been heralded by the authors of the three studies as 'the largest and most comprehensive investigation of the causes and correlates of delinquency ever undertaken' (Thornberry *et al.* 2004: 1). The project has, through an intensive exploration of the nature of the risk factor-delinquency relationship (particularly by examining the temporal precedence of risk factors), claimed to have contributed to RFR through the systematic exploration of developmental pathways into delinquency. In this respect, the partnership has begun to address (intentionally or otherwise) Farrington's concerns that there has been an absence of understanding of the 'processes or developmental pathways that intervene between risks factors and outcomes' (Farrington 2000: 7). However, the artefactual nature of the methodologies and analyses employed have provided little to validate risk as a dynamic process (rather than as a static factor) or to begin to explain or evidence the actual processes that link factors to outcomes at different points in time.

In contrast to claims that the studies covered 'a wide range of factors', the developmental aims of the Causes and Correlates studies, guided by some of the most prominent developmental criminologists within the RFR field, have inevitably privileged the investigation of psychosocial risk factors and the exploration of universally-applicable, deterministic, predictive relationships between risk factors and delinquency. This bias has been reflected in the use of a set of standardised psychosocial measures (e.g. the Child Behaviour Checklist), demographically-biased samples (high-risk samples from high-risk neighbourhoods), and common analytical techniques (multivariate regression measures to identify correlations between risk at time A and delinquency at time B). Consequently, with an equivalent body of 'risk' factors measured in an equivalent way in each study for equivalent groups of high-risk young people, it was inevitable that a degree of replicability and universalism would emerge. This replicability is, therefore, likely to be the product of standardisation of methodology (the same restricted set of questions, targeted on artificially constructed samples and crudely, often cross-sectionally, analysed between groups) (D. Smith 2006). In the words of Case (2007: 92) 'if you do what you've always done, you'll get what you've always got'.

The Causes and Correlates studies have been an intensive, yet self-fulfilling exercise in validating the tenets of developmental RFR. The identification of different developmental pathways and their portrayal as causal and explanatory has been reliant on statistical control, imputation and face validity – extrapolating dynamic and causal processes from the identification of statistical correlates and analyses of quantified and aggregated variables which cannot be experimentally controlled or isolated in the real-world context. As such, the interpretive leap involved in understanding correlates as causes has been unjustified in the light of the methodological and analytical limitations of the participant studies.

Sex Differences in Antisocial Behaviour: exploring risk from birth

The Dunedin Multidisciplinary Health and Development Study, or the Dunedin Study as it has come to be known, began in 1972 in Dunedin, New Zealand. The study set out to conduct 'a longitudinal investigation of the health, development and behaviour of a complete city-wide cohort of births between 1 April 1972 and 31 March 1973' with the central aims of:

- the prediction of childhood correlates of future health and behaviour outcomes;
- the developmental study of continuity and change in health and behaviour;
- the epidemiological study of the prevalence and incidence of health problems and behaviour problems.

(Mofitt *et al.* 2001: 10–11)

Moffitt *et al.* (2001, 2006) have pursued their third aim through a specific study of 'the developmental epidemiology of sex differences and antisocial behaviour during the first two decades of life ... [with a] focus on antisocial behaviour during adolescence both as the prime outcome of childhood risk and as an important predictor of subsequent adult outcomes' (Moffitt *et al.* 2001: 2–3). The methods, results and conclusions from this study have been mainly disseminated in a book entitled *Sex*

Differences in Antisocial Behaviour: Conduct Disorder, Delinquency and Violence in the Dunedin Longitudinal Study (Moffitt *et al.* 2001).

The Sex Differences in Antisocial Behaviour methodology

The Dunedin Study sample represented a complete cohort of children born between 1 April 1972 and 31 March 1973 in Dunedin, New Zealand. Sample members have been assessed on 11 occasions thus far – at age 3, 5, 7, 9, 11, 13, 15, 18, 21, 26 and 32 years.

Data for the Sex Differences in Antisocial Behaviour study has been collected from multiple sources (sample members, observers, parents, teachers, partners, peers, police, courts) using multiple, 'age-appropriate' methods (e.g. observation, behavioural problem checklists, cognitive tests of memory and reading, diagnostic interviews, official records) and multiple measures of antisocial behaviour (Moffitt *et al.* 2001: 14):

- *Psychometric ratings* of difficult temperament (at age three and five years).
- *Teacher and parent ratings* of antisocial behaviour problems using the Rutter Child Scale (at ages five, seven, nine and 11 years) and the Revised Behaviour Problem Checklist (at ages 13 and 15 years).
- *Diagnostic scales* measuring conduct and personality disorder (age 11, 13, 15, 18 and 21 years).
- *Self-reported delinquency* measured using the Self-Reported Early Delinquency interview (Elliott *et al.* 1983) (at ages 13 and 15 years) and the Self-Reported Delinquency interview (Elliott *et al.* 1985) (aged 18 and 21 years), both of which are standardised instruments measuring self-reported 'illegal' activity in the past 12 months.
- *Official records* of police arrests (age 11, 13 and 15 years) and court convictions (age 13, 15, 18 and 21 years).
- *Peer reports* of 'delinquent reputation' (age 18 and 21 years), asking whether the sample member has problems with aggression, offending, alcohol use and drug use.
- *Self-report and partner report* of domestic abuse (age 21 years).

From the multiple sources of data collected, a 'dependent variable' of *adolescent antisocial behaviour* was formulated as a composite of standardised measures taken at seven separate points: parent reports (at age 13 and 15 years), teacher reports (at age 13 years), self-reports (at age 13, 15 and 18 years) and peer reports (at age 18 years). The aggregated, composite measure of adolescent antisocial behaviour was constructed to provide a single dependent variable against which to measure the statistical impact of the so-called risk predictors. According to the authors:

> Aggregation is not always appropriate, of course, but in the service of obtaining more reliable estimates of risk and protective factors in development, investigators are better off creating aggregated scores by combining, within specified developmental periods, several measures of the same construct. (Moffitt *et al.* 2001: 93)

In terms of independent 'risk' variables, the researchers focused on what they saw as 'the most important risk factors for antisocial behaviour' discerned from large scale reviews of RFR (e.g. Rutter *et al.* 1998). They labelled these risk factors as 'risk predictors' and measured them in the 'most important domains' of risk factor influence at a range of different ages (based on suppositions about when different factors are most likely to be relevant or active at different times in the child's life):

- *Parental (maternal)* – young motherhood (measured at birth of sample child), low maternal IQ and poor maternal reading skills (when sample members were aged three years), poor maternal mental health (age seven, nine and 11 years), mother's neuroticism (when sample members were aged three years), maternal criminality (when sample members were aged 21 years).
- *Family* – deviant (negative, inappropriate) mother–child interaction (when sample members were aged three years), harsh discipline, inconsistent discipline, family conflict (all measured when sample members were aged seven and nine years), number of caregiver changes (when sample members were aged 11 years), number of residence moves (measured when sample members were aged five, seven, nine and 11 years), family socioeconomic status (averaged across the first 15 years of the study), relationship with parents (when sample members were aged 13 and 15 years).
- *Cognitive and neurological* – neurological abnormalities (when sample members were aged three years), intelligence (when sample members were aged three years), low neuropsychological memory scores (when sample members were aged 13 years), poor reading achievement (when sample members were aged seven, nine and 11 years), low resting heart rate (when sample members were aged seven, nine and 11 years).
- *Behavioural (individual)* – difficult temperament (when sample members were aged three and five years), hyperactivity (when sample members were aged five, seven, nine and 11 years), internalising problems (when sample members were aged five, seven, nine and 11 years).

- *Peer relationships* – peer rejection (when sample members were aged five, seven, nine and 11 years), peer attachment (when sample members were aged 13 years), peer delinquency (when sample members were aged 13 years), lack of involvement in school activities (when sample members were aged 15 years).

With the exception of five variables measured at age 13 and 15 years (relationship with parents, attachment to peers, peer delinquency, involvement in school, neuropsychological memory scores), the measurement of so-called *risk predictors* pre-dated the measurement of adolescent antisocial behaviour (as assessed between the ages of 13 and 18 years). Thus, most of the supposed predictive relationships identified are really only indicative of a temporal precedence in the measurement of risk factors (i.e. they were measured some years before the offending measure was taken), rather than necessarily indicating precedence in their onset and/or position in the relationship with offending. Even when the five variables were measured contemporaneously with offending, which would have enabled analysis of the direction of their relationship with offending, there was no examination of their age of onset relative to offending onset, so predictive relationships were not explored.

The first stage of analysis examined correlations between the risk predictors and adolescent antisocial behaviour. Subsequently, multiple regression was employed to establish 'whether the effect of the risk predictor on adolescent antisocial behaviour varies as a function of the Study member's sex' (Moffitt *et al.* 2001: 101).

Although the authors provided brief explanations of how each risk factor may influence antisocial behaviour, they stated that an 'extensive review' of the presumed risk-factor–antisocial behaviour relationship in each case was beyond the scope of the book (Moffitt *et al.* 2001). Such a conclusion illustrates what is implicit throughout the Moffitt *et al.* study, namely that the authors' primary interest was the exploration of sex differences in exposure to risk factors rather than a detailed exploration of the existence, extent and nature of any relationships between risk factors and offending for young people of both sexes.

The Sex Differences in Antisocial Behaviour findings and conclusions

Correlational analysis identified that every *maternal* risk predictor was significantly associated with antisocial behaviour by both males and females (except for mother's neuroticism, which was not associated with female antisocial behaviour). The multiple regression analysis identified no significant gender differences, indicating that maternal risk factors exercised similar levels of (statistical) influence on antisocial behaviour for both genders.

Similarly, all of the *family* risk predictors were significantly correlated with male and female antisocial behaviour, except for 'number of residence moves' (which was not correlated with female antisocial behaviour). The authors found that most of the family risk predictors had stronger effects on male antisocial behaviour than female antisocial behaviour.

In terms of *neuro-cognitive* risk predictors, most were significant predictors of male and female antisocial behaviour, although 'neurological abnormalities' and 'low resting heart rate' had very modest correlations with antisocial behaviour. The predictor of 'intelligence' was found to be more significantly associated with antisocial behaviour for males than females.

Every *behavioural* predictor was significantly correlated with antisocial behaviour by both genders, apart from 'child internalising problems', which was unrelated to antisocial behaviour for either gender. Multiple regression discovered that, in particular, 'difficult temperament' and 'hyperactivity' were more predictive of antisocial behaviour among males than females.

The *peer-relationships* risk factors found to link to antisocial behaviour in boys and girls were 'rejection by other children' during primary school years, 'affiliation with delinquent peers' and 'feeling marginalised from school and conventional peers'. 'Peer rejection in childhood' was more predictive of male antisocial behaviour than antisocial behaviour by females. However, the authors cautioned that unlike in the other domains, peer-relationships risk factors were measured at the same time as antisocial behaviour. Consequently, the direction of the relationship between the two could not be established and thus correlations should be taken to taken to indicate peer-related risk *factors* rather than risk *predictors*.

The authors concluded that:

- the same risk factors predict antisocial behaviour in both males and females, no replicable sex-specific risk factors for antisocial behaviour were identified;
- female antisocial behaviour does not require special attention within aetiological research;
- the risk measures selected from the Dunedin Study archive accounted for most of the variation in antisocial behaviour by males and females;
- temperament, hyperactivity, peer relationships and personality traits can account for most of the sex differences in antisocial behaviour amongst young people;
- developmental contexts are crucial to understanding the influence of risk factors across the life course.

(see Moffitt *et al.* 2001)

Sex Differences in Antisocial Behaviour as RFR

The Sex Differences in Antisocial Behaviour study aimed to contribute to developmental RFR by exploring the influence of risk factors measured from birth – more than satisfying the recommendations of certain developmental risk factor researchers (e.g. Richard Tremblay – see the Montréal Longitudinal and Experimental Study below) that longitudinal RFR begin at earlier ages. This has enabled measures of risk to be obtained several years before measures of antisocial behaviour, enabling the authors to test a wider range of factors (e.g. the under-explored potential of biological/neurological factors – although how much the authors have actually done this is moot) over a longer period and to have more confidence in their temporal precedence and predictive validity than has been possible in other RFR.

Beyond this important difference between the Sex Differences in Antisocial Behaviour study and other developmentally-biased RFR, the study exemplified the methodological weaknesses of its sister studies (psychosocial reductionism, crude factorisation, developmental static determinism etc). However, there are two further matters that strike at the heart of the quality of the Sex Differences in Antisocial Behaviour study that require sustained attention, namely: assumptions of causality based on temporal precedence and the validity of the statistical correlations between risk predictors and antisocial behaviour.

Firstly, the developmental emphasis of the authors has led them to impute predictive relationships between psychosocial variables and antisocial behaviour on the basis of a temporal precedence in the *measurement*, rather than the *onset*, of risk relative to the measurement of antisocial behaviour (an equivalent imputation to that found in the Causes and Correlates studies). The emphasis on measurement periods as indicative of the temporal relationship between risk and antisocial behaviour overlooks the possibility that antisocial behaviour was present in young people's lives prior to age 13 years and, as such, may have pre-dated, overlapped or even become conflated with several of the early childhood risk factors measured from age three to 11 years. In other words, there is no direct link between the presence (measurement) of a risk and the behaviour it is supposed to cause – they are simply measured sequentially and implied to be causally related. The mere statistical identification of temporal precedence of risk predictors over antisocial behaviour does not necessarily indicate an actual relationship between the two beyond the statistical – although this relationship is imputed and used to form the basis of the conclusions of the study (cf the 'psychosis of positivists'). The simple identification of exposure to risk in childhood and an episode of antisocial behaviour in adolescence does not indicate unequivocally that one led to or can explain the other. For example, even if a factor (e.g. harsh parental discipline) was first measured prior to antisocial behaviour, specific episode of/exposure to the factor may have had no actual impact on antisocial behaviour *at that point* (except for statistically) and may actually have been predicted/caused/exacerbated/reintroduced by antisocial behaviour at a later stage or have predicted or caused antisocial behaviour when manifesting itself again later in life. In the absence of detailed temporal and qualitative data, the statistical correlational techniques used in the Sex Differences in Antisocial Behaviour study can only highlight superficial relationships, rather than having any capacity to explain them. Much greater methodological sophistication, than was evident in the Sex Differences in Antisocial Behaviour study, is needed to show that temporal precedence and causality are both present and linked.

Secondly, the uncritical use of aggregation of multiple measures/constructs has produced a dependent variable (antisocial behaviour) so broadly-defined and non-discriminatory that multiple risk factors are inevitably correlated with it, particularly when explored superficially through basic correlational analysis. Although they argue that their approach was justified, Moffit *et al.* artificially constructed the dependent variable of antisocial behaviour so broadly that, in fact, almost every variable in their study was positively correlated with it. Consequently, it is very difficult to read their results as anything other than the crude and simplistic product of weak methodology and an extreme lack of statistical sophistication. Thus the Sex Differences in Antisocial Behaviour study actually contributes little or nothing to our understanding of risk factors and their relationship to antisocial behaviour.

The Montréal Longitudinal and Experimental Study: childhood risk and risk-focused intervention

Originating in 1984, the Montréal Longitudinal and Experimental Study (MLES) aimed 'to study the development of antisocial behaviour from kindergarten to high school with a specific focus on the role of parent–child interactions' (Tremblay *et al.* 2003: 205). The MLES authors espoused an explicitly developmental and psychosocial theoretical basis to their understanding of the impact of risk factors on antisocial behaviour, citing the theoretical influences of the Cambridge-Somerville Youth Study and the Cambridge Study in Delinquent Development. The study's central thesis was that boys with a low socio-economic status (due to their parents' occupations and/or the neighbourhood they live in) who show disruptive behaviour at kindergarten age are most 'at risk' of frequent and serious antisocial behaviour in the future compared to other children from the same environment (Tremblay *et al.* 2003). To examine this thesis, the MLES focused on the impact of parent–child interactions, psychological problems (hyperactivity, anxiety), substance use, school performance, poverty and 'physical factors' (e.g. health, nutrition, pre-natal complications, maturation, hormone levels).

The MLES methodology

In the first year of the study, a purposive sample of 1,161 boys aged six years was taken from kindergartens in 53 schools in 'low socioeconomic status' areas of Montréal, Canada. To control for cultural effects, boys in the sample had to have biological parents born in Canada and had to speak French as their first language. The behaviour of each of the sample members was rated by their teachers using the Preschool Behaviour Questionnaire (Tremblay *et al.* 1987), a 13 item checklist containing indicators of disruptive behaviour: bullying, kicking, biting, hitting, fighting, being disobedient, blaming others, irritability, being destructive, restlessness, being inconsiderate, lying, being 'squirmy', not sharing and being unpopular. The 125 boys rated above the seventieth percentile on the disruptive behaviour scale were classified as 'disruptive'. From this group, 82 boys were allocated to a longitudinal group receiving intensive observation from which 43 were allocated to an experimental intervention/treatment group, which would receive a preventative intervention consisting of parent training and social skills training. A further 41 'non-disruptive' boys (defined by falling below the seventieth percentile on the disruptive behaviour scale) from the original sample constituted a control group against which the findings from the experimental intervention would be evaluated.

On an annual basis, all boys in the three sample groups (control, longitudinal and treatment) were interviewed to investigate (largely psychosocial) factors relating to family relationships, parenting, attitudes to school, peer relationships, leisure time, personality and the impact of life events. These interviews were supplemented by annual questionnaires with mothers that collected information on family background, family relationships, parenting, social support, life events and the child's delinquency over the past 12 months.

Serious delinquency and the frequency of delinquency were measured annually from the ages of ten to 17 years and once again when the boys were aged 20 years. The MLES employed a self-report inventory of 27 delinquent acts, with the boys required to report how often they had committed delinquent acts in the past 12 months, using a four-point Likert-scale: 'never, once or twice, often, very often'.

The annual rounds of interviews have been augmented at various stages in the study by *ratings of behaviour* (physical aggression, opportunism, conduct problems, anxiety, inattention, hyperactivity, prosocial behaviour) by mothers and classroom peers (when the boys were aged ten, 11 and 12 years), *psychiatric interviews* with boys and mothers (when boys were aged 15 years), *direct observation of social interactions* in school, home and in a laboratory setting (between the ages of 7–15 years) and *physiological and neuropsychological tests* with sub-samples of boys (between the ages of 7 and 20 years old).

Logistic regression analysis was conducted to identify ('predictive') statistical relationships between psychosocial factors measured at each data collection episode and delinquency measured in later data collection episodes (Nagin and Tremblay 2005), with the implication being that temporal precedence in the measurement of risk factors equated to (i.e. enabled imputation of) the temporal precedence of risk factors in their relationship of influence with delinquency (i.e. risk factors could be interpreted as predictive and/or causal).

The MLES findings and conclusions

A series of key findings have emerged from the MLES regarding the predictive influence on delinquency of the psychosocial factors measured through the different data collection episodes, in particular:

- *Kindergarten disruptive behaviour* – teacher ratings of physical aggression, hyperactivity and non-prosocial behaviour (but not anxiety or inattentiveness) predicted self-reported delinquency during the transition from childhood to early adolescence (Pulkkinen and Tremblay 1992).
- *Kindergarten personality* – teacher ratings of high levels of impulsivity, low anxiety and lack of regard for others, predicted delinquency during the transition from childhood to adolescence, irrespective of the deviant characteristics of peers (Tremblay *et al.* 1994).
- *Family poverty* – boys from families experiencing economic hardship scored lower on measures relating to learning, physical health, emotion, family and environment. Family poverty predicted serious delinquency (breaking and entering, arson, theft of objects over $100, vandalising a car, beating someone up) but did not predict other types delinquency (e.g. petty theft).
- *Parenting process* – low levels of parental monitoring (e.g. poor supervision, lack of rule-setting in the home) was associated with an increased risk of self-reported serious delinquency.
- *School failure* – there was an association between not being in an age-appropriate classroom at the age of 16 years and delinquency at that age, which suggested a 'significant relationship between academic failure and delinquency'.

(see Tremblay *et al.* 2003)

In relation to the original study aim of exploring the development of antisocial behaviour from kindergarten to school, the authors concluded that the factors they identified were *associated* with delinquency, not causal of this behaviour. Tremblay and colleagues stated that factors were not 'causal' because, 'longitudinal studies are still only correlational studies, and the strong association between a predictor variable at time A and an outcome variable at time B does not necessarily imply a causal relationship. In fact, most time A–time B correlations are probably not causal' (Tremblay *et al.* 2003: 224). However, they did argue that these factors do play a predictive role in either sustaining or reducing antisocial behaviour.

There has been somewhat limited dissemination of the factors identified in the experimental portion of the study, Tremblay *et al.* (2003) reported that three years post-intervention, when most boys were in their final year of elementary school (nine to ten years old), self-reported delinquency amongst members of the treatment group had decreased, as had (teacher- and peer-rated) levels of disruptive behaviour and association with disruptive friends. More members of the treatment group were in an age-appropriate classroom and had fewer disruptive friends than the longitudinal group and this was considered to exert a positive impact at that time and on into high school on different aspects of development such as self-esteem, positive attitudes to school and reduced delinquency (see Vitaro and Tremblay 1994). The frequency of self-reported delinquency was significantly lower in the treatment group compared to the control group three to six years later between the ages of 13 and 16 years, a finding that the authors attributed to the effects of the intervention.

It was concluded by Tremblay and colleagues that 'the importance of the beneficial impact (of the intervention) on elementary school adjustment should not be overlooked' (2003: 232) and that 'comparative changes in delinquent behaviour and the significantly higher levels of academic adjustment observed in youngsters from the experimental group may be attributable to the treatment' (Tremblay *et al.* 2003: 235). However, the authors noted that this positive impact at age ten years had apparently disappeared by the age of 15 years, exemplified by the finding that the majority of the experimental group boys (59 per cent) were not in an age-appropriate classroom by that time. Tremblay *et al.* attempted to explain this 'disappointing' finding by offering a pessimistic conclusion that seems contradictory to their support for the efficacy of the preventative experiment:

> Given that poor school adjustment at age 15 is the norm for this sample of boys from low SES environments, it was unlikely that an intervention directed at disruptive behaviour would have enabled disruptive kindergarten boys to have more success in high school than the majority of their peers. (Tremblay *et al.* 2003: 232)

Notwithstanding their pessimism regarding the potential of the experimental intervention, the authors interpreted (imputed) their findings as suggesting that improvements in parental practices and in the child's social competence/social skills, which were both apparently encouraged by the intervention, were operating as 'protective factors' that discouraged the onset of delinquency and encouraged desistance from delinquency.

The MLES authors recommended the continued use of longitudinal designs within RFR on the basis that correlational (cross-sectional) studies can continue to correlate putative causal variables, assessed at a given point in time, with antisocial behaviour assessed at another point in time (Tremblay *et al.* 2003: 242). Indeed, the study's authors have claimed that their findings highlighted the need for more valid and potentially practical longitudinal exercises 'to start earlier than school entry to understand and prevent the development of antisocial behaviour' (Tremblay *et al.* 2003: 236). Indeed, the authors go on to claim that:

> The MLES still appears, at the beginning of the twenty-first century, to be the largest longitudinal and experimental study specifically designed to understand the development and prevention of delinquency with subjects first assessed before Grade 1. (Tremblay *et al.* 2003: 208)

The MLES as RFR

The MLES design has been, to a point, typical of longitudinal, developmental RFR, in that 'risk' factors have been measured in early childhood and their 'predictive' power has been analysed in adolescence (similar to the approach taken by the Causes and Correlates studies, for example). Where the MLES has sought to be different has been in beginning to measure 'preadolescent' risk (beginning at age six years), so exploring developmental pathways of risk for a longer period (albeit still terminating the main study at 20 years). The MLES has also acknowledged clearly that its attempt to measure the temporal ordering of risk and delinquency has not identified risk factors that can be considered 'causal'. However, risk has been interpreted as predictive of (i.e. prefiguring) delinquency. Stating that factors are predictive of delinquency is a less strong, although more accurate, conclusion to draw than claiming causal relationships. Consequently, the research findings should be interpreted with a lower level of confidence or certainty in the expressed linkages between factors and outcomes than a study which demonstrated causality.

In an attempt to demonstrate the strength of these predictive linkages between childhood developmental risk factors and adolescent outcomes, the MLES adopted an experimental design – with a treatment group receiving interventions targeted on pre-established risk factors. The outcomes of this experiment were, however, mixed, with some benefits in outcomes being enjoyed by the treatment group in the pre-teen years, but these improved outcomes were not evident at age 15 years. How can these results be explained? There are a number of different and sometimes competing possible explanations:

- *Imprecision* – that the imprecise (e.g. aggregated, homogenised, factorised) measurement and imputations of temporal precedence (rather than precise measurement of the timing of risk and offending) inevitably produced multiple correlations that could be interpreted selectively, but which had no validity or explanatory utility for individual young people. For example, the temporal precedence of risk was imputed in the absence of definitive information that the sample boys had not committed delinquent acts before the age of ten years (the first time at which delinquency was measured). Such behaviour may have prefigured, even caused, the onset of risk, but neither preadolescent delinquency nor the age of onset a risk was measured. Furthermore, the psychosocial bias in the MLES has become psychosocial reductionism due to the widespread factorisation of risk, the quantitative, statistical analysis (and consequent deterministic interpretation) of the relationship between risk and delinquency and the portrayal of protective factors as risk-dependent – all to the detriment of more in-depth exploration of risk and protection as processes that can explain delinquency and/or that can be explained and constructed by the young people who commit delinquent acts.
- *Psychosocial reductionism* – that the study actually failed to measure/assess the most relevant factors in early childhood. The developmental focus of the MLES has induced a psychosocial bias within the data collection, to the neglect of, for example, socio-structural factors, thus perpetuating an over-simplified and restricted view of the scope and nature of risk in young people's lives. For example, family poverty (measured by economic hardship) was taken to distinguish young people who were actually poor from those who just lived in the poor/low socio-economic status neighbourhoods (measured by average family income) from which the sample was taken. However, there was little exploration of the specific characteristics of these poor neighbourhoods or the effects of these characteristics on individual risk factors. It was as if low neighbourhood socio-economic status was ascribed the status of a demographic variable/static risk factor (like gender or ethnicity) that could be taken for granted and did not warrant further investigation.
- *Flawed theory* – that the simple developmental model is actually flawed and a young person's life is more shaped by their current circumstances and/or agency than childhood developmental deficits.
- *Invalidity* – that there is, in fact, no causal relationship between factors and outcomes.

- *Artefact* – that the predictive relationship between factors and outcomes exists only in the results of the statistical tests used and not in the real world.
- *Misdirection* – that the interventions targeted the wrong factors (because they did not emerge from study of the group who were actually submitted to them but from prior research) or the interventions themselves were not effective in remedying the attributed deficits.

The MLES set out to utilise its longitudinal design and developmental preconceptions in order to 'test causal hypotheses and identify effective interventions' (Tremblay *et al.* 2003: 230). However, the results actually tell us very little about risk factors and their relationship to delinquency. Although Tremblay *et al.* produced lists of factors that they considered 'predictive' of future delinquency, the test of the validity and relevance of these factors in causing delinquency showed no discernable relationship. It seems likely, therefore, that on the basis of these results that the predictive factors were not predictive at all. Therefore, Tremblay *et al.*'s implication that young people are crash test dummies on an inevitable developmental pathway to delinquency does not bear the weight of much confidence. It is arguable that the MLES actually promulgated a 'black box' (see Porteous 2007) approach to understanding he relationship between both risk factors and delinquency and between risk-focused interventions and the prevention of delinquency. Therefore, the MLES has contributed little substantive knowledge of the risk factors that may predict delinquency, what is happening inbetween intervention and outcome (i.e. delinquency or decreases in delinquency) or *how* the intervention may have changed behaviour (if it did so at all) beyond existing differences between the samples compared, the unmeasured influence of life events or the young person simply growing out of crime.

The Seattle Social Development Project: childhood risk factors, risk-focused intervention and the Social Development Model

In 1985, the prospective longitudinal Seattle Social Development Project (SSDP) was established under the guidance of David Hawkins, the originator of the Social Development Model. The SSDP set out to understand and prevent youth crime and violence by conducting a panel study and by implementing a linked risk-focused intervention. Both the risk factor study and the risk-focused intervention were constructed to test the tenets and constructs of the Social Development Model (Hawkins and Weis 1985); a distinct strand of RFR that 'organises a broad range of risk and protective factors into a model specifying causal hypotheses to capture key elements of socialization' (Hawkins *et al.* 2003: 279). Through a synthesis of various explanatory theories, the Social Development Model has hypothesised parallel and developmentally-specific processes producing prosocial and antisocial behaviours (see Chapter 2). For Hawkins and his colleagues, an empirical investigation into the constructs of the Social Development Model was necessary – for two main reasons:

- the Social Development Model had been established as a hypothetical model with a limited evidential basis;
- the theoretical constructs of the Social Development Model (social control theory, social learning theory and differential association theory), when taken in isolation, could not fully account for the aetiological processes of delinquency, nor were they able to adequately explore delinquency across different developmental stages (see Hawkins *et al.* 2003).

The SSDP methodology

The SSDP drew a purposive, multi-ethnic sample of 808 children aged ten years old from schools in high crime neighbourhoods in Seattle, US. Sample members and their parents were regularly interviewed in the first 12 years of the project (sample members nine times; parents six times). In addition, the children's teachers completed the Child Behaviour Checklist (Achenbach and Edelbrook 1983) for the first five years of the project (1985–1989). Interviews at each data collection point obtained data relating to psychosocial 'risk and protective factors' for offending that overlapped with social development constructs (see Chapter 2), with the measurement of new items relating to sexual activity, work, marriage, pregnancy and parenting being added when the children were over 16 years of age. The factors measured were:

- *Involvement, interaction and perceived rewards/costs* – in relation to school, family, neighbourhood, peer, work and intimate relationships.
- *Skills* – social, academic and work-related.
- *Bonding* – commitment and attachment to school, parents and peers, intimate/marital relationships.
- *Belief in the moral order/antisocial opportunities* – drug availability, antisocial behaviour of others, parental and peer substance use, parental attitudes favourable to drug use.
- *Exogenous variables* – position in the social structure (income, economic deprivation, living arrangements, ethnicity, gender, age), external constraints (parenting, neighbourhood characteristics, victimisation) and individual constitutional factors (cognitive functioning, temperament, factors relating to: school, family, peer network, work and relationships).

The individual variables of aggression, anxiety and depression were measured and factorised through teacher ratings on the Child Behaviour Checklist. Family, school and peer factors were measured in interviews through dichotomous (yes/no) measures of agreement with a series of sub-questions/statements. For example, 'attachment to parents' was a composite of:

- Would you like to be the kind of person your mother is?
- Do you share your thoughts and feelings with your mother?
- Would you like to be the kind of person your father is?
- Do you share your thoughts and feelings with your father?

The factor 'school commitment' was a composite of agreement with two statements:

- I do extra work on my own in class;
- When I have an assignment to do, I keep on working on it until it is finished.

Whereas, the 'low neighbourhood attachment' factor was an aggregation of yes/no responses to three statements:

- I know many people in my neighbourhood;
- I like my neighbourhood;
- I feel safe in my neighbourhood.

(Chung *et al.* 2002: 85–6)

Frequency and seriousness of *delinquency* was measured from age 13 with a self-report inventory asking the children if they had committed any of a series of offences (and if so, how often), namely: vandalism/criminal damage, theft/robbery, assault/violence, use of weapons, selling drugs, being in trouble with the police, traffic offences, white-collar crime, gambling, gang involvement and domestic violence. Offences were broken down into minor, moderate and serious categories (see Chung *et al.* 2002). For example, assault was recorded in terms of picking fights or throwing objects at people (minor), hitting parents, hitting teachers or hitting someone with serious intent (moderate) and using force to get money from people (serious). Similarly, theft was divided into taking things worth less than $5 (minor), taking things with more than $5 but less than $50 (moderate) and taking things worth more than $50 (serious).

The SSDP has collected additional psychosocial risk data from a range of sources, notably *official records* from *schools* (information regarding test scores, special educational needs and disciplinary proceedings collected annually until 1991), the *police* (arrest records collected annually until 1993) and the *courts* (annual collection of sentencing records until sample members were aged 21 years).

Critical of the way in which other studies have adopted crude and/or homogenised offending outcome measures (that, for example, do not offer anything more specific than 'offender' or 'non-offender'), Hawkins *et al.* (2003) were concerned to be more specific in measuring their target outcomes. The authors emphasised the importance of understanding the different developmental trajectories of offending, rather than making oversimplified and generalised comparisons between aggregated groups of 'offenders' and 'non-offenders'. They believed that 'there are distinctive groups that follow distinctive trajectories of offending with distinctive etiologies ... [so] different causal mechanisms and pathways may be needed to understand distinct patterns of criminal behavior over time' (Hawkins *et al.* 2003: 265).

Group-based statistical modelling (Chung *et al.* 2002) identified five groups of young people, each with their own developmental trajectory of offending between the ages of 13 and 21 years:

- *non-offenders* (never offended);
- *late onsetters* (offended after age 13 years);
- *desistors* (had offended at age 13 or older, but were not offending at age 21 years);
- *escalators* (were offending more at age 21 than at age 13 years);
- *chronics* (were offending at equivalent levels at ages 13 and 21 years).

The so-called psychosocial 'predictors' of delinquency for the full sample were measured by using logistic regression to analyse the statistical relationship between risk factors measured at time A (e.g. at ten years old) and a dichotomous (yes/no) measure of delinquency taken at time B (e.g. 18 years old). For each of the developmental trajectory groups, risk factors measured at age 10–12 years were analysed against delinquency measured at 13 years of age and beyond. For example, once the 'late onsetter' group had been established, the psychosocial risks reported by these individuals at age ten years were analysed against their subsequent offending at the age of 13 years and any statistical links were taken to indicate risk factors for these group.

The SSDP findings and conclusions

The psychosocial risk factors and social development model constructs identified as significantly-related to offending in the study were:

- *Family* – positive external constraints imposed by the family (e.g. consistent rules, clear behavioural boundaries) were associated with the absence of delinquency during adolescence (Kosterman *et al.* 2000). However, bonding to the family was *not* statistically-linked to non-delinquency (Hill *et al.* 2002), in opposition to a central tenet of the Social Development Model that family bonding exerts a protective influence. That said, the authors acknowledged that because they did not ensure that the bonding measured was to prosocial family members, the SSDP analyses failed to account for the existing criminality, violence or antisocial attitudes of family members, which themselves could have been modelled by sample members, in accordance with Social Learning Theory (Hawkins *et al.* 2003).

- *School* – low academic achievement measured at age 12–13 years predicted delinquency at age 15–16 years (Herrenkohl *et al.* 2000), whilst high academic achievement was linked to the absence of delinquency (Ayers *et al.* 1999). A lack of bonding to school was also a risk factor for later delinquency (Ayers *et al.* 1999) and violent behaviour at age 18 years (Herrenkohl *et al.* 2000), especially when combined with low academic achievement.

- *Peer group* – association with delinquent peers (along with delinquent siblings and adults) statistically-predicted future delinquent behaviour, notably serious delinquency at age 12–13 years (O'Donnell *et al.* 1995).

- *Individual* – having poor social skills at age 12–13 years was predictive of delinquency at age 15–16 years, whilst young people with higher levels of social skills and substance use refusal skills were significantly less likely to report delinquent behaviours between the ages of 12 and 14 years than young people without these interaction skills (Ayers *et al.* 1999).

- *Developmental trajectories* – according to Chung *et al.* (2002), late onsetters at age 13 years were significantly more likely than non-delinquents to report individual risk factors (especially aggression, anxiety and depression) at age 10–12 years, whereas escalators from age 13 years were more likely than desisters to report peer, school and neighbourhood factors (especially lack of attachment/bonding to school, availability of drugs in the neighbourhood and antisocial peers) at age 10–12 years. Chung *et al.* (2002) went on to analyse risk factors (measured at age 10–12) for each offending trajectory group in relation to the seriousness of their offending. They found that poor family management was a risk factor for minor offending by the late onsetter group only, aggressive behaviour was a risk factor for both minor and serious offending amongst the late onsetter and chronic offender groups, whilst having antisocial peers, low academic achievement, low school bonding, low neighbourhood attachment and availability of drugs in the neighbourhood were all risk factors associated with minor and serious offending amongst the escalator, desister and chronic offender groups.

Hawkins and colleagues concluded that their analysis of the interview data and additional data sources had enabled them to pinpoint the 'indicators of major psychosocial risk factors for crime' (Hawkins *et al.* 2003: 257) and to establish the large degree to which social development model constructs are able to predict delinquency. The authors also concluded (from the identification of developmental offending trajectories) that early intervention was crucial in order to prevent the development of delinquency and other problem outcomes (e.g. violence) and multiple interventions should be prioritised as responses to the multiple pathways into delinquency. Most importantly, it was concluded that 'developmental trajectories do not require different etiological theories. Constructs from the social development model can account for somewhat different factors contributing to different behavioral trajectories' (Chung *et al.* 2002: 82).

The linked SSDP intervention

In order to explore experimentally the influence of the psychosocial risk factors identified (see above) and their malleability within risk-focused intervention, students in the SSDP sample were assigned to one of four groups: a *control* group that received no interventions, a *parent-training only* group (parents received training when the child was in grades 5–6, i.e. aged 10–11 years), a *late intervention* group (the child received a social development intervention and parents received parent training when the child was in grades 5–6 only) and a *full intervention* group (which received social development intervention and parent training when the child was in grades 1–6, i.e. aged 4–11 years).

The SSDP evaluation compared the effect of risk and protective factors on delinquency once sample members had been exposed (or not exposed in the case of the control group) to the type(s) of interventions offered to their group, which consisted social development and/or parent training:

- The *social development intervention* 'sought to reduce specific risk factors and to increase protective factors for adolescent health and behaviour problems specified in the social development model' (Hawkins *et al.* 2003: 284). Particular focus was given to risk factors in the domains of family (clarity of parental norms and rules for behaviour, consistently enforced behavioural expectations, poor family management practices, favourable parental attitudes towards problem behaviour, family conflict, family bonding), school (academic failure, attachment and commitment to school) and peers (delinquent and antisocial peer influence).

Classroom teachers were trained in proactive classroom management, interactive teaching and co-operative learning techniques, combined with giving social skills training to students. In particular, the teaching interventions aimed to increase the protective factors of clarity of school behavioural norms and rules, consistently enforced expectations for behaviour, academic achievement and attachment to school. The social skills element was focused on increasing resistance to delinquent peers.

- The *parent training* consisted of parenting evenings for 'developmentally-adjusted' training in effective parenting skills and supporting children's success – in order to enhance the alleged protective efficacy of effective family management, bonding to the family, avoiding/dealing with family conflict and constructive parental attitudes to problem behaviour.

The SSDP intervention results

Two years following completion of the interventions, the full intervention group (compared to the control group) demonstrated significantly lower levels of delinquency and aggression, but significantly higher levels of family management, involvement with family, attachment to family and attachment/commitment to school (Hawkins *et al.* 1991). These findings remained consistent at age 18 years, six years following the interventions (Hawkins *et al.* 1999). At the age of 18 years, young people who had been in the full intervention group were significantly more likely than control group members to be more attached and committed to school, to have demonstrated higher academic achievement and to display lower levels of delinquency and violence.

According to Hawkins *et al.* (2003), the SSDP demonstrated an intervention 'dose effect', with greater reductions in offending and more positive outcomes evidenced in the full intervention group, followed by the late intervention group, then the parent training only group and finally the controls. The authors concluded that risk and protective factors were equivalent to 'causal processes' that should be addressed using multiple interventions, because there are multiple direct and indirect paths to offending and violence. They emphasised the importance of intervening early in the development of delinquent pathways and the need for a dual focus on interrupting negative pathways and promoting positive pathways (Hawkins *et al.* 2003). Moreover, the risk and protective factors identified in the SSDP were considered to be viable foci for preventative interventions in childhood and adolescence because 'interventions that change the course of development during childhood can have long-term positive effects in promoting prosocial bonding and reducing violence' (Hawkins *et al.* 2003: 303).

The SSDP as RFR

Hawkins and his colleagues do not appear to be developmentalists in the traditional sense (i.e. advocates of childhood risk factors leading to adolescent offending). Their focus has been on identifying influential risk *processes*, including those leading to *pro*social behaviour, and their strand of RFR is not as reductionist and oversimplified as much extant RFR, largely due to the attempts to identify different developmental trajectories ranging from adolescence through to young adulthood. However, a degree of reductionism has remained which has undermined the depth and complexity of the resultant understandings of risk that have been produced. The major limitations of the ongoing SSDP have been (and continue to be) the pervasive psychosocial bias that results in the authors pre-empting the most important risk factors to measure, along with the factorisation and aggregation of potentially complex and multi-faceted risk and social development constructs that are specific to individual young people; procedures that wash away much of the dynamic, qualitative and nuanced nature of both constructs. This bleaching out of complexity has been exacerbated by the aggregation of risk data across a series of broadly-framed groups (i.e. the experimental intervention groups and the developmental trajectory groups) such that the mooted antisocial and prosocial pathways are not representative (or necessarily relevant to) any specific individuals in the study sample. Furthermore, the different offending trajectories identified and explored actually emerged from a single, 'general' measure of offending which, as the authors acknowledged, lacked sensitivity to the potentially-diverse aetiologies of different forms of offending (Chung *et al.* 2002).

A central weakness in the SSDP research conclusions was the overly-basic and literal use of temporal precedence to indicate the predictive effects of risk factors and social development constructs. Information relating to risk and social development was collected annually from when the sample members were aged ten (i.e. Time A), whilst offence data was not collected until sample members were aged 13 (i.e. Time B). Subsequently, predictive relationships between risk factors/social development constructs and offending/offending trajectories were identified on the basis of temporal precedence (i.e. that measures taken at Time A predated those taken at Time B). However, as has been discussed at length previously, basic temporal precedence such as this does not necessarily indicate predictive influence, nor does it tell us anything about causal relationships or dynamic processes, the latter of which was claimed by the study authors. All that was established conclusively by the SSDP research was that risk factors/social development constructs could be measured prior to offending and statistically associated with different offending trajectories and differing levels of offence seriousness, with no consideration that (unmeasured) offending episodes could have pre-dated and therefore influenced the onset of risk factors/social development constructs and no definitive explanation as to how, if at all, risk factors/social development constructs were related to offending. There was certainly little evidence provided to support the claim that risk factors are 'causal processes' in the pathways to offending. This final point suggests a criticism of the conclusions from the intervention element of the SSDP; the forming of confident conclusions based on a lack of available empirical evidence to explain (as opposed to impute) how, if at all, the different interventions were related to and/or influenced risk factors/social development constructs and ultimately brought about changes in offending.

The SSDP offered some bold claims as to the positive and independent effects of its interventions on offending pathways (with the potential influence of extraneous factors not even acknowledged), but there were weak links between the breadth of these conclusions, the findings from the research element of the study and the design of the project. Therefore, the supposed validation of the Social Development Model constructs in the SSDP research and intervention elements appears to have rested on the replication of traditional developmental risk and protective factors and the apparent success of the social development interventions, rather than on any validated, definitive understandings of substantive relationships with offending or the actual processes of change precipitated by risk and protective factors/social development constructs.

The Edinburgh Study of Youth Transitions and Crime: towards a synthesised, integrated explanation of risk

The prospective longitudinal Edinburgh Study of Youth Transitions and Crime was co-directed by David J. Smith, Lesley McAra and Susan McVie in the School of Law at the University of Edinburgh. The Edinburgh Study, as it has become known, began in 1998 with funding from the ESRC (1998–2002) and has been subsequently funded by the Scottish Executive (2002–2005) and the Nuffield Foundation (2002–2005). Although Scotland is part of the UK, this Scottish research is included in the international chapter partly because the focus of much of this book is on England and Wales, but for other reasons too. Scotland has a distinctive culture, legal system, criminal justice system and polity which is reflected in the study's design and intention to speak to an international audience. The Edinburgh Study was 'not concerned with early childhood influences, but with transitions and personal transformations during adolescence and adulthood' (Smith and McVie 2003: 169–70) on the basis that earlier RFR had demonstrated the predictive ability of childhood risk factors, but with a worrying number of 'false positives' (children predicted to offend in the future who did not), which highlighted the significance of *adolescent* influences on offending. Thus the authors set out explicitly to build on but go beyond existing research. The research team's desire to broaden the scope and ambition of traditional RFR by addressing previously-neglected foci was reflected in their statement of the key aims of the Edinburgh Study:

> Unlike previous studies, it focuses in particular on explaining gender differences, and on the mechanisms leading to serious, long-term, and frequent offending. It aims to assess the influence of contact with the official systems on subsequent criminal careers. Finally it integrates explanations at the level of the individual and local community. (Smith and McVie 2003: 169)

Therefore, the study team sought to extend RFR by formulating an holistic, integrated understanding of risk influence that could be applied to the study of youth offending universally in different contexts for different samples of young people. Accordingly, the Edinburgh Study deliberately adopted a broad and comprehensive methodology. The study team was particularly interested in exploring individual development (i.e. developmental strand of RFR), young people's interactions with formal and informal agencies of control (compatible with the Social Development Model and the life course strand of RFR), how young people negotiated their pathways into and out of offending (cf. the pathways approach) and the interactions between individualised, psychosocial (risk) factors (e.g. personality, family) and socio-structural neighbourhood factors (e.g. social controls in the community, physical environment) such as those typically explored by ecological RFR. By integrating knowledge and perspectives drawn from across the disparate strands of RFR, the Edinburgh Study aimed to better 'understand the causes of youth crime and how offending emerges in the process of development from childhood to adulthood' (Smith and McAra 2004: 14).

The Edinburgh Study methodology

The Edinburgh Study cohort consisted of 4,317 young people aged between 11½ and 12½ years who entered Edinburgh secondary schools in autumn 1998. In total, 40 of the 49 secondary schools in Edinburgh participated (including all state-funded mainstream schools and most of the independent sector and special educational schools) in the six annual sweeps of data collection from 1998–2003. Data has thus far been collected from multiple sources using multiple methods:

- *Pastoral teacher questionnaire* (1999 only): an abbreviated version of the Goodman's Strengths and Difficulties Questionnaire (Goodman 1997), which measures problem and prosocial behaviour by 4–16 year olds by rating young people on ten statements about their behaviour and emotional state.

- *Parent/carer survey* (2001 only): assessed family structure, relationships, conflict, parental supervision and discipline, parental contact with the school, knowledge of the child's leisure activities and offending behaviour.
- *Official records*: collected from the local Social Work Department (1998–2006), Children's Hearings system (1998–2005), police (2001–2002), schools (1998–2003) and Scottish Criminal Records Office (2006).
- *Neighbourhood information*: police recorded crime data, census data such as migration and high youth population statistics (indicating neighbourhood instability) and rates of unemployment, overcrowding, renting and single-parent households (indicating economic deprivation), and information collected from a community survey of Edinburgh residents carried out in 2001. Overall, the Edinburgh team categorised 91 local neighbourhoods based on six census characteristics producing indicators of levels of social stress and official (police-recorded) offending statistics.

The main data collection instruments have been:

- *Young person questionnaire*: measuring prevalence and frequency of self-reported offending and a set of 'explanatory' factors seen as increasing the 'risk' of offending. These factors were identified following 'extensive consultation with researchers in the UK and those involved in longitudinal studies of crime and young people in the US and New Zealand' (D.J. Smith *et al.* 2001: 10).
- *Young person interview*: individual qualitative interviews following up the questionnaires by measuring a range of more specific issues, including reasons for involvement in, and desistance from, offending.

In the questionnaire, active delinquency (i.e. in the past 12 months) has been measured using an inventory of 18 offences. From sweep three onwards, the general delinquency category was sub-divided into *broad* delinquency (having committed any of the offences on the inventory) and *serious* delinquency (having committed any serious delinquent act – joyriding, carrying a weapon, robbery with force or threats, car breaking, arson).

Explanatory factors in the questionnaire have been measured in terms of:

- *Family* – parental supervision, autonomy/parental trust, conflict with parents, parental discipline, activities with parents;
- *School* – attachment to school, parents' commitment to school, misbehaviour at school and punishment, truancy;

- *Neighbourhood* – cohesion (being friendly with people in the neighbourhood), problems (e.g. vandalism, selling drugs, fighting), policing;
- *Lifestyle* – experience of bullying and victimisation, hanging around the streets, substance use, contact with the police;
- *Peers* – peer pressure, friendship groups and relationships, peer delinquency and substance use;
- *Individual* – self-esteem, alienation, impulsivity, moral reasoning, future aspirations, worries and coping strategies.

(see D.J. Smith *et al.* 2001; Smith and McVie 2003)

Each 'explanatory' element was a composite measure of responses to a set of sub-statements (covering the past 12 months) with which young people had to indicate their strength of agreement on a Likert-scale, with high scores indicating a high level of that (risk) factor. For example, 'parental supervision' was a composite of four items (how often your parents know where you are going, who you are with, what time you will be home and whether you came back on time) scored on a four point scale of 'always', 'usually', 'sometimes' or 'never'. The same scale was used to factorise 'parent/child conflict', which was a composite of responses to the question 'how often do you argue with your parents about' followed by a series of issues ('how tidy your room is', 'what you do when you go out', 'what time you come home', 'who you hang about with', 'your clothes and appearance'). On the other hand, 'police contact' (measured as yes or no), has been a conflation of children's hearings records of police referral for 15 year olds, whether the young person self-reported being charged by the police before age 15 years (yes or no) and number of times in trouble with the police in the last year (from none to 11 and above).

At sweeps one and two (when the young people were aged 12 and 13 years), baseline measures of delinquency and explanatory factors were taken and simple correlations between the two were examined statistically using binary regression (D.J. Smith *et al.* 2001). From sweep three onwards 'the study provided the first real opportunity to carry out more sophisticated analysis of the data, making use of the longitudinal design of the study and testing the effects of explanatory and potentially causal factors on later delinquency' (McVie 2003: 24). Consequently, multivariate analyses have been employed to investigate relationships between factors measured at earlier ages (e.g. during sweeps one and two) and delinquency (general and serious) measured at a later stage and to 'estimate the effect of each of the explanatory variables as a predictor of delinquency, after taking into account the effect of all of the others' (Smith and McAra 2004: 17).

The Edinburgh Study researchers were also interested to explore the potential for system contact to amplify deviance. In the Scottish context, the 'system' comprised contact with the police (stage one of the system), referral by a police Juvenile Liaison Officer to the reporter (stage two) and reporter referral (stage three) to a children's hearing (a welfare-based, needs-orientated decision-making system predicated on early and minimal intervention). At sweep four of the study (with young people aged 14½–15½ years – the peak age of referral to the reporter in the study and nationally across Scotland), binary logistic regression was used to identify the psychosocial characteristics of young people referred to each stage of the system. To control for selection effects and to highlight the characteristics of young people moving through the system, propensity score matching was conducted, whereby individuals in the system were statistically-matched with a comparable (control) group from the original Edinburgh sample who were not in the system (McAra and McVie 2007).

The Edinburgh Study findings and conclusions

In relation to the *family*, poor parental supervision and parent/child conflict at both sweeps one and two was significantly correlated with later delinquency (D.J. Smith *et al.* 2001). Smith and McAra (2004) discovered that parenting style and family functioning (parents tracking and monitoring behaviour, child's willingness to disclose information, parental consistency, parent/child conflict, excessive punishment) measured at age 13 years (sweep two) predicted delinquency at age 15 years (sweep four), which 'demonstrates that parenting had a genuine causal influence on the later behaviour of teenagers' (Smith and McAra 2004: 3).

In terms of *school*: attitudes to school, relationships with teachers and school-based misbehaviour were all closely correlated with delinquency in the first two sweeps of the study (D.J. Smith *et al.* 2001). Attachment to school (particularly attachment to teachers and the belief that school success will bring later rewards) measured at age 13 years was predictive of delinquency at age 15 years, as was parental commitment to school, which suggested that 'there is a role for schools in preventing the development of delinquent behaviour' (D.J. Smith 2006: 4).

There were significant correlations between different indicators of deprivation in the *neighbourhood* and delinquency in sweeps one and two (D.J. Smith *et al.* 2001). This finding was reinforced at sweep five (when young people aged 16 years), which used ordinal regression to identify correlations between concurrent measures of delinquency and measures of neighbourhood deprivation (high unemployment, dense local authority housing, dissatisfaction with the neighbourhood, living in a disorderly neighbourhood), as opposed to measures of individual deprivation (e.g. separation from parents, unemployment (D.J. Smith 2006). In contrast, young people who reported delinquency at age 12 years were more likely to have desisted by the age of 17 years if they lived in a socially advantaged neighbourhood and reported bonding with parents and teachers and parental involvement in school in the intervening period (D.J. Smith 2006).

The main *peer-* and *lifestyle*-related factor highlighted was gang membership, which predicted delinquency at age 17 years when measured at age 12 years (Bradshaw and Smith 2005). Contact with the police and local criminal justice agencies was also significantly-correlated with continued delinquency (D.J. Smith 2006; McAra and McVie 2007).

At the *individual* level, impulsivity (measured at age 16 years) was more strongly-correlated with delinquency measured at the same age than was neighbourhood deprivation (D.J. Smith 2006).

At sweep four, a detailed analysis of gender-specific explanatory factors (using ordinal regression to measure the explanatory variables and delinquency concurrently) concluded that 'the pattern of findings were similar for boys and girls, suggesting that for the most part the same model of explanation for delinquency is likely to apply to both' (Smith and McAra 2004: 16).

The system contact/deviancy amplification element of the study initially identified ten variables (experienced in the past year) that statistically predicted selection at each stage of the system, namely: gender (male), non-two parent family, free school meal entitlement (a measure of poverty), drug use, hanging out most days, truancy, neighbourhood deprivation, early police contact, number of times in trouble with police and volume of serious offending (McAra and McVie 2007: 331), which suggests that system contact and progression through the system was the product of particular decision-making processes. The most notable finding was that although the self-reported serious offending of both groups (those in the system and matched controls) decreased between sweeps four and five, young people exposed to children's hearings at sweep four were significantly more likely to report serious offending one year later. This suggested to the authors that 'repeated and more intensive forms of contact with agencies of youth justice may be damaging to young people in the long-term' (McAra and McVie 2007:333) due to, *inter alia*, labelling, creating a master status of offender, exacerbating socio-structural factors already outside of the young person's control (e.g. family structure, social deprivation, gender) and targeting intervention on the family and education rather than on the individual and the offence (McAra and McVie 2007).

The Edinburgh Study as RFR

The Edinburgh Study has most assuredly *not* been atheoretical, as other RFR studies have claimed to be (cf. Glueck and Glueck 1950; Farrington 1988). It has been an ambitious project that has explicitly aimed to incorporate and evaluate several different strands of RFR in one comprehensive study. The authors have set out to develop more comprehensive 'explanatory models' of how risk factors operate (e.g. with reference to a broader set of micro-and macro-level influences) than have been explored in more restricted forms of RFR. For example, the integrated Edinburgh approach has moved beyond typical ecological considerations of neighbourhood 'collective efficacy' (Sampson *et al.* 1997), community functioning and neighbourhood socio-economic status (Wikström and Loeber 1998) to explore broader and much-neglected socio-structural factors (e.g. gender, family structure, social deprivation) and deleterious impact of contact with criminal justice agencies, using official data sources, self-reports and innovative statistical techniques such as propensity score matching.

A key conclusion from the Edinburgh Study has been that the 'explanatory variables' for broad and serious offending form 'explanatory models' which can be used to guide policy and practice with young people. However, what are these explanatory models and, if they exist, what are they actually explaining? The Edinburgh Study has addressed the temporal ordering of risk and delinquency through regression analyses of risk measured at time (sweep) A and delinquency measured at time (sweep) B and supplemented this procedure with multivariate analysis of the individual influence of each factor when controlling for the effects of all others. However, like other longitudinal RFR studies, the Edinburgh Study has not measured the onset of risk in relation to the onset of delinquency, so conclusions of temporal precedence and explanatory power have been restricted to imputations based on the temporal ordering of *measurements* of risk and delinquency rather than any necessary *actual* real world relationship. Therefore, the researchers have been unable to demonstrate or model any definitive real-world (non-statistical) relationship between the two, unable to demonstrate the direction, intensity and duration of any relationships and unable to offer detailed, evidenced, qualitative explanations of the processes by which factors may impact on delinquency or vice versa.

Indeed, this explanatory problem is common to much RFR. For the most part the Edinburgh Study researchers are sensitive to this issue. For example, they have employed ordinal regression techniques to produce explanatory 'models' which they have acknowledged to be 'contemporaneous models (the explanatory and the outcome variables described the same time period) not longitudinal models showing the effects . . . on later delinquency' (Smith and McAra 2004: 17). However, again in common with much RFR, the slip to claims of causality is never far away (cf. Smith and McAra 2004: 3). The problem of demonstrating causality between risks and outcomes (and the associated imputed strength of relationship between variables) is endemic to artefactual RFR. On the other hand, demonstrating statistically predictive relationships between factors and outcomes is a realistic product of RFR, but it must be recognised that the strength of these relationships is far from certain. The strength, even of predictive relationships and the degree of confidence we can place in them is dependent on a range of additional matters. Quality of measurement, specificity of factorisation, clear temporal precedence and the appropriate use of statistical tests are all issues shown to have an impact on the veracity of findings and conclusions from RFR. So too, theoretical influence, researcher bias and the age-related collection of data, plus the types of data collected (psychosocial, structural etc) all have an impact on the confidence that should be placed in the findings from the Edinburgh Study.

The Edinburgh Study was explicitly designed and developed to address the known weaknesses of much previous RFR, but as yet, success has been limited. The focus on socio-structural influences and the influence of system contact has been a welcome challenge to the reductionist psychosocial bias of much artefact RFR. However, the Edinburgh Study has retained a predominantly psychosocial, factorised and cross-sectional view of risk in line with the limitations of much previous developmental and artefactual research.

A vast amount of data has been collected within the Edinburgh Study and it should be recognised that to date the analysis of this data remains in its early stages. Befitting their comprehensive strategy and the critical, reflexive approach the authors say they are taking, they have eschewed a simple developmental hypothesis in analysing the data and have stated a desire to test different theoretical models and hypotheses using increasingly complex statistical modelling techniques, even employing a designated statistician for this purpose. However, this remains a nascent process and results to date remain limited.

The explanatory models in the Edinburgh Study have been extricated from a patchwork of theories and methodologies from across the gamut of RFR; research that has been characterised by a theoretical, methodological, analytical and interpretive diversity. Therefore, it is debatable as to whether these various strands are able to hang together in a coherent and consistent integrated model, particularly one intent on factorising complex risk measures and fitting diverse theoretical explanations into a developmental paradigm for analysing and interpreting the 'predictive' and 'explanatory' power of these 'risk factors'. Consequently, it is difficult to evaluate whether the Edinburgh Study represents an evolution of RFR through a coordinated and internally valid approach or whether it is merely a collection of loosely-connected theories and approaches within a study, each examining different aspects of risk within a methodology that remains devoutly developmental in orientation (although having its origins in adolescence rather than childhood) and interpreting findings through the post-hoc application of 'relevant' theories or whether the study has set out to 'test' the validity and veracity of different models, but has not done so as yet. The diverse, disparate theoretical foci have, to an extent, robbed the research of a clear and coherent theoretical identity and have had their central tenets over-simplified by a reductionist approach to measurement and analysis, which has limited the definitiveness with which conclusions can be supported.

The universal risk factor: hunted down or created?

RFR has certainly become a global enterprise (see France and Homel 2007); at least if 'global' is taken to mean spanning the industrialised 'Western' World. From its origins in the US in the work of the Gluecks, through to the hugely influential Cambridge Study of West and Farrington in the UK and beyond, RFR has spread to many, if not most, Western countries. RFR studies across the globe have made use of longitudinal and cross-sectional research designs, typically consisting of survey methods (questionnaires and interviews) followed by the factorisation and statistical analysis of psychosocial background factors and factors in current life as a way of understanding and explaining youth offending. Perhaps quite naturally, even inevitably, as this disparate body of international research findings has emerged, researchers have looked at the overall body of knowledge and drawn out commonalities in their findings. However, has the widespread global replication and apparent commonality of risk factors in (largely developmental) RFR ignored or disregarded the vast 'contextual and cultural variations' between (and within) different countries (Hargreaves 2007: 5), not to mention individual differences in relation to age, gender, ethnicity, locality and type of offence?

The global enterprise of RFR that has replicated largely the same body of psychosocial risk factors across time, place and sample and fostered claims to generalisable, universalised risk factors has not been an entirely homogenous, coordinated international research effort, but rather a series of heterogeneous studies informed by divergent theoretical underpinnings and a range of aims and objectives. However, substantive homogeneity has been evident in the narrow range of psychosocial risk factors measured, the pervasive (often crude) factorisation of risk and the use of statistical analyses to impute temporal precedence – the majority of which have encouraged developmentalist conclusions regarding the predictive validity of risk factors and their existence as potential globally-applicable 'universal truths' (D. Smith 2006). The consistent replication of developmental understandings of psychosocial measures of risk across location, context, developmental stage, sample and time has fuelled claims of the existence of universal 'risk factors', which are typically understood as present in childhood and exerting a deterministic, predictive and comparable impact on offending in adolescence for all young people. Subsequent 'successful' risk-focused intervention programs (e.g. MLES, SSDP) have reinforced and valorised developmental understandings of how risk factors influence offending universally – sometimes against the evidence.

However, in reaching these conclusions, the international RFR movement has uncritically assumed that replicability across countries implies *comparability*, in the face of differences between- and within-studies in terms of, *inter alia*:

- sample composition and age range;
- socio-political context (which impacts on diverse definitions of offending, delinquency and antisocial behaviour in different countries);
- constructions of risk and protection by young people;
- constructions of risk and protection by researchers choosing the factorisation processes and standardised instruments with which to measure and interpret risk;
- the precise timing of data collection episodes and analyses;
- the theoretical bases that have informed the study;

Subsequent conclusions regarding the efficacy of risk-focused interventions have simply compounded the extant limitations and weaknesses of RFR by imputing explanations for successful outcomes, equivalent to how much RFR has imputed the nature of the relationship between risk factors and offending.

Farrington (2002) has maintained that if cross-national differences are evident in RFR then criminologists need to identify the 'active ingredients' that explain them (e.g. social, cultural, legal, or criminal justice processes in different countries). However, researchers simply have not looked for these ingredients and have preferred to impute any causal/explanatory linear influence of risk and risk-focused interventions using superficial statistical manipulations and the uncritical acceptance of temporal ordering as a basis for the developmental influence of risk on current behaviour and developmental pathways. There has been little consideration that factors may actually *post-date* and *be caused by* offending/delinquency/antisocial behaviour, occur concurrently to these behaviours (either maintaining a relationship with them or not at that time) or *pre-date* the target behaviours but have no influence on them at the time of their measurement (e.g. the factor causes offending during exposure at a later point, possibly when exposure is more intense and/or over a longer duration).

A global RFR movement has attempted to identify risk factors as universal in influence and replicable across the globe. However, standardised cross-sectional RFR and longitudinal replications of generalised, developmental and artefactual understandings of risk have eschewed analysis of the validity of risk factors in young people's lives and has arguably washed away the cultural, political, social, national and local differences that impact on:

- different constructions and understandings of 'childhood', 'youth', 'gender', 'ethnicity' and 'offending';
- the definitions and interpretations of risk that influence how they are responded to by young people, families, communities and countries;
- the ability of different groups of young people to resist, negotiate and influence risk at different stages in their lives.

Studies have, therefore, largely ignored 'the historical and social context and . . . the importance of diversity and local knowledge rather than only searching for universal relationships' (Pearce 1996: 682). International RFR has demonstrated a similar insensitivity to between- and within-individual differences in the risk–offending relationship relating to, *inter alia*, age, gender, ethnicity, type/seriousness/duration/frequency of offending and the intensity, duration and frequency of exposure to risk and protection. Therefore the 'universalism' of understandings of risk has been artificially restricted by the psychosocial bias, reductionism and determinism inherent to the hegemonic developmental strand of RFR. Much international RFR has been oversimplified by its 'developmentocentric' and positivistic nature, which has understood risk and protection through crude factorisation, aggregation and imputation. Across the Western world, a dominant form of largely developmental RFR has privileged the investigation of childhood factors and their predictive influence on offending in adolescence over the influence of these or other factors in current life.

International RFR has characterised the risk-factor–offending relationship as predetermined at an early age, implying that children are crash test dummies inextricably bound for deleterious outcomes in the absence of risk-focused intervention at earlier and earlier ages. Neither the methodological validity of these deterministic conclusions, nor the validity of measuring the salience of childhood risk factors in the lives of older children and young people, has been adequately questioned or evaluated by developmentalists. A developmental determinism has attained clear hegemony in the field, reflected in and perpetuated by the predominance of developmental studies within major reviews of international RFR. However, the chosen studies, the selected definitions of 'risk' factors and the preferred interpretations of the relationship between these factors and offending included in these reviews have been dictated by two of the most prominent developmental risk factor researchers since the inception of the paradigm (David Farrington and Michael Rutter). This inherent bias has been overlooked and the reviews have become established as ostensibly independent and comprehensive depictions of the state of RFR knowledge.

The global 'movement' of RFR has been typified by a mismatched power struggle between high profile developmental research and a small, almost invisible body of qualitative, ethnographic studies, predominantly in England and Wales (e.g. the pathways studies discussed in Chapters 2 and 3). Developmental devotees committed to the (often government supported) investigation of globally applicable, universal risk factors in the form of clinical (e.g. 'objectively' measured, amenable to treatment), psychosocial *variables* have established proprietary rights over RFR. The mid-1950s hegemony of sociological, explanatory theories of the risk–offending relationship appears a distant memory. There is a clear theoretical and methodological hegemony of artefact-based models of risk 'factors' over qualitative understandings of risk *processes* of influence in a more complex relationship between young people and offending. The ongoing international agenda and dominant paradigm for RFR has been misguided – reflective of an aggressive attempt by psycho-developmentalists to dominate aetiological explanations of youth offending. However, the resultant 'explanations' have imputed and extrapolated more than they can explain through the over-simplified factorisation and aggregation of risk (largely confined to psychosocial domains), the over-generalised and unrepresentative analysis of statistical differences between-groups rather than within-individuals, the imputation that risk factors have temporal precedence over the onset of offending and the consequent imputation that these factors exert a causal or predictive influence on offending. The self-perpetuating developmentalism and artefactualism of much international RFR undermines any claims that explanations of risk, risk factors and risk-focused interventions are universally-applicable. More importantly, the biases and limitations of international RFR question the validity of the label of 'risk factor' on two levels:

- whether risk and its relationship with offending can or should be explored and understood quantitatively in terms of 'factors'?
- whether the factors identified in RFR actually indicate 'risk' of offending in any explanatory or predictive sense beyond the statistical?

If the answer to either question is no, then the feasibility, validity and appropriateness of the very notion of 'risk factor research' is open to question. Crucially, neither of these questions can be answered adequately with reference to the existing international body of RFR. The reason for this answer is, however, largely because the methodological and analytical quality of this research is so inconsistent and weak that it is impossible to make a reasoned judgement. Consequently, whilst the intention (at the outset of this chapter) was to investigate international RFR and to explore/evaluate the notion of the universal risk factor, what was discovered was a range of studies so flawed that, in fact, they preclude definitive conclusions because the research itself has not produced findings or conclusions robust enough to base conclusions on.

Bibliography

Achenbach, T.M. and Edelbrock, C. (1983) *Manual for the Child Behavior Checklist and Revised Child Behavior Profile*. Burlington, VT: Queen City Printers.

Ayers, C.D., Williams, J.H.W., Hawkins, J.D., Peterson, P.L., Catalano, R.F. and Abbott, R.D. (1999). 'Assessing correlates of onset, escalation, deescalation, and desistance of delinquent behavior', *Journal of Quantitative Criminology*, 15: 277–306.

Bradshaw, P. and Smith, D.J. (2005) *Gang Membership and Teenage Offending*, Edinburgh Study of Youth Transitions and Crime Research Digest No. 8. Edinburgh: The University of Edinburgh.

Browning, K., Huizinga, D., Loeber, R. and Thornberry, T. (1999) *Causes and Correlates of Delinquency Program. OJJDP Fact Sheet*. Washington, DC: Office of Juvenile Justice and Delinquency Prevention.

Case, S.P. (2007) 'Questioning the "evidence" of risk that underpins evidence-led youth justice interventions', *Youth Justice*, 7(2): 91–106.

Catalano, R.F. and Hawkins, J.D. (1996) 'The Social Development Model: A theory of anti-social behaviour', in J. Hawkins (ed.) *Delinquency and Crime: Current Theories*. Cambridge: Cambridge University Press.

Chung, I-J., Hill, K.G., Hawkins, J.D., Gilchrist, L.D. and Nagin, D (2002) 'Childhood predictors of offence trajectories', *Journal of Research in Crime and Delinquency*, 39: 60–90.

Elliott, D.S., Huizinga, D. and Ageton, S.S. (1985) *Explaining Delinquency and Drug Use*. Beverly Hills, CA: Sage.

Elliott, D.S., Ageton, S.S., Huizinga, D., Knowles, B.A. and Canter, R.J. (1983) *The Prevalence and Incidence of Delinquent Behaviour. The National Youth Survey Report No. 26*. Boulder, CO: Behavioral Research Institute.

Farrington, D.P. (1988) 'Studying changes within individuals: The causes of offending', in M. Rutter (ed.) *Studies of Psychosocial Risk: The Power of Longitudinal Data, 158–183*. Cambridge: Cambridge University Press.

Farrington, D.P. (1996) *Understanding and Preventing Youth Crime*. York: Joseph Rowntree Foundation.

Farrington, D.P. (2000) 'Explaining and preventing crime: The globalization of knowledge', *Criminology*, 38(1): 1–24.

Farrington, D.P. (2002) 'Developmental criminology and risk-focused prevention', in M. Maguire, R. Morgan and R. Reiner (eds) *The Oxford Handbook of Criminology*, 3rd edn. Oxford: Oxford University Press.

Farrington, D.P. (2007) 'Childhood risk factors and risk-focused prevention', in M. Maguire, R. Morgan and R. Reiner (eds) *The Oxford Handbook of Criminology*, 4th edn. Oxford: Oxford University Press.

Farrington, D.P. and Loeber, R. (1999) 'Transatlantic replicability of risk factors in the development of delinquency', in P. Cohen, C. Slomkowski and L. Robins (eds) *Historical and Geographical Influences on Psychopathology*. Mahwah, NY: Lawrence Erlbaum.

France, A. and Homel, R. (2007) *Pathways and Crime Prevention: Theory, Policy and Practice*. Cullompton: Willan Publishing.

Glueck, S. and Glueck, E. (1950) *Unraveling Juvenile Delinquency*. New York: Commonwealth Fund.

Goodman, R. (1997) 'The strengths and difficulties questionnaire: A research note', *Journal of Child Psychology and Psychiatry*, 38: 581–6.

Graham, J. and Bowling, B. (1995) *Young People and Crime*. Home Office Research Study 145. London: Home Office.

Hagell, A. and Newburn, T. (1994) *Persistent Young Offenders*. London: Policy Studies Institute.

Hargreaves, D. (2007) 'Teaching as a research-based profession: Possibilities and prospects', in M. Hammersley (ed.) *Educational Research and Evidence-based Practice*. London: Sage.

Hawkins, J.D. and Weis, J.G. (1985) 'The social development model: An integrated approach to delinquency prevention', *Journal of Primary Prevention*, 6: 73–97.

Hawkins, J.D., Catalano, R.F., Kosterman, R., Abbott, R. and Hill, K.G. (1999) 'Preventing adolescent health-risk behaviours by strengthening protection during childhood', *Archive of Paediatrics and Adolescent Medicine'*, 153: 226–34.

Hawkins, J.D., Smith, B.H., Hill, K.G., Kosterman, R., Catalano, R.F. and Abbott. R.D. (2003) 'Understanding and preventing crime and violence. Findings from the Seattle Social Development Project', in T.P. Thornberry and M.D. Krohn (eds) *Taking Stock of Delinquency: An Overview of Findings from Contemporary Longitudinal Studies*. New York: Kluwer.

Hawkins, J.D., Von Kleve, E. and Catalano, R.F. (1991) 'Reducing early childhood aggression: Results of a primary prevention program', *Journal of the American Academy of Childhood and Adolescent Psychiatry*, 30: 208–17.

Herrenkohl, T.I., Maguin, E., Hill, K.G., Hawkins, J.D., Abbott, R.D. and Catalano, R.F. (2000) 'Developmental risk factors for youth violence', *Journal of Adolescent Health*, 26: 176–86.

Hill, K.G., Collins, L.M. and Hawkins, J.D. (2002). 'Examining the progression of offenses in the behavioral repertoire: A Latent Transition Analysis of the development of delinquency and substance use'. Unpublished.

Hirschi, T. (1969) *Causes of Delinquency*. Berkeley, CA: University of California Press.

Huizinga, D. and Espiritu, R. (1999) *Delinquent Behavior of Youth in the Juvenile Justice System*. Pittsburgh, PA: National Center for Juvenile Justice.

Huizinga, D., Esbensen, F. and Weiher, A. (1991) 'Are there multiple paths to delinquency?' *Journal of Criminal Law and Criminology*, 82: 83–118.

Huizinga, D., Weiher, A.W., Espiritu, R. and Esbensen, F. (2003) 'Delinquency and crime. Some highlights from the Denver Youth Survey', in T.P. Thornberry and M.D. Krohn (eds) *Taking Stock of Delinquency: An Overview of Findings from Contemporary Longitudinal Studies*. New York: Kluwer.

Junger-Tas, J., Marshall, I.H. and Ribeaud, D. (2003) *Delinquency in an International Perspective: The International Self-Reported Delinquency Study*. The Hague: Kugler.

Kosterman, R., Hawkins, J.D., Guo, J., Catalano, R.F. and Abbott, R.D. (2000) 'The dynamics of alcohol and marijuana initiation: patterns and predictors of first use in adolescence', *American Journal of Public Health*, 90: 360–6.

Krohn, M.D. (1986) 'The web of conformity: A network approach to the explanation of delinquent behavior', *Social Problems*, 33: 581–93.

Loeber, R. and Hay, D.F. (1997) 'Key issues in the development of aggression and violence from childhood to early adulthood', *Annual Review of Psychology*, 48: 371–410.

Loeber, R., Farrington, D.P., Stouthamer-Loeber, M., Moffitt, T.E., Caspi, A., White, H. Wei, E. and Beyers. J.M. (2003) 'The development of male offending. Key findings from fourteen years of the Pittsburgh Youth Study', in T.P. Thornberry and M.D. Krohn (eds) *Taking Stock of Delinquency: An Overview of Findings from Contemporary Longitudinal Studies*. New York: Kluwer.

Loeber, R., Farrington, D.P., Stouthamer-Loeber, M. and Van Kammen, W.B. (1998) 'Multiple risk factors for multi-problem boys: Co-occurrence of delinquency, substance use, attention deficit, conduct problems, physical aggression, covert behaviour, depressed mood, and shy/withdrawn behavior', in R. Jessor (ed.) *New Perspectives on Adolescent Risk Behavior*. Cambridge: Cambridge University Press.

Loeber, R., Stouthamer-Loeber, M., Van Kammen, W.B. and Farrington, D.P. (1989) 'Development of a new measure of self-reported antisocial behavior for young children: Prevalence and reliability', in M. Klein (ed.) *Cross-National Research in Self-Reported Crime and Delinquency*. Boston, MA: Kluwer-Nijhoff.

Lynam, D., Moffitt, T, and Stouthamer-Loeber, M. (1993) 'Explaining the relation between IQ and delinquency: Class, race, test motivation, school failure, or self-control?', *Journal of Abnormal Psychology*, 102: 187–96.

McAra, L. and McVie, S. (2007) 'Youth Justice? The impact of system contact on patterns of desistance from offending', *European Journal of Criminology*, 4(3): 315–45.

McCord, J. (1979) 'Some child-rearing antecedents of criminal behaviour in adult men', *Journal of Personality and Social Psychology*, 37: 1477–86.

McVie, S. (2003) *Edinburgh Study Technical Report: Sweeps 3 and 4* [Online]. Available at: http://www.law.ed.ac.uk/cls/esytc/findings/technicalreport3and4.pdf [accessed 17 March 2009].

Moffitt, T.E. (2006) 'Life-course persistent versus adolescence-limited antisocial behavior', in D. Cicchetti and D. Cohen (eds) *Developmental Psychopathology*, 2nd edn. New York: Wiley.

Moffitt, T.E., Caspi, A., Rutter, M. and Silva, P.A. (2001) Sex *Differences in Antisocial Behaviour*. Cambridge: Cambridge University Press.

Moffitt, T.E. and Silva, P.A. (1988) 'IQ and delinquency: A direct test of differential detection hypothesis', *Journal of Abnormal Psychology*, 97: 330–3.

Nagin, D.S. and Tremblay, R.E. (2005) 'Developmental trajectory groups: Fact or a useful statistical fiction?', *Criminology*, 43(4): 873–904.

O'Donnell, J., Hawkins, J.D. and Abbott, R.D. (1995) 'Predicting serious delinquency and substance use among aggressive boys', *Journal of Consulting and Clinical Psychology*, 63: 529–37.

O'Mahony, D. (2008) 'The risk factors prevention paradigm and the causes of crime: A deceptively useful blueprint', *Youth Justice 2008: Measuring Compliance with International Standards Conference*, Cork University, Republic of Ireland, April 2008.

Pearce, N. (1996) 'Traditional epidemiology, modern epidemiology, and public health', *American Journal of Public Health*, 86: 678–83.

Porteous, D. (2007) 'The prevention of youth crime: A risky business?', in B. Thom, R. Sales and J. Pearce (eds) *Growing Up With Risk*. Bristol: Policy Press.

Pulkkinen, L. (1988) 'Delinquent development: Theoretical and empirical considerations', in M. Rutter (ed.) *Studies of Psychosocial Risk*. Cambridge: Cambridge University Press.

Pulkkinen, L. and Tremblay, R.E. (1992) 'Patterns of boys' social adjustment in two cultures and at different ages: A longitudinal perspective', *International Journal of Behavioural Development*, 15(4): 527–53.

Rutter, M. and Giller, H. (1983) *Juvenile Delinquency: Trends and Perspective*. Harmondsworth: Penguin.

Rutter, M.J., Giller, H. and Hagell, A. (1998) *Antisocial Behaviour by Young People*. Cambridge: Cambridge University Press.

Sampson, R.J. and Laub, J.H. (1993) *Crime in the Making: Pathways and Turning Points through Life*. Harvard: Harvard University Press.

Sampson, R.J., Raudenbush, S.W. and Earls, F. (1997) 'Neighborhoods and Violent Crime: A Multilevel Study of Collective Efficacy', *Science*, 15: 918–24.

Smith, C. and Krohn, M. (1995) 'Delinquency and family life amongst male adolescents. The role of ethnicity', *Journal of Youth and Adolescence*, 24: 64–93.

Smith, D. (2006) 'Youth crime and justice: Research, evaluation and evidence', in B. Goldson and J. Muncie (eds) *Youth Crime and Justice*. London: Sage.

Smith, D.J. (2006), *Social Inclusion and Early Desistance from Crime*. Edinburgh Study of Youth Transitions and Crime Research Digest No.12. Edinburgh: The University of Edinburgh.

Smith, D.J. and McAra, L. (2004) *Gender and Youth Offending*, Edinburgh Study of Youth Transitions and Crime Research Digest No. 2. Edinburgh: The University of Edinburgh.

Smith, D.J. and McVie, S. (2003) 'Theory and Method in the Edinburgh Study of Youth Transitions and Crime', *British Journal of Criminology*, 43(1):169–95.

Smith, D.J., McVie, S., Woodward, R., Shute, J. and McAra, L. (2001) *The Edinburgh Study of Youth Transitions and Crime: Key Findings at Ages 12 and 13*. Edinburgh Study of Youth Transitions and Crime Research Digest No. 1 [Online]. Available at: http://www.law.ed.ac.uk/cls/esytc/findings/digest1.htm [accessed 17 March 2009].

Stouthamer-Loeber, M., Loeber, R., Wei, E., Farrington, D.P. and Wikström, P-O. (2002) 'Risk and promotive effects in the explanation of persistent serious delinquency in boys', *Journal of Clinical and Consulting Psychology*, 70: 111–23.

Thornberry, T.P. (1987) 'Toward an interactional theory of delinquency', *Criminology*, 25(4): 863–92.

Thornberry, T.P. (1994) *Violent Families and Youth Violence. OJJDP Fact Sheet 21*. Washington: Office of Juvenile Justice and Delinquency Prevention.

Thornberry, T.P., Huizinga, D. and Loeber, R. (2004) 'The Causes and Correlates studies: Findings and policy implications', *Juvenile Justice*, 10(1): 3–19.

Thornberry, T.P. and Krohn, M.D. (2003) *Taking Stock of Delinquency: An Overview of Findings from Contemporary Longitudinal Studies*. New York: Kluwer.

Thornberry, T.P., Lizotte, A.J., Krohn, M.D., Farnworth, M. and Jang, S.J. (1991) 'Testing interactional theory: An examination of reciprocal causal relationship among family, school, and delinquency', *Journal of Criminal Law and Criminology*, 82(1): 3–35.

Thornberry, T.P., Lizotte, A.J., Krohn, M.D., Smith, C.A. and Porter, P.K. (2003) 'Causes and consequences of delinquency. Findings from the Rochester Youth Development Study', in T.P. Thornberry and M.D. Krohn (eds) *Taking Stock of Delinquency: An Overview of Findings from Contemporary Longitudinal Studies*. New York: Kluwer.

Thornberry, T.P., Lizotte, A.J., Krohn, M.D., Farnworth, M. and Sung Joon Jang (1994). 'Delinquent Peers, Beliefs, and Delinquent Behavior: A Longitudinal Test of Interactional Theory', *Criminology* 32:47–83.

Tremblay, R.E., Desmarais-Gervais, L., Gagnon, C. and Charlebois, P. (1987) 'The Preschool Behaviour Questionnaire: Stability of its factor structure between cultures, sexes, ages and socioeconomic classes', *International Journal of Behavioral Development*, 10(4): 467–84.

Tremblay, R.E., Phil, R.O., Vitaro, F. and Dobkin, P.L. (1994) 'Predicting early onset of male antisocial behavior from preschool behavior', *Archives of General Psychiatry*, 51: 732–39.

Tremblay, R.E., Vitaro, F., Nagin, F., Pagani, L. and Seguin, J. (2003) 'The Montréal Longitudinal Experimental Study. Rediscovering the power of descriptions', in Thornberry, T.P. and Krohn, M.D. (2003) *Taking Stock of Delinquency: An Overview of Findings from Contemporary Longitudinal Studies*. New York: Kluwer.

Vitaro, F. and Tremblay, R.E. (1994) 'Impact of a prevention program on aggressive children's friendships and social adjustment', *Journal of Abnormal Child Psychology*, 22 (4): 457–75.

Wikström, T. and Loeber, R. (1998) 'Individual risk factors, Neighbourhood SES and juvenile offending', in M. Tonry (ed.) *The Handbook of Crime and Punishment*. New York: OUP.

[2]

Power and powerlessness in transition

Monica Barry

> I think I've learnt ... I was just a wee laddie then. I'm now a young man. More the man I want to be.
>
> (Derek, 21)

Introduction

As was suggested in Chapter 2, there are few criminological theories that are successful in fully understanding offending as a *process* of change for the individual in the transition to adulthood. By 'process' I mean that offending and non-offending combine to make up a series of interrelated actions through time and space to achieve a desired outcome. Offending is not, generally speaking, a lifelong phenomenon, since the vast majority of people who start offending also stop offending after a relatively short period in youth. Offending could thus be seen during this period as a means, however misguided, of achieving economic, social or personal ends. The short-term end result, for many of the young people in this book at least, was interaction and integration with others of similar age in the transition to 'adulthood'. Non-offending – following successful desistance – was a further means to an end, namely wider social integration.

It is argued here that combining criminological theory with youth transitions enables linkages and consistencies to be identified between the process of starting and stopping offending and the process of the transition to adulthood. Whilst theories of youth transitions (e.g. Coles, 1995; Jones, 1996; Wyn and White, 1997) cannot explain offending behaviour *per se*, they can help us understand offending and desistance as a process and demonstrate more fully the extent to which offending may help to rectify, in the short term, the unequal distribution of power for young people in transition. Given the emphasis within the desistance literature on employment and relationships as a stimulus to stopping offending, a parallel investigation of transitions (where employment and relationships are two key components) would also seem pertinent. Likewise, the widening debate over the need to combine agency and structure in the criminological literature (Farrall and Bowling, 1999) has commonalities with more recent youth transitions research highlighted in this chapter. Before exploring youth transitions research more fully, the following section first examines broader anthropological literature relating to 'rites of passage' which have relevance to the concept of youth transitions.

The liminal status of youth

The terms 'youth' and 'youth transitions' are concepts which have attracted increasing sociological interest since the 1980s in understanding the extended and fragmented period that young people may go through before attaining full 'adult' status (Chisholm, 1993; Coles, 1995). The term 'youth' has become an additional stage between childhood and adulthood to exemplify this protracted transition (see, for example, Bynner *et al.*, 1997). However, prior to this increasing sociological interest in youth transitions, anthropologists had been examining the experiences of adolescents in small-scale societies and the 'rites of passage' that they progress through in preparation for adulthood. Whilst the term 'youth' was not seen as a middle phase between childhood and adulthood in such anthropological studies, Van Gennep (1960, cited in Turner, 1967) nevertheless identified three elements in the transition from childhood to adulthood in terms of 'rites of passage'. These are:

- *separation* – 'symbolic behaviour signifying the detachment of the individual or group either from an earlier fixed point in the social structure or a set of cultural conditions (a "state")';
- *margin* – 'during the intervening "liminal" period, the characteristics of the ritual subject (the "passenger") are ambiguous; [s/he] passes through a cultural realm that has few or none of the attributes of the past or coming state';
- *aggregation* – 'the passage is consummated. The ritual subject... is in a stable state once more and, by virtue of this, has rights

and obligations of a clearly defined and "structural" type' (Turner, 1967: 94–5).

Whilst Van Gennep focused on the more positive aspects of 'ritual' and 'ceremony' for young people in making the transition to adulthood, his middle 'liminal' phase has been adapted here to emphasize the more negative interpretations of youth which have been usurped by governments to restrict or forestall young people's movements as full citizens. The rites of passage of girls and young women in different cultures tended to be played down in this anthropological literature, although the liminal period was often described in terms of stereotypical feminine traits such as weakness and passivity. Turner (1969) describes individuals within the liminal phase as: 'persons or principles that (1) fall in the interstices of social structure, (2) are on its margins, or (3) occupy its lowest rungs' (ibid.: 125). Cloward and Ohlin (1961: 55) also see adolescence as a crucial marginalizing phase in the transition to adulthood: '... male adolescents are cut off from adult roles and relegated to a prolonged preparatory status in which they are no longer children but are not yet adults'. Whilst these authors were speaking some forty years ago along with their counterparts in anthropology, the status of young people in transition has changed little in the interim, and arguably has deteriorated.

Whilst the term 'youth' has more recently offered a sociological bridge between the widening poles of childhood and adulthood in the Western world, the phase of 'youth' is more than the 'liminal' phase described in the rites of passage literature. As James and Prout (1997) suggest, growing up nowadays involves several transitional processes rather than a one-off initiation process: youth transitions extend 'over considerable periods of time rather than being concentrated into ritual moments' (ibid.: 248). Nevertheless, it is in the late teens and early twenties that many people experience discrimination, socially, legally and economically, as a direct result of their age, and hence their status as 'liminal beings'.

The phases of transition

MacDonald and Marsh (2005) suggest that much criminal career research is overly deterministic and positivistic and that it would benefit from also considering the wider experiences of young people in transition. Whilst youth transitions research has not been used systematically in the field of criminology to date, these authors argue that such literature can provide a better understanding of youth offending as perceived and experienced by young people themselves. Not only are the phases of transition important markers to young people, but they should also be important markers to criminologists keen to understand the usually temporary and youthful nature of offending. Studying youth transitions in parallel with youth offending enables an exploration of the dynamics of age, power, interdependence and integration in the transition to full citizenship in adulthood.

Youth transitions research tends to adhere to a differentiation of the various phases of transition by chronological age, namely, 'childhood' (0–14), 'youth' (15–24) and 'adulthood' (25+) (see, for example, Jones, 1996). It is acknowledged that these transitional phases, like those of onset, maintenance and desistance used in this book, are zigzagging, overlapping and contentious, and as such, are merely heuristic devices, used as markers of change or development for children and young people. The factors which do, however, differentiate them one from the other are described briefly below.

Childhood

Childhood as a distinct and separate phase in the lifecycle was seen to emerge in the seventeenth century to distinguish children from their older counterparts (Aries, 1962). Aries's seminal work on childhood, although based on minimal empirical data and using modern (and masculine) conceptions of childhood (Archard, 1993; Wiltshire, 2003, pers. comm.), was nevertheless influential in its time in suggesting that children needed to be protected for moral as well as educational reasons. Aries (1962: 412) described children as being 'subjected to a special treatment, a sort of quarantine', and even though recent Children's Acts and the UN Convention on the Rights of the Child have attempted to diffuse the sense of 'quarantine', the term 'childhood' still differentiates children from adults in terms of risk, protection and rights and emphasizes the 'otherness' of children (Brown, 1998; Franklin, 2002). Children are increasingly given legal and protected status which separates them out from their older counterparts and which both enables and restricts their access to rights and responsibilities as citizens (Barry, 2001a). Children are almost totally dependent in a legal sense on adults, in particular on their families or carers, but once they reach school age, this dependence on families dissipates (albeit often temporarily) as the school milieu takes over, not only in terms of education and daytime supervision but also for leisure and social interaction. It is within the school environment that children increasingly relate to other children rather than family for leisure, identity and companionship. For many children from disadvantaged communities, 'childhood' does not offer the same type of protection that it offers young people from more affluent communities, against, for example, poverty, marginalization or taking on responsibilities as carers, thus questioning the traditional image of childhood as being a time of innocence and protection.

Youth

As mentioned above, the term 'youth' is a relatively new sociological concept, and indeed it was only in the eighteenth century that changing social conventions and tighter social legislation '*made* the adolescent' (Musgrove, 1964: 34, emphasis in original). The term 'youth' has now come to exemplify the extended transition from childhood to adulthood as a result of increasing restrictions on school leavers within the labour market as well as the commodification of this section of the population by consumer and other markets (Roberts, 2003). According to Coles (1995: 4), youth is 'an interstitial phase' between childhood and adulthood, during which young people are treated 'neither as children nor as adults' (ibid.: 6). Musgrove (1964) is more specific in suggesting that youth is an oppressed group, rejected by adults, and that young people's exclusion from 'adulthood' has been engineered for adverse rather than benign reasons.

Youth could be described as a time of distancing from, initially, the family environment and subsequently, the school environment, offering increased levels of autonomy and enabling experimentation with identities. The main milieu within which young people congregate is the friendship group, both within and outside the school environment, although many young people may still retain strong links with their families and the wider community during the youth phase.

The concept of 'youth' has been criticized for segregating and problematizing young people to the exclusion of the wider social and political environment of which they are a part. Jeffs and Smith (1998: 45) argue: 'that "youth" has limited use as a social category and that it characteristically involves viewing young people – mainly young men – as being in deficit, from a developmental perspective, and in need of training and control'. This is particularly apparent in relation to young offenders, who are being swept into a more punishment- and adult-oriented criminal justice system.

Adulthood

All individuals aged 25 and over are deemed to come under the rubric of 'adulthood', irrespective of their competence, since from that age all legal rights are in place (Jones, 1996). At the age of 25, individuals have full responsibilities as citizens, they are expected to support themselves through paid employment or other income, although they are also eligible for state benefits, and they are liable to pay taxes towards services for themselves and others. However, adulthood is not necessarily an 'end point' when specific rights and privileges are bestowed, but is a social construct dependent on social, legal, historical, cultural and personal contexts.

The key factors which young people equate with adulthood are parenthood, a home of one's own and stable employment, but these vary in importance for young people depending on social class and gender (Thomson and Holland, 2002). Adults are also more likely to interact with a wider social network, not least because of a wider range of contacts and commitments relating to employment, housing or child-rearing, and to have a greater power/influence over their own destiny because of increased equality and rights within the wider society.

Research on youth transitions

The advent in the UK of Thatcherism in the late 1970s marked a turning point not only for children and young people who became increasingly confined to the family and marginalized from the labour market, but also for sociologists of youth who had hitherto concentrated their attention on youth subcultures at the expense of structural constraints on youth transitions (MacDonald *et al.*, 2001). In an attempt to focus more on the socio-economic climate in which youth transitions took place, transitions research in the 1980s and early 1990s focused more on structural constraints than on individual choice. However, such research has more recently been criticized for being overly deterministic and throwing the proverbial baby out with the bath water in analysing the structure-agency debate. As Miles (2000: 10) argues:

> The tendency ... to adopt a structural perspective on transitions has been counter-productive, primarily because of its failure to prioritize the actual views, experiences, interests and perspectives of young people as they see them, in favour of bland discussions, most commonly of trends in employment and education patterns.

Traditionally, therefore, transitions research has portrayed a linear, psychosocial movement towards conventional goals. The main transitional pathways or 'careers' identified by such sociologists in the 1980s and early 1990s have been summarized by Coles (1995) as follows:

- the transition from full-time education and training to a full-time job in the labour market (the school-to-work transition);
- the transition from family of origin (mainly the biological family) to family of destination (the domestic transition);
- the transition from residence with parents (or surrogate parents) to living away from them (the housing transition).

Cohen and Ainley (2000: 81) suggest that the above categories of transition are no longer applicable to young people's position in society: 'education no longer relates necessarily to work, nor home-making to marriage or marriage to child-rearing'. Indeed, some say that transitions are no longer a youth phenomenon nor uni-directional, but apply to all people of all ages at different times. Roberts (2003: 6) suggests that: 'Most sociologists have abandoned trying to define youth in terms of chronological age. Nowadays we say that we study youth transitions which may occur at age 12, 16, 20, 30 or even when individuals are older than this'. He goes on to argue that 'Some people never establish themselves in jobs which will support an adult lifestyle. Some remain unmarried and childless, and continue to live in their parents' homes until the latter's death' (ibid.: 8).

Nevertheless, the period of youth – as in the age range 15–25 – is a time of life when there are major changes and decisions made which often impact irretrievably on young people's futures. Whilst for Turner's (1967; 1969) small-scale traditional societies referred to earlier, this period was a planned-for stage pending a 'new beginning', for many disadvantaged young people in Britain this phase in the lifecycle holds no status and there are few supportive structures to guide their transition to adulthood. This lack of support in the liminal phase leaves young people precariously poised between the two stools of protected children and autonomous adults (Barry, 2002).

The elements of transition described by, *amongst others*, Van Gennep and Coles are predominantly structurally defined and determined, whereas one further element less often cited in the youth transition literature is that of the transition from dependence to independence (Jones, 1996). This more individualized description of the transition phase allows young people's own narratives to come to the fore, and it is these narratives that have recently made academics question the linear approach to transitions which had hitherto been the norm. Stephen and Squires (2003), for example, argue that young people's transitions in late modernity are neither linear nor predictable but are fragmented, prolonged and cyclical. Equally, young people are increasingly seen as being proactive in defining, negotiating and making sense of their own transitions. Many recent accounts of young people's experience of youth transitions (*amongst others*, Holland *et al.*, 1999; Barry, 2001a and 2001b) suggest that their narratives and transitional experiences are guided as much by personal agency and responsibility as they are by structural factors.

According to Beck (1992), the certainties associated with industrial society have been eroded by a new age of modernity consisting of uncertain risks and opportunities, resulting in what he terms 'individualization'. This suggests that young people now have to resolve their own problems, overcome structural constraints and 'individualize' their own life projects (Cote, 2002). This fragmentation of past stability has resulted, in the last decade or so, in the transition research pendulum swinging away from structuralism and back towards a 'new freedom' of individualized lifestyles and reflexive construction of one's own biography (Holland *et al.*, 1999). Whilst the concept of individualization describes both structure and agency, the individual is nevertheless at the centre (albeit structurally defined), and factors such as class, gender and social networks are peripheral. Furlong and Cartmel (1997), however, warn against an over-emphasis on individualization at the expense of social and structural change, suggesting it would be an epistemological fallacy to focus on individual responsibility and self-determination without taking into account the powerful impact of existing social structures.

If, as Beck (1992) suggests, agency has superseded structure in youth transitions through the 'individualization' of young people, then it would seem reasonable to assume that the timing of such transitions would vary greatly between individuals, depending on their capacity to progress their life projects. Nevertheless, there tends to be a continuity in the overall timing of transitions, not least as illustrated by the age–crime curve, and this general continuity suggests that structural factors are more constraining than individual factors are enabling. Young people from disadvantaged backgrounds have had to resort increasingly to using agency (or more exactly 'entrepreneurial skills') in the transition to adulthood because of the presence of structural barriers. For example, MacDonald *et al.* (2001: 3.5) argue that transitions research needs to explore the 'alternative careers' adopted by many disadvantaged young people, such as criminal careers and parenting (Craine, 1997) or 'fiddly work' (MacDonald *et al.*, 2001: 3.5).

An ethos of individualization also tends to legitimate the marginalization of young people by the state (Wyn and White, 1997). Wyn and White argue that age is 'socially constructed, institutionalized and controlled in historically and culturally specific ways' (ibid.: 11). This social construction of age, and the impact of postmodern thinking regarding individualization, has lessened the impact of class inequalities and resulted in young people generally viewing failure in the transition to adulthood as a personal problem rather than a public issue (Bates and Riseborough, 1993). The developmental approach to both youth transitions, 'at risk' youth and offending behaviour by young people may have been usurped by the state to mask or legitimate structural inequalities. Such an approach places emphasis on the process of adolescent development which is seen as divorced from structural factors. Wyn and White conclude that the marginalization and criminalization of young people in particular is deliberate and sustained, a means of 'deflecting attention away from the structural reasons for poverty and unemployment' (ibid.: 135). Wyn and White (1997) also argue that disadvantaged young people should not be seen as any different from other age groups, having the same conventional goals as most people in society: '... in many cases the "resistance" exerted by "disadvantaged" young people is not necessarily *against* mainstream institutions but constitutes struggles for a place *within* them' (ibid.: 92, emphases in original).

Transitions research seems to have become preoccupied with the structure/agency dichotomy within an extended and increasingly adverse socio-economic environment. This preoccupation seems to be at the expense of the notion of power, citizenship and rights. The political and social power imbalances operating within our society, not least in the transition phase between childhood and adulthood, tend to be played down in favour of identifying localized structural constraints and individual choice at the expense of the macro-level issue of young people's rights in the transition to full citizenship. It is thus to the concept of power – or capital – that this discussion now turns.

The concept of capital

It has been suggested here that criminological theory alone cannot offer a comprehensive and all-encompassing approach to the mainly temporary nature of offending amongst a mainly transient section of a mainly youthful population. A broader, more dynamic approach is needed that depicts offending behaviour as a process of change and development amongst young people. This book deploys the concept of youth transitions to enable this more comprehensive and all-encompassing approach to be developed.

Criminological literature has hitherto emphasized blocked aspirations, subcultural association or the labelling and prejudice of the wider society, but has not specifically focused on the socio-legal constraints of disparities of power and participation of young people in transition. MacDonald and Marsh (2005) argue that subcultural theories are useful in understanding youth transitions, and by drawing on youth transitions in this book, subcultural affiliations amongst young people can be viewed as more political than individual, more transient than durable, and more interdependent than rebellious. Youth subcultural affiliations can offer a temporary reprieve in the transition to more sustainable and durable sources of power and reciprocity in adulthood. Equally, participation through consumerism often acts as a source of power where no other sources of power may exist in youth (Jones and Wallace, 1992). Offending is one means of acquiring such consumer power where no legitimate financial means are available.

Matza suggests that powerlessness is a key factor in producing drift and therefore delinquency: 'Being pushed around puts the delinquent in a mood of fatalism... In that condition he is rendered irresponsible' (Matza, 1964: 89). Such powerlessness, it could be argued, manifests itself in the transition phase of youth when young people fall between the two stools of relative protection as children and interdependence as adults. Whilst offending is not just a problem for young people but is also concentrated in communities and cultures more generally that are disempowered through increasing unemployment and poverty, powerlessness is perhaps most acutely felt by young people in transition, and offending is often an escape from such disempowerment (Ferrell and Sanders, 1995).

Power is not a concept reducible to one single definition; indeed its meaning differs according to the context in which it is used. For example, it can imply force, manipulation, authority and economic or political influence, and according to Haugaard (2002: 2): '[t]here will always be specific usages which are particularly suitable to certain theoretical projects'. In denoting the type of power available to individuals within their social world, Bourdieu utilizes the concept of capital, a term which goes back to the beginning of the twentieth century, notably in relation to 'social capital'.

The term 'social capital' has a chequered history and seems to have first arisen in the USA in 1916, when the schools reformer, Hanifan, coined the phrase to denote the 'good will, fellowship, sympathy and social intercourse among the individuals and families who make up a social unit' (Putnam, 2000: 19). Whilst Bourdieu appropriated the concept of capital in the 1970s in Europe, two North American sociologists, Coleman (1988) and Putnam (1993; 2000) have also given prominence to the concept of social capital. To Coleman, social capital combines rational action with social structure, includes obligations, trust, expectations, norms and information-sharing, and whilst productive, is not always benign: 'A given form of social capital that is valuable in facilitating certain actions may be useless or even harmful for others' (Coleman, 1988: 98). Coleman suggests that social capital allows individuals to 'establish relations purposefully and continue them when they continue to provide benefits' (ibid.: 105). He thus infers that if social capital is proving more damaging than beneficial, then that particular source of social capital will cease to be utilized. However, Coleman's interpretation of social capital is rational and utilitarian

– he stresses the 'indebtedness' aspect of such capital rather than the social aspect.

Following on from Coleman's communitarian interpretation of social capital, Putnam (2000) identified four strands of social capital as follows: 1) civic community networks; 2) a 'sense of belonging' to a civic community; 3) norms of reciprocity and trust; and 4) positive attitudes towards, and engagement in, voluntary, state and personal networks (Morrow, 1999). More recently, he has identified two sub-categories of social capital: bonding social capital (exclusive and inward-looking group identities) and bridging social capital (inclusive and outward-looking group identities): 'Bonding social capital constitutes a kind of sociological superglue, whereas bridging social capital provides a sociological WD-40' (Putnam, 2000: 23). Again, he acknowledges the adversarial as well as the consensual impact of both types of capital. Webster *et al.* (2004: 30) also comment on the adversarial nature of some sources of bonding social capital, which can 'exclude, marginalize, constrain and entrap' young people. MacDonald and Marsh (2005), who worked closely with Webster and colleagues on a recent study of young people's transitions in Northern England, talk of 'the paradox of networks' (ibid.: 203), where poorer areas are seen as lacking bridging social capital but are nevertheless a major source of support and legitimate opportunities for young people. They quote Kearns and Parkinson (2001: 2105) who argue that because people from more disadvantaged communities tend to draw on bonding rather than bridging social capital within such communities, they can only 'get by' rather than 'get on'. MacDonald and Marsh also point out the negative influences of social networks amongst dependent heroin users and their greater need for bridging social capital beyond the milieu of their drug-using peers.

Putnam, like Coleman (1988), argues that social capital is both the individual and collective face of reciprocal social relations. It can be both 'warm and cuddly' and 'malevolent, antisocial' (Portes and Landolt, 1996: 21–2), depending on whether such capital's support, cooperation, trust and institutional effectiveness are aimed at positive or negative outcomes. However, Putnam's concept of social capital is seen as inappropriate to the experiences of young people, not least because young people tend to be excluded from civic participation and develop their own individualized social networks (Morrow, 2001; Raffo and Reeves, 2000). Morrow (2001: 55) argues that Putnam's concept is 'a woolly, catch-all category' and ignores the historical and economic context, is gender-blind (in that women's employment goes against the romanticized ethos of community), is culturally specific to the USA only and tends to ignore individual agency and one's capacity to generate one's own social capital. Morrow (2001: 54) further argues that these individualized social networks are more important to young people than communities *per se*:

> For children and young people, 'community' is more often a 'virtual' community of friends based around school, town centre and street, friends' and relatives' houses, and sometimes homes in two different towns, rather than a tightly-bound easily-identifiable geographical location.

Bourdieu's theory of social practice

With the bad press associated with the broader concept of capital, it is perhaps surprising that the work of the French sociologist, Pierre Bourdieu, has attracted so much attention in sociological and educational circles, although little to date in criminological circles. Bourdieu is principally interested in the *relational* context of everyday actions and perceptions: the struggle for identification and recognition (Bourdieu, 1989; May, 1996), a major resource for which is capital. Bourdieu attempts to bridge the gap in social theory between agency and structure, without losing the 'major contribution of the structuralist legacy to social science' (May, 1996: 125). The disciplines contained within the social sciences have long argued that there is a dichotomy between what Callinicos (1999: 79) has described as 'the anti-humanist dissolution of the subject practised by structuralism and post-structuralism... [and] the reduction of social structures to emanations of individual subjectivity common to both Rational Choice Theory and the phenomenological tradition'. Bourdieu (1990) suggests that individual and collective constructions of the social world are not developed in a vacuum but are reproduced by, and themselves reproduce, social structures and are thus subjected to structural constraints. There is a constant interplay between structural constraints and individual choice, and the importance of time, space, agency and the individual's capacity to change are all implicated in the construction and reconstruction of the social world (Bourdieu, 1990).

Bourdieu's theory of social practice (1986) stresses personal networks and focuses as much on agency and sociability as on structure and institutionalization as well as on power relationships and the inevitability of the unequal distribution of capital amongst different groups and societies. Bourdieu argues that throughout their lives, individuals accrue capital – social, cultural, economic and symbolic – through their social practice (Bourdieu, 1984). These forms of capital, as utilized by Bourdieu, are described in more detail below.

Social capital is defined by Bourdieu (1997: 51) as:

> the aggregate of the actual or potential resources which are linked to possession of a durable network of more or less institutionalized relationships of mutual acquaintance and recognition – or in other words, to membership in a group – which provides each of its members with the backing of the collectively-owned capital, a 'credential' which entitles them to credit.

In other words, social capital is valued relations with significant others and is generated through relationships which in turn bring resources from networks and group membership. To Bourdieu, social capital includes not only social networks but also 'sociability' – 'a continuous series of exchanges in which recognition is endlessly affirmed' (1986: 250). As will be seen from the stories of the young people in this book, social capital gained within the peer group is a crucial source of support and recognition for young people in transition.

Economic capital is the financial means to not only the necessities but also the luxuries of everyday living, including inheritance, income and assets. Bourdieu stresses the dominance of economic capital in the market place because such capital can be transmitted, preserved and rationally managed (Bourdieu, 1990). Economic capital is not a major source of capital for young people generally, given their transient status between childhood and adulthood, their confinement to full-time education and their resulting segregation from the adult labour market, although it is acknowledged that young people from middle class backgrounds will be able to draw more readily on the economic and other capitals accruing from their families. For young people who have few responsibilities or commitments, economic capital may bring short-term status rather than longer-term financial security. However, for those offenders who commit crime as a means of earning a living, which Stewart *et al.* (1994: 19) refer to as 'professional' offenders, a successful criminal career may be consciously chosen as a viable alternative source of economic capital to employment.

Cultural capital is legitimate competence or status and comes from knowledge of one's cultural identity in the form of art and education in particular: 'language use, manners and orientations/ dispositions... and formal qualifications' according to Jenkins (1992: 116). It exists in three forms – in an embodied state of long-lasting dispositions of mind and body (e.g. styles and modes of presentation and identity); in an objectified state, as in cultural goods; and in an institutionalized state, through educational and other qualifications or status. To Bourdieu, cultural capital is not easily acquired or transmitted and is seen as an established form of capital that only truly gains legitimacy over time and via institutionalized or objectified means. It does not lend itself readily, therefore, to the relatively short (in terms of the lifecycle) transition period between childhood and adulthood.

Symbolic capital, to Bourdieu, is an overarching resource that brings prestige and honour gained from the collective, legitimate and recognized culmination of the other three forms of capital (Bourdieu, 1989): 'Capital has to be regarded as legitimate before it can be capitalized upon' (Skeggs, 1997: 8). Symbolic capital is 'the power granted to those who have obtained sufficient recognition to be in a position to impose recognition' (Bourdieu, 1989: 23), and is primarily accrued through: 'services, gifts, attention, care, affection' (Bourdieu, 1991: 128). It is, in effect, the 'recognition' received from a group:

> ... struggles for recognition are a fundamental dimension of social life and... what is at stake in them is the accumulation of a particular form of capital, honour in the sense of reputation and prestige, and ... there is, therefore, a specific logic behind the accumulation of symbolic capital, as capital founded on cognition [*connaissance*] and recognition [*reconnaissance*].
>
> (Bourdieu, 1990: 22, emphases in original)

However, Bourdieu argues that symbolic capital is basically unstable in comparison with economic capital: 'being based on reputation, opinion and representation ... [it] can be destroyed by suspicion and criticism, and is particularly difficult to transmit and to objectify' (Bourdieu, 1990: 93).

Field, habitus and practice

In an attempt to bridge the gap between structure and agency, Bourdieu utilizes three key underlying concepts in his theory of social practice, namely field (objectivity), habitus (subjectivity) and practice (interaction). Jenkins (1992: 85) defines a *field* as 'a network, or a configuration, of objective relations between positions objectively defined ... a structured system of social positions'. Fields are the site of struggles between holders of capital and are constituted by the distribution of different types of capital or power within them: they reflect the 'unequal distribution of capital' (Bourdieu, 1986: 46).

Habitus is both 'an internalization of reality' and, through practice, 'an externalization of self as constituted through past experience' (Haugaard, 2002: 225). Habitus is the unconscious shaping of actions and interactions and can change over time. The habitus bridges the gap between history and sociology in that it is 'history embodied in human beings' (May, 1996: 126), but external circumstances interplay with individual practice to create expectations and aspirations; individuals cannot of themselves influence how or when external circumstances change. This makes habitus seem like a self-fulfilling prophecy, and hence lays Bourdieu open to the criticism of being overly deterministic (Jenkins, 1992).

Finally, *practice* is the conscious result of the interplay between habitus and field. Whilst practice is often unquestioned – as interaction, behaviour or everyday life – Bourdieu attempts to construct a theoretical model of social practice (Jenkins, 1992). Social practice is not merely what people say and do, but why, when and where they say and do it. The interplay between the habitus (agency or subjectivity) and the field (structure or objectivity) results in a congruence between the individual and his/her social world that makes the latter seem self-evident and thus acceptable to the individual.

The methods by which individuals accrue capital within their practice are predominantly strategic. To Bourdieu, strategies are an important link between fields, habitus and practice, even though the habitus is mainly made up of 'tacit' knowledge. To Bourdieu, strategies are less rigid and circumscribed than rules, and include rational calculation (tempered by the constraints of limited resources) and the achievement of objectives in the medium to long term (Jenkins, 1992). However, strategizing is not only about rational choice but incorporates the needs/expectations of significant others. Bourdieu describes it as 'a feel for the game: a practical sense' which emanates from the habitus (Fowler, 2000: 77).

The durability and legitimacy of capital

The concepts of durability and legitimacy are crucial to an understanding of the effects of capital accumulation on the individual or group in society and will be discussed further in Chapter 7. Meantime, these two concepts are described briefly below in relation to the significance of capital accumulation for young people in transition.

Capital of whatever kind takes time and effort to accumulate and to transmit. Its potential for profit and reproduction is therefore, through time, dependent on the structure, dynamics and constraints of the social world (Bourdieu, 1986). *Durability* is an important element in Bourdieu's concept of capital. He describes social capital as being a 'durable network' (1997: 51) and recognition as being a 'durable feeling' (1998: 102). However, whilst social, cultural, economic and symbolic capital are readily identifiable forms of potential power for young people, it is argued here that for many young people *in transition*, they are not durable, not least because they are not recognized as legitimate by the wider society as a result of the paucity of opportunities available at this stage in their lives.

Capital thus takes on a less durable profile in relation to young people who are in transition. Young people, by dint of their status as 'transitional beings' (Turner, 1967: 98) and especially those from working class backgrounds, tend to have few, if any, fixed or permanent obligations towards, responsibilities for, or expectations of gaining capital beyond their immediate environment of friends and family. Durability of capital, along with collective legitimacy (see below) is one of the crucial elements that is missing within the childhood and youth phases, partly because of young people's liminal state both economically and socially, but also because they are not seen as full citizens with the longer-term obligations, independence and responsibilities associated with adulthood (Jones, 1995). Turner (1967: 100), in describing the 'liminal phase' – albeit in relation to primitive societies but arguably of relevance in modern society – has identified equality as being a strong factor in relationships between individuals in transition: 'The liminal group is a community or comity of comrades'. Turner argues that this equality is based on a negation, amongst young people in transition, of the factors which characterize status in society:

> transitional beings... *have* nothing. They have no status, property, insignia, secular clothing, rank, kinship, position, nothing to demarcate them structurally from their fellows.
> (Turner, 1967: 98–9, emphasis in original)

Bourdieu's definition of *legitimacy* is sociological rather than legal and refers to recognition and acceptance more than to authority and compliance. Sennett and Cobb (1972: 265) suggest that legitimacy is related to 'social rights': 'the source of social legitimacy in capitalist society comes primarily from what a person produces... and who he essentially *is*' (ibid.: 267–8, emphasis in original). It is one's identity rather than what one produces that is the key to Bourdieu's understanding of legitimacy. Bourdieu defines 'legitimacy' as '[a]n institution, action or usage which is dominant, but not recognized as such, that is to say, which is tacitly accepted' (Bourdieu, 1984: 110). In other words, capital of whatever form is legitimate or 'symbolic' only in an implied sense. The concept of legitimacy is important in the gaining and imposition of symbolic capital. Symbolic capital accrues when one's actions or power are acknowledged, legitimated and finally recognized but since, to Bourdieu, the nation state 'is the site par excellence of the concentration and exercise of symbolic power' (Bourdieu, 1998: 47), it is less effective in a 'restricted market' (Fowler, 2000: 41) where official legitimation is unlikely outside of the 'mainstream'.

Capital accumulation in transition

Whilst Bourdieu infers that the accumulation of symbolic capital requires both durability and *official* legitimacy within the wider society, I argue that for young people in transition, in the possible absence of other forms of capital, symbolic capital is also a viable and vital source of identity, status, recognition, reputation and power within the friendship group and although not necessarily durable, can accrue once legitimated by other young people in the short term rather than by the wider society in the longer term. Such 'informal' legitimation could offer children and young people from disadvantaged backgrounds improved access to continuity and recognition in an otherwise decompartmentalized and potentially unstable set of transitional experiences and networks.

The discussion in this book is based on an appropriation of various of Bourdieu's concepts in order to demonstrate the possible relationship between the phases of offending and those of transition. It could be argued, for example, that Bourdieu's concept of field could apply equally to the constructs of childhood, youth and adulthood, in that these phases of transition are 'a structured system of social positions' (Jenkins, 1992: 85) embedded within age- and status-determined power relations within society. Bourdieu (1986: 46) suggests that the field reflects an 'unequal distribution of capital' and indeed, in the analysis used in this book, the forms, sources and levels of capital accumulation vary between each phase of transition, depending on the value placed on such capital by both the holders of it and those significant others who contribute towards, or restrict, its accumulation. Bourdieu also suggests that the habitus may become torn between two or more fields, resulting in the possibility of heterodoxy or orthodoxy (May, 1996) – respectively, an undermining or an acceptance of the status quo. Offending behaviour in childhood and youth could be argued to be a manifestation of heterodoxy, whilst desistance in adulthood could be argued to be a manifestation of orthodoxy, based on a redistribution of capital. The internalization of new norms and values by young people, their progression through the fields of transition and the accumulation of different and extended forms of capital in adulthood can enable the modification of the habitus and the eventual orthodoxy of practice.

Table 3.1 demonstrates the various ways in which young people can accumulate capital *through conventional means*, whilst still acknowledging that capital can also be accumulated through offending. These conventional sources of capital for young people in transition are deduced both from Bourdieu's definitions of each type of capital and from the literature on youth transitions (for example, Coles, 1995; Jones, 1995) and youth culture (Brake, 1985; Miles, 2000; Willis, 1990). Such sources of capital are pertinent, but not necessarily available, to *all* young people, depending on the ease with which they can make the transition to adulthood, both from an agency and a structural perspective.

The analysis in the following chapters is based on the experiences, views and aspirations of the young people in this study. Case study

Table 3.1 Potential sources of conventional capital accumulation for young people

Capital	*Onset/childhood*	*Maintenance/youth*	*Desistance/ adulthood*
Social	Family, friends	Friends, relationships	Family, wider social networks
Economic	Family income	Personal income	Employment
Cultural	Schooling	Consumption, acquisition of skills and qualifications	Further education
Symbolic	Family, friends, dependence	Friends, reputation, independence	Family, interdependence

material is drawn upon to illustrate the linkages between offending and transition and the relevance of capital. The case studies were chosen because they represent a cross-section of the overall sample in terms of age ranges and lengths of offending history. They also represent two ends of the spectrum in terms of desistance and persistence, in order to compare the varying levels of capital accumulation in the transition to adulthood and to explore these young people's levels of capital expenditure. Each respondent's classification of himself/herself as a 'persister' or 'desister' at the time of interview is acknowledged at the start of each case study.

Their reasons and explanations for offending at onset (Chapter 4), in the maintenance phase (Chapter 5) and in the desistance phase (Chapter 6), were subsumed under four different categories, which illustrate these young people's interpretation of their offending behaviour. These categories are: relational, monetary, practical and personal. Relational reasons include interactions with others whether such interactions are positive or negative. Monetary reasons include the need for money for general or specific purposes, e.g. survival, consumables or drugs. Practical reasons pertain to structural or external factors, such as the 'hassle factors' resulting from offending and its detection, health reasons and the employment and education implications of procuring a criminal record. Personal reasons relate to the individual's own needs and feelings. Whilst these categories emerged naturally from the primary analysis, it was found subsequently that these categories closely matched the concepts of capital espoused by Bourdieu described above, namely social, economic, cultural and symbolic capital. Whilst the analysis in the following chapters remains primarily true to the voices of the young people participating in the research, Bourdieu's interpretation is interspersed with the young people's perceptions in order to illustrate the potential of the concept of capital in understanding offending in transition.

References

Archard, D. (1993) *Children: Rights and Childhood*, London: Routledge.

Aries, P. (1962) *Centuries of Childhood*, London: Jonathan Cape.

Barry, M. (2001a) *A Sense of Purpose: Care Leavers' Views and Experiences of Growing Up*, London: Save the Children/Joseph Rowntree Foundation.

Barry, M. (2001b) *Challenging Transitions: Young People's Views and Experiences of Growing Up*, London: Save the Children/Joseph Rowntree Foundation.

Barry, M. (2002) 'Minor rights and major concerns: the views of young people in care', in B. Franklin (ed.) *The New Handbook of Children's Rights: Comparative Policy and Practice*, London: Routledge.

Bates, I. and Riseborough, G. (1993) *Youth and Inequality*, Buckingham: Open University Press.

Beck, U. (1992) *Risk Society: Towards a New Modernity*, London: Sage.

Bourdieu, P. (1984) *Distinction: A Social Critique of the Judgement of Taste*' (trans. Richard Nice), London: Routledge.

Bourdieu, P. (1986) 'The forms of capital', in J.G. Richardson (ed.) *Handbook of Theory and Research for the Sociology of Education*, Westport, CT: Greenwood Press.

Bourdieu, P. (1989) 'Social space and symbolic power', *Sociological Theory*, Vol. 7: 14–25.

Bourdieu, P. (1990) *In Other Words: Essays Towards a Reflexive Sociology* (trans.M. Adamson), Cambridge: Polity Press.

Bourdieu, P (1991) *Language and Symbolic Power*, edited and introduced by J.B. Thompson, (trans G. Raymond and M. Adamson), Cambridge: Polity Press.

Bourdieu, P. (1997) 'The forms of capital', in A.H. Halsey, H. Lauder, P. Brown and A. Stuart Wells (eds) *Education: Culture, Economy, Society*, Oxford: Oxford University Press.

Bourdieu, P. (1998) *Practical Reason*, Cambridge: Polity Press.

Brake, M. (1985) *Comparative Youth Culture*, London: Routledge and Kegan Paul.

Brown, S. (1998) *Understanding Youth and Crime: Listening to Youth?*, Buckingham: Open University Press.

Bynner, J., Chisholm, L. and Furlong, A. (eds) (1997) *Youth, Citizenship and Social Change in a European Context*, Aldershot: Ashgate.

Callinicos, A. (1999) 'Social theory put to the test of politics: Pierre Bourdieu and Anthony Giddens', *New Left Review*, Vol. 236: 77–102.

Chisholm, L. (1993) 'Youth transitions in Britain on the threshold of a "New Europe", *Journal of Education Policy*, Vol. 8, No. 1: 29–41.

Cloward, R. and Ohlin, L. (1961) *Delinquency and Opportunity: A Theory of Delinquent Gangs*, London: Routledge and Kegan Paul.

Cohen, P. and Ainley, P. (2000) 'In the country of the blind? Youth studies and cultural studies in Britain', *Journal of Youth Studies*, Vol. 3, No. 1: 79–95.

Coleman, J.S. (1988) 'Social capital in the creation of human capital', *American Journal of Sociology*, Vol. 94, Supplement: S95–S120.

Coles, B. (1995) *Youth and Social Policy: Youth Citizenship and Young Careers*, London, UCL Press.

Cote, J. (2002) 'The role of identity capital in the transition to adulthood: the individualization thesis examined', *Journal of Youth Studies*, Vol. 5, No. 2: 117–34.

Craine, S. (1997) 'The "Black Magic Roundabout": cyclical transitions, social exclusion and alternative careers', in R. MacDonald (ed.) *Youth, the 'Underclass' and Social Exclusion*, London: Routledge.

Farrall, S. and Bowling, B. (1999) 'Structuration, human development and desistance from crime', *British Journal of Criminology*, Vol. 39, No. 2: 253–68.

Ferrell, J. and Sanders C. (eds) (1995) *Cultural Criminology*, Boston, MA: Northeastern University Press.

Fowler, B. (ed.) (2000) *Reading Bourdieu on Society and Culture*, Oxford: Blackwell.

Franklin, B. (ed.) (2002) *The New Handbook of Children's Rights: Comparative Policy and Practice*, London: Routledge.

Furlong, A. and Cartmel, F. (1997) *Young People and Social Change: Individualization and Risk in Late Modernity*, Milton Keynes: Open University Press.

Haugaard, M. (ed.) (2002) *Power: A Reader*, Manchester: Manchester University Press.

Holland, J., Gillies, V. and McCarthy, J.R. (1999) 'Living on the Edge: Accounts of Young People Leaving Childhood Behind', paper presented to the ESA Conference, Amsterdam, August.

James, A. and Prout, A. (1997) 'Re-presenting childhood', in A. James and A. Prout (eds) *Constructing and Reconstructing Childhood*, London: Falmer Press.

Jeffs, T. and Smith, M. (1998) 'The problem of "youth" for youth work', *Youth and Policy*, No. 62: 45–66.

Jenkins, D. (1992) *Pierre Bourdieu*, London: Routledge.

Jones, G. (1995) *Leaving Home*, Buckingham: Open University Press.

Jones, G. (1996) 'Deferred citizenship: a coherent policy of exclusion?', *Young People Now*, 26 March: 26–7.

Jones, G. and Wallace, C. (1992) *Youth, Family and Citizenship*, Milton Keynes: Open University Press.

Kearns, A. and Parkinson, M. (2001) 'The significance of neighbourhood', *Urban Studies*, Vol. 38, No. 12: 2103–10.

MacDonald, R. and Marsh, J. (2005) *Disconnected Youth? Growing up in Britain's Poor Neighbourhoods*, Basingstoke: Palgrave Macmillan.

MacDonald, R., Mason, P., Shildrick, T., Webster, C. Johnston, L. and Ridley, L. (2001) 'Snakes and ladders: in defence of studies of youth transition', *Sociological Research Online*, Vol. 5, No. 4, http://www.socresonline.org.uk/5/4/macdonald.html.

Matza, D. (1964) *Delinquency and Drift*, New York: Wiley.

May, T. (1996) *Situating Social Theory*, Buckingham: Open University Press.

Miles, S. (2000) *Youth Lifestyles in a Changing World*, Buckingham: Open University Press.

Morrow, V. (1999) 'Conceptualising social capital in relation to the well-being of children and young people: a critical review', *The Sociological Review*, Vol. 47: 744–65.

Morrow, V. (2001) 'Young people's explanations and experiences of social exclusion: retrieving Bourdieu's concept of social capital', *International Journal of Sociology and Social Policy*, Vol. 21, No. 4/5/6: 37–63.

Musgrove, F. (1964) *Youth and the Social Order*, London: Routledge and Kegan Paul.

Portes, A. and Landolt, P. (1996) 'The downside of social capital', *The American Prospect*, No. 26: 18–21.

Putnam, R.D. (1993) *Making Democracy Work: Civic Traditions in Modern Italy*, Princeton NJ: Princeton University Press.

Putnam, R.D. (2000) *Bowling Alone: The Collapse and Revival of American Community*, New York: Simon and Schuster.

Raffo, C. and Reeves, M. (2000) 'Youth transitions and social exclusion: developments in social capital theory', *Journal of Youth Studies*, Vol. 3, No. 2: 147–66.

Roberts, K. (2003) 'Problems and priorities for the sociology of youth', in A. Bennett, M. Cieslik and S. Miles (eds) *Researching Youth*, Basingstoke: Palgrave Macmillan.

Sennett, R. and Cobb, J. (1972) *The Hidden Injuries of Class*, Cambridge: Cambridge University Press.

Skeggs, B. (1997) *Formations of Class and Gender: Becoming Respectable*, London: Sage.

Stephen, D. and Squires, P. (2003) '"Adults don't realise how sheltered they are": a contribution to the debate on youth transitions from some voices on the margins', *Journal of Youth Studies*, Vol. 6, No. 2, June: 145–64.

Stewart, J., Smith, D. and Stewart, G. (1994) *Understanding Offending Behaviour*, Harlow: Longman.

Thomson, R. and Holland, J. (2002) *Inventing Adulthood: Young People's Strategies for Transition*, Swindon: ESRC.

Turner, V. (1967) *The Forest of Symbols: Aspects of Ndombu Ritual*, Ithaca, NY: Cornell University Press.

Turner, V. (1969) *The Ritual Process: Structure and Anti-Structure*, Chicago: Aldine.

Webster, C., Simpson, D., MacDonald, R., Abbas, A., Cieslik, M., Shildrick, T. and Simpson, M. (2004) *Poor Transitions: Social Exclusion and Young Adults*, Bristol: Policy Press.

Willis, P. (1990) *Common Culture*, Milton Keynes: Open University Press.

Wyn, J. and White, R. (1997) *Rethinking Youth*, London: Sage.

Part II
Punishment and Juvenile Offenders

[3]

Juvenile offenders

Thom Brooks

Introduction

When we think about punishment we tend to think about how it affects adults and not juveniles.[1] Questions about what a thief might deserve or the most appropriate punishment for murderers tend to assume the thief and murderer are adults. Many believe that an offender's age may justify different punishments for the same crimes. But why should youth matter and what difference should it make? Do juvenile offenders deserve different punishments?

This chapter examines the punishment of juvenile offenders. I will explain why justice requires different consideration given to youths and what this might look like. I will also challenge traditional conceptions about youth justice and how we should conceive punishment for non-adults. The idea of having a stake in society takes on central importance. Juveniles are in a transition to becoming full members of political society. One concern is how best to ensure that they see themselves as coming to have a stake in society as a means to tackle juvenile offending. This is best addressed by the unified theory of punishment which is based upon the idea of stake-holding. Furthermore, the unified theory best addresses relevant multiple penal goals within a coherent framework. We are able to make better sense of juvenile offending and its punishment. The unified theory offers us a compelling view about how this is best achieved.

What is a juvenile?

The idea of 'the juvenile' is relatively recent. This is perhaps best explained by improvements in record keeping: 'Compulsory registration of births was not introduced until 1836, and thus it was not until the 1850s that birth certificates would have been available for the purpose of determining whether someone qualified as a juvenile'.[2] It did not take long for new courts to emerge that tailored punishment specifically to juvenile offenders. The first was launched in the United States with the passing of the Illinois Juvenile Court Act of 1899.[3] It established the first separate court hearing cases involving juvenile defendants and it could sanction different penal outcomes. The aims of the court were not punitive, but aimed at rehabilitation.[4] The idea was that youth offenders require reformation. This idea of youth and the need for reformation is based upon the view that juveniles are in a developmental transition to adulthood: to be a juvenile is to be a non-adult. This background provides the framework for how juvenile offending is understood today.

A juvenile is a non-adult often less than 18 years old.[5] But why should age make a difference? Antony Duff says:

> we should understand 'juvenile' offenders to be those who are neither so immature that they can certainly not be held criminal responsible, nor so mature that they are certainly as fit as any other adult to be held criminally responsible.[6]

Juvenile offenders are persons who are not fully responsible for their crimes because of their immaturity. Put differently: 'to treat someone like a child is, roughly, to treat her as if her life is not quite her own to lead and as if her choices are not quite her own to make'.[7]

Youth are in a transition to adulthood. Perhaps many adults will share a similar lack of maturity and foresight. The issue is that we give all persons a reasonable life chance to acquire these traits by distinguishing between adults and non-adults in the criminal justice system. We do not have the legal expectation that persons below a set age limit will develop a more complete transition to adult maturity. So while some underage people might well be treated as if they were adults, they are the exceptions rather than the rule. Unless there are grounds for doing otherwise, all persons underage are treated as juvenile offenders.[8] Those who are above a set age limit may well lack full maturity as well, but they are the exceptions rather than the rule on that side of the legal border. Unless there are grounds for doing otherwise, all such persons are treated as adults.[9]

While there is little controversy surrounding the need for youth courts, there is wide variation between legal systems on who should be considered a relevant non-adult.[10] Legal systems often distinguish between children, juveniles, and adults. *Children* are persons who cannot be held criminally liable for their actions.[11] *Juveniles* are persons who may be held partially responsible and *adults* may be held fully responsible.[12] The age of criminal responsibility differs widely, especially in the United States. The Federal government holds that persons under 11 years old cannot be criminally liable. Individual states each accept considerable variation from 6 to 12 years. The age of criminal responsibility is 13 in France, 14 in Germany, 15 in Scandinavian countries, and 16 in Spain and Portugal. It is 10 in England and Wales and 12 in Scotland. Those under the age of criminal responsibility may not be held criminally liable, but there are some powers in place to address relevant matters arising. For example, children under

10 years old may be subjects of civil care and supervision orders in England and Wales, where children may be taken into care by a local authority.[13] So while children may lack criminal responsibility, there may still be sufficient reason for the state to intervene and perhaps have children put under state supervision.

The primary distinction between children and juveniles is that the former are incapable of rendering minimally satisfactory judgements about permissible actions. Children are persons who are 'genuinely at sea on the question of right and wrong'.[14] Juveniles are believed capable of minimally satisfactory judgements which might render them partly criminally responsible for any offences. However, these judgements are merely minimally satisfactory and not more substantially satisfactory where the latter might render them fully responsible for any crimes. The difference between them is a difference in degree. Minimally satisfactory judgement is necessary, but not sufficient, for possession of some partial degree of criminal responsibility that will never be more than incomplete. Only substantially satisfactory judgement may entail some degree of criminal responsibility that may be complete. For example, a youth and an adult otherwise similarly situated may possess very different degrees of criminal responsibility for the same crimes whereby the youth may never be found more criminally responsible for the same act all things considered.[15]

There are at least three reasons why juveniles are believed to fall short of full criminal responsibility. First, youth are believed to have underdeveloped cognitive abilities. This may impair their understanding of the consequences stemming from their actions. Second, juveniles are believed to have underdeveloped control mechanisms. Teenage years are often a time where we learn self-control and mature in our understanding about how we might work with others to overcome obstacles. Third, youth are believed to be developing their sense of self-identity and relationships with others. Juveniles are learning how they may see themselves as part of a societal fabric. This process of identity formation faces inevitable environmental pressures from family and peer groups that may often play a positive role, but not always.

Juveniles face several developmental challenges in terms of their cognitive abilities, control mechanisms, and self-identity where each may be fragile and relatively malleable. One prison governor is reported to have said: 'Adolescents are impulsive, confused about their own identities and relationships'.[16] Of course, adults may have these characteristics as well. But adults seem less excusable because we might expect them to have achieved a more satisfactory development after reaching a certain age. The idea of juvenile justice is the expectation that most juveniles will not achieve full responsibility.[17] We must then consider how justice should be managed for persons who are not expected to possess full criminal responsibility.[18] Note that this need not entail that youth are punished less than they may deserve. The fact they may not possess full responsibility for their crimes may justify a punishment less severe than what might have been retributively deserved if the youth had full criminal responsibility.

Much hangs on which side of the line a person finds herself. The categories of child, juvenile, and adult represent groups defined by age, but justified by other factors. Age is a crude, but convenient and broadly effective, means by which the law may pronounce clear judgements about whether a person may be held criminally responsible and which court is most appropriate. It is not that a person becomes significantly better developed in her own judgements about lawful conduct on the day she becomes 18 years old reaching legal adulthood. Instead, the significance of becoming 18 is that by this date she will be expected to be held fully accountable for her actions. There is often a legal significance attached to reaching a particular age, such as 18 years, and achieving legal adulthood. Its significance lies in the attached behavioural expectations from a legal point of view to be reached at that time. So the borders between child and juvenile as well as juvenile and adult are porous from the standpoint of the facts of development, but not law. While the law gives fixed determinations about when each stage is reached by attaining a particular age, different people may develop at different paces. This may warrant exceptional treatment for exceptional persons.

Punishing juveniles as if adults

Some legal systems permit juvenile offenders to be prosecuted and punished as adults. This is usually set within a clear framework that is rarely employed. For example, in the United States there are over 80,000 juveniles in residential placement on any given day. The following conditions apply:

A person may be tried as an adult if:

(a) a juvenile is charged with a violent felony or drug trafficking or importation offense and if the offense was committed after the person's 15th birthday;
(b) a juvenile possessed a firearm during a violent offense and the offense was committed after the person's 13th birthday; or
(c) a juvenile had been previously adjudicated delinquent of a violent felony or drug offense.[19]

This framework is not entirely unusual for other jurisdictions. A juvenile may be tried as an adult under specific conditions that normally include violence towards others, including use of a firearm. The main factor is not his responsibility or mature development, but rather the dangerousness of his alleged crime. Let us first reflect on this fact before considering a critique.

This idea about when youth may be punished as if an adult is more sympathetic to some theories of punishment than others. Deterrence proponents might argue that general deterrence is best secured by ensuring that all persons engaged in violent crimes are punished severely. The benefit that flows from general deterrence and future crime reduction through fear of strong punishment has priority over the cost of punishing juveniles as adults independently of any clear evidence that their capacity for judgement is satisfactorily advanced for non-adults. Expressivists, including communicative theorists, might argue major violent crimes are events to be avoided however possible. Their occurrence understandably commands widespread public condemnation. It is possible that juveniles may be punished as adults where this is necessary to convey justified public disapproval. Finally, a unified theory of punishment might claim that the actions of some juveniles may pose more substantial than normal threats to rights under exceptional circumstances that might warrant punishing juveniles as adults. Punishment is a response to crime that aims at the restoration of rights. There may be exceptional circumstances that give rise to the justification of treating some youth differently than most others in less exceptional circumstances.

So some theories may justify punishing juveniles as adults. It is unclear how far below the age of legal adulthood each might extend. Expressivism would require punished juveniles to be capable of understanding the message of public disapproval conveyed to them by the political community through punishment. Furthermore, some expressivists, such as communicative theorists, would additionally require that juveniles be capable of returning some communication of secular apology in reply. The unified theory of punishment is based around the idea of the stakeholder society. We punish with the aim of the restoration of rights in order to best maintain and protect rights. This is done with a view towards promoting stakeholding which includes the offender. The punishment of juveniles as adults should not make less likely her ability to realize her coming to have a stake in society and its future. This is a major constraint. If we believe that in most, if not virtually all, cases juveniles will be best served in being punished as a non-adult, then the punishment of juveniles as adults will be limited to exceptional circumstances that meet the condition that they best promote stakeholding for all including the juvenile offender.

These examples are meant to illustrate that perhaps expressivists and unified theorists might justify the punishment of juveniles as adults, but this would be limited to fairly exceptional circumstances within robust limitations where such punishment is understood to be deserved and proportionate. Thus, the punishment of juveniles as adults may be exceptional, but it must also crucially be deserved and proportionate.[20]

Nevertheless, the unified theory may offer a more compelling view because it remains unclear how expressivism differs from retributivism. Expressivists argue that punishment must be proportionate to what is deserved and justified as the expression of public disapproval. But are there cases where expressivists might argue punishment is proportionate to what is deserved, but unjustified because it does not express public disapproval? No, there are not and the two issues of retributivist desert and justified public disapproval are not distinctly separate. So it is unclear what precise contribution expressivism offers beyond what retributivism might offer us already. The unified theory does not run into any such problem.

The deterrence theory of punishment might justify the punishment of juveniles as adults on different grounds. The central importance for most deterrence theorists is how punishment might best promote deterrence. If deterrence may be promoted best by punishing juveniles as adults in some circumstances, then this may be justified. This need not be in exceptional cases only although widespread use might lead to public confusion about the expected penal threats issued by the state which would undermine general deterrence. One remaining problem is that it is difficult to know whether deterrence takes place. While we may measure the reduction in recorded crimes over time, correlation is not causation: the fact that crime is reduced is not necessarily evidence that crime reduction is a result of popular fear of threatened punishment if they chose to perform crimes. This fundamental problem about deterrence is one reason to prefer an alternative theory of punishment. A second reason is that we may reject the punishment of juveniles as adults in non-exceptional circumstances. This may be justified by deterrence, but not by other approaches including the unified theory as noted previously. A third reason is that deterrence may require us to punish juvenile offenders more than adults similarly situated for the same crimes. If juveniles are more likely to commit offences, then there is a need for punishment to have a greater penal threat in order to serve as a more effective deterrent. So deterrence proponents may justify greater punishment for juveniles because they require a greater threat to be deterred from criminal offending.[21]

Rehabilitation theories of punishment and retributivism present a somewhat different situation. Rehabilitation theorists argue that the goal of punishment is to help rehabilitate offenders. Some offenders will require more reformation than others. This need not be related to age. While juvenile offenders may have much more to learn, some adult offenders may be more difficult to teach on how to break from problematic behaviours. The rehabilitation of offenders should be tailored to their particular needs. The question is not so much about their age, but rather about their need to achieve satisfactory rehabilitation.

Similarly, retributivists argue that punishment should be proportionate to what is deserved. An offender's punishable desert is our central concern and not her age although this may impact upon her desert. It may be the case that juvenile offenders on the whole deserve less punishment than adults similarly situated for the same crime. But the reason is not that juveniles deserve less punishment because they are non-adults. Instead, the reason that any juvenile who is punished less than an adult similarly situated for the same crime must be because the juvenile possesses less punishable desert.[22] Ido Weijers and Antony Duff argue:

> It is thus plausible that juvenile offenders are often less culpable for the crimes that they commit than are normal adult offenders, and less competent to understand and participate in their trials than adults are supposed to be.[23]

Juvenile offenders may often possess less desert than adults similarly situated. This difference may arise where juvenile offenders lack minimal competence and, thus, lack similar desert. But the fact that an offender is not yet an adult does not entail he will always possess less desert than an adult.[24] Retributivists may justify the punishment of juveniles as adults where juveniles posses sufficient desert. Thus, rehabilitation theorists and retributivists might punish juveniles as adults, but this need not be in exceptional cases only and must be determined on a case by case basis.[25] This may provide an important reason to support an alternative theory, such as the unified theory of punishment, which would only justify such punishment in exceptional circumstances. Moreover, the unified theory does not run into the problems of possible cases where rehabilitative needs may require greater punishment than what is deserved or offenders who cannot be rehabilitated. Nor does the unified theory accept the problematic link between retributivism and morality.

Most legal systems acknowledge the importance of supporting a separate youth court for juvenile justice that is distinct from the criminal justice system that applies to adults. Nevertheless, there may be circumstances where juveniles are punished as if they were adults. The reasons may differ widely across various theories of punishment. However, it is clear that each may justify the punishment of juveniles as if they were adults under certain circumstances with some exceptions. There is also strongest support for the unified theory of punishment. This theory does not run into the problems faced by other theories while only justifying the punishment of juveniles as adults under exceptional circumstances.

Age and crime

There is a link between crime and the age of offenders. Richard L. Lippke says:

> Criminal offending is overwhelmingly the province of the young, with the vast majority of offenders consisting of those 16–35 years of age. Teenagers and young adults, while not altogether incapable of moral responsibility, are perhaps best viewed as moral works in progress.[26]

Consider the following facts about young offenders. About 40 per cent of all first time offenders are aged between 18 and 20 years.[27] Roughly 70 per cent of persistent youth offenders have been in contact with the police over the past year. Criminal offending tends to peak when offenders are in their teens or early twenties before soon tapering off. Criminal offending tapers off more slowly for more violent criminals.[28] This evidence strongly suggests that the most effective way to achieve crime reduction overall is to reduce offending by youths. Criminal offending is not only 'the province of the young', but the youth offenders of today compose most of the adult offenders of tomorrow. If we may reduce juvenile offending, then we may best reduce all offending.

A reduction in juvenile offending will contribute to fewer victims. Juveniles are both more likely to be offenders and victims than adults. For example, youth between the ages of 12 and 17 were twice as likely as adults 18 or older to be the victim of a violent crime.[29] In a study examining annual rates of violent victimization between 1993–2003 in the United States, the annual average rate for all violence per 1,000 persons was about 84 for juveniles between the ages of 12 and 17 and about 32 for adults aged 18 years or older. Rates of assault, robbery, serious violence, rape, and sexual assault were much less for those 18 years or older compared with youth between 12 and 17 years old.[30]

This speaks to a powerful truth in criminological research: most offenders share a broadly similar profile to their victims. The problem is not so much the dangerous stranger, but the dangerous neighbour or relative. The probability of being the victim of someone from a similar socio-economic background and ethnicity is high. There is also a high probability that offenders and victims will be similar in age and young. One study of victims aged between 12 and 19 years found that more than half of their offenders were perceived to be in the same age range and only about 20 per cent perceived to be 21 or older.[31] Juvenile offenders are most likely to engage in violent crimes against other youth.[32] Furthermore, younger teens are more likely to suffer violent crime at school than elsewhere.[33]

So why do juveniles offend? The standard view is that juveniles are more likely than adults to engage in risky behaviour, including criminal offending. The reason is that juveniles are generally less aware of the costs associated with potentially risky behaviour. Furthermore, juveniles are believed to be generally less aware of the likelihood of their incurring costs associated with their behaviour. Even where potential costs are known, their likelihood is dismissed. Juveniles may know they should not engage in offences, such as criminal damage or drug possession. The problem is that they may fail to acknowledge the risk of their behaviour by discounting the likelihood of their being convicted and sentenced for their crimes.

The common approach to the standard view is to improve education about risks. The idea is that juveniles might be less likely to engage in risky behaviour if they better understood the associated risks involved. The problem is that these efforts have met with limited success and not been found that effective. This is because youth may already understand the relevant potential risks. The issue is that they may remain unconvinced that the costs of risky behaviour might be imposed upon them.[34] Improved education about risks remains important, but it is insufficient. What is required is more efforts to convince potential youth offenders that there may be real consequences for them that are likely if they were to engage in criminal behaviour: 'Only when offending is seen to have more social costs than personal benefits will young people attempt to modify their behaviour so as to adapt to their current social situation'.[35] This is the challenge we face.

One idea about how to better convince potential youth offenders is through the lens of stakeholding. Youth must come to see the attraction about their coming to have a stake in society. Stakeholding is an idea about mutual recognition and reciprocity where we acknowledge others as fellow stakeholders. If we view ourselves as having a stake in society, then we may become much less likely to engage in criminal behaviour that may damage our stake and common rights. This perspective seeks to foster crime reduction through constructions of self-identity with others.[36] The stakeholder society is a political community where members choose to engage with each other to address common issues.

Stakeholding comes in stages. Children are persons who have a stake, but are unable to participate on minimally equal terms with other stakeholders. The child's relation to society is more akin to a patient rather than an agent. So while children are affected in substantial ways by the decisions made by the political community, they lack the ability to contribute on a minimally equal basis with others. Adults are those who may engage with other stakeholders on equal terms. Juveniles are at a transitional stage between children and adults. While juveniles have a stake and some ability for engagement, their stake and engagement ability are in a process of development. This process may breed a certain amount of inevitable frustration for youth as they acquire and develop new self-identities of themselves and their relation to others.

While there has been much research into the idea of recognition and how it may contribute to our understanding of criminology, there has been precious little attention into how we might best foster stakeholding to more effectively reduce crime. This is not too surprising. The idea of stakeholding originally addressed how we might better conceive corporate responsibility and strategic communications in the area of business ethics: we should understand various parties as stakeholders and this should contribute to new management structures for collective decision-making that are more democratic, transparent, and ethically robust.[37] Much work has centred on how corporate governance might be improved if we adopted stakeholder theory, but it has also extended further into other domains. For example, there has since been interest in how economic justice might be improved through stakeholding: the idea of the property-owning democracy defended by John Rawls is perhaps one important example of this.[38]

These accounts are useful for showing us how we might reform our institutions, but much more research is needed into the social psychology and socio-legal project of fostering stakeholding for fellow citizens. There is a particular need for how we might best foster stakeholding specifically for juveniles.

Stakeholding comes in stages of development. While the stages may be sufficiently clear, their membership ages are not. Stage membership may differ from one society to the next. For example, one proposal is that membership is set in terms of children (0 to 14 years), juveniles (15 to 24 years), and adults (25 years and older).[39] This is one of many such ways that age membership might be attributed to each group. Its importance is highlighting the need for thinking beyond binary considerations of adult and non-adult, and developing further categories. For example, those who are children will lack some, if not all, criminal responsibility, and so this group deserves individual attention. Those who are adults may possess full responsibility, but they are not most likely to engage in criminal behaviour. These are reasons why this group deserves individual attention as well.

The more problematic category is the juveniles group. This is because they are most at risk. This is further complicated by the fact that this group will contain persons deemed legal adults and those who are not if defined as persons between 15 and 24 years. So there may be good reason to consider crime reduction policies within this broad category, but then tailored more specifically for 15 to 17 year olds and persons between 18 and 24 years. This need not require establishing new courts, but it will require new considerations about how to better address juvenile offending by both minors and young adults more effectively than we have. There are already procedures in place for children, juveniles, and adults to receive different treatment in most legal systems. These procedures should be reconsidered, specifically in terms of how stakeholding and restoration might be better promoted for juvenile and young adult offenders through punishment.

Juveniles and restorative recognition

Juvenile offending is an issue of central importance for any criminal justice policy. One major factor is that juveniles are most likely to be first-time offenders.[40] If offending can be reduced for juveniles, then this may yield major benefits in terms of greater crime reduction in general. Successive governments have initiated different penal experiments to best address juvenile offending through various piloted schemes.[41]

Restorative justice has received increasing attention as the approach of choice for confronting youth justice.[42] There are at least two reasons behind its popularity. The first is that most juvenile offenders commit non-violent crimes. Juvenile offenders are more potentially dangerous in the longer term where any future offending may become more serious if not satisfactorily addressed. But juvenile offenders do not commit many serious violent crimes when underage. There is greater public support for less punitive approaches, such as restorative justice, if it may effectively end non-violent criminality. Such support might vanish in cases where juveniles have committed more serious violent crimes. Restorative justice is less often used in such cases generally. A second reason behind the popularity of restorative justice for juvenile offenders is that it has been shown to be highly likely to reduce crime among adults. Fewer juvenile offenders often leads to fewer adult offenders in future. So restorative justice has become increasingly popular for juvenile offenders because it is likely to contribute to crime reduction in the longer term while its use is often confined to addressing non-violent offenders. Studies have found reoffending rates still high, but restorative justice for youths has been found to lead to far less reoffending than community sentences and about half as much as custodial sentences.[43] While such studies are inconclusive, the evidence thus far is promising.

Restorative justice aims to restore what crime has damaged between offender, victim, and the local community. This approach has proven widely popular for all participants and effective in reducing crime. However, the use of restorative justice for juvenile offenders raises specific issues. Juveniles are not adults and their parents may decide that they participate in a restorative conference on their behalf. Most victims who agreed to take part in restorative conferences are satisfied by the experience and its conclusion. There is less satisfaction for underage victims who have not agreed to take part, but participated because of the decision by their parent or guardian.[44] A similar problem may arise for juvenile offenders. Restorative justice becomes possible where offenders accept responsibility for their crimes. But what if participation is determined by the decision of a parent or guardian instead of the underage offender?

It is unclear how best to address this problem. On the one hand, restorative justice works best where all persons present who have a stake in the outcome come together to address how what has been damaged by crime may be resolved. So it is important that all parties choose to participate to ensure the process is successful. On the other hand, juveniles are not deemed fully legally autonomous. Their parents or guardians have a responsibility to protect and promote their interests. There may be inevitable conflicts on occasion between what a juvenile and his parents believe is the best response to an invitation to participate in a restorative conference. Many problems with restorative conferences are resolved by better management of likely expectations about the purpose of a conference, its conduct, and possible results. Perhaps the best way to address the specific needs arising in restorative justice cases involving youth is to take further measures to ensure that all potential underage participants and their parents or guardians receive additional support and information about likely expectations from participation. Juveniles may be unable to make fully informed decisions, but this is not a reason to be more diligent about ensuring they have as much information as reasonably advisable.

Restorative justice conferences for juvenile offenders often end with the agreement of a contract that the offender must fulfil. These contracts may include acceptable behaviour contracts, anti-social behaviour orders (ASBOs), curfews up to 90 days, and child safety orders for children under ten years old. The contracts are an acknowledgement of responsibility and accountability. Offenders often become more aware about how their actions have impacted upon others negatively with an action plan for how they might best restore what they have damaged. This may include financial contributions to repay any material losses.

Restoration appears to work well because it brings together relevant stakeholders to a crime and its penal outcome into constructive dialogue with one another. It is tempting to view its success as fostering a sense of recognition in juvenile offenders: they gain a sense of inclusive membership in the community through restorative justice. Recognition then plays a central role in making restorative justice a success. However, it is not recognition as such that has this role, but rather recognition *of a particular kind*. What counts is not only that I am recognized, but recognized *as a stakeholder*. Restorative justice conference members are persons with a stake in the decision.

The idea of stakeholding as *restorative recognition* best captures the specific form of recognition that plays such a central role in these contexts. This leads to practical results. One result is that contracts agreed to in restorative conferences should have regard to how they promote future stakeholding. A second practical result is there must be a greater focus on ensuring a satisfactory provision of support networks, such as family, friends, and local community. Youth offenders often lack such provision which may contribute to their failure to see themselves as future stakeholders.[45] Restorative recognition is better achieved where satisfactory support networks are available.

Finally, stakeholding is important for all members in a political community and not exclusive to non-violent offenders. Restorative justice proponents limit the applicability of their approach by rejecting the justification of hard treatment. Non-custodial sentences may not always command public confidence. There is perhaps a greater need for violent juvenile offenders to acknowledge their crimes and accept accountability for their actions in dialogue with fellow stakeholders. There is much potential benefit for victims, offenders, and others engaging in restorative dialogue. This may require a different membership, such as a magistrate or judge conducting the conference. The benefits of restorative conferences should not be limited to non-violent offenders only, but extended to potentially most, if not all, offenders. Furthermore, these conferences may warrant possible custodial sentences for violent offenders. This understanding of more punitive restorative justice is closest to the unified theory of punishment. If our aim is the restoration of rights, then we should not limit ourselves to non-custodial sentences where these may improve our ability to satisfy our penal aims.

Juvenile gender justice

The problem of crime is often a problem of males and crime. The difference between men and women is striking. The crime rates are broadly similar from around the ages of 12 to 13, but they rise only slightly for young women before dropping significantly from the age of about 21.[46] This is in stark contrast with young men. The male crime rate doubles at 14 years and then tapers off more slowly. There is also a major difference in crimes performed. For example, young women are more likely to engage in criminal damage or purchasing stolen goods when under the age of 16. Young men are also more likely to engage in these crimes, but also fighting, which begins to increase sharply in likelihood as they approach adulthood. Nevertheless, nearly 75 per cent of all youth crime is property related. Young men are four times more likely to engage in these crimes than young women.

The evidence about juvenile offending highlights an important fact often overlooked in relevant debates. Juvenile offending is largely a problem of crime performed by young men; adult offending is largely a problem of crimes performed by many young men later in life. There is a clear gender dimension to juvenile justice which we might call *juvenile gender justice*.[47]

There are many arguments given about why young women are much less likely to offend after their teenage years. One argument is the influence of relational factors, such as the responsibility for raising children, the positive impact of a new relationship or support from family and friends. For example, Monica Barry interviewed one women who had previously offended. She says: 'Reasons for stopping? Well the kids, know what I mean. To try and make a family … [My daughter] had seen so much … She hadn't seen the needle or nothing, know what I mean, but kids aren't stupid'.[48] This passage is suggestive of the importance of stakeholding. The change in this woman's life is she has come to view herself as having a stake in society because of the importance she gives to her responsibilities to her children. Her self-identification in constructive 'pro-social' relations to others is one important route to understanding herself as a stakeholder.[49]

Juvenile offending and the unified theory

The courts have generally adopted a multiple penal goals framework for the punishment of juvenile offenders. For example, some courts claims four goals should be pursued in these cases: the punishment of juvenile offenders; the reform and rehabilitation of juvenile offenders; the protection of the public; and the making of reparations by juvenile offenders to persons affected by their crime.[50] Punishment should be determined with regard to these different goals. Note the absence of any explicit inclusion of deterrence. This is explained by the decisions of many courts to find it unlawful for the purpose of youth punishment.[51] Deterrence assumes a cost–benefit analysis that is believed to be inapplicable for juvenile offenders.

One potential problem is that these goals may come into conflict with each other. The goal of reform may be undermined by the need to protect the public, for instance. Should we reject a multiple penal framework for the punishment of juvenile offenders because it is incoherent? The unified theory may best address this commonly used framework. The potential conflict between multiple penal goals is possible in the absence of a principled context which the unified theory provides. It argues that punishment is a response to crime that aims at the restoration of rights within the context of promoting stakeholding. Punishment may address multiple penal goals to promote the aim of restoring rights. Different penal goals are justified insofar as they help promote the aim of restoration. The unified theory has the flexibility to address this framework and it is able to best explain its justification. By contrast, other theories of punishment would insist on some alternative framework employing some, but not all, of these principles. For example, rehabilitation theorists might endorse the goal of rehabilitating juvenile offenders and communicative proponents may support payment of reparations, but neither may offer a compelling justification for how these multiple penal goals may be defended in a coherent theory which the unified theory provides us.

The unified theory best addresses the multiple penal goals often brought to bear on the punishment of juvenile offenders. The theory may also best account for the risk factors that may contribute to the need for punishment.[52] One risk factor is a troubled home life where the parents or guardians are regularly in contact with the police. This risk factor is linked with another: a lack of adequate housing or homelessness. The struggle for satisfactory accommodation may contribute to criminal behaviour in order to secure it. Other risk factors include drug and alcohol abuse and often undetected mental illness, such as manic depression or schizophrenia. These four risk factors for criminal behaviour are common for adults, too.

There are a further two risk factors that are specific to juvenile offenders.[53] The first is peer group pressure. Youth are engaged in the process of self-identity formation and their 'self-concept'.[54] This may make them more vulnerable to render poor judgements than adults. One way to tackle juvenile offending is to target leaders in peer networks, including gangs.[55] Changes at the 'top' may flow down to benefits at the 'bottom'. Youth may find some networks attractive because of their perceived importance in terms of social status. Networks that promote anti-authority attitudes, such as gang membership, may contribute to higher crime rates.[56] A second risk factor is poor performance or attendance at school, especially school exclusion.

Together, these six risk factors are united in illuminating a problem we have discussed previously: the problem of persons failing to see themselves as having a stake in society. If young persons are not in school with other students, then they may fail to see how engaging with others in a constructive environment may be conducive to their future. Lacking opportunities for lawful behaviour may provide incentives for creating opportunities for unlawful behaviour. Overcoming these problems is the project of helping ensure youth see themselves as coming to have a stake in society and its future. This is more than mere recognition, but recognition as a stakeholder. It is important that all juveniles see themselves as coming to have a legitimate stake in society.[57] Criminal justice policy should help remove obstacles to stakeholding where possible.[58] One finding is that crime reduction is better achieved through non-custodial sentences wherever possible and greater use of community penalties where juvenile offenders may have punishment tailored more to their individual needs.[59] The idea is that youth who view themselves as coming to have a legitimate future stake in society may find membership in peer networks, including gangs, that oppose legitimate stakeholding an unattractive option.

Punishment is a response to crime that often becomes necessary for offenders who lack positive support networks. This is no less true for juvenile offenders. It is important to help create and maintain such support to promote restorative recognition through stakeholding.[60] This sense is often lacking for many young adults. For example, one recent British study of over 2,200 persons between 16 and 24 years old found that more than a third 'do not feel part of their local community'.[61] One in five felt isolated 'most of the time' and about 10 per cent felt like an outcast. Nearly a third did not believe there was a future for them in their local area. The problem is that many youth feel some loss of control over their lives and future direction.[62] There is a central need to promote stakeholding and assist young adults in taking greater control over their lives by helping them to see themselves as having a future stake in society.

The unified theory of punishment occupies a unique position. It is best placed to defend the multiple penal goals that are often employed in determining punishments for youth. The unified theory is also best placed to explain the central issue behind the risk factors associated with potential future offending for adults and juveniles as a problem concerning stakeholding. The unified theory best accounts for the problem of youth crime as well as its flexible and effective punishment.

Conclusion

This chapter has examined the punishment of juvenile offenders. The issue is highly important because juvenile offenders are most likely to commit crimes and the youth offenders of today are often the adult offenders of tomorrow. We require an approach that might best address the specific issues associated with juvenile justice that promote an effective criminal justice policy.

The unified theory of punishment offers the most compelling theory for thinking about juvenile justice. Juvenile offending is often a product of a failure of youths understanding themselves as having a stake in society. This may be best addressed by promoting restorative recognition through shared stakeholding which the unified theory advances. Offenders engage with others to become more aware of how their actions impact upon others and receive assistance with forging and maintaining positive support networks. Juvenile offenders may be developing into legal adulthood. Punishment may become justified, but it should not contribute to creating further obstacles for offenders to view themselves as stakeholders. Instead, punishment aims at the restoration of rights and promotion of stakeholding for adult and juvenile offenders although each may require different treatment according to what restoration may require.

Notes

1 I shall refer interchangeably to 'juveniles' and 'youths'.
2 J. J. Tobias, *Crime and Industrial Society in the Nineteenth Century* (London: B. T. Batsford, 1967): 12.
3 Illinois Juvenile Court Act, 1899 Ill. Laws 132.
4 See Blackburn, *The Psychology of Criminal Conduct*, 10–11.
5 While adulthood is normally reached when someone becomes 18 years old, some jurisdictions may permit persons who are 16 or 17 to become adults and the rules may vary.
6 R. A. Duff, 'Punishing the Young' in R. A. Duff and Ido Weijers (eds), *Punishing Juveniles: Principle and Critique* (Oxford: Hart, 2002): 116.
7 Tamar Shapiro, 'What Is a Child?' *Ethics* 109 (1999): 715.
8 This chapter will later turn to the question of under which circumstances, if any, should youth offenders be tried and punished as adults.
9 There may be several such grounds, potentially including the defence of diminished responsibility (i.e. 'an abnormality of mental functioning'). See Coroners and Justice Act 2009, s. 52 and Simester et al., *Simester and Sullivan's Criminal Law*, 714–22.
10 See Easton and Piper, *Sentencing and Punishment*, 187.
11 This is sometimes referred to in terms of the defence of infancy. See Simester et al., *Simester and Sullivan's Criminal Law*, 722–4.
12 Please note the relevant qualifications. Juveniles *may* be held partially responsible, but there may be circumstances that justify their being held fully responsible. We will come to this issue shortly. Adults *may* be held fully responsible, but there may be circumstances where they are not.
13 See Children Act 1998.
14 Solicitor General cited in *Hansard*, Lords, 16 December 1997, col. 596.
15 The qualification of 'all things considered' is important. Of course, it may be possible that a youth may be found more criminally responsible than an adult where they are not similarly situated and the same crime performed under very different circumstances.
16 Quoted in Trevor Grove, *The Magistrate's Tale: A Frontline Report from a New JP* (London: Bloomsbury, 2002): 117.
17 See Hegel, *Elements of the Philosophy of Right*, §10 Addition: 'The child … is only the potentiality of reason and freedom'.

Notes

18 For example, see Grove, *The Magistrate's Tale*, 118: 'But even Sharon had misgivings. Gruffly but with feeling she told us about the appalling circumstances most of "the boys" were going back to after their release. In the essays they wrote about what they'd do first when they got out, the priorities were invariably the same: a McDonalds hamburger, a spliff, a beer and sex, roughly in that order'.

19 US Bureau of Justice Statistics (http://www.ojp.usdoj.gov/bjs/). See Brian D. Johnson and Megan C. Kurlychek, 'Transferred Juveniles in the Era of Sentencing Guidelines: Examining Judicial Departures for Juvenile Offenders in Adult Criminal Court', *Criminology* 50 (2012): 1–40.

20 This perspective may also be accepted by restorative justice proponents that we will discuss later. Restoration aims at the restoration of what is damaged by crime. This must be tailored to the circumstances where juveniles may often be treated differently than adults similarly situated, but not always, such as in exceptional circumstances although there must be robust limitations in place.

21 This possible objection to deterrence theories is strongly relevant because juveniles are more likely than adults to engage in criminal behaviour. No deterrence theorist advances the position that juveniles should be punished more than adults under normal circumstances. However, this may clearly follow from the arguments. A potential reply is that the criminal law shouldn't offer multiple threats for the same crimes. On balance, there should not be one penal system for adults and another for juveniles because this may be counterproductive to deterrence. Such a view would reject the idea that deterrence should be specific, not general, and tailored to particular individuals. The problem with this potential reply to the original objection is that it rejects the objection at a cost. It denies that deterrent punishment would justify greater punishment of juveniles than adults, but the cost is that it accepts that juveniles should normally be punished as if they were adults. If we wish to defend the view that the punishment of juveniles as adults should be limited to exceptional circumstances at best, if at all, then we should reject deterrence on the grounds that deterrence may lead to punishing juveniles more than adults in normal cases or punishing juveniles as adults in normal cases.

22 There is also the problem that older offenders are more likely to have past convictions that may lead to their being punished more for the same crimes than younger offenders. See Shawn Bushway and Anne Piehl, 'The Inextricable Link between Age and Criminal History in Sentencing', *Crime and Delinquency* 53 (2007): 156–83.

23 Ido Weijers and Anthony Duff, 'Introduction: Themes in Juvenile Justice' in *Punishing Juveniles*, 11.

24 On competence and adulthood, see Thom Brooks, 'Can We Justify Political Inequality?' *Archiv für Rechts und Sozialphilosophie* 89 (2003): 426–38 and Thom Brooks, 'Equality and Democracy: The Problem of Minimal Competency', *Ethical Perspectives* 14 (2007): 3–12.

25 I have said nothing about the negative retributivism of Rawls, Hart, and others. This is because the application of their theories – which we have explained are often incoherent at their core – will depend upon the particular mix found in a theory. This makes it somewhat difficult to state with any confidence how such theorists might grapple with the punishment of juvenile offenders.

26 Lippke, *Rethinking Imprisonment*, 92.

27 Home Office, *Justice for All*, 111.

28 See Margaret F. Severson, Kimberly Bruns, Christopher Veeh, and Jaehoon Lee, 'Prisoner Reentry Programming: Who Recidivates and When?', *Journal of Offender Rehabilitation* 50 (2011): 345.

Notes

29 See US Bureau of Justice Statistics, *Juvenile Victimization and Offending*, 1.
30 Ibid. 2.
31 See Michael R. Rand and Jayne E. Robinson, *Criminal Victimization in the United States, 2008 – Statistical Tables* (Washington, DC: Bureau of Justice Statistics, 2011): table 41.
32 See US Bureau of Justice Statistics, *Juvenile Victimization and Offending*, 7.
33 See Stephen Roe and Jane Ashe, 'Young People and Crime: Findings from the 2006 Offending, Crime and Justice Survey', *Home Office Statistical Bulletin* (London: Home Office, 2008): 15, 30 and US Bureau of Justice Statistics, *Juvenile Victimization and Offending*, 5.
34 See Dhami and Mandel, 'Crime as Risk Taking'.
35 Monica Barry, *Youth Offending in Transition: The Search for Social Recognition* (Abingdon: Routledge, 2006): 134.
36 See Eleonora Patacchini and Yves Zenou, 'Juvenile Delinquency and Conformism', *Journal of Law, Economics and Organization* 28 (2012): 1–31.
37 On the origins of stakeholding in business ethics, see Nigel de Bussy, 'Stakeholder Theory', in Wolfgang Donsbach (ed.), *The International Encyclopedia of Communication* (Oxford: Blackwell, 2008): 4815–17. See also Hutton, *The Stakeholder Society* and Will Hutton, *Them and Us: Changing Britain – Why We Need a Fair Society* (London: Little, Brown, 2010).
38 On the idea of a property-owning democracy, see Rawls, *Justice as Fairness*, 137–9. See also James Meade, *Efficiency, Equality, and the Ownership of Property* (London: George Allen and Unwin, 1964).
39 See Barry, *Youth Offending in Transition*, 26. While Barry does not explicitly endorse the idea of the stakeholder society, she does argue for the related idea of mutual recognition.
40 For example, see Ministry of Justice, *Adult Re-Convictions*.
41 See Easton and Piper, *Sentencing and Punishment*, 265.
42 One example is the UK's Youth Justice Board (http://www.justice.gov.uk/about/yjb).
43 For example, one study of youth and restorative justice in Northern Ireland found reoffending rates of 37.7 per cent (restorative justice), 52.1 per cent (community sentences), and 70.7 per cent (custodial sentences). See Jessica Jacobson and Penelope Gibbs, *Making Amends: Restorative Youth Justice in Northern Ireland* (London: Prison Reform Trust, 2009).
44 See Gal and Moyal, 'Juvenile Victims in Restorative Justice', 1025–7.
45 See Rebecca S. Siegel, Annette M. La Greca, and Hannah M. Harrison, 'Peer Victimization and Social Anxiety in Adolescents: Prospective and Reciprocal Relationships', *Journal of Youth and Adolescence* 38 (2009): 1096–109.
46 These crime rates are not uncommon. Rates summarized have been drawn up with UK Home Office studies of self-reported crimes. The purpose of noting findings is purely indicative: the importance is to highlight various contours of criminal behaviour and not to promote any particular social science empirical study.
47 For example, see Traquina Emeka and Jon Sorensen, 'Female Juvenile Risk: Is There a Need for Gendered Assessment Instruments?', *Youth Violence and Juvenile Justice* 7 (2009): 313–30. On gender and essentialism, see Alison Stone, 'Essentialism and Anti-Essentialism in Feminist Philosophy', *Journal of Moral Philosophy* 1 (2004): 135–53 reprinted in Thom Brooks (ed.), *Ethics and Moral Philosophy* (Leiden: Brill, 2011): 385–407.
48 Barry, *Youth Offending in Transition*, 113.
49 It is relatively uncontroversial that stark differences exist between male and female offenders. It is controversial why this stark difference exists. One possible explanation is that young women are more likely to form pro-social attitudes

Notes

earlier than young men. This might be partially explained by the idea that women are more likely to see themselves as having a stake in society although more must be said about why this might be the case. For example, see S. Bennett, D. P. Farrington, and L. R. Huesmann, 'Explaining Gender Differences in Crime and Violence: The Importance of Social Cognitive Skills', *Aggression and Violent Behavior* 10 (2005): 263–88. Such factors may not always play a positive constructive role. For an illuminating critique, see Elizabeth Caufmann, 'Understanding the Female Offender', *Future of Children* 18 (2008): 119–42.

50 For example, see Ashworth, *Sentencing and Criminal Justice*, 391.

51 See ibid. 392.

52 See Stephen Case and Kevin Haines, *Understanding Youth Offending: Risk Factor Research, Policy, and Practice* (Portland: Willan, 2009).

53 See Blackburn, *The Psychology of Criminal Conduct*, 160–80.

54 See ibid. 197.

55 See Patacchini and Zenou, 'Juvenile Delinquency and Conformism', 1–31.

56 See Emma Alleyne and Jane L. Wood, 'Gang-Related Crime: The Social, Psychological, and Behavioral Correlates', *Psychology, Crime, and Law* (2012) (DOI: 10.1080/1068316X.2012.658050).

57 See Barry, *Youth Offending in Transition*, 2, 161, 166. Se also ibid. 156–8.

58 See Green, *Lectures on the Principles of Political Obligation*, §209.

59 See Laura S. Abrams, Diane Terry, and Todd M. Franke, 'Community-Based Juvenile Reentry Services: The Effects of Service Dosage on Juvenile and Adult Recidivism', *Journal of Offender Rehabilitation* 50 (2011): 492–510.

60 See Independent Commission on Youth Crime and Antisocial Behaviour, *Time for a Fresh Start: The Report of the Independent Commission on Youth Crime and Antisocial Behaviour* (London: The Police Foundation, 2010).

61 BBC News, 'Young People Feel "Isolated" in Their Community', (27 October 2010) (http://www.bbc.co.uk/news/education-11629544).

62 See Barry, *Youth Offending in Transition*, 130.

Bibiography

Abrams, Laura S., Diane Terry, and Todd M. Franke (2011). 'Community-Based Juvenile Reentry Services: The Effects of Service Dosage on Juvenile and Adult Recidivism', *Journal of Offender Rehabilitation* 50: 492–510.

Alleyne, Emma and Jane L. Wood (2012). 'Gang-Related Crime: The Social, Psychological and Behavioral Correlates', *Psychology, Crime and Law*. DOI: 10.1080/1068316X.2012.658050.

Ashworth, Andrew (2010). *Sentencing and Criminal Justice, 5th ed.* Cambridge: Cambridge University Press.

Barry, Monica (2006). *Youth Offending in Transition: The Search for Social Recognition*. Abingdon: Routledge.

Bennett, S., D. P. Farrington, and L. R. Huesmann (2005). 'Explaining Gender Differences in Crime and Violence: The Importance of Social Cognitive Skills', *Aggression and Violent Behavior* 10: 263–88.

Blackburn, Ronald (1993). *The Psychology of Criminal Conduct: Theory, Research and Practice*. New York: Wiley.

Brooks, Thom (2007). 'Equality and Democracy: The Problem of Minimal Competency', *Ethical Perspectives* 14: 3–12.

Bushway, Shawn and Anne Piehl (2007). 'The Inextricable Link between Age and Criminal History in Sentencing', *Crime and Delinquency* 53: 156–83.

Bibliography

Case, Stephen and Kevin Haines (2009). *Understanding Youth Offending: Risk Factor Research, Policy and Practice.* Portland: Willan.

Caufmann, Elizabeth (2008). 'Understanding the Female Offender', *Future of Children* 18: 119–42.

de Bussy, Nigel (2008). 'Stakeholder Theory' in Wolfgang Donsbach (ed.), *The International Encyclopedia of Communication.* Oxford: Blackwell, pp. 4815–17.

Dhami, Mandeep K. and David R. Mandel (2011). 'Crime as Risk Taking', *Psychology, Crime and Law* (2011): 1–15.

Duff, R. A. (2002). 'Punishing the Young' in R. A. Duff and Ido Weijers (eds), *Punishing Juveniles: Principle and Critique.* Oxford: Hart, pp. 115–34.

Easton, Susan and Christine Piper (2005). *Sentencing and Punishment: The Quest for Justice.* Oxford: Oxford University Press.

Emeka, Traquina and Jon Sorensen (2009). 'Female Juvenile Risk: Is There a Need for Gendered Assessment Instruments?', *Youth Violence and Juvenile Justice* 7: 313–30.

Gal, Tali and Shomrom Moyal (2011). 'Juvenile Victims in Restorative Justice', *British Journal of Criminology* 51: 1014–34.

Green, Thomas Hill (1941). *Lectures on the Principles of Political Obligation.* London: Longmans.

Grove, Trevor (2002). *The Magistrate's Tale: A Frontline Report from a New JP.* London: Bloomsbury.

Hegel, G. W. F. (1991) *Elements of the Philosophy of Right*, ed. A. W. Wood, trans. H. B. Nisbet. Cambridge: Cambridge University Press.

Home Office (2002). *Justice for All.* London: Home Office.

Hutton, Will (1998). *The Stakeholding Society: Writings on Politics and Economics.* Cambridge: Polity.

—— (2010). *Them and Us: Changing Britain – Why We Need a Fair Society.* London: Little, Brown.

Independent Commission on Youth Crime and Antisocial Behaviour (2010). *Time for a Fresh Start: The Report of the Independent Commission on Youth Crime and Antisocial Behaviour.* London: The Police Foundation.

Jacobson, Jessica and Penelope Gibbs (2009). *Making Amends: Restorative Youth Justice in Northern Ireland.* London: Prison Reform Trust.

Johnson, Brian D. and Megan C. Kurlychek (2012). 'Transferred Juveniles in the Era of Sentencing Guidelines: Examining Judicial Departures for Juvenile Offenders in Adult Criminal Court', *Criminology* 50: 1–40.

Lippke, Richard L. (2007). *Rethinking Imprisonment.* Oxford: Oxford University Press.

Meade, James (1964). *Efficiency, Equality, and the Ownership of Property.* London: George Allen and Unwin.

Ministry of Justice (2011). *Adult Re-Convictions: Results from the 2009 Cohort (England and Wales).* London: Her Majesty's Stationery Office.

Patacchini, Eleonora and Yves Zenou (2012). 'Juvenile Delinquency and Conformism', *Journal of Law, Economics and Organization* 28: 1–31.

Rand, Michael R. and Jayne E. Robinson (2011). *Criminal Victimization in the United States, 2008 – Statistical Tables.* Washington, DC: Bureau of Justice Statistics.

Bibliography

Rawls, John (2001). *Justice as Fairness*, ed. Erin Kelly. Cambridge, Mass.: Harvard University Press.

Roe, Stephen and Jane Ashe (15 July 2008). 'Young People and Crime: Findings from the 2006 Offending, Crime and Justice Survey', *Home Office Statistical Bulletin*. London: Home Office.

Severson, Margaret F., Kimberly Bruns, Christopher Veeh, and Jaehoon Lee (2011). 'Prisoner Reentry Programming: Who Recidivates and When?', *Journal of Offender Rehabilitation* 50: 327–48.

Shapiro, Tamar (1999). 'What is a Child?', *Ethics* 109: 715–38.

Siegel, Rebecca S., Annette M. La Greca, and Hannah M. Harrison (2009). 'Peer Victimization and Social Anxiety in Adolescents: Prospective and Reciprocal Relationships', *Journal of Youth and Adolescence* 38: 1096–109.

Simester, A. P., G. R. Sullivan, J. R. Spencer, and Graham Virgo (2010). *Simester and Sullivan's Criminal Law: Theory and Doctrine, 4th ed.* Oxford: Hart.

Stone, Alison (2004). 'Essentialism and Anti-Essentialism in Feminist Philosophy', *Journal of Moral Philosophy* 1: 135–53.

Tobias, J. J. (1967). *Crime and Industrial Society in the Nineteenth Century.* London: B. T. Batsford.

US Bureau of Statistics (2005). *Juvenile Victimization and Offending, 1993 – 2003.* Washington, DC: US Department of Justice (NCJ 209468). Available online at http://www.usdoj.gov.bjs/.

Weijers, Ido and Antony Duff (2002). 'Introduction: Themes in Juvenile Justice' in R. A. Duff and Ido Weijers (eds), *Punishing Juveniles: Principle and Critique.* Oxford: Hart, pp. 1–19.

Part III
Juvenile Offending and Sentencing

[4]

The Inextricable Link Between Age and Criminal History in Sentencing

Shawn D. Bushway
University at Albany, NY
Anne Morrison Piehl
Rutgers University, New Brunswick, NJ

In sentencing research, significant negative coefficients on age research have been interpreted as evidence that actors in the criminal justice system discriminate against younger people. This interpretation is incomplete. Criminal sentencing laws generally specify punishment in terms of the number of past events in a defendant's criminal history. Doing so inadvertently makes age a meaningful variable because older people have had more time to accumulate criminal history events. Therefore, two people of different ages with the same criminal history are not in fact equal. This is true for pure retributivists, as the fact that the younger offender has been committing crimes at a higher rate of offending may make the younger offender more culpable, and is also true for those with some utilitarian aims for sentencing. Simulation results illustrate the stakes. To a certain extent, the interests of low-rate older offenders are opposed to those of high-rate younger offenders.

Keywords: *sentencing; age discrimination; criminal history*

Characteristics of the current offense and of the offender's criminal history play large roles in determining sentencing outcomes in most systems in the United States. But the extent to which other factors are considered as aggravating or mitigating circumstances varies substantially across jurisdictions (Tonry, 1993). Among these other factors is age, and its use in sentencing is

---

Authors' Note: The authors contributed equally to this article. The research described herein was supported under Award NIJ 2002-IJ-CX-0023 from the U.S. Department of Justice, National Institute of Justice, Office of Justice Programs. Points of view in the article are those of the authors and do not necessarily represent the views of the Department of Justice. Correspondence concerning this article should be addressed to Anne Piehl, Department of Economics, Rutgers University, 75 Hamilton St., New Brunswick, NJ 08901; e-mail: apiehl@economics.rutgers.edu.

controversial. On one hand, age is clearly considered relevant to sentencing decisions: Juveniles are sanctioned and punished under laws and by institutions that are generally separate from those punishing adults.[1] On the other hand, there is a weak consensus that age should not be considered a relevant and legitimate factor in sentencing for adults. Empirical studies of sentencing outcomes generally find that, on average, younger defendants receive longer sentences, controlling for other attributes of the crimes and the defendants' criminal histories (Bushway & Piehl, 2001; Engen & Gainey, 2000; Ulmer, 2000). This finding is often interpreted as evidence of age discrimination and negative stereotyping (Kurlychek & Johnson, 2004; Steffensmeier, Ulmer, & Kramer, 1998; Ulmer & Johnson, 2004).

Because older people have had more time to accumulate a criminal history than younger people, age affects the meaning of criminal history. Consider two defendants, one of whom is 25 years old and the other of whom is 35 years old, with the same current offense and the same numbers and types of past adult convictions. Assume both of whom began offending at the same age. A sentencing law based on only criminal history and current offense would treat these defendants identically. But are these two defendants equally culpable or equally dangerous? Is such a law really treating like cases alike?

In our example, the younger defendant has committed the same number of offenses in a shorter period of exposure than has the 35-year-old; in other words, the younger defendant offended at a higher rate. Under some theories of retribution, the higher rate of offending would make the younger offender more culpable (von Hirsch, 1985). Theories based on maximizing incapacitation would also favor more prison space for the (younger) higher rate offender because more crimes would be averted for the same spell of incarceration. In addition, the defendant's age provides other information that might help facilitate the goal of incapacitation. From years of research on criminal careers, it is well known that those with higher offense rates are more likely to persist in offending (not desist), further increasing the incapacitation benefits from incarcerating the younger offender rather than the older offender. Finally, older offenders, because of simple maturation, are less likely to persist in offending.[2] These three characteristics of the age–criminal history relationship support sentences that are negatively correlated with age.[3]

In this article, we explore these various meanings of age in criminal sentencing. We turn to the research literature on criminal careers to form hypotheses about how a court might want to consider age in setting sentences. Fortunately, that literature is well developed and has a number of findings that have been confirmed in repeated analyses of multiple data sets. We use these findings to simulate data that allow us to study the relationship between age and criminal history. Although a defendant's age is of varying relevance depending on the philosophy of punishment, we show that courts can improve their performance relative to their goals by punishing younger offenders more severely, conditional on criminal history, when setting criminal punishments.

Based on these results, we suggest that the finding of a significant coefficient on this extralegal variable not necessarily be taken as evidence of unwarranted disparity, bounded rationality, or limitation of court functioning requiring explanation. If incapacitation is a legitimate sentencing goal, then one would expect to see younger defendants sentenced to longer terms conditional on the count of prior offenses. Similarly, if retribution depends on rates of offending rather than the absolute number, one would expect the same result. Neither of these conclusions relies on discrimination, limited information, or resource constraints. Instead, our findings argue that age is a legitimate source of variation in sentencing and should be formally incorporated into sentencing policy.

Literature Review

Age, Criminal History, and Sentencing

According to Savelsberg (1992), the goal of formal rational criminal law is "simply to be just, retributive, and to punish equal and free individuals equally for equal offenses" (p. 1348). Sentencing guidelines based only on severity of the current offense and criminal history (measured as the number and type of past offenses) are seen by most scholars as a way to implement a formally rational system. The inclusion of criminal history to determine "just deserts" is somewhat controversial. Savelsberg, Fletcher (1978), and Singer (1979) are among those who argue that a criminal history is irrelevant for determining retribution and suggest that its inclusion in sentencing guidelines represents explicit consideration of the substantively rational goal of incapacitation.

Others, including von Hirsch (1985), Wasik (1987), and Ulmer and Kramer (1996), argue that criminal history can and should be used to determine culpability above and beyond the seriousness of the current offense. The logic of this argument can be summed up as "the more repetitive a behavior, the more blameworthy." There are several different predicates for such an argument (Wasik, 1987). One is that blameworthiness increases when behavior persists, even after punishment has been imposed. Another is the Bayesian or "evidentiary" reason—later offending increases one's assessment that the defendant was truly guilty of the previous crime or is truly guilty of offending more generally. These two predicates suggest a monotonic relationship between blameworthiness and criminal convictions. A third predicate is that with repeated offending, one becomes less deserving of leniency. Thus, some retributivists would increase sentences for the second, third, or later offense but not incrementally for subsequent offenses.

Criminal history can also play a role in achieving the goal of incapacitation (Albonetti, 1991; Steffensmeier & Demuth, 2000; Ulmer & Kramer, 1996). The basic assumption in this framework is that individuals with longer criminal histories pose a greater danger because of future offending. This logic was formalized in the idea of selective incapacitation (Greenwood, 1982), which offered the hope that sentencing officials could formally predict who would be among the most chronic offenders and "selectively" incapacitate the worst offenders. This idea has generated a great deal of opposition. Some objected because of philosophical concerns regarding the appropriate goals of sentencing and others because of the potential for false positives in prediction (see especially Auerhahn, 1999; Chaiken & Chaiken, 1982; Farrington, 1985; Gottfredson, 1987; Gottfredson & Gottfredson, 1986, 1994).

Others criticize any incapacitation strategy as inherently unfair because it punishes people based on what they might do rather than what they already have done (Tonry, 1999). In contrast to this position, Schauer (2003) argues that there is no moral imperative for individualized sentencing—generalizations such as those routinely contained in sentencing guidelines are common and frequently necessary. Furthermore, sentencing on group characteristics may lead to fewer errors than leaving discretion in the hands of individuals (Silver & Chow-Martin, 2002).

And, in reality, informal incapacitation strategies are almost certainly being utilized in most courts. In standard empirical sentencing research, the existence of significant coefficients on criminal history factors, and extralegal factors such as age, race, sex, education, employment, and community ties, are all viewed as evidence of judges' attempts to assess an offender's future behavior and punish accordingly (Albonetti, 1991; Steffensmeier & Demuth, 2000). Moreover, although it is indisputable that there is a tension between the goals of incapacitation and retribution in terms of their philosophical origins (von Hirsch, 1983, 1985), it is also true that both goals are frequently present in sentencing decision making either informally as one of the focal concerns of the courtroom community (Steffensmeier et al., 1998; Ulmer & Kramer, 1996) or formally as part of the structure of the sentencing law promulgated by legislatures or sentencing commissions (Tonry, 1993).

The question in this article is whether age deserves a place at the table as a legitimate factor for decisions about retribution and incapacitation or if it deserves to be placed into the same category as race—an illegitimate, extralegal variable. On this point, the existing literature is mixed. Steffensmeier, Kramer, and Ulmer (1995) were among the first to seriously study age in sentencing, and they documented a nonlinear relationship between age and sentence length. Very young adult offenders (younger than 21) were treated leniently, but punishment rapidly increased as offenders passed through their 20s and into their 30s, only to begin to decline again as offenders began to age into their 40s and 50s. In that paper, they were agnostic about the age effect, concluding that if "age-based considerations reflect 'real' differences in crime propensity or blameworthiness, they can be viewed as legitimate antecedents of judicial decision making" (p. 600). There is a general finding in the sentencing literature that older offenders are sentenced to more lenient sentences (Spohn, 2000). In fact, there are a few instances in which sentencing laws explicitly instruct on the use of age. Most notably, the Virginia sentencing guidelines include a penalty for youth in the calculation used to determine sentence enhancements.

Since the initial paper, Steffensmeier and colleagues (1995) have changed their position somewhat in response to further evidence based on interactions of age, race, and gender. Steffensmeier et al. (1998) find that the age effect is particularly strong for young Black men, a finding that they interpret as evidence of the use of a stereotype by judges. Spohn and Holleran (2000) go a bit further than Steffensmeier et al. (1998), arguing that this is evidence of a "punishment penalty" for being young, minority, and male, and they make the explicit link to illegitimate statistical discrimination. Ulmer and Johnson (2004) use much the same language, and Kurlychek and Johnson (2004) explicitly interpret their finding that youth who are transferred to adult court are punished more severely than older offenders as age discrimination. In this context, Virginia's explicit use of age in sentencing is particularly troubling. Tonry (1999), in particular, has objected to the formal use of age. Specifically, Tonry states that "giving greater punitive weight to offenders' ages than to their past criminality violates basic and widely shared culpability notions" (p. 1782).

We hope to sharpen the debate about the ways in which age can and should be considered in the determination of punishment. Tonry (1999) has drawn a sharp distinction between age and criminal history, arguing, in effect, that age tells us nothing about culpability that the count of past offenses has not already told us. In fact, Tonry treats criminal history and criminality as if they are identical concepts. In contrast, we argue that age and criminal history together provide information about criminality that is not available in simple counts of past offending. As such, age conveys information that may be useful to policy makers motivated by retribution or by incapacitation. This information can be incorporated into general sentencing rules of various forms or for determining punishment in a particular case. Bearing this context in mind, we now turn to a discussion of what information age may convey, beginning with the role of age in offending patterns.

The Research Literature on the Role of Age in Offending

Age is a key feature of the literature on criminal careers and the life course. The goal of the literature is to describe the pattern of offending as people age, both at the individual and the aggregate levels (the age–crime curve). The formal criminal career paradigm divides a criminal career into four dimensions: onset, frequency of offending, severity of offending, and desistance. The most prominent statistical feature is lambda (λ), the offending rate, used to characterize an individual's offending frequency. Rate is simply a count of events divided by exposure time. In characterizing a criminal career, much of the effort was directed at looking at the relationship between λ and age and the relationship between λ and other dimensions of the criminal career such as onset and desistance. The emphasis on rates is now ubiquitous in criminology; for example, prominent empirical techniques in modern life course criminology, such as semi-parametric trajectory analysis (Nagin, 2005) and hierarchical linear modeling (Raudenbush, 2001), focus on estimating rates of offending over time.

In the life course context, the only truly identical people in terms of perceived criminality are two people of the same age, same age of onset, and same rate of offending. It is therefore true that two people with the same number of past criminal events are not necessarily identical and do not necessarily deserve equal punishment. Consider again the two people in the introduction. These two people began offending at the same age, have identical criminal histories (each having committed the same 5 crimes starting at age 20), and have committed the identical instant offense. Person A is 25 years old, and Person B is 35 years old. In terms of either blameworthiness or dangerousness, are these two people equivalent? The answer from the criminal career and life course literature is a resounding no—these two individuals do not have the same offending rate. Person A has committed 5 offenses in 5 years (rate = 1 crime per year), whereas Person B has committed the same 5 offenses in 15 years (0.33 crimes a year). The difference in rates is caused not by the difference in age per se but rather the difference in exposure time. In this case, exposure time is perfectly correlated with age because the age of onset is the same and because neither has been incarcerated.[4] Based solely on what we know about offending rates, it is rational and reasonable to conclude Person A is more culpable and likely to commit more crimes than Person B in the same period.

The fact that Person A is a higher rate offender than Person B provides additional information that might be useful from an incapacitation perspective. According to a recent comprehensive review of the criminal career literature by Piquero, Farrington, and Blumstein (2003), there is a consensus from the empirical work in this area that high rate offenders are less likely to stop offending (desist) than are lower rate offenders. Thus, higher rate offenders have higher expected future offending because they are more likely to offend and, conditional on offending, have higher expected offending rates.

In the criminal career literature, desistance was traditionally parameterized as the probability that an individual will stop offending in the next period and all subsequent periods (λ becomes 0). This was done by estimating the desistance probability for individuals at a given point in their career. Blumstein, Cohen, and Hsieh (1982) assessed the probability that one would desist given that an individual had 1 offense, 2 offenses, and so on. They found that the probability of desisting decreases with the early offenses, before leveling off and finally increasing dramatically as the career becomes very lengthy. This basic shape can be accounted for by describing the correlation between the probability that someone will drop out and the underlying offending propensity. The reason desistance drops at the beginning is that people with very low rates of offending are more likely to drop out than those who offend at higher rates. In other words, there is a negative correlation between the desistance probability and the offending rate.

Barnett, Blumstein, and Farrington (1987) described this phenomenon in a model in which they estimated both a conviction rate and a desistance rate for a group of young British offenders through age 25. To accurately describe the data, they found they needed to divide all offenders into two groups, the "occasional" and "frequent" offenders. The groupings were assigned probabilistically, and each group was assigned a different frequency rate and desistance rate. The frequent group was estimated to have a conviction rate of 1.14 offenses per year, with a termination probability of 0.1 per conviction—there was a 10% chance the individual would never be convicted again after each conviction. The occasional group was estimated to have a conviction rate of 0.41 offenses per year and a termination probability of 0.33. This research clearly corroborates earlier findings that the probability of desisting and the rate of offending are negatively correlated.

The final piece of the age–criminal history relationship lies with the possibility that age may also play an independent role in predicting recidivism.

Although Barnett et al. (1987) assumed that the rates of offending and the probability of recidivating were constant over the course of a criminal career, neither is likely to be true. Recidivism studies help illuminate this point. Among current offenders, older offenders have lower rates of offending in the preceding period than younger offenders and are less likely to recidivate (Gottfredson & Gottfredson, 1994; Langan & Levin, 2002). There is also strong consensus in the literature that the single best predictor of desistance among all offenders is age, so much that one of the main theoretical explanations of desistance is aging or maturation (Gottfredson & Hirschi, 1990; Laub & Sampson, 2001).

Analysis

Generating the Data

In this section, we create a simulation data set based on the existing literature about offending over the life course. Our goal is to abstract from crime severity to focus only on the role of age in providing information about criminality. Although we could make the same points with actual data, it would be less clear to the reader what feature of the data was generating the result. By using simulated data based on estimates from real data, we can isolate the observed relationship between age and criminality and therefore isolate the role age plays in describing criminality. Although we recognize this approach is somewhat unconventional, we believe this approach is useful for clarifying how age can be used in sentencing to improve outcomes. We proceed by first building our virtual data set and showing that these data replicate key features of sentencing data sets. We then conduct a series of policy experiments to illustrate a number of important points regarding the role of age in sentencing outcomes. In particular, we show that failure to use age explicitly in the sentencing process does not mean that age is uncorrelated with sentence length—in fact, it means that older offenders with the same rate of offending (the same criminality) as younger offenders are punished more harshly.

In empirical applications, researchers use probabilistic models to estimate (unobserved) rates of offending (Blumstein, Cohen, Roth, & Visher, 1986; Osgood & Rowe, 1994). The observed counts of offenses are the combination of this parameter with random chance embodied in a probability distribution. Including randomness in the model makes it more realistic: Two people with the exact same criminality (or offending rate) may commit a different number of crimes in a given observation period. Or to put it another way, two people with the same number of offenses in a given period may have different underlying rates of offending. The longer these individuals are observed, the more the randomness averages out and the easier it is to distinguish who has the higher criminality. Although it may not be terribly unusual for a low-rate offender to have one offense at a young age, it would be unusual for him or her to have one offense per year by the time he or she is middle aged. This follows from the rules of basic probability.

We simulate offending data based on only one type of crime. This allows us to abstract from crime seriousness when we analyze the accumulation of criminal history. This is an important simplification.[5] We also ignore age of onset and the complications of a juvenile court system that punishes younger offenders according to different rules.

Given the recent growth of trajectory analysis to estimate rates of offending over time (Nagin, 2005), there are a number of papers from which we can choose empirical estimates. All of these models use Poisson models to estimate rates of offending from observed counts. In other contexts, researchers use the negative binomial to model offending (Osgood, 2000). Negative binomial models are essentially mixture models in which the population is allowed to have a continuous distribution of Poisson offending rates over time. Semi-parametric trajectory models with a Poisson distribution are also mixture models, where different groups are allowed to have different Poisson offending rates over time.

For the sake of simplicity, we will use an ad hoc, group-based approach here with Poisson distributions and assign different rates of offending to people in different groups. Specifically, we rely on the Barnett et al. (1987) estimates of stable offending rates with separate desistance probabilities for two groups. This reflects a clear choice on our part because estimates using trajectory methods from the same Cambridge data are available in Nagin and Land (1993). The advantage with the Barnett et al. estimates is that there are separate parameters for the rate of offending and probability of desistance. These two parameters map onto the two relationships between age and observed criminality that we wish to analyze: (a) that age is a control for exposure time and (b) that desistance is correlated with the rate of offending, which means that there will be a different relationship between age and desistance for people with different rates of offending. The combination of these two parameters (rate of offending and probability of desistance) creates downward trajectories, as found in the Nagin and Land paper. Having two parameters (as opposed to one time-varying parameter in the Nagin and Land formulation) allows us, through robustness tests, to highlight the importance of each of these two distinct mechanisms.

We use the parameters from the Barnett et al. (1987) study to generate 4,000 simulated sample members of each single year of age from age 16 through 40, for a total of 100,000 offenders (4,000 × 25 age cohorts). Among these 100,000 offenders, 43% are high-rate offenders (called *frequent*) and 57% are low-rate offenders (called *occasional*), the relative proportions estimated in the study. The frequent group is less likely to desist and more likely to offend, conditional on not desisting.

For each of our simulated offenders, we randomly draw a number of convictions from a Poisson distribution with the appropriate mean (1.14 for frequent, 0.41 for occasional), allowing offenders to have multiple convictions in a particular year. Then, we draw a binomial desistance variable for each person to determine whether or not he or she continues to offend in subsequent periods (desistance is permanent). The only thing that differentiates successive cohorts is how many years he or she has "lived" (i.e., how many times conviction and desistance parameters were randomly drawn). For example, the 40-year-old cohort was started at age 16, and we allowed the model to run until age 40. We then reported the data for this cohort at age 40.

Table 1 introduces the results of the simulation by reporting the characteristics of those who offended in the current period. The bottom right-hand corner shows that the 100,000 offenders were responsible for 31,926 convictions in the current period. The young cohorts were responsible for more offending than were the older cohorts, as those at older ages have had time to desist (and we did not model any late onset into criminal activity). For all cohorts, the frequent group is responsible for more offending than is the low-rate group despite the fact that there are more members in the occasional group. Among 40-year-olds, there are few members of the low-rate group who are still offending: The 49 people represent just 2% of the members of the cohort.

Table 2 shows descriptive statistics for the 20,844 individuals with convictions in the current period. These offenders had an average of 1.5 convictions this year, just more than 7 convictions in previous years and an average age of nearly 24. Sixty-nine percent of them were frequent offenders. The right-hand column treats each offense as a separate case, as a court generally would. Of course there are more cases than offenders ($N = 31{,}926$). Among cases, the average age and the number of past convictions are both somewhat higher, and a higher proportion (75%) is attributable to frequent offenders.

Table 3 illustrates how criminal history accumulates with age for the two types of offenders. Among 16-year-olds, no one has a criminal history, as this is the age of onset. Over time, though, those in the frequent group accumulate criminal history quite quickly. Those in the occasional group also generally have longer criminal histories at older ages, as this population includes only

Table 1
Current Offending, by Cohort

Age	Frequent	Occasional	Total
16	2,017	883	2,900
17	1,890	835	2,725
18	1,679	744	2,423
19	1,552	705	2,257
20	1,477	621	2,098
21	1,368	513	1,881
22	1,330	414	1,744
23	1,234	387	1,621
24	1,127	373	1,500
25	1,085	328	1,413
26	931	307	1,238
27	837	243	1,080
28	821	229	1,050
29	780	209	989
30	777	179	956
31	676	129	805
32	697	147	844
33	546	122	668
34	593	117	710
35	488	78	566
36	530	74	604
37	439	87	526
38	421	57	478
39	354	70	424
40	377	49	426
Total	24,026	7,900	31,926

Note: Each age cohort contains 4,000 members, 43% of whom are high-rate offenders and 57% of whom are low-rate offenders (exact number varies by cohort because of random noise). Frequent offenders have an average of 1.14 convictions per year, with a 0.1 probability of permanent desistance. For occasional offenders, the average is 0.41 convictions and 0.33 chance of permanent desistance. Parameters are drawn from Barnett, Blumstein, and Farrington (1987).

those who offended in the current period and, by definition, have therefore not desisted. It is easy to compare offending rates across these columns, as we have not yet modeled any incapacitation, so exposure times are constant across the groups. Moving down the columns, frequents accumulate just more than one offense per year, and occasionals accumulate history at about one third that rate.

From this table, several correlations of interest are apparent. Criminal history is strongly positively correlated with age ($r = .84$, $p < .0001$). This

Table 2
Descriptive Statistics: Current Offenders and Current Offenses

	Offenders		Offenses	
	M	*SE*	*M*	*SE*
Number of offenses this period	1.532	(0.006)	1	
Criminal history (past convictions)	7.042	(0.052)	7.530	(0.043)
Age	23.855	(0.045)	24.014	(0.037)
Percentage frequent	0.688	(0.003)	0.753	(0.002)
N	20,844		31,926	

Table 3
Average Criminal History for Current Offenders (by Cohort and Offending Group)

Age	Frequent	Occasional	Overall
16	0.00	0.00	0.00
17	1.07	0.27	0.83
18	2.20	0.59	1.70
19	3.25	0.98	2.54
20	4.58	1.24	3.59
21	5.51	1.51	4.42
22	6.46	1.93	5.38
23	7.70	2.35	6.42
24	8.56	2.44	7.04
25	9.99	2.93	8.35
26	11.27	3.03	9.22
27	12.31	3.33	10.29
28	13.15	3.72	11.09
29	14.29	4.22	12.16
30	15.26	4.26	13.20
31	16.62	4.42	14.67
32	17.71	4.78	15.45
33	18.26	5.25	15.88
34	19.64	5.50	17.31
35	20.60	6.37	18.64
36	21.66	6.22	19.77
37	23.40	6.83	20.66
38	24.56	6.47	22.40
39	25.28	6.79	22.23
40	26.11	7.37	23.96
Total	9.34	2.03	7.53

Note: $N = 31{,}926$ overall offenses in the current period, 24,026 by frequent offenders, and 7,900 by occasional offenders.

correlation is higher among frequents ($r = .92$) than among occasionals ($r = .77$). Furthermore, criminal history is positively correlated with the offending rate ($r = .54$, $p < .0001$), as is age ($r = .23$, $p < .0001$). The other important correlation is that between age and frequent status among current offenders. This correlation is smaller in magnitude but strongly statistically significant ($r = .13$, $p < .0001$). Although these data are not "real," they share key characteristics observed in virtually all current analysis of offending over the life course. This is not surprising given that the simulation is based on parameters estimated from the Cambridge data.

Sentencing in the Shadow of Lambda

We now imagine a situation in which a judge is asked to sentence the people who have entered the system in this period. We take as given that the task of the judge (for both retribution and incapacitation reasons) is to identify, and punish more harshly, the more criminal offenders. We also take as given, as argued previously, that the rate of offending is the proper measure of criminality. In our stylized data, there are only two rates of offending, so the judge's problem is to identify members of the two groups using the information that is generally available at sentencing.

Table 4 organizes the data to approximate the situation faced by judges in the face of a sentencing protocol based on criminal history categories. Most sentencing guidelines account for prior offending by including the number of prior criminal offenses (Tonry, 1993). Counts of prior offending are generally the mechanism to trigger criminal history enhancements (e.g., three-strikes laws) in other criminal sentencing systems.[6] In our analysis, we divide criminal history into four categories based on the number of convictions prior to the current period. The categories are modeled on the categories in the Maryland sentencing guidelines and are defined in the note to Table 4. The final column of the table shows the conditional probability of being a high-rate offender given a particular criminal history category. Obviously, among those in categories for longer criminal histories, the probability of being a high-rate offender is very high.

But this table does not take into consideration the age of the offenders, which, as we saw in Table 3, is highly correlated with the length of criminal history. Figure 1 plots the percentage frequent in each criminal history category by single year of age. For the major criminal history category, it is always highly likely that an offender is a high-rate one. But for the other groups, the probability an offender is high rate falls sharply with age. The rate of decline is fairly linear for the no history and minor history categories

Table 4
Criminal History Categories and Offending Groups: Population of Current Offenders

Adult Record	Frequent	Occasional	Frequent (%)
No history	2,932	2,712	52.0
Minor	5,615	4,051	58.1
Moderate	5,479	1,047	84.0
Major	10,000	90	99.1
Total	24,026	7,900	75.3

Note: The no history group contains current offenders with no criminal history, minor includes those with 1-4 past offenses, moderate is those with 5-9 past convictions, and major contains those with more than 9 convictions prior to the current period.

but appears nonlinear for the moderate category. In fact, at young ages, most of those in the moderate history group are frequent offenders. But as people age, those in this category are very unlikely to be frequents. Accurate inference about the criminality of the frequent offender is obviously easier when age information is available.

These relationships are also readily seen in a regression framework. Column 1 of Table 5 reports the results of probit models of the probability that someone is a frequent offender on age and measures of criminal history. The table reports coefficients as changes in probability, calculated at sample means.

When whether an offender is frequent or occasional is regressed only on age, the coefficient is positive, meaning that older offenders are more likely to be high-rate offenders. Column 2 reports that without age in the model, each additional past conviction raises the probability that a defendant is frequent by three percentage points. When both age and criminal history are included in the model, as in column 3, age takes on a negative sign and the magnitude of the effect of the number of past convictions drops by more than one third. These shifts are because of the strong correlation between these two variables. There is also a huge jump in the log likelihood from column 2 to column 3, suggesting that it is much easier to predict frequency of offending if age is included in addition to criminal history.

Columns 4 and 5 replace the number of past convictions with the conviction rate, and column 6 adds an interaction between age and the conviction rate. The rate of offending is highly positively correlated with being a frequent offender. Column 6 shows that for the same conviction rate, a

Figure 1
Probability of Current Offender Being Frequent (by Criminal History)

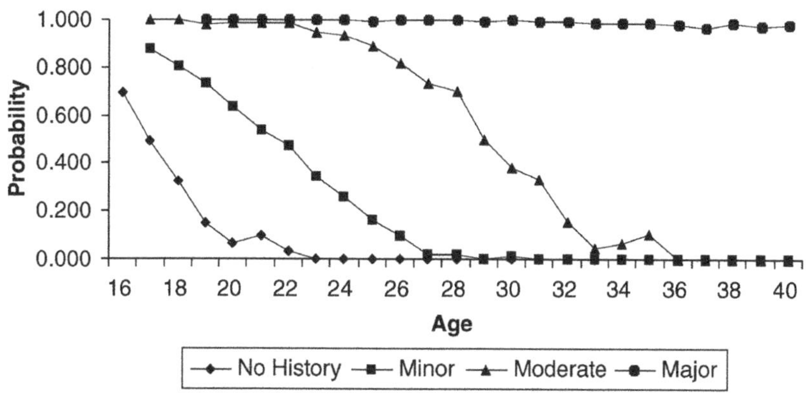

person 1 year older has a two percentage point increase in the probability of being a frequent offender. The bottom panel of Table 5, in which we add higher order polynomials for rates of offending, reveals that there are non-linearities in the relationships of each of these variables with probability of the current defendant being frequent, as was visible in Figure 1.

Note that the fit for the regression with rates but not age in column 4 is substantially worse than the fit in column 3, where age and criminal history are included separately. This is clear evidence that age plays two roles. First, it controls for exposure time. This is the only function included in the specification with criminal history as a rate, column 4. Second, it predicts desistance.[7] In column 5, when we add age, the fit improves relative to column 4. Here, age predicts desistance, but not fully, because desistance varies with the rate of offending. Notice what happens in column 6 when we interact rate of offending with age—the fit returns to the same level as we had previously accomplished with age and criminal history counts.[8]

It is interesting that we can accomplish the same thing with counts and age as with the more complicated model with age and rates. This exercise illustrates the meaning that should be ascribed to the coefficients in the various models. In these analyses, recall that the offending rates and desistance probabilities are time stable. Although the parameters are stable, our inference is not. We learn about people and make better decisions about their criminality as we observe them over longer periods.

Table 5
Probability of Being Frequent Offender: Current Offenders

	1	2	3	4	5	6
A. Model with linear terms						
Age	0.009**		–0.012**		–0.007**	–0.012**
	(0.0004)		(0.0008)		(0.0003)	(0.0008)
Past convictions		0.034**	0.020**			
		(0.0004)	(0.001)			
Conviction rate				0.412**	0.440**	–0.322**
				(0.004)	(0.005)	(0.021)
Age × Conviction Rate						0.020**
						(0.001)
–Log likelihood	17,583.405	13,618.852	8,648.175	12,201.431	12,016.852	8,647.003
B. Model with nonlinear terms						
Age	–0.022		–0.016		–0.608**	–0.084**
	(0.019)		(0.009)		(0.021)	(0.018)
Age^2	0.116		0.038		2.143*	0.166**
	(0.075)		(0.021)		(0.077)	(0.061)
Age^3	–0.138		–0.043		–2.436**	–0.185*
	(0.093)		(0.023)		(0.094)	(0.078)
Past convictions		0.012**	0.012			
		(0.002)	(0.007)			
Past $convictions^2$		0.212**	–0.038**			
		(0.018)	(0.019)			
Past $convictions^3$		–0.508**	0.148**			
		(0.063)	(0.055)			

(continued)

Table 5
(continued)

	1	2	3	4	5	6
Conviction rate		0.138**	0.732**	−1.114**		
				(0.014)	(0.025)	(0.227)
Conviction rate^2				0.244**	−0.139**	0.051
				(0.109)	(0.017)	(0.062)
Conviction rate^3				−0.046**	0.0012	0.010
				(0.002)	(0.002)	(0.015)
Age × Conviction Rate						0.071**
						(0.014)
Age × Conviction Rate^2						−0.0003
						(0.0002)
Age × Conviction Rate^3						−0.00001
						(0.0001)
–Log likelihood	17,581.893	13,560.074	8,620.366	11,970.436	10,999.769	8,602.465

Note: $N = 31{,}926$. Cells report changes in probability evaluated at sample means. Standard errors in parentheses.
*Significant at 5%. **Significant at 1%.

Distributional Implications of Sentencing Policy

Whether a judge is trying to more severely punish people who are more criminal (i.e., have a greater propensity to commit criminal acts) or more heavily punish those who are more likely to offend in the future, consideration of age will reduce the weight placed on the number of past convictions. Conditional on criminal history, older offenders will be punished more leniently, and people who are both older and have offended at a high rate will be particularly subject to punishment. A punishment system based on the models underlying column 3 or column 6 will reproduce the general findings from empirical studies of sentencing outcomes: Those who are younger generally receive longer sentences, and this effect is sometimes found to be nonlinear; criminal history matters a great deal to punishment; and sometimes interactions among characteristics are found to be important. Thus, our findings provide an understanding of the relationship of age to punishment that reflects either retributive or incapacitation motivations on behalf of sentencing agents. Some have interpreted statistically significant coefficients on age as evidence of discrimination against young people. Others have interpreted this as evidence that judges are boundedly, not formally, rational. Our illustration shows that rational decision makers trying to discern underlying criminality produce similar empirical relationships.

The implications of these results are perhaps seen most clearly if we undertake policy experiments to analyze the resulting distributions of punishment. Table 6 reports the results of using the estimates in Table 5 to sentence to terms of prison those with the highest predicted probabilities of being frequent offenders. Those with low predicted probabilities are assumed to have a sentence that does not leave them incapacitated or deterred (think of "continued without a finding," a dismissal, or a term of probation with little enforcement of conditions). These experiments are similar in spirit to those performed in the selective incapacitation literature. They should be taken as illustrative of the major policy implications, as it is likely that a continuous distribution of offending rates (rather than two groups) better represents the true population.

The columns in Table 6 line up with those in Table 5. Column 1 reports the outcomes of sentencing to prison for a year the top half of the offenders (in terms of the likelihood they are frequent) based on a model using only age. Under this policy, 80% of the incarcerated group will be frequent, the average age will be 29, there will be an average of nearly 13 prior convictions, and incapacitation benefits average 0.92 crimes during the period of incarceration. These characteristics can be compared to the descriptive

Table 6
Properties of Those Sentenced to Prison if Half With Greatest Probability of Being Frequent Offender Are Sentenced to 1 Year Incarceration

	Policy					
	1	2	3	4	5	6
Frequent	0.799	0.939	0.990	0.975	0.973	0.990
	(0.003)	(0.001)	(0.001)	(0.001)	(0.001)	(0.001)
Age	29.38	28.41	27.19	25.71	25.04	27.06
	(0.039)	(0.045)	(0.049)	(0.053)	(0.049)	(0.050)
Past convictions	12.74	13.46	13.10	11.98	11.30	13.03
	(0.060)	(0.054)	(0.057)	(0.063)	(0.063)	(0.057)
Average crimes incapacitated	0.917	1.022	1.052	1.043	1.025	1.058
	(0.009)	(0.009)	(0.009)	(0.009)	(0.009)	(0.009)
Frequents not incarcerated	0.706	0.566	0.515	0.530	0.532	0.515
	(0.004)	(0.004)	(0.004)	(0.004)	(0.004)	(0.004)
N incarcerated in 2 but not in *X*	2,720	0	1,740	3,713	4,024	1,970

Note: *N* = 31,926. For each model in Panel A of Table 5, the top half of all predicted values are assigned 1 year of incarceration. The statistics above are calculated over those assigned to prison for each model corresponding to the same column in Table 5.

statistics in Table 2 to see which part of the population is getting selected for punishment by the model of sentencing used.

Other models provide some substantial improvement over this age-only model, and all of the predictions perform pretty well, as suggested by Gottfredson and Gottfredson (1994). In Table 6, the models in column 3 (age and number of past convictions) and column 6 (age, rate, and the interaction) identify the largest proportion frequent. The second-to-final row (frequents not incarcerated) tells the proportion frequent who were not punished under the given sentencing scheme. This shows the extent to which the policy results in false negatives.

All of the models that have age and past offending represented in some way do fairly well in terms of the proportion frequent among incarcerated offenders. However, these results reveal that different models punish different types of offenders. For example, the models based on rate are more likely to select younger offenders—there are clearly distributional consequences to the choice of functional form. The final row in the table reveals how many people are differentially affected by changing sentencing rules. The same total bed space is used in all models. But, for example, relative to the policy in column 2 in which the prediction is based only on the count of past convictions, column 3 punishes 1,740 different people (which also means that 1,740 people punished under column 2 are not punished under column 3). Those punished under column 3 and not column 2 are somewhat younger, with somewhat fewer convictions and somewhat higher incapacitation benefits. The last row of Table 6 demonstrates that there are huge distributional consequences in moving from the count to the rate, in particular.[9]

Figure 2 shows how the prediction works by age for the model with only the count of prior convictions (column 2) and for the model that adds the consideration of age (column 3). The percentage frequent overall increases with age, as shown by the squares. The column 2 prediction does pretty well at young ages, but older people do not do so well under this policy, as shown by the lower proportion of frequents incarcerated at older ages. That is, punishing the accumulated number of prior convictions has a differential impact on offenders of different ages, hurting older offenders with low rates of criminality relative to more criminal younger offenders. Contrast this to the predictions based on column 3 (the *X*s), where we find quite constant performance of the model over the life course.

There are, of course, additional policies that could be modeled. One interesting approach is to drop consideration of criminal events if they have occurred in the distant past. Use of a "decay factor" to weigh more recent events more heavily than more distant events will go part of the way to resolving the issues modeled above. The policies could also be made more realistic by considering multiple types of offending, with differences in terms of blameworthiness and predicted future offending. The basic insights of this section will carry through to those settings.

Robustness

To investigate the sensitivity of these conclusions to reasonable alternative parameter values, we conducted two additional simulations. For the first, we decreased the spread between the two groups, and for the second, we increased the spread. In both cases, we maintained the two-group model and kept the proportion frequent the same as above (57%). In addition, we matched the level of first-period offending and desistance to the main model.

Specifically, for the first robustness check, we increased the rate of offending and decreased the desistance rate for the occasional group by 10% each and adjusted the rates for the frequent group to offset these while keeping constant the overall offending for the population.[10] We then created 100,000 population members as before, using randomness and the Poisson

Figure 2
Percentage Frequent in Two Policy Experiments

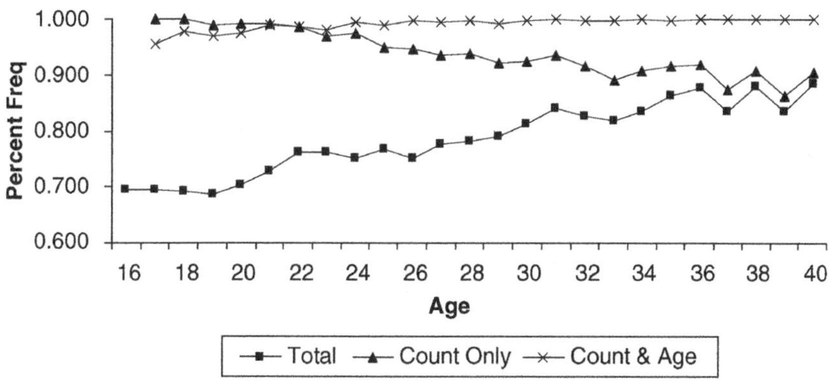

Note: The count only series comes from the policy experiment in Table 6, column 2, a model that uses the count of past convictions alone. The column 3 series comes from the experiment in column 3 that adds age to past convictions when forming the predictions.

model to create the sequences of offending and desistance. For the second robustness check, we increased the spread in a symmetric fashion: decreased the offending and increased the desistance for the occasional group with offsetting adjustment for the frequents. Note that the chosen parameters continue to exhibit negative correlation in both robustness simulations.

With less spread between the two groups, as in the first robustness check, the challenge of distinguishing between offender types is greater. As offenders age, more of the occasional offenders continue to offend whereas fewer of the frequent group do, relative to the base model. Nonetheless, the major features of the analysis carry through. This is most easily seen in Figure 3, which plots the percentage frequent in each criminal history category by single year of age. As was the case for the base model plotted in Figure 1, in this population with less spread between the two groups, it is easier to distinguish offender types as offenders age. In the graph, there are hints that the major criminal history category can sometimes contain occasional offenders. In addition, the slope of the lines for minor and moderate criminal history are less steep than in the base case.

Figure 4 shows the comparable figure for the robustness check with greater difference between the two groups. Here, the percentage frequent in the major history group is always greater than 0.98. The slopes for the intermediate

Figure 3
Robustness: Less Spread Between Groups: Probability of Current Offender Being Frequent (by Criminal History)

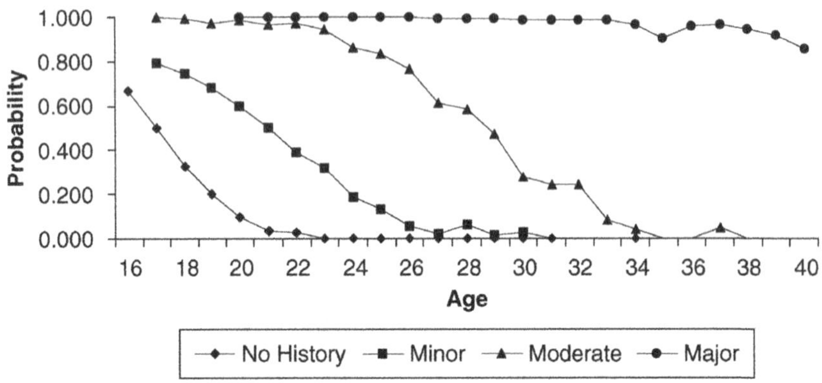

Figure 4
Robustness: More Spread Between Groups: Probability of Current Offender Being Frequent (by Criminal History)

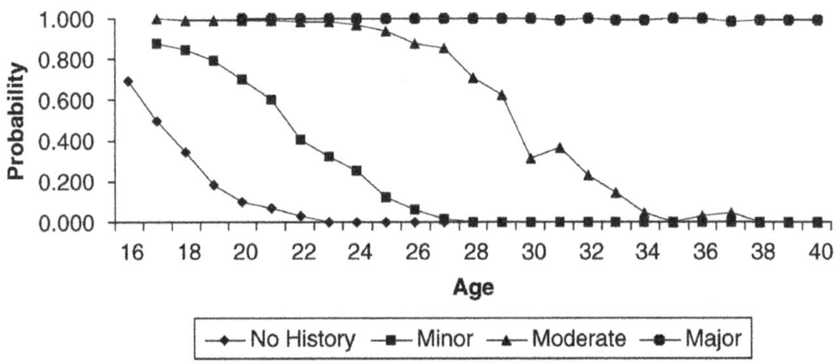

criminal history categories are somewhat steeper than in the base case (and by extension the first robustness sample). But again, the major findings are observed.

These robustness checks provide evidence that the main results are not specific to the particular draw of the data or the specific parameter values.

Furthermore, the simulations confirm that having less difference between groups makes it harder to distinguish between them. But for reasonable parameter values, the practical impact is small.

Conclusion

The sentencing literature suggests that age is not appropriate for decisions about sentencing except in the case of juveniles (Steffensmeier & Demuth, 2000; Steinberg & Cauffman, 1996; Steinberg & Scott, 2003). But offending patterns are strongly correlated with age, which means that age and criminal history have a number of almost inextricable links. This leads to some confusion about how to punish younger offenders. Many policy makers want to offer leniency to first-time (and second-time) offenders in the hopes that they have already learned their lesson and in the fear that severe punishment might harden their criminality. Of course, at young ages, those who are highly criminal cannot be reliably discerned from those who were simply unlucky or acted inconsistently with their general character. It is possible to draw such distinctions more reliably at older ages because with more accumulated experience these types of offenders are unlikely to have similar official offending profiles.

To make better decisions about the appropriate use of age and criminal history, it would be useful to understand the individual contributions of both to culpability and to predictions about future criminal behavior. This cannot be easily done in a real setting because of the complex set of interrelationships under study. Fortunately, simulated data can take us part of the way to understanding the various meanings of age in criminal sentencing.

In this article, simulations have revealed how criminal history evolves in the set of offenders caught in any given period. Because the simulation abstracts from many features of the real world, it is easy to see here that offender type becomes more clearly revealed over time. Punishment decisions need to be made in real time, however, and the simulation shows that uncertainty about offender type is great at young ages and falls over time. Predictions of type are more reliable when age and the number of past events are used; "more reliable" does not imply perfection, though. In the past, research in the criminal career literature was criticized because of the high false positive rate (Gottfredson & Gottfredson, 1994). The argument here is not that all predictions will be correct—only that accuracy will improve over standard practice when age is included.

Is it reasonable to believe that the simulation captures important features of real sentencing data? Earlier in this article, we reported a very high correlation between age and criminal history. In real data on convicted offenders, this bivariate correlation is much lower. Comparing our simulated data to a sample of sentenced offenders in Maryland, we found a correlation of about .8 in the simulation and .1 to .2 in the real data. But this discrepancy is largely accounted for by the fact that the simulation abstracts from crime severity. When the Maryland data are restricted to a given level of crime severity, the correlation doubles or even triples, depending on what level of crime severity we choose; the correlation is much higher for more serious offenders (whether measured by a sentence to prison or by the seriousness of the current offense). Much of the remainder of the discrepancy can be accounted for by realistic assumptions about measurement error in the real data (specifically by assuming some offending is not captured on administrative records and by the use of conviction charges, which are determined by plea bargaining). In both simulated and real data, the correlation between age and criminal history is weaker among older offenders. These facts provide our simulation with face validity. In addition, they suggest that the link between age and criminal history will be obscured in heterogeneous samples. Work in this area using real data that seek to focus on the value of using characteristics of age in conjunction with criminal history will need to isolate groups of offenders who have committed fairly similar crimes.

Perhaps the greatest contribution of our simulations involves the investigation of various policy alternatives. We have shown that not considering age in setting criminal sentences will punish severely older offenders with low-level criminality (especially relative to young, high-rate offenders with a similar number of past offenses). Thus, whether age is encouraged as a basis for decision making or ruled to be an illegitimate factor has direct, tangible consequences for the distribution of punishment, the fairness of the criminal justice system, and crime control.

How should age be used in the determination of punishment? One who believes (a) that culpability depends only on the number of past criminal events (and not on the frequency of offending) and (b) that incapacitation is not a goal of punishment policy would argue strongly that age be excluded from consideration. At the other extreme, a person who is (a) a strong believer in the role of incapacitation and (b) unconcerned about the uncertainty in the prediction at younger ages will argue for a policy that explicitly considers the age of the offender, with no accommodation for younger offenders. It is possible to design any number of policies that fall between the two extreme policies described above, trading off some uncertainty for some gains in targeting.

Because the mix of prisoners, crime rates, and criminal justice resources will determine the ability of age to improve sentencing policy, we do not feel it is wise or feasible to provide a detailed recommendation for exactly how age should be used in sentencing. But we do strongly believe that members of guideline commissions and other policy makers who are concerned about assigning punishment in a way that reflects criminality should formally consider age when assigning punishment. In our opinion, the actions of the Virginia Criminal Sentencing Commission in using age in the risk assessment tool are justified given their desire to release the least criminal members of the incarceration population.

The large existing literature on recidivism repeatedly has shown that age and criminal history are the two best predictors of recidivism. Our simulation clearly shows that age, in combination with criminal history, provides information about criminality, even in an artificial world where rates of offending do not decrease with age. Age in sentencing is not simply age but is also a control for exposure time that is useful for making inferences about rates of offending and desistance probabilities that are not available from simple counts of offending. Recognizing this fact should lead to more accurate and therefore fairer sentencing policy. Failure to recognize this fact will continue a system that disproportionately punishes older offenders despite their lesser criminality and fails to make use of all available information when seeking to assign punishment that is proportionate to the criminality of the individual.

Notes

1. The cutoff varies across states and runs from 16 to 18 (Strom, 2000). Whether these cutoffs are at the appropriate point for presuming culpability is a debated matter (Steinberg & Cauffman, 1996, 2001; Steinberg & Scott, 2003).

2. At the youngest ages, it is possible that the probability of continuing to offend increases for several years. We consider the details of these predictions in the empirical section of the article.

3. Throughout the article, we set aside the issue of juvenile offenders who may not be considered fully culpable for their crimes and restrict our attention to adults.

4. Relaxing either of these assumptions would mean that age is no longer perfectly correlated with exposure time. However, age will continue to be strongly and positively correlated with exposure time. Below, we document that age and exposure time are highly correlated in real data.

5. Note that this abstraction means that the simulated data will not look just like actual data. Specifically, the simple correlation between age and criminal history in actual conviction data will be modest, given that people are selected into the criminal justice system by both offending severity and criminal history.

6. There are exceptions where prior offending information is used more subtly, including the use of a decay factor where prior offenses that are more than a certain number of years old (10 in the case of the federal guidelines) are discarded.

7. In simulations not reported here, we generated two groups with different offending rates but no desistance probability. In that case, a regression of the form in column 4 had almost

identical fit to the regression in column 3 because in that setting age served only as a control for exposure.

8. In simulations not reported here, we allowed the desistance probabilities to be the same for the two groups. In this case, the regressions reported in columns 5 and 6 were identical.

9. Models with nonlinear terms give very similar predictions to the linear models discussed here. The additional results are available from the authors on request.

10. Details of the simulations and additional results are available from the authors.

References

Albonetti, C. A. (1991). An integration of theories to explain judicial discretion. *Social Problems*, *38*, 247-266.

Auerhahn, K. (1999). Selective incapacitation and the problem of prediction. *Criminology*, *37*, 703-734.

Barnett, A., Blumstein, A., & Farrington, D. (1987). Probabilistic models of youthful criminal careers. *Criminology*, *25*, 83-107.

Blumstein, A., Cohen, J., & Hsieh, P. (1982). *The duration of adult criminal careers*. Washington, DC: National Institute of Justice.

Blumstein, A., Cohen, J., Roth, J., & Visher, C. A. (Eds.). (1986). *Criminal careers and career criminals*. Washington, DC: National Academy Press.

Bushway, S. D., & Piehl, A. M. (2001). Judging judicial discretion: Legal factors and racial discrimination in sentencing. *Law & Society Review*, *35*, 733-764.

Chaiken, J. M., & Chaiken, M. R. (1982). *Varieties of criminal behavior*. Santa Monica, CA: RAND.

Engen, R. L., & Gainey, R. R. (2000). Modeling the effects of legally relevant and extralegal factors under sentencing guidelines: The rules have changed. *Criminology*, *38*, 1207-1229.

Farrington, D. P. (1985). Predicting self-reported and official delinquency. In D. P. Farrington & R. Tarling (Eds.), *Prediction in criminology* (pp. 150-173). Albany: State University of New York Press.

Fletcher, G. P. (1978). *Rethinking criminal law*. Boston: Little, Brown.

Gottfredson, S. D. (1987). Prediction: An overview of selected methodological issues. In D. M. Gottfredson & M. Tonry (Eds.), *Crime and justice: An annual review of research* (Vol. 9, pp. 21-52). Chicago: University of Chicago Press.

Gottfredson, S. D., & Gottfredson, D. M. (1986). Accuracy of prediction models. In A. Blumstein, J. Cohen, J. Roth, & C. Visher (Eds.), *Criminal careers and career criminals* (pp. 212-290). Washington, DC: National Academy of Sciences.

Gottfredson, S. D., & Gottfredson, D. M. (1994). Behavioral prediction and the problem of incapacitation. *Criminology*, *32*, 441-474.

Gottfredson, M. R., & Hirschi, T. (1990). *A general theory of crime*. Stanford, CA: Stanford University Press.

Greenwood, P. W. (1982). *Selective incapacitation*. Santa Monica, CA: RAND.

Kurlychek, M., & Johnson, B. (2004). The juvenile penalty: A comparison of juvenile and young adult sentencing outcomes in a criminal court. *Criminology*, *42*, 485-517.

Langan, P. A., & Levin, D. J. (2002). *Recidivism of prisoners released in 1994*. Washington, DC: Bureau of Justice Statistics.

Laub, J. H., & Sampson, R. J. (2001). Understanding desistance from crime. In M. Tonry (Ed.), *Crime and justice: A review of research* (Vol. 28, pp. 1-69). Chicago: University of Chicago Press.

Nagin, D. S. (2005). *Group-based modeling of development over the life course*. Cambridge, MA: Harvard University Press.

Nagin, D. S., & Land, K. C. (1993). Age, criminal careers, and population heterogeneity—Specification and estimation of a nonparametric, mixed poisson model. *Criminology, 31*, 327-362.

Osgood, D. W. (2000). Poisson-based regression analysis of aggregate crime rates. *Journal of Quantitative Criminology, 16*(1), 21-43.

Osgood, D. W., & Rowe, D. C. (1994). Bridging criminal careers, theory, and policy through latent variable models of individual offending. *Criminology, 32*, 517-554.

Piquero, A. R., Farrington, D. P., & Blumstein, A. (2003). The criminal career paradigm: Background and recent developments. In M. Tonry (Ed.), *Crime and justice: A review of research* (Vol. 30, pp. 137-283). Chicago: University of Chicago Press.

Raudenbush, S. (2001). Comparing personal trajectories and drawing causal inferences from longitudinal data. *Annual Review of Psychology, 52*, 501-525.

Savelsberg, J. J. (1992). Law that does not fit society—Sentencing guidelines as a neoclassical reaction to the dilemmas of substantivized law. *American Journal of Sociology, 97*, 1346-1381.

Schauer, F. (2003). *Profiles, probabilities, and stereotypes*. Cambridge, MA: Belknap.

Silver, E., & Chow-Martin, L. (2002). A multiple models approach to assessing recidivism risk: Implications for judicial decision making. *Criminal Justice and Behavior, 29*, 538-568.

Singer, R. (1979). *Just deserts: Sentencing based on equality and desert*. Cambridge, MA: Ballinger.

Spohn, C. (2000). Thirty years of sentencing reform: The quest for a racially neutral sentencing process. In *Policies, processes, and decisions of the criminal justice system* (pp. 427-501). Washington, DC: U.S. Department of Justice.

Spohn, C., & Holleran, D. (2000). The imprisonment penalty paid by young, unemployed Black and Hispanic male offenders. *Criminology, 38*, 281-306.

Steffensmeier, D., & Demuth, S. (2000). Ethnicity and sentencing outcomes in US federal courts: Who is punished more harshly? *American Sociological Review, 65*, 705-729.

Steffensmeier, D., Kramer, J., & Ulmer, J. (1995). Age differences in sentencing. *Justice Quarterly, 12*, 583-602.

Steffensmeier, D., Ulmer, J., & Kramer, J. (1998). The interaction of race, gender, and age in criminal sentencing: The punishment cost of being young, Black, and male. *Criminology, 36*, 763-797.

Steinberg, L., & Cauffman, E. (1996). Maturity of judgment in adolescence: Pyschosocial factors in adolescent decision making. *Law and Human Behavior, 20*, 249-272.

Steinberg, L., & Cauffman, E. (2001). Adolescents as adults in court: A developmental perspective on the transfer of juveniles to criminal court. *Social Policy Report, 15*, 3-14.

Steinberg, L., & Scott, E. (2003). Less guilty by reason of adolescence: Developmental immaturity, diminished responsibility and the juvenile death penalty. *American Psychologist, 58*, 1009-1018.

Strom, K. J. S. (2000). *Profile of state prisoners under age 18, 1985-97*. Washington, DC: Bureau of Justice Statistics.

Tonry, M. (1993). Sentencing commissions and their guidelines. In M. Tonry (Ed.), *Crime and justice: A review of research* (Vol. 17, pp. 137-195). Chicago: University of Chicago Press.

Tonry, M. (1999). Rethinking unthinkable punishment policies in America. *UCLA Law Review, 46*, 1781-1791.

Ulmer, J., & Johnson, B. D. (2004). Sentencing in context: A multilevel analysis. *Criminology, 42*(1), 137-177.

Ulmer, J. T. (2000). The rules have changed—So proceed with caution: A comment on Engen and Gainey's method for modeling sentencing outcomes under guidelines. *Criminology, 38*, 1231-1243.

Ulmer, J. T., & Kramer, J. H. (1996). Court communities under sentencing guidelines: Dilemmas of formal rationality and sentencing disparity. *Criminology, 34*, 383-408.

von Hirsch, A. (1983). Criminology: Commensurability and crime prevention: Evaluating formal sentencing structures and their rationale. *Journal of Criminal Law & Criminology, 1983*, 209.

von Hirsch, A. (1985). *Past or future crimes: Deservedness and dangerousness in the sentencing of criminals*. New Brunswick, NJ: Rutgers University Press.

Wasik, M. (1987). Guidance, guidelines, and criminal record sentencing reform: Guidance or guidelines? In M. Wasik & K. Pease (Eds.), *Sentencing reform: Guidance or guidelines?* (pp. 105-115). Manchester, UK: Manchester University Press.

Shawn D. Bushway is an associate professor of criminal justice in the School of Criminal Justice, University at Albany. Much of the work for this article was completed while he was a professor at the University of Maryland. He received his PhD in public policy analysis and political economy in 1996 from the H. John Heinz III School of Public Policy and Management at Carnegie Mellon University. His current research focuses on the process of desistance, the impact of a criminal history on subsequent outcomes, and the distribution of discretion in the criminal justice sentencing process.

Anne Morrison Piehl is an associate professor in the Economics Department and a member of the Program in Criminal Justice at Rutgers University. She conducts research on the economics of crime and criminal justice, including the relationship between immigration and crime, impacts of incarceration, and distribution of discretion in criminal sentencing. She received her PhD in economics from Princeton University.

[5]

Deterrence as a Principle of Youth Sentencing: No Effect on Youth, but a Significant Effect on Judges

Carla Cesaroni[*] and Nicholas Bala[**]

The use of deterrence as a factor in youth sentencing is controversial. Social science research consistently indicates that an increase in the severity of punishment imposed on adolescents does not affect the youth crime rate: youth who are prone to committing offences do not consider the likelihood or consequences of being apprehended. A survey of Canadian youth court judges' attitudes regarding sentencing under the Young Offenders Act (YOA) *reveals substantial variation in the extent to which they took deterrence into account. Judges' own views on deterrence, rather than the nature of the offence, were most likely to influence the sentence. Even in light of these realities, deterrence is still being put forward, particularly within the political arena, as a means of reducing youth crime.*

In order to help address sentencing variation and the overuse of youth custody, the Youth Criminal Justice Act (YCJA) *refrains from including deterrence as a principle of youth sentencing. The Supreme Court of Canada, in* R. v. B.W.P., *recently confirmed this position. Under the* YCJA *there has been a very significant decline in the use of youth custody, without an overall increase in the level of youth crime. Despite the large body of research doubting the value of deterrence in reducing youth crime, the Conservative government has proposed new legislation which will reintroduce deterrence as a principle of youth sentencing. The authors argue that the assumptions underlying this proposal are flawed, and further submit that if such a law is enacted, judges should take a narrow approach to the use of deterrence as a factor in sentencing youths. There is concern that using deterrence as a factor in youth sentencing will not reduce levels of youth crime, but will instead increase the use of custody. This will unnecessarily expose incarcerated youths to a culture of criminality and impose heavy personal costs on them, as well as financial burdens upon society.*

Introduction

I. Deterrence in Sentencing under the *Young Offenders Act*

[**] Professor, Faculty of Law, Queen's University. The authors would like to acknowledge the research assistance of Lindsay Kenalty, Queen's J.D. candidate 2009, and the helpful review comments of Peter J. Carrington.

Introduction

Two serious problems arose under the *Young Offenders Act* (*YOA*):[1] substantial variation in sentencing of youthful offenders and the overuse of youth courts and custody.[2] The *Youth Criminal Justice Act* (*YCJA*),[3] which came into force in 2003, was intended to address these problems with the *YOA*. One of the central goals of the *YCJA* is a more limited and principled use of custody for young offenders. To that end, it provides more direction for judges in sentencing youths, restricts the use of custodial sentences and encourages the use of community-based responses to youth crime. Since the *YCJA* came into force, there has been less disparity among judges in sentencing and a very significant decline both in the use of courts and in the use of custody for Canadian youth, with no overall increase in reported levels of youth crime.[4]

1. *Young Offenders Act*, R.S.C. 1985, c. Y-1 [*YOA*].

2. Anthony N. Doob & Jane B. Sprott, "Youth Justice in Canada" in Michael Tonry & Anthony N. Doob, eds., *Youth Crime and Youth Justice: Comparative and Cross-National Perspectives* (Chicago: University of Chicago Press, 2004) 185 at 220-21.

3. *Youth Criminal Justice Act*, S.C. 2002, c. 1 [*YCJA*].

4. There have been a number of federal government studies and statistical releases on the effect of the implementation of the *YCJA*. They all reveal similar trends, though there are some differences in exact numbers due to different measures and data sources. The youth crime rate in Canada, as reported by the police, has fluctuated considerably over the past 20 years, yet it has changed very little since the *YCJA* came into force in April 2003. The police-reported rate of youth crime in 2006 was 7 876 per 100 000, which is 1 per cent lower than the rate in 2002, the last full year that the *YOA* was in effect. The youth crime rate in 2006 was practically identical to the rate in 1986, which was 7 877 per 100 000. The *YCJA* resulted in a very substantial reduction in police charging with greater use of diversion. In 2003, when the *YCJA* came into force, there was a dramatic change in the relative use of charges and extrajudicial measures: the rate of youths charged dropped by 18 per cent, and the rate of apprehended youths dealt with by alternatives to charging

Custody is an expensive and intrusive response to youth crime. It should be reserved for the more serious offenders, and for those youth who repeatedly offend despite the imposition of community-based sentences. In addition to the financial burdens that unnecessary custodial sentences impose on society are the possible short-term and long-term impacts on a young person's well-being and propensity to reoffend. Evidence from several Canadian reports and reviews reveals that youth in custody may be subject to peer abuse while incarcerated,[5] and studies of incarcerated youth in Ontario show that a significant number (10 to 15 per cent) are fearful for their safety and experience severe depression

increased by a similar amount. By 2006, 56 per cent of cases were diverted and 44 per cent charged. The rate of custodial youth sentences in 2003/04 was 342 per 100 000 — a drop of 35 per cent from the rate in 2002/03, the last year that the *YOA* was in effect. The rate of custodial sentences declined by a further 13 per cent in 2004/05 and 16 per cent in 2005/06. The result was that the rate of custodial sentences in 2005/06 was less than half (47 per cent) of the rate in 2002/03. See Julian V. Roberts, Nicholas C. Bala & Peter J. Carrington, "Reducing the Use of Courts and Custody for Young Offenders in Canada: Evaluating the Youth Criminal Justice Act" (under review 2008); Statistics Canada, *Youth Crime in Canada, 2006* by Andrea Taylor-Butts & Angela Bressan (Ottawa: Juristat Centre for Justice Statistics, May, 2008); and Statistics Canada, *Youth Custody and Community Services in Canada, 2005/2006* by Shelly Milligan (Ottawa: Juristat Centre for Justice Statistics, July 2008). See also Statistics Canada, *Youth Court Statistics 2003-04* by Jennifer Thomas (Ottawa: Juristat Centre for Justice Statistics, June 2005); Statistics Canada, *Youth Custody and Community Services in Canada, 2004/2005* by Donna Calverley (Ottawa: Juristat Centre for Justice Statistics, March 2007); Statistics Canada, *Crime Statistics in Canada, 2005* by Maire Gannon (Ottawa: Juristat Centre for Justice Statistics, July 2006); Peter J. Carrington & Jennifer L. Schulenberg, *The Impact of the Youth Criminal Justice Act on Police Charging Practices with Young Persons: A Preliminary Statistical Assessment* (Ottawa: Department of Justice, 2005); Anthony N. Doob & Jane B. Sprott, *The Use of Custody under the Youth Criminal Justice Act* (Ottawa: Department of Justice, 2005).

5. See *e.g.* Law Commission of Canada, *Restoring Dignity: Responding to Child Abuse in Canadian Institutions* (Ottawa: Minister of Public Works and Government Services, 2000). See also A.W. Leschied, A. Cunningham & N. Mazaheri, *Safe and Secure: Eliminating Peer-to-Peer Violence in Ontario's Phase II Secure Detention Centres* (North Bay: Ministry of Solicitor General and Correctional Services, 1997); Ombudsman of British Columbia Public Report no. 34, *Building Respect: A Review of Youth Custody Centres in British Colombia* (British Columbia: Office of the Ombudsman, 1994).

and anxiety.[6] Perhaps most importantly, a number of studies suggest that custodial sentences may also result in an increase in recidivism rates of incarcerated youths.[7] Those youths who have pro-social values at the time of incarceration may be placed with others who have anti-social attitudes; after their release, youths may be likely to associate with other adolescents whom they have met in custody, and may therefore be more likely to join gangs.[8] Being in custody also appears to have a negative impact on their long-term job stability, and hence may contribute to reoffending.[9]

Since most young offenders are likely to outgrow anti-social behavior,[10] and since criminal justice processing may actually amplify such behaviour, concerns about the high rates of custody under the *YOA* were understandable. Sections 38 and 39 of the *YCJA* establish a set of principles to govern youth sentencing, emphasizing rehabilitation, proportional sentencing and limited accountability, in comparison to adult sentencing.[11] There is no explicit mention in the *YCJA* of deterrence, a sentencing objective that clearly applies to adults. In its

6. Carla Cesaroni & Michelle Peterson-Badali, "Young Offenders in Custody: Risk and Adjustment" (2005) 32 Criminal Justice & Behavior 251. This is consistent with research from other Western jurisdictions which suggest that between 20-45 per cent of adolescents in custodial facilities report they have been victimized during the course of their current sentence. See Graham Beck, "Bullying Among Young Offenders in Custody" in Noel K. Clark & Geoffrey M. Stephenson, eds., *Criminal Behaviour: Perceptions, Attributions and Rationality* (Leicester: British Psychological Society, 1995) 54.

7. See *e.g.* J. Kraus, "Remand in Custody as a Deterrent in Juvenile Jurisdiction" (1978) 18 Brit. J. Crim. 285.

8. R. Peacock & A. Theron, "Identity Development of the Incarcerated Adolescent with Particular Reference to Prison Gang Membership" (2007) 20:3 Acta *Criminologica* 61.

9. Robert J. Sampson & John H. Laub, "A Life-Course Theory of Cumulative Disadvantage and the Stability of Delinquency" in Terence P. Thornberry, ed., *Advances in Criminological Theory: Developmental Theories of Crime and Delinquency*, vol. 7 (New Brunswick, NJ: Transaction Publishers, 1997) 133. See generally Mark Halsey, "Pathways into Prison: Biographies, Crimes, Punishment" (2008) 20 Current Issues in Criminal Justice 95.

10. The peak years of offending behaviour for girls are 15 and 16 years of age, and for boys are 17 and 18 years of age: see *e.g.* Elizabeth S. Scott & Thomas Grisso, "The Evolution of Adolescence: A Developmental Perspective on Juvenile Justice Reform" (1997) 88 J. Crim. L. & Criminology 137.

11. *Supra* note 3, ss. 38(1), 39(1).

early years, one of the most contentious issues in the interpretation of the *YCJA* was whether deterrence should be a factor in the sentencing of young offenders. In June 2006, the Supreme Court of Canada ruled, in *R. v. B.W.P.*,[12] that deterrence was not to be taken into account in sentencing under that *Act.*

The issue of deterrence as a factor in youth sentencing has remained controversial. In January 2006, the federal Liberal government, which had been responsible for the enactment of the *YCJA*, was replaced by a minority Conservative government. An important plank of the Conservatives' 2006 election platform was the promise to "get tough" with criminals, especially those committing violent offences. The Conservatives pledged that "serious crime must mean serious time," and that they would "ensure truth in sentencing and put an end to the Liberal revolving door justice system."[13] In November 2007, the Conservative government introduced Bill C-25 to honour that pledge.[14] The Bill was short. One provision was intended to expand the range of situations in which youth can be detained before trial.[15] The other provided:

> (f) subject to paragraph [38(2)] (*c*) [which establishes the principle of proportionality for youth sentencing], the sentence may have the following objectives:
>
> (i) to denounce unlawful conduct, and
>
> (ii) to deter the young person and other young persons from committing offences.[16]

Bill C-25 was not passed before the 2008 election was called and Parliament was dissolved.

12. 2006 SCC 27, [2006] 1 S.C.R. 941 [*B.W.P.*].

13. Conservative Party of Canada, *Stand Up for Canada: Federal Election Platform* (2006) at 22.

14. Bill C-25, *An Act to amend the Youth Criminal Justice Act*, 2nd Sess., 39th Parl., 2007 (First Reading 17 November 2007).

15. This provision was a response to a recommendation from a public inquiry into this tragic case: Nova Scotia, *Spiralling out of Control: Lessons Learned from a Boy in Trouble — Report of the Nunn Commission of Inquiry* (Nova Scotia: Nunn Commission of Inquiry, 2006).

16. *Supra* note 14, cl. 2(f)(i)-(ii).

In the 2008 election campaign, the Conservatives again made toughening Canada's youth justice laws an important issue, pledging to enact "new, balanced legislation."[17] Prime Minister Stephen Harper stated that a "primary goal of [youth] sentencing . . . [should be] to discourage others from committing crimes."[18] Deterrence would be explicitly included as a "primary" objective of such sentencing. Other proposals included provisions for "automatic, stiffer sentences for persons 14 and older convicted of serious and violent crimes such as murder and manslaughter."[19] The names of youths 14 years and older who commit such crimes would be made public. The Conservatives also proposed to change the law to make it easier for prosecutors to apply for pre-trial detention of young people.

The rationale for deterrence-based sentencing is that imposing a more severe sentence for an offence not only demonstrates the unpleasant consequences of offending to the particular person being sentenced, and thereby reduces the likelihood of recidivism (specific or individual deterrence), but that it also warns other potential offenders of what may happen if they offend, and thereby results in less offending by other youth (general deterrence). Deterrence-based sentencing of young offenders is premised on a particular view of how such offenders, and potential offenders, will respond to sanctions.

This article explores the role of deterrence as a principle of youth sentencing in Canada, and asks whether it will result in less youth crime. We have chosen to focus on deterrence because the impact of deterrence-based sentencing principles raises empirical questions that have been offered by social scientists and considered by judges. We begin with a review of the case law on the role of deterrence in sentencing under the *YOA*. Then we present and analyze previously unpublished data on the

17. Prime Minister Harper announced the Conservative proposals for *YCJA* reform in a speech: see "Balancing Rehabilitation and Responsibility" (22 September 2008), online: Harper Leadership 08 <http://www.conservative.ca/EN/1091/106115> ["Balancing Rehabilitation"]. For media reports, see *e.g.* Campbell Clark, Carolyn Alphonso & Les Perreaux, "Harper pitches two-tier youth justice plan" *The Globe and Mail* (23 September 2008) A1.

18. "Balancing Rehabilitation", *ibid.*

19. *Ibid.*

attitudes of Canadian youth court judges toward deterrence, and the effect of these attitudes on their sentencing practices under that *Act*.

We next discuss the controversy about the role of deterrence under the *YCJA*, and we review the criminological literature, which clearly establishes that increasing the severity of youth sentences does not significantly affect youth crime rates. We conclude that the reintroduction of deterrence as a principle of youth sentencing is misguided. It would not result in any reduction in youth crime, and it could have the effect of increasing the number of youth in custody, thereby undermining the significant gains that have been made under the *YCJA*.

I. Deterrence in Sentencing under the *Young Offenders Act*

The *YOA*, which was in effect from 1984 to 2003, did not clearly articulate the principles that would govern youth sentencing, and there was controversy among judges about whether to use deterrence as a factor. The Supreme Court of Canada resolved this controversy in 1989 in *R. v. J.J.M.*, concluding that deterrence should be considered in sentencing, albeit to a lesser extent than for adults. Justice Cory wrote:

> There is reason to believe that *Young Offenders Act* dispositions can have an effective deterrent effect. The crimes committed by the young tend to be a group activity. . . .If the activity of the group is criminal then the disposition imposed on an individual member of the group should be such that it will deter other members of the group. For example the sentence imposed on one member of a "swarming group" should serve to deter others in the gang.
>
> Having said that, I would underline that general deterrence should not, through undue emphasis, have the same importance in fashioning the disposition for a youthful offender as it would in the case of an adult. One youthful offender should not be obliged to accept the responsibility for all the young offenders of his or her generation.[20]

20. *R. v. J.J.M.*, [1993] 2 S.C.R. 421 at 434.

Although Justice Cory accepted the argument that more severe sentences can have "an effective deterrent effect" on levels of youth offending, he cited no authority for this proposition. Despite the fact that, as discussed below, the proposition is inconsistent with a significant body of social science research, the Court's approach was understandably influential with youth court judges working under that *Act*, and it undoubtedly contributed to the high rate of use of custodial sentences under the *YOA*.

II. Survey of Youth Court Judges on Deterrence under the *Young Offenders Act*

There are few studies on how the use of deterrence as a factor in sentencing affects judicial decision making, and no published Canadian research offers a detailed examination of the extent to which deterrence affects the sentencing of adolescent offenders.[21] The following discussion addresses this gap in the literature, analyzing previously unpublished data on judicial attitudes toward deterrence as a factor in sentencing under the *YOA*.

As preparations were being made to enact the *YCJA* in 2001, Justice Canada sponsored an extensive survey of youth court judges in Canada to learn about judicial attitudes to youth sentencing under the *YOA*. Judges were asked questions on a range of matters, including their evaluation of the contributions of other justice system professionals, the use of diversion from court, their theories of youth sentencing, the use of custody and the administration of sentences for youth.[22] While some

21. For one of the few studies of judicial attitudes towards sentencing in juvenile court, see Gordon Bazemore & Lynette Feder, "Judges in the Punitive Juvenile Court: Organizational, Career and Ideological Influences on Sanctioning Orientation" (1997) 14 Justice Quarterly 87.

22. Surveys were sent to youth court judges in all jurisdictions in the country by Justice Canada (with a cover letter from the researcher). Although most provincially appointed judges in Canada deal with youth matters, some of these judges do not hear youth cases. The questionnaire was sent to all provincially appointed judges, however, as from the lists provided it was not possible to ascertain which judges dealt with youth court cases. Therefore, in addition to the mailing being over-inclusive, there was no reliable way of estimating the population size (of judges who have heard youth court matters in the

data from that survey have been published and analyzed, a detailed analysis of the responses to questions about deterrence has not previously been published.[23]

There were 238 respondents from all of the provinces and two of the three territories. Seventy-four per cent of the respondents were male. The 238 youth court judges had from one to thirty-five years of judicial experience, with a median of eleven years. Most of them heard adult court cases on a regular basis as well as youth cases. Thirty-four per cent sat in large metropolitan areas of 500 000 or more, while 38 per cent sat in smaller communities with populations of 25 000 or less. Twenty-five per cent regularly sat in aboriginal communities.

The respondent judges were asked a series of questions about sentencing for various kinds of offences. For each of three offences of different types and levels of sentences — "a moderately serious violent offence (such as an assault causing bodily harm)," "a property offence such as break-and-enter of a business establishment" and "an administration of justice offence such as 'failure to appear' or 'failure to comply with a disposition'" — they were asked to rate, on a five-point scale,[24] the importance of each of the following principles or purposes of sentencing: denunciation, general deterrence, specific deterrence,

---

previous 12 months). Hence, a response rate cannot be calculated. In order to be able to assure anonymity of the responses, and to alleviate potential concerns by judges that their answers would become the property of the government, the questionnaires were returned to the Centre of Criminology, University of Toronto. Surveys were mailed on 27 December 2000 and were sent to all provincial court judges in Canada listed on a document obtained from the National Judicial Institute. This survey was carried out by Anthony N. Doob with support from the Department of Justice, Canada. The authors would like to thank Professor Doob for making the data available to us for secondary analysis. The first author of this article was involved with Professor Doob in the analysis of other parts of this data: Anthony N. Doob & Carla Cesaroni, *Responding to Youth Crime in Canada* (Toronto: University of Toronto Press, 2004) at 198-224.

23. Significant parts of the survey data dealing with other issues have been analyzed and reported upon. See Anthony N. Doob, *Youth Court Judges' Views of the Youth Justice System: The Results of a Survey* (Ottawa: Department of Justice, 2001); Doob & Cesaroni, *ibid.*

24. A small number of judges simply checked factors that were important to them rather than rating the importance of factors. Instead of eliminating these judges, a "checked" factor was scored as 4, and an "unchecked" factor as 2.

proportionality, rehabilitating the young person, incapacitation and protection of the public.[25]

The results set out in Table 1 reveal significant variation in how the respondent judges viewed the importance of general deterrence when sentencing youth. For example, for a moderately serious violent offence, 23 per cent considered general deterrence to be an important factor in sentencing, 30 per cent considered it to be somewhat important, and 47 per cent considered it to be not important. It is noteworthy that this pattern was similar across the three different offences. This suggests that the views of the sentencing judge were more influential than the nature of the offence in determining whether a young offender would get a sentence in which general deterrence was a factor.[26]

Table 1: The Importance of General Deterrence in Sentencing for Different Types of Offences[27]

Offence	Not Important	Somewhat Important	Important	Total
Moderately Serious Violent	47%	30%	23%	100%
Property	50%	27%	23%	100%
Administration of Justice	49%	27%	24%	100%

Judges were also asked the following question: "When sentencing a young person, how often do you take into account the prevalence of youth crime (or this particular type of youth crime) in the community?" Not surprisingly, as indicated in Table 2, youth court judges who ranked general deterrence as "important" in sentencing decisions were

25. For each of the ratings, a high number signified that the factor was important (1: "not at all important" and 5: "very important").

26. In order to further explore the relationship between judges' ratings of general deterrence in sentencing, a summed scale of ratings of general deterrence was created by adding judges' ratings of importance (from 1: "not important" to 5: "very important") of general deterrence in sentencing for all three offences. Ratings of deterrence were then divided into low (for summed scores of 3 to 6), medium (for summed scores of 7 to 9) and high ratings (for summed scores of 10 to 15). The low ratings group comprised 35 per cent of the sample; the medium comprised 34 per cent; and the high comprised 31 per cent.

27. Responses are collapsed such that 1 ("not at all important") and 2 (unlabelled) are combined as "not important"; and 5 ("very important") is combined with 4 (unlabelled) as "important."

the most likely to take into account the prevalence of youth crime in the community. Table 2 shows that among youth court judges who ranked general deterrence as high in importance, 95 per cent either always or usually considered the prevalence of youth crime in the community; only five per cent "rarely or never" considered that factor. Of those who ranked general deterrence as "not important," 21 per cent "rarely or never" considered the prevalence of youth crime.

Table 2: Relationship Between Judges' Views on General Deterrence and the Prevalence of Youth Crime

Importance of General Deterrence	Prevalence of Youth Crime Considered When Sentencing		
	Always/Often	Rarely/Never	Total
Low	79%	21%	100%
Medium	90%	10%	100%
High	95%	5%	100%
Total	88%	12%	100%

$\chi^2 = 9.141$; df $= 2$; $p = .010$

It would seem that judges who rated general deterrence as having a high importance, and who took the prevalence of youth crime into account, were likely to believe that there was a connection between lower crime rates and harsher punishments.

In anticipation of the coming into force of the *YCJA*, judges were asked what portion of their youth court cases they thought could be dealt with just as adequately outside of the court (for example, informally, by the use of diversion, or through what were called "alternative measures" under the *YOA*[28] and are called "extrajudicial sanctions" under the *YCJA*[29]). Overall, a judge's belief in the importance of deterrence as a factor in youth sentencing was significantly related[30] to the belief that there was little scope for diversion of youth cases from the courts. More specifically, of the judges who rated general deterrence as high in importance, 59 per cent were of the view that few or none of their cases could be handled outside of court, whereas only 27 per cent of those who rated deterrence as "not important" were of that view.

28. *Supra* note 1, s. 4.
29. *Supra* note 3, s. 10.
30. $\chi2$ (6, $N = 212$) $= 16.467$, $p. <.05$

III. Survey Results on General Deterrence and the Use of Custody

The *YOA* stated, rather vaguely, that "[t]he youth court shall not commit a young person to . . . custody unless the court considers a committal to . . . custody to be necessary for the protection of society . . . ."[31] The ambiguous language of the *YOA* regarding when to impose custody, such as "whenever appropriate" and when "reasonable in the circumstance,"[32] resulted in great disparities in the extent to which different judges imposed custodial sentences.

In contrast, the *YCJA* established significant restrictions on the use of custody. Under section 39(1), custodial sentences can only be imposed if one or more of four conditions are met (the so-called four "gateways" to custody):

- the youth has committed a "violent offence";
- the youth has "failed to comply with [previously imposed] non-custodial sentences";
- the youth has been found guilty of a moderately serious offence[33] and has a "history that indicates a pattern of findings of guilt"; or
- "in exceptional cases," where the youth has committed an indictable offence and the "aggravating circumstances . . . are such that the imposition of a non-custodial sentence would be inconsistent with the purpose and principles" of youth sentencing.[34]

The second condition — previous failure "to comply with non-custodial sentences" — is noteworthy. This criterion indicates that a repeat offender found guilty of a non-violent offence should not receive

31. *Supra* note 1, s. 24(5).

32. *Ibid.*, ss. 24(1.1)(b)-(c), enacted by S.C. 1995, s. 19. See Anthony N. Doob & J. B. Sprott, "Changes in Youth Justice Sentencing in Canada" (1999) 11 Federal Sentencing Reporter 262 at 263.

33. An indictable offence for which an adult could receive a sentence of more than two years.

34. *Supra* note 3, s. 39(1).

a custodial sentence if the youth has complied with previous non-custodial sentences. Earlier, under the *YOA*, however, judges may have been inclined to increase the severity of responses with a "step-up" in the sentence for a repeat non-violent offender to a custodial sentence.[35] Data from the Justice Canada survey summarized in Table 3 shows that judges who ranked general deterrence as important under the *YOA* were more likely to impose a custodial sentence if a youth reoffended after being given a non-custodial sentence. Sixty-four per cent of judges who ranked general deterrence of high importance, but only 46 per cent of those who ranked it as low in importance, said that a youth's failure to comply with a previous non-custodial sentence was a significant factor, in at least half of the cases in which they ordered a custodial sentence. Only six per cent of judges who ranked general deterrence as of high importance reported that they never took account of a previous non-custodial sentence in deciding when to order custody, as compared to 28 per cent of those who ranked general deterrence as low in importance.

Table 3: Relationship Between Judges' Views on General Deterrence in Sentencing and on the Relevance of Previous Non-Custodial Disposition

Importance of General Deterrence	Previous Non-Custodial Disposition a Relevant Factor[36]				
	All/Most	Half	Few	None	Total
Low	36%	10%	26%	28%	100%
Medium	44%	25%	27%	4%	100%
High	43%	21%	30%	6%	100%
Total	41%	19%	27%	13%	100%

$\chi^2 = 24.431$; df $= 6$; $p < .001$

Previously published research offers strong evidence that under the *YOA* prior convictions had a significant impact on the likelihood of receiving a custodial sentence, regardless of the seriousness of the

35. Anthony Matarazzo, Peter J. Carrington & Robert D. Hiscott, "The Effect of Prior Youth Court Dispositions on Current Disposition: An Application of Societal-Reaction Theory" (2001) 17 Journal of Quantitative Criminology 169.

36. This question was probing the "theory" of individual judges on sentencing, and the extent to which they saw specific deterrence as a factor in ordering custody. It read as follows: "The youth had successfully completed non-custodial sentences in the past but had clearly not learned from that experience and was continuing to commit offences."

offence.[37] It is not surprising that judges who felt that general deterrence was an important sentencing principle would also support an escalation in sanctions: in Julian V. Roberts' words, "Advocates of general or specific deterrence support a recidivist premium on the grounds that recidivists are more likely to reoffend and need stronger disincentives."[38] As Roberts notes, this can mean "that a defendant who otherwise would receive a non-custodial penalty is incarcerated, not for . . . his current conduct, but for crimes committed earlier."[39]

Often related to specific deterrence is the view that it may be appropriate to impose a custodial sentence as a "short, sharp, shock," because it can deter youth from future offences. Under the *YOA*, youths were often sentenced to custody, but usually for relatively short stays. In 1999-2000, 34 per cent of custodial sentences were for one month or less, and 78 per cent were for three months or less.[40]

Tables 4 and 5 illustrate that judges' views of general deterrence were related to the use of short custodial sentences or "short, sharp, shocks" (to deter both the particular offender and other youth). Table 4 shows that 76 per cent of judges who rated general deterrence as high in importance said that delivering such a "shock" was an important factor in handing down short sentences, while only 14 per cent said that it was not. By way of contrast, among those judges who saw general deterrence as of low importance, only 47 per cent rated the "short, sharp, shock" as important, and 22 per cent as not important.

---

37. See Peter J. Carrington & Sharon Moyer, "Factors Affecting Custodial Dispositions under the Young Offenders Act" (1995) 37 Can. J. Crim. 127; Melanie Kowalski & Tullio Caputo, "Recidivism in Youth Court: An Examination of the Impact of Age, Gender, and Prior Record" (1999) 41 Can. J. Crim. 57 at 66-67.

38. Julian V. Roberts, "The Role of Criminal Record in the Sentencing Process" (2004) 22 Crime & Justice: A Review of Research 303 at 303.

39. *Ibid.* at 316.

40. Statistics Canada, *Youth Court Data Tables 1999-00* (Ottawa: Minister of Industry, 2001).

Table 4: Relationship Between Judges' Views on General Deterrence in Sentencing and Short Custodial Sentences

Importance of General Deterrence	Custodial Sentence Would Deter Youth Through "Short, Sharp, Shock"			
	Not Important	Somewhat Important	Important	Total
Low	22%	31%	47%	100%
Medium	16%	22%	62%	100%
High	14%	10%	76%	100%
Total	17%	22%	61%	100%

$\chi^2 = 12.818$; df = 4; $p < .05$

Table 5 shows that 37 per cent of the judges who gave significant weight to general deterrence in youth sentencing saw deterrence of other youths as an important consideration when imposing short custodial sentences; only eight per cent of those who gave little weight to general deterrence saw it as an important consideration.

Table 5: Relationship Between Judges' Views on the Importance of General Deterrence in Sentencing, and on the Importance of Deterring Other Youth by Imposing Short Custodial Sentences

Importance of General Deterrence	Short Sentence Would Deter Other Youth			
	Not Important	Somewhat Important	Important	Total
Low	81%	11%	8%	100%
Medium	50%	29%	21%	100%
High	26%	37%	37%	100%
Total	53%	25%	22%	100%

$\chi^2 = 42.637$; df = 4; $p < .001$

The data from the survey reveal that under the *YOA*, judges who ranked general deterrence as a significant factor in their sentencing decisions were:

- more likely to take the perceived prevalence of youth crime in the community into account when sentencing;
- more likely to escalate a sanction to custody for youth who failed to comply with a previous non-custodial sentence;
- less likely to favour community-based responses to youth crime; and

- more likely to support the use of "short, sharp, shocks" in the form of short custodial sentences.

These findings help to predict the probable effect of the proposal in Bill C-25 and the 2008 Conservative election platform to add deterrence as a "primary goal" of youth sentencing. They suggest that adding general deterrence as a sentencing principle will lead to more custodial sentences — at least for judges who will adopt deterrence as an important sentencing factor.

IV. The Courts on Deterrence under the *Youth Criminal Justice Act*

The *YCJA* gives judges much more direction in sentencing than the *YOA* did. Although the *YCJA* continues to recognize a role for custody, it was intended to reduce the level of incarceration from that under the *YOA*, as well as to encourage the use of community-based sentencing. Further, although the *YCJA* continues to give judges significant discretion in particular sentencing decisions, it sought to reduce the wide disparities in youth court sentencing that occurred under the *YOA*.[41] Specifically, section 38(1) of the *YCJA* establishes the *purpose* of sentencing in youth court; sections 38(2) and 38(3) articulate specific *principles* to govern youth sentencing; and section 39 establishes detailed *restrictions* on the use of custody.

At the adult level, section 718 of the *Criminal Code* lists all of the conventional purposes of sentencing: denunciation, *deterrence*, incapacitation, rehabilitation, restoration to victims and acknowledgment of harm.[42] This list is not prioritized, and as a result has been criticized as failing to give judges clear guidance and as having

41. See Statistics Canada, *Youth Custody and Community Services in Canada, 2000/01* by Julie Marinelli (Ottawa: Juristat, Centre for Justice Statistics, 2002), reporting that the incarceration rate per 10 000 young persons in 2001 ranged from nine in Quebec to as high as 36 in the Northwest Territories.

42. *Criminal Code*, R.S.C. 1985 c. C-46, s. 718.

had little real effect on adult sentencing practices.[43] In contrast, section 38(1) of the *YCJA* establishes the purpose of sentencing in youth court in a relatively precise fashion: "The purpose of sentencing under section 42 (youth sentences) is to hold a young person accountable for an offence through the imposition of just sanctions that have meaningful consequences for the young person and that promote his or her rehabilitation and reintegration . . . ."[44]

In commenting on this provision in *R. v. B.W.P.*, Justice Charron of the Supreme Court of Canada wrote:

> It is apparent from a plain reading of s. 38(1) that "protection of the public" is expressed, not as an immediate objective of sentencing, but rather as the long-term effect of a successful youth sentence. Likewise, s. 3(1) sets out the three specific means by which sentencing is intended to "promote the long-term protection of the public". These specific means do not include general deterrence.[45]

Holding young offenders accountable and ensuring the proportionality of sentences to offences are central themes under the *YCJA*. It is also clear that rehabilitation is more important in the sentencing of youths than of adults: under section 38(1), youth court judges are always required to consider what sentence is most likely to rehabilitate a young offender.[46] This emphasis on rehabilitation requires the judge to consider carefully whether non-custodial alternatives would be sufficient to hold a youth accountable in the particular circumstances.

Section 718(b) of the *Criminal Code* explicitly provides that one of the objectives of the sentencing of adults is specific and general deterrence: "to deter the offender and other persons from committing offences."[47] Similarly, the *YCJA* has detailed provisions articulating the principles that are to govern sentencing, sentencing review and release from custody. Section 50 of the *YCJA* states that Part XXIII (sentencing) of the *Criminal Code* (which includes section 718) generally "does *not*

43. See *e.g.* Julian V. Roberts & Andrew von Hirsch, "Statutory Sentencing Reform: The Purpose and Principles of Sentencing" (1995) 37 Crim. L.Q. 220.

44. *Supra* note 3, s. 38(1).

45. *Supra* note 12 at para. 31.

46. *Supra* note 3, s. 38(1).

47. *Supra* note 42, s. 718(b).

apply" to the sentencing of young offenders under the *YCJA*. It also states, however, that the provisions of Part XXIII are to apply to youths if explicitly mentioned in section 50 of the *YCJA*, such as the explicit reference in section 50 of the *YCJA* to section 718.2(e) of the *Code* (special consideration for sentencing of aboriginal offenders).

After the *YCJA* came into force, some youth court judges initially concluded that, although not mentioned in the *Act*, general and specific deterrence have not "been eliminated entirely" in youth sentencing. These judges, however, recognized that these deterrence-related objectives are of "lesser importance in youth justice court sentencing" than in adult court.[48] For example, Justice Mackenzie of the British Columbia Court of Appeal noted in *R. v. B.V.N.*[49] that the *YCJA* "implies a reduced emphasis on general deterrence compared to adult sentencing," but does not require judges "to completely disregard general deterrence in particular cases." In the same case, Justice Oppal stated:

> In spite of the recognition and the acceptance of the general principle that young offenders are not generally possessed with the same degree of moral blameworthiness as adult offenders, the fact remains that not all young offenders are unaware of the sanctions imposed by the criminal justice system . . . . [I]t would be unrealistic and unwise to conclude that the principle of general deterrence has no application in dealing with young offenders.[50]

Shortly after the British Columbia Court of Appeal decided *R. v. B.V.N.*, the Manitoba Court of Appeal took a different approach in *R. v. B.W.P.*,[51] holding that deterrence is *not* to be a factor in youth sentencing. The Manitoba court upheld a sentence of one day in custody, followed by 15 months of community supervision, for an aboriginal youth who pleaded guilty to manslaughter and had served 108 days in detention before sentencing. On the issue of deterrence,

48. *R. v. M.(T).*, 2003 CarswellOnt 4024 at para. 42. (Ont. Ct. J.) (WLeC). See also *R. v. N.(B).*, 2004 BCPC 22, 2004 CarswellBC 241 (Prov. Ct.) (WLeC).

49. 2004 BCCA 266, [2004] 196 B.C.A.C. 100.

50. *Ibid.* at para. 23. A similar conclusion was reached in *R. v. T.M.D.*, 2003 NSCA 151, [2004] 220 N.S.R. (2d) 109 at para. 31.

51. 2004 MBCA 110, [2004] 187 Man. R. (2d) 80.

Hamilton J.A. wrote, "A judge cannot sentence one young person with the aim of sending a message to other youth. This would be at variance with the required focus on the young person being sentenced. I am also of the view that specific deterrence is not a principle of sentencing in light of the exclusion of this principle under s. 50(1) of the *YCJA*."[52]

After hearing simultaneous appeals from the conflicting British Columbia and Manitoba Courts of Appeal judgments, the Supreme Court upheld the approach of the Manitoba Court of Appeal, and ruled that deterrence is not to be a factor in sentencing youth. In *R. v. B.W.P.*, Justice Charron began by explaining the concepts of specific and general deterrence:

> Deterrence, as a principle of sentencing, refers to the imposition of a sanction for the purpose of discouraging the offender and others from engaging in criminal conduct. When deterrence is aimed at the offender before the court, it is called "specific deterrence", when directed at others, "general deterrence". The focus of these appeals is on the latter. General deterrence is intended to work in this way: potential criminals will not engage in criminal activity because of the example provided by the punishment imposed on the offender. When general deterrence is factored in the determination of the sentence, the offender is punished more severely, not because he or she deserves it, but because the court decides to send a message to others who may be inclined to engage in similar criminal activity.[53]

The Court relied on the Preamble to the *YCJA*, the Declarations of Principle in section 3, the Sentencing Principles in section 38, and the specific words of section 50. Justice Charron said:

> The *YCJA* introduced a new sentencing regime . . . it sets out a detailed and complete code for sentencing young persons under which terms it is not open to the youth sentencing judge to impose a punishment for the purpose of warning, not the young person, but others against engaging in criminal conduct. Hence, general deterrence is not a principle of youth sentencing under the present regime. The *YCJA* also does not speak of specific deterrence. Rather, Parliament has sought to promote the long-term protection of the public by addressing the circumstances underlying the offending behaviour, by rehabilitating and reintegrating young persons into society and by holding young persons

52. *Ibid.* at para. 64. A similar conclusion was reached in *R. v. L.R.P.*, 2004 NBCA 76, [2005] 200 C.C.C. (3d) 472.

53. *Supra* note 12 at para. 2.

> accountable through the imposition of meaningful sanctions related to the harm done. Undoubtedly, the sentence may have the effect of deterring the young person and others from committing crimes. But, by policy choice, I conclude that Parliament has not included deterrence as a basis for imposing a sanction under the *YCJA*.[54]

As Justice Charron recognized, sentencing can have a deterrent effect (both specific and general) by holding the accused youth "accountable" and by imposing a sentence that is "proportionate" to his or her circumstances and to the harm done to a victim (principles of sentencing that are explicitly recognized in sections 3 and 38 of the *YCJA*). The difference between deterrence as an *effect* rather than a *purpose* of sentencing is subtle, but very important. For example, not considering deterrence as a purpose of sentencing means that the prevalence of an offence in a particular community is not to be considered as an aggravating factor. However, the court can consider the harm suffered by the victim, and if youths are aware that they will be held accountable for the harm they have caused, this should have some effect on behaviour.[55]

Although the focus of the appeals before the Supreme Court in *R. v. B.W.P.* was on general deterrence, the Court also excluded specific deterrence as a sentencing factor under the *YCJA*. The Court noted that "specific deterrence calls for the incapacitation of the offender in order to prevent further commission of crime, usually . . . through incarceration . . . [and since] Parliament has imposed specific restrictions on . . . custodial sentences . . . . th[e]se provisions must govern."[56] Although the Court was presented with a significant amount of social science research on the inefficacy of more severe sentences as a deterrent to youth crime, the Court did not refer to this material in its judgment. Rather, it treated the issue of whether deterrence is a permissible purpose for sentencing under the *YCJA* as a matter of statutory interpretation, not as a matter of social policy.

In its May 2008 decision in *R. v. D.B.*,[57] the Supreme Court unanimously recognized that youths' right to liberty and security of the

54. *Ibid.* at para. 4.
55. *R. v. B.R.S.*, 2003 SKPC 84, [2003] 235 Sask. R. 113 at para. 24.
56. *Supra* note 12 at para. 40.
57. *R. v. B.(D.)*, 2008 SCC 25, 293 D.L.R. (4th) 278.

person, enshrined in section 7 of the *Canadian Charter of Rights and Freedoms*, may be compromised by a statutory presumption in favour of adult sentencing, contrary to the principles of fundamental justice, as youths have "reduced moral blameworthiness" for their offences, when compared to adults. However, the Court was split five to four on whether fundamental justice was violated by the provisions of the *YCJA*, which create a presumption of adult sentencing for youths found guilty of the most serious offences. Writing for the five-member majority, Abella J. concluded that the presumption in favour of adult sentencing in section 72 of the *YCJA*[58] violates section 7 of the *Charter*, but accepted that adult sentences could still be imposed on youth if the Crown satisfied the onus for justifying such sentences. In the course of her decision, Justice Abella noted that social science research justifies disregarding deterrence as an explicit aggravating factor in the sentencing of adolescents:

> It is widely acknowledged that age plays a role in the development of judgment and moral sophistication .... "Adolescents also lack the intellectual capacity to appreciate fully the consequences of their acts. In many contexts, youths will act without foresight or self-awareness, and they may lack empathy for those who may be the victims of their wrongful acts." ... There is, moreover, evidence suggesting that as a result of this reduced judgment and maturity, young persons respond differently to punishment than adults, and that harsher penalties do not, by themselves, reduce youth crime. See A. N. Doob, V. Marinos, and K. N. Varma, *Youth Crime and the Youth Justice System in Canada: A Research Perspective* (1995), at pp. 56-71. This helps explain why, in s. 3(1)(*b*)(i) of the *YCJA*, "rehabilitation and reintegration", not general deterrence, are emphasized and why, in s. 3(1)(*b*)(ii), accountability should be "fair and proportionate ... consistent with the greater dependency of young persons and their reduced level of maturity."[59]

As noted above, the *YCJA* brought about a very noteworthy decline in the use of courts and custody for Canadian youth without any overall increase in youth crime. Although a number of factors have likely contributed to this decline in custodial sentences, the move away from deterrence as a sentencing principle is in our view a significant one.

58. Section 72 of the *YCJA* created a presumption that an adult sentence would be imposed for a young person aged 14 or older and found guilty of murder, attempted murder, aggravated sexual assault or a "third serious violent" offence.

59. *Supra* note 57 at paras. 62, 64-65.

Furthermore, the fact that the overall youth crime rate has not increased suggests that youth court sentencing practices have no appreciable effect on youth crime rates. This raises serious doubts about whether more severe punishments would reduce youth crime rates.

V. Deterrence and the Nature of Adolescence: Social Science Research

Deterrence theory is based on the assumption that punishment can prevent future offending, and it is linked to a belief that harsher punishments will reduce levels of crime. It is also based on the premise of rational choice: the premise that potential offenders will rationally weigh the costs and consequences of possible penalties against the benefit they derive from the crime. While it is recognized that certain types of adult offending behaviour may be deterred by more severe sanctions, a growing body of criminological research concludes that increasing the severity of sentences imposed for adolescent offenders does not affect their behaviour.[60] However, increasing the *likelihood of being apprehended*, which thereby increases the immediate consequences of offending, may have some effect on adolescents.

A number of factors related to adolescent cognition and psychosocial development negate the possibility of reducing youth crime by increasing the severity of sanctions. The biggest obstacle to that sort of deterrent effect lies in the fact that youths who commit offences generally do not consider the likelihood of being caught and punished. Many adolescents, especially those who are likely to engage in serious or repeat offending, are at a stage in life when they have a sense of invulnerability, and therefore have a significant likelihood of engaging in high risk behaviour. The reality is that youth who are prone to commit offences do not think about the consequences of their acts; making their consequences more severe if they are apprehended will not

60. See discussion in Doob & Cesaroni, *supra* note 22 at 241-53. For an excellent summary of the literature on deterrence in adult sentencing, see Anthony N. Doob & Cheryl M. Webster, "Sentencing Severity and Crime: Accepting the Null Hypothesis" (2003) 30 Crime & Justice: A Review of Research 143.

affect their behaviour.[61] Further, due to cognitive limitations and more limited life experiences, adolescents have difficulty in thinking about future events.[62] Short-term excitement and the perceived psychological, social or monetary rewards of offending can outweigh potential long-term penal consequences, which may be seen as only a remote possibility.[63]

The cognitive and psychosocial reality is that adolescents have less judgment and greater impulsivity than adults. In the words of American psychologists Elizabeth Cauffman and Laurence Steinberg:

> [Society] cannot claim that adolescents "ought to know better" if, in fact, the evidence indicates that they do not know better, or, more accurately, cannot know better, because they lack the abilities needed to exercise mature judgment. To the extent . . . that maturity of judgment goes hand in hand with a consolidation of a sense of identity, research . . . suggests that most individuals would not be expected to display consistently mature judgment until the age of eighteen, at the earliest.[64]

---

61. See *e.g.* Laurence Steinberg & Elizabeth S. Scott, "Less Guilty by Reason of Adolescence: Developmental Immaturity, Diminished Responsibility, and the Juvenile Death Penalty" (2003) 58 American Psychologist 1009; Elizabeth Cauffman & Laurence Steinberg, "The Cognitive and Affective Influences on Adolescent Decision-Making" (1995) 68 Temp. L. Rev. 1763. See also *R. v. F.M.*, 2008 BCCA 111, [2008] 231 C.C.C. (3d) 57, where the British Columbia Court of Appeal upheld a decision that youths aged 13 and 15 years who killed a man in an assault should only be found guilty of manslaughter, as opposed to second degree murder, on account of their "diminished capacity" to foresee the consequences of their acts. Smith J.A. wrote (at paras. 24-27):

> Just as it is common knowledge that intoxication can affect the ability of persons to foresee the consequences of their actions, it is common knowledge that lack of life experience affects the level of maturity and can affect the ability of youths to foresee the consequences of their actions . . . The trial judge was entitled to view this and similar evidence as demonstrating a level of immaturity that could cause him to reasonably doubt whether the appellants subjectively foresaw the consequences of their actions.

62. See Elizabeth S. Scott, N. Dickon Reppucci & Jennifer L. Woolard, "Evaluating Adolescent Decision Making in Legal Contexts" (1995) 19 Law and Human Behavior 221.
63. See *ibid.* See also Steinberg & Scott, *supra* note 61.
64. Laurence Steinberg & Elizabeth Cauffman, "The Elephant in the Courtroom: A Developmental Perspective on the Adjudication of Youthful Offenders" (1999) 6 Va. J. Soc. Pol'y & L. 389 at 404; Cauffman & Steinberg, *supra* note 61 at 1776-77.

For many youth, gaining acceptance with peers is much more salient than any possible future criminal justice sanction. Their ability to act independently and resist peer influences is weaker than that of adults. Fear of social rejection may lead youths to commit acts in groups that they would not commit alone.[65]

Interestingly, and perhaps not surprisingly, recent neurobiological research has established that the behaviour and attitudes of adolescents are reflected in their level of brain development.[66] While physical growth generally stops between the ages of 14 and 16 years, growth and development of the brain normally continues well past the age of 18. In particular, the prefrontal cortex — the part of the brain that governs judgment and self-control, as well as functions such as response inhibition, emotional regulation, planning and organization — develops quite significantly in late adolescence. An American law professor, Antoinette Clarke, has recently said:

> One of the main tasks of the brain, particularly of the prefrontal cortex, is to inhibit actions. As the brain develops through childhood and adolescence, it is this very inhibition machinery that is being fine-tuned. What can we expect of adolescents if that inhibition machinery, the prefrontal cortex, is not yet fully tuned? Children, including teenagers, may simply not be as capable at inhibiting behavior as adults. Coupled with a biological inability to understand the consequences of their actions, it has now become clear that adolescents are far less capable of choosing to obey the law than was previously thought.[67]

The incomplete brain development of adolescents helps to explain why they do not exercise better judgment about risk-taking and

65. Steinberg & Scott, *supra* note 61 at 1012; Scott & Grisso, *supra* note 10 at 162.

66. See *e.g.* C. Antoinette Clarke, "Bridging The Gap: An Interdisciplinary Approach To Juvenile Justice Policy" (2007) 56 DePaul L. Rev. 927; Robert M. Sapolsky, "The Frontal Cortex and the Criminal Justice System" in Semir Zeki & Oliver Goodenough, eds., *Law and the Brain* (New York: Oxford University Press, 2006) 227; Linda Patia Spear, "Neurobehavioral Changes in Adolescence" (2000) 9 Current Directions in Psychological Science 111; Elizabeth R. Sowell *et al.*, "*In Vivo* Evidence for Post-Adolescent Brain Maturation in Frontal and Striatal Regions" (1999) 2 Nature Neuroscience 859.

67. Clarke, *ibid.* at 935.

offending, and do not respond to the threat of sanctions in the same way as do adults.

VI. Deterrence and Youth Offending: Social Science Research

The weight of criminological research clearly rejects the view that harsher sentences can reduce levels of youth crime.[68] In addition, social science research concludes that changes in the *severity* of punishment of youth are ineffective in changing behaviour. However, the research also suggests that increasing the *likelihood* of apprehension and punishment may affect the behaviour of at least some youthful offenders.

For some anti-social youth, even a perceived increase in the likelihood both of being apprehended and of getting a severe sanction does not affect their offending behaviour.[69] Similarly, some studies on youth recidivism find no relationship between youths' perceptions of the likelihood of being sanctioned by the courts and their later criminal acts.[70] The authors of a study of 125 male street youth in Edmonton

68. See Marc Mauer & Malcolm C. Young, *Truths, Half-Truths, and Lies: Myths and Realities About Crime and Punishment* (Washington D.C.: The Sentencing Project, 1996); Daniel S. Nagin & Greg Pogarsky, "Integrating Celerity, Impulsivity, and Extralegal Sanction Threats into a Model of General Deterrence: Theory and Evidence" (2001) 39 Criminol. 865; Andrew Von Hirsch *et al.*, *Criminal Deterrence and Sentence Severity: An Analysis of Recent Research* (Oxford: Hart, 1999). There is an article by an economist who argues that youth are deterred by sanctions, though the study uses macro data and does not clearly distinguish between the effects of increasing the severity of sanctions (deterrence through sentencing) and increasing the likelihood of arrest (deterrence through law enforcement): Steven D. Levitt, "Juvenile Crime and Punishment" (1998) 106 Journal of Political Economy 1156. For a more polemical and theoretical piece advocating more severe sanctions on youth as a means of deterring youth crime, see Moin A. Yahya, "Deterring *Roper*'s Juveniles: Using a Law and Economics Approach to Show that the Logic of *Roper* Implies that Juveniles Require the Death Penalty More than Adults" (2006) 111 Penn St. L. Rev. 53.

69. Anne L. Schneider & Laurie Ervin, "Specific Deterrence, Rational Choice, and Decision Heuristics: Applications in Juvenile Justice (1990) 71 Social Science Quarterly 585.

70. *Ibid.* See also Wanda D. Foglia, "Perceptual Deterrence and the Mediating Effect of Internalized Norms Among Inner-City Teenagers" (1997) 34 Journal of Research in Crime and Delinquency 414.

concluded that serious violent activities on the street are guided by impulse and emotion.[71] The results of this study suggest that violent offences by homeless male street youth will not be deterred by policies that focus on the threats of criminal sanctions. However, their offending may be reduced by policies that increase youths' bonds to conventional society.[72] At least one study suggests that tough legal sanctions may actually lead to an increase in offending by members of "social out groups," who respond with defiance to the perceived illegitimacy of law enforcement officials.[73]

Politicians regularly propose changing the law to make it more likely that youths charged with the most serious offences will be treated as adults. Indeed, making it easier to impose adult-like sentences on young offenders was a part of the 2008 Conservative election platform. However, a significant amount of the research documenting the lack of deterrent effect of sentencing policy on youth behaviour has come from studies on the effects of adult sentences for serious adolescent offenders.

In the latter part of the twentieth century, a number of American states changed their legal regimes to facilitate adult sentences for adolescents. However, a number of studies arrive at similar conclusions about the lack of deterrent effect of the increase in the likelihood of an adult sanction being imposed on an adolescent offender.

A study of the effect of a change in New York law, which resulted in mandatory adult court trials and sanctions for certain serious violent offences committed by youths, concluded that the new law had no deterrent effect, despite the fact that it was widely used and publicized.[74] A study of the effect of a similar change in Idaho's law — mandatory adult trials, and adult sentences for certain violent crimes — found a 13 per cent *increase* in arrest rates for those offences after the law was

71. Stephen W. Baron & Leslie W. Kennedy, "Deterrence and Homeless Male Street Youths" (1998) 40 Can. J. Crim. 27.

72. *Ibid.*

73. Lawrence W. Sherman, "Defiance, Deterrence, and Irrelevance: A Theory of the Criminal Sanction" (1993) 30 Journal of Research in Crime and Delinquency 445.

74. Simon I. Singer & David McDowall "Criminalizing Delinquency: The Deterrent Effects of the New York Juvenile Offender Law" (1988) 22 Law & Soc'y Rev. 521.

implemented.[75] A more recent study, published in 2006, examined the effects of changes in the laws of 14 American states which made it easier to sanction serious juvenile offenders as adults.[76] This study found that the changes had no effect on levels of serious youth crime and concluded that this type of reform has no deterrent effect.

A number of American studies have concluded that the imposition of adult sentences does not reduce reoffending by youths who are given such sanctions, and the punishment may actually be criminogenic, in that it increases the likelihood of their reoffending. A Pennsylvania-based study, published in 2003, compared outcomes from a group of adolescents who received adult sentences with outcomes from another group who committed the same offences and had similar records but received youth sentences. Those who received adult sentences were more likely to be rearrested for a violent offence than those who were sentenced in youth court.[77] A Florida study published in 1997 came to a similar conclusion: youths transferred to adult court recidivated earlier and more often than a comparator group who had been dealt with in youth court.[78] These studies clearly support the conclusion that imposition of adult sentences does not have a specific deterrent effect but may actually increase the likelihood of further offending, especially if young offenders are placed in an adult facility where they are likely to be subject to stronger negative effects from other inmates.

There is, however, evidence that some youth can be deterred from offending by changes in the enforcement of the law. In Jacksonville, Florida, the local prosecutor instituted a policy of much more aggressive prosecution of serious youth offenders. This was reportedly

75. Eric L. Jensen & Linda K. Metsger, "A Test of the Deterrent Effect of Legislative Waiver on Violent Youth Crime" (1994) 40 Crime and Delinquency 96 at 101.

76. Benjamin Steiner & Emily Wright, "Assessing the Relative Effects of State Direct File Waiver Laws on Violent Juvenile Crime: Deterrence or Irrelevance?" (2006) 96 J. Crim. L. & Criminology 1451.

77. David L. Myers, "The Recidivism of Violent Youths in Juvenile and Adult Court: A Consideration of Selection Bias" (2003) 1 Youth Violence and Juvenile Justice 79.

78. Lawrence Winner *et al.*, "The Transfer of Juveniles to Criminal Court: Reexamining Recidivism Over the Long Term" (1997) 43 Crime and Delinquency 548.

accompanied by a 30 per cent reduction in youth crime in that city.[79] There is also evidence that some youth who pass the age of adult criminal responsibility (whether that age is 16 or 18) reduce their offending behaviour, or desist completely from it, because they know they will face completely different treatment if apprehended. This is the type of sentencing "bright line" that may have an effect on some adolescents.[80]

Recently, the United States Supreme Court considered the deterrent effect of the most serious sanction possible, the death penalty, on youthful offenders. In *Roper v. Simmons*, the Supreme Court ruled that the death penalty could not be used on persons under 18 years of age at the time of the offence because it is cruel and unusual punishment, and is hence unconstitutional. Writing for the majority of the Court, Justice Kennedy cited a body of sociological and psychological research which found that, compared to adults, juveniles lack maturity and a sense of responsibility. Justice Kennedy said:

> Once the diminished culpability of juveniles is recognized, it is evident that the penological justifications for the death penalty apply to them with lesser force than to adults. We have held there are two distinct social purposes served by the death penalty: "retribution and deterrence . . . ." As for deterrence, it is unclear whether the death penalty has a significant or even measurable deterrent effect on juveniles . . . In general we leave to legislatures the assessment of the efficacy of various criminal penalty schemes . . . Here, however, the absence of evidence of deterrent effect is of special concern because the same characteristics that render juveniles less culpable than adults suggest as well that juveniles will be less susceptible to deterrence. In particular . . . "[t]he likelihood that the teenage offender has made the kind of cost-benefit analysis that attaches any weight to the possibility of execution is so remote as to be virtually nonexistent."[81]

In sum, as the United States Supreme Court recognized in this judgment, there is now a significant body of social science research calling seriously into question the view that imposing heavier sanctions on adolescent offenders achieves either general or specific deterrence.

---

79. William J. Bennett, John J. Diiulio & John P. Walters, *Body Count: Moral Poverty . . . and How to Win America's War Against Crime and Drugs* (New York: Simon & Schuster, 1996) at 123.

80. Levitt, *supra* note 68.

81. *Roper v. Simmons*, 543 U.S. 551 at 571-72 (2005).

VII. Politics, Deterrence and Youth Crime

Before the coming into force of the *YOA* in 1984, youth justice policy in Canada was not heavily influenced by partisan concerns or public opinion;[82] the *YOA* was enacted with unanimous support in Parliament. However, over the last two decades, the emergence of public concern about the perceived level and seriousness of youth crime has been a significant catalyst for change in the Canadian youth justice system. Opinion polls in most Western nations reveal that the need for government responses to youth crime is now widely seen as an important issue.[83] Even though youth crime rates in Canada have not changed appreciably over the past few years, opinion polls repeatedly show that the public, at least outside of Quebec, perceives youth sentencing to be too lenient.[84] The idea that deterrence should be a main goal of sentencing is generally popular in Canada, though interestingly the public and government of Quebec have a less punitive and more rehabilitative approach to youth offending.[85]

As noted earlier in this paper, Bill C-25 and the 2008 Conservative election platform proposed to amend the *YCJA* by making deterrence an explicit principle of youth sentencing. The Conservative government clearly believes that this proposal has widespread public support, and that it is an expedient way to satisfy the political pressure to "get tough" on youth crime.[86] Justice Minister Rob Nicholson made the following comments in Parliament during second reading of Bill C-25 in November 2007:

---

82. Sanjeev S. Anand, "Catalyst for Change: The History of Canadian Juvenile Justice Reform" (1999) 24 Queen's L.J. 515.

83. Julian V. Roberts, Nicole Crutcher & Paul Verbrugge, "Public Attitudes to Sentencing in Canada: Exploring Recent Findings" (2007) 49 Can. J. Crim. 75 at 77.

84. *Ibid.*

85. Anthony N. Doob *et al.*, *An Exploration of Ontario Residents' Views of Crime and the Criminal Justice System* (Toronto: University of Toronto, Centre of Criminology, 1998). See also Anthony N. Doob, "Transforming the Punishment Environment: Understanding Public Views of what Should be Accomplished at Sentencing" (2000) 42 Can. J. Crim. 323.

86. Michael G. Turner *et al.*, "Public Tolerance for Community-Based Sanctions" (1997) 77 The Prison Journal 6.

> Last year the Supreme Court of Canada [in *R. v. B.W.P.*] ruled that the *Youth Criminal Justice Act* does not allow deterrence and denunciation to be considered by the courts as specific objectives of the courts when they are sentencing youth. These are important objectives we believe for judges to have when considering an appropriate sentence. Deterrence means imposing a sanction for the purpose of discouraging the offender and others from engaging in criminal conduct. Denunciation refers to society's condemnation of the offence. My proposed sentencing amendment would allow courts to consider both deterrence and denunciation as objectives in youth sentences . . . *Many Canadians are concerned about youth crime and believe that changes to sentences can be very helpful.* They want to stem the reported recent increase in violent youth crime . . . .[87]

Conservative Prime Minister Stephen Harper has been an outspoken critic of the *YCJA*, despite its success in dramatically reducing the use of courts and custody without increasing the overall youth crime rate. In June 2008, Prime Minister Harper characterized Canada's approach to handling young offenders as "an 'unmitigated failure,'" in that it did not "hold young lawbreakers responsible for their behaviour and . . . make them accountable to their victims and [society]."[88] Public opinion polls suggest that, outside Quebec, there is significant public support for this type of legislative change.[89]

The Conservative Party's 2008 election platform policy on youth crime went beyond the limited amendments in Bill C-25. That platform called for the changes set out in Bill C-25: that is, adding deterrence and denunciation as sentencing principles and changing the law on pre-trial detention. It also went much further to propose "automatic, stiffer sentences for persons 14 and older convicted of serious and violent crimes"[90] and provisions that would allow increased publication of the

87. *House of Commons Debates*, No. 021 (21 November 2007) at 1535 (Hon. Rob Nicholson) [emphasis added].

88. See James Cowan, "Harper vows changes to 'failed' youth justice act" *The Star Phoenix* (6 June 2008), online: CanWest News Service <http://www.canada.com/saskatoonstarphoenix/story.html?id=a69024fb-c635-4b23-af82-2ee5cb7ddea1>, reporting on a speech given by the Prime Minister to the Canadian Crime Victims Foundation in Vaughan, Ontario. See also "Cracking down on criminals and putting victims first" (6 June 2008), online: Office of the Prime Minister <http://www.pm.gc.ca/eng/media.asp?category=1&id=2137>.

89. Gloria Galloway, "Poll shows support for Tories' justice plan for youths" *The Globe and Mail* (26 September 2008) A13.

90. "Balancing Rehabilitation", *supra* note 17.

names of serious youthful offenders. Although there has been no general increase in youth crime since the *YCJA* came into effect, serious violent crimes have increased in some localities, most notably in Toronto. In 2006, the youth homicide rate in Canada spiked to its highest level in decades,[91] though it remains much lower than in the United States.[92] While there is public support for "toughening" the law, the other political parties rejected the Conservative approach in the 2008 election campaign on the basis that it would not reduce youth crime, with particularly strong opposition from the Quebec-based Bloc Québécois.[93]

Conclusion

We are not arguing that imposing sanctions on youth has no deterrent effect for adolescent offenders, but rather that *increasing the severity* of sanctions, by taking account of deterrence as an aggravating factor, will not reduce youth crime. As recognized in the *YCJA*, it is

---

91. Taylor-Butts & Bressan, *supra* note 4.

92. See *e.g.* Nicholas C. Bala *et al.*, *Juvenile Justice Systems: An International Comparison of Problems and Solutions* (Toronto: Thompson Educational, 2002).

93. See "Conservatives vow to toughen youth justice act" (22 September 2008), online: CBC News <http://www.cbc.ca/news/canadavotes/story/2008/09/22/harper-elxn.html>:

> Liberals said the Conservative proposal won't make Canada safer and compared it to attempts in several U.S. states, where they claim slapping young people with harsher sentences failed to reduce crime rates.
>
> "It's the wrong approach," Liberal Leader Stéphane Dion said . . . Dion said his party's platform contained a crime-reduction strategy based on the approaches of previous Liberal governments, which he said have brought the lowest crime rate in 20 years.
>
> Bloc Leader Gilles Duceppe also decried the Tory plan.
>
> "This is the Republican way of the United States, more people in prison, more arms in circulation," Duceppe said Monday. "I don't want to live in that society."

See also *e.g.* John Barber, "Ontario and Quebec: Partners in crime-fighting" *The Globe and Mail* (8 October 2008), online: Globe and Mail <http://www.theglobeandmail.com/servlet/story/GAM.20081008.BARBER08/TPStory/TP Comment>; and see Shannon Kari, "Candidates still believe crime pays: Play on public's concerns to win votes" *National Post* (6 October 2008), online: National Post <http://www.nationalpost.com/news/canada/election-2008/story.html?id=862382>.

important that young offenders are held accountable for their acts, and that sentences are proportionate to the seriousness of their crimes. To the extent that youths are aware of the fact that they will be held accountable, as Justice Charron noted in *R. v. B.W.P.*, the youth justice system may have "the effect of deterring the young person [being sentenced] and others from committing crimes," even if deterrence is not an explicit aggravating factor in youth sentencing.[94] Although the weight of social science evidence establishes that increases in the *severity* of sanctions imposed on youth offenders will not reduce youth crime rates, an awareness of an increased *likelihood* of apprehension may well deter youth crime.

If this type of law is enacted, its impact on the youth justice system will of course depend on the exact wording of the new provisions and any other changes to the *YCJA*, as well as on the attitudes of the youth court judges who are applying the law. The survey data in this paper suggests that, at least initially, a significant number of youth court judges will take any change in the law that reintroduces the concept of deterrence as a principle of youth sentencing as a signal to increase the use of custody, though other judges may give this factor little or no weight. The ultimate impact of any changes will depend on the interpretation by the appellate courts. Given the historical controversy over the significance of deterrence in youth sentencing, the issue of the interpretation of the new law will very likely have to be resolved by the Supreme Court of Canada.

It can be argued that the provisions in Bill C-25 were not intended to dramatically increase the use of custody. If this had been the intention, Parliament would have also amended section 39(1) and expanded the "custody gateways," or even eliminated them and allowed custodial sentences for any offence. Bill C-25 did not remove any of the sentencing principles now set out in section 38, nor did it change any of the statements in the Preamble and Declaration of Principle (section 3), all of which continue to emphasize the limited use of custody for youth. Further, as recognized by the Supreme Court in *R. v. J.J.M.*, if deterrence is included as a principle of youth sentencing, it is to be given less

94. *Supra* note 12 at para. 4.

weight than for adults.[95] While Bill C-25 was intended to honour the Conservative commitment in the 2006 election campaign to add deterrence (and denunciation) as sentencing principles, it does not seem to have been intended to significantly increase the use of custody.

It has been said that it is easier to be "tough on crime" than to be "smart on crime."[96] The prevailing rhetoric, and most recent proposed Conservative amendments, suggest that there is a desire to be seen as "getting tough" on youth crime, even though social science research raises very serious doubts about whether tougher sanctions will reduce youth crime rates.[97] This paper has presented survey data on the impact that deterrence-based policies may have on levels of custody. Judges under the *YOA* who believed in the importance of deterrence were more likely to escalate sanctions toward custody and to use custody as a

95. *Supra* note 20.

96. *Supra* note 2 at 214.

97. A recent report from England raises serious doubts about the effect of youth justice policy on youth crime: see Enver Solomon & Richard Garside, *Ten Years of Labour's Youth Justice Reforms: An Independent Audit* (London: Centre for Crime and Justice Studies, King's College, May 2008). Prior to the 1997 general election, youth crime had become a major political battleground. The youth justice system in England was criticized by commentators from across the political spectrum as being too soft on young criminals. In 1997 the Labour government was elected on a platform that promised a "root and branch reform" of youth justice "to prevent offending" and tackle what it described as the emergence of "an excuse culture." The *Crime and Disorder Act* ((U.K.), 1998, c. 37) introduced major changes to the youth justice system. Since then, spending on youth justice has substantially increased, but much of the new money is being spent on custody. Between 2003 and 2006 there was an eight per cent increase in use of youth custody, but there has been no apparent effect on youth crime as measured by either police statistics or self-report studies. Solomon and Garside conclude (at 13-14, 16-17):

> [I]t is far from clear what impact the youth justice system, however reformed, will have on levels of youth crime and on levels of safety and victimisation experienced by children and young people. It has long been recognised by many criminologists that crime levels and crime patterns are a product of a complex interplay of social processes. At any given time, factors such as employment levels, relative levels of income inequality, demographic breakdown, cultural practices and a society's technological progress will have an impact on levels of crime and safety . . . . It is significant that Labour chose to place great emphasis on the youth justice system as a means of dealing with deeply rooted social problems. As will become clear at various stages in this report, this emphasis was arguably misplaced, even if the aspiration to deal with such social problems was appropriate.

"short, sharp, shock." We recognize that adding deterrence as a principle of youth sentencing may, superficially, be good politics, but it is not good public policy and will not increase public safety. It may, however, have an effect on some youth court judges, who may impose more severe sentences and increase the use of custodial sentences for youth offenders.

The post-election Conservative government will undoubtedly try to introduce some type of new youth justice legislation, but it remains to be seen whether it will be generally consistent with the modest reforms of Bill C-25 or will be a major and much broader revision of the *YCJA*. We submit that it would be preferable not to enact a law that reintroduces deterrence as a principle of youth sentencing.[98] If such a law is enacted, we would argue that judges should apply the principle of deterrence in a narrow fashion, consistent with the interests of youth and society, recognizing that youth crime is not deterred by the imposition of more severe sentences. If, despite the arguments made here, amendments are made to the *YCJA* that result in a considerable

98. The Conservative proposal was also recently criticized by retired Nova Scotia Supreme Court Justice Merlin Nunn, who wrote a major report on the youth justice system in that province. The Conservatives maintained that his report influenced their proposals. See Cristin Schmitz, "Ex-judge slams election pledge to hike prison terms for youths" *The Lawyers Weekly* (10 October 2008). She writes:

> Sentencing young offenders to longer jail terms may be "politically appealing" to some, but it's ineffective, "revenge-based" criminal justice policy, says the retired judge who did an in-depth review of the *Youth Criminal Justice Act* (*YCJA*) two years ago.
>
> Former Nova Scotia Supreme Court Justice Merlin Nunn spoke out after Prime Minister Stephen Harper pledged during the federal election campaign last month to scrap the *YCJA*, while "enhancing" prison sentences for young offenders, including hiking the maximum youth sentence for murder from 10 years to life in prison and up to 14 years for other violent offences.
>
> Harper stated "many" of his reforms were based on the 2006 Nunn Report, but Nunn . . . flatly disagrees with the thrust of the Conservative plan to bring forward harsher sentences and longer jail terms.
>
> "I don't think it's a good idea. I don't think it's wise," he opined . . . .
>
> "There is no proof that long sentences are going to do anything except sometimes make things worse because the young kid sentenced to a longer term in prison [to be served partially] in an adult prison, is going to come out. And he may very well be a lot worse than he was when he went in," observed Nunn.

increase in the use of custody for youth, this would impose serious human costs on youth, and substantial financial costs on provincial correctional authorities, without increasing public safety.

[6]

ENVISIONING A JUVENILE JUSTICE SYSTEM THAT SUPPORTS POSITIVE YOUTH DEVELOPMENT†

JAMES M. FRABUTT*
KRISTEN L. DI LUCA**
KELLY N. GRAVES***

INTRODUCTION

Is it possible to envision a juvenile justice system in this country that seeks to uphold and protect community safety but also offers youth an opportunity for change, restitution, and rehabilitation? Should we envision such a possibility? And, would we even be satisfied with it if it came to fruition? We believe that we can and should. Moreover, we are not alone in advocating for a significant paradigm shift in re-framing the role and function of the American juvenile justice system. Numerous child advocates, scholars, and practitioners have issued a clarion call for an integrated system that meets youths' needs with a system of services and support wholly focused on helping them become sta-

† On November 7, 2007, the *Notre Dame Journal of Law, Ethics & Public Policy* hosted a panel discussion entitled, "Lost Innocence: Hope and Punishment in the Juvenile Justice System." Dr. Frabutt's remarks have been revised and incorporated into this article.

* Faculty member in the Alliance for Catholic Education Leadership Program and Concurrent Associate Professor of Psychology at the University of Notre Dame; B.A., Psychology, University of Notre Dame; M.A. & Ph.D., Human Development and Family Studies, University of North Carolina at Greensboro.

** Research Associate and Evaluation Manager for the Center for Youth, Family, and Community Partnerships at the University of North Carolina at Greensboro; B.A., Psychology, Humboldt State University. Mrs. Di Luca serves as a research partner for the Middle District of North Carolina Project Safe Neighborhoods initiatives, a data-driven strategy to reduce gun- and gang-related violence in eight city- and county-wide collaboratives in the District.

*** Associate Director of the Center for Youth, Family, and Community Partnerships at the University of North Carolina at Greensboro; B.A., Psychology, Virginia Polytechnic Institute; M.A., Psychology, Wake Forest University; Ph.D., Psychology, University of North Carolina at Greensboro.

ble, competent adults.[1] This article reaffirms the case for a positive youth development orientation in the juvenile justice system. The juvenile system of North Carolina is used as a frame of reference to describe several leverage points for building a justice system that makes such an approach a reality:

- engaging a system-wide focus and commitment to treatment, rehabilitation, and restoration;
- proactively addressing the mental-health issues of court-involved youth;
- granting specialized attention to the facility-to-community transition process for incarcerated youth;
- investing fiscal, social, and human capital in the power of prevention, relying on a network of evidence-based, cost-effective, community-based programs.

I. Linking Positive Youth Development with Juvenile Justice

Positive youth development, an approach that gained significant traction beginning in the 1990s, upholds the notion that youth are one of our most significant assets. And like all assets that one cherishes, youth as a whole must be developed, protected, cultivated, and secured.[2] More than just a series of programs or interventions, positive youth development "is a new philosophical foundation for youth services that views youth as resources rather than only the recipients of services, and also seeks to involve youth actively in the programs and activities designed to benefit them."[3] Butts, Mayer, and Ruth described positive youth development as an "alternative to viewing adolescent development through the lens of problems and deficits."[4] Instead, positive youth development focuses on strengthening protection in youths' lives while simultaneously reducing risk.

1. *E.g.*, William H. Barton, *Bridging Juvenile Justice and Positive Youth Development*, *in* The Youth Development Handbook 77 (Stephen F. Hamilton & Mary Agnes Hamilton eds., 2004); Gordon Bazemore & W. Clinton Terry, *Developing Delinquent Youths: A Reintegrative Model for Rehabilitation and a New Role for the Juvenile Justice System*, 75 Child Welfare 665 (1997); Jeffrey Butts et al., *Focusing Juvenile Justice on Positive Youth Development*, Chapin Hall Issue Brief, Oct. 2005; Robert Schwartz, *Juvenile Justice and Positive Youth Development*, *in* Applied Developmental Science 353 (Richard M. Lerner et al. eds., 2004).

2. For an overview on positive youth development, see The Youth Development Handbook, *supra* note 1; Trends in Youth Development (Peter L. Benson & Karen Johnson Pittman eds., 2001).

3. George E. Capowich, *Implementing Positive Youth Development in Juvenile Justice*, *in* Am. Youth Pol'y Forum et al., Contract with America's Youth 54, 54 (Samuel Halperin et al. eds., 1995).

4. Butts et al., *supra* note 1, at 4.

The notion is to move beyond simple risk avoidance—for that will never be enough to ensure well-being—and capitalize on building resilience through competency development.[5] This notion stands in contrast to traditional approaches: "While service programs based on deficit or 'medical model' assumptions have come to dominate the youth policy landscape, most people become conventional adults as they gain experience in responsible institutional roles at work, in the family, and through key community networks."[6] Therefore, it is imperative to cultivate youth competencies across cognitive, social, moral, emotional, and behavioral domains such as interpersonal social skills, positive identity development, academic competency, personal contentment, and social engagement.

Several emergent frameworks encapsulating the processes of positive youth development exist. Villarruel and colleagues have outlined the Community Youth Development Model.[7] Their conceptualization is important because it underscores the role of the community and the importance of community institutions to foster opportunities for youth engagement. The Search Institute has developed another well-known approach focused on forty developmental assets.[8] External assets are the positive experiences received from peers, adults, parents, and social/educational settings. These assets are focused on support and empowerment, boundaries and expectations, and constructive use of time. Internal assets are the characteristics possessed by individual youth that elicit positive growth and development. These assets are focused on positive values, social competencies, and commitment to learning. A model developed by Lerner and colleagues is a third integrative approach to positive youth development that emphasizes youth-environment interactions and highlights attributes among youth known as the five Cs—competence, confidence, connection, caring, and character.[9]

5. *See* Stephen F. Hamilton et al., *Principles for Youth Development, in* THE YOUTH DEVELOPMENT HANDBOOK, *supra* note 1, at 3, 10.

6. Bazemore & Terry, *supra* note 1, at 666.

7. Daniel F. Perkins et al., *Community Youth Development: Partnership Creating a Positive World, in* COMMUNITY YOUTH DEVELOPMENT 1 (Franscisco A. Vallarruel et al. eds., 2003).

8. *See* Peter L. Benson & Peter C. Scales, *Developmental Assets, in* ENCYCLOPEDIA OF APPLIED DEVELOPMENTAL SCIENCE 342 (Celia B. Fisher & Richard M. Lerner eds., 2005).

9. Richard M. Lerner et al., *Toward a New Vision and Vocabulary About Adolescence: Theoretical and Empirical Bases of a "Positive Youth Development" Perspective, in* CHILD PSYCHOLOGY 445, 448–49 (Lawrence Balter & Catherine S. Tamis-LeMonda eds., 2006).

All these frameworks have several elements in common: a reliance on youth strengths instead of deficits; clear acknowledgement that youth are shaped by (and have the ability to shape) multiple social contexts beyond their family (schools, neighborhood organizations, churches, and social programs); and an understanding that youth pro-social development is greatly fostered through high-quality relationships with caring adults. With that array of convictions in place, isn't it time to more fully integrate the tenets of positive youth development with juvenile justice? As Schwartz noted, "embracing the principles of [positive youth development] remains our best hope for creating a future that welcomes the majority of our children."[10]

II. Focusing on Treatment

The first leverage point for embracing a positive youth development approach is to create a juvenile justice system that is essentially focused on treatment and rehabilitation. Although true to its roots and firmly planted in the bedrock of the American system of juvenile justice, rehabilitation has not always been embraced as a guiding mantra. In fact, when the history of the juvenile justice system in this country is reviewed, one observes dramatic shifts of the pendulum from punishment to rehabilitation.[11] Not surprisingly, some of these pendulum swings often coincide with election cycles. In the not-too-distant past, for example, in various states across the country, policymakers and leaders in the corrections field felt that "nothing works" in terms of correctional treatment,[12] so there was a subsequent movement away from rehabilitation and a focus on being "tough on crime." There was a "lock 'em up" mentality, in which out of sight meant out of mind; treatment efforts languished while punishments and sanctions reigned. However, offenders almost always go back to the families, neighborhoods, and communities from which they came, and if their mindset is not changed while incarcerated, the criminal cycle simply begins again. This is particularly disheartening in light of the fact that the correctional community is well aware of several approaches that do work, especially

10. Schwartz, *supra* note 1, at 372.

11. *See* Schwartz, *supra* note 1, at 355–60.

12. *See* James C. Howell, Youth Violence and Juvenile Justice 20 (1997) (discussing the "Just Deserts" reform movement); Panel on Research on Rehabilitative Techniques, Nat'l Research Council, The Rehabilitation of Criminal Offenders 88 (Lee Sechrest et al. eds., 1979) (taking the position that contemporary rehabilitative techniques are limited, if not altogether ineffective, and require more study and innovation).

for juvenile offenders, and they all fall broadly under the category of treatment and rehabilitation.[13]

One example from a system that is equally focused on public safety and youth rehabilitation can be observed in new approaches to secure confinement in North Carolina. A movement toward juvenile justice reform in North Carolina began in earnest during the 1990s with changes to the state juvenile code. In 2000, then-Governor Jim Hunt created a cabinet-level department to carry forth the new code, entrusted to the new Department of Juvenile Justice and Delinquency Prevention (DJJDP). Since that time, North Carolina has completely revamped its approach to juvenile prisons in the state. These facilities—called Youth Development Centers (YDCs)—used to be large institutional facilities much like adult prisons. In response to H1414-Sec. 16.3, the DJJDP recommended that small, community-connected facilities replace YDCs. Originally there were only five such facilities to serve the entire state; new plans called for the construction of thirteen smaller, more geographically dispersed facilities. With the backing of the state legislature, the DJJDP adopted a new model featuring YDCs that are markedly different on several levels: size, design, campus layout, schedule, staffing patterns, and an array of on-site services and supports.[14] All of those changes were conceived with one goal in mind: creating a therapeutic environment to break the cycle of criminal offenses.[15]

More than just a buzzword or the latest fad, creating a "therapeutic environment" represents a paradigm shift in treating youthful offenders. To cast a therapeutic environment in a state's most secure facilities, reserved for the most challenging juvenile offenders, requires a commitment that transcends environmental space, resources, and time allocation. As described by the DJJDP, "The environment is the treatment; therefore, every part of every

13. *See* Clive R. Hollin, *Treatment Programs for Offenders: Meta-Analysis, "What Works," and Beyond*, 22 INT'L J.L. & PSYCHIATRY 361 (1999) (describing meta-analysis methods to provide data on rehabilitation programs that work); Mark Lipsey & David B. Wilson, *Effective Intervention for Serious Juvenile Offenders: A Synthesis of Longitudinal Research*, *in* SERIOUS & VIOLENT JUVENILE OFFENDERS 313 (Rolf Loeber & David P. Farrington eds., 1998) (utilizing meta-analysis to identify and evaluate the effectiveness of intervention for serious juvenile offenders).

14. George Sweat, N.C. Dep't of Juvenile Justice & Delinqency Prevention, North Carolina's Juvenile Justice Reform: Keys to Success (Aug. 2006) (accompanying slides on file with author).

15. *See* N.C. DEP'T OF JUVENILE JUSTICE & DELINQENCY PREVENTION, ANNUAL REPORT 2 (2006), *available at* http://www.ncdjjdp.org/resources/pdf_documents/annual_report_2006.pdf.

day is planned and implemented to support treatment and development."[16] The prevailing notion is that every staff member, every interaction, every activity that transpires within the YDC is an agent of change. Focused therapeutic interactions, coupled with educational, clinical, health, and other services should thereby comprise a majority of youths' in-facility time, up to 80%.[17] Key elements of the therapeutic approach in practice are outlined below.[18]

- Youth receive thorough assessment of strengths and needs at intake. Prior to entering a YDC, each youth spends time at the Assessment and Treatment Planning Center to derive an individualized service plan. Each youth thus arrives at the YDC with clearly articulated goals, recommended strategies and interventions to reach those goals, and guidelines to monitor progress.
- There is a four-to-one staffing ratio within the YDC. Building on the notion that adult role models serve as the basis of positive, pro-social interactions, youth have the opportunity to develop deeper, more constant relationships with staff members. Through regular, consistent, one-on-one interactions, staff uphold high expectations for youth along with support and firmness to reach them. Interactions with every staff member in the building are possible teachable moments, predicated on the rationale that modifying youths' thinking is what ultimately changes their behavior.
- Since youth admitted to YDCs are, on average, three to four grade levels behind their peers in reading and mathematics, the educational needs of the juveniles are addressed through developmentally appropriate approaches to instruction. This may include differentiated instruction, integrative education, and an interdisciplinary studies curriculum. On any given day, youth will spend seven hours in a structured, school-like instructional environment.

16. *Therapeutic Environment Training Gets Underway*, DJJDP NEWS EXPRESS (N.C. Dep't of Juvenile Justice & Delinqency Prevention, Raleigh, N.C.), Feb. 2006, at 1, *available at* http://www.ncdjjdp.org/resources/pdf_documents/news_express_archive/2006_february.pdf.

17. *See* Lawrence W. Sherman et al., *Preventing Crime: What Works, What Doesn't, What's Promising*, NAT'L INST. OF JUST.: RES. IN BRIEF (U.S. Dep't of Justice, Wash. D.C.), July 1998, at 1.

18. For further discussion of the therapeutic approach, see Sweat, *supra* note 14; N.C. Dep't of Juvenile Justice & Delinqency Prevention, DJJDP Response to H1414-16.3 (Nov. 23, 2004), http://www.ncdjjdp.org/facilities/future_facilities.html (follow title hyperlink).

- Every youth in a YDC receives intensive services such as counseling, therapy, and instruction in critical life skills. Depending on the needed services outlined in their individualized plan, youth may receive treatment for substance abuse, serious emotional disturbance, and/or sexual behavior problems. Intensive case management supports the proper array of programming to ensure efficacy.
- YDCs are purposely being built in closer proximity to the population centers that have typically had the most youth in treatment. More community connectedness means that the facilities are open to parent and family involvement in the rehabilitation process. This may take the form of parenting groups, family therapy, and programs to enhance family communication and discipline practices. Caregivers are encouraged to commit to ongoing involvement in their child's treatment through regular visits, participation in service team meetings, and frequent phone contact with staff.
- Planning for release from the YDC begins on the day that a youth arrives there. That is, community reintegration is not viewed as a discrete, culminating event. Instead, progress toward goals is monitored all along with an eye toward the transition from secure confinement to one's home community. Advance planning is crucial to making sure that necessary services and supports are in place in the designated discharge environment.

The full theoretical framework and slate of treatment options is more extensive than elaborated upon here. In addition to the highlighted points, the YDC programming continuum provides health services, a recreation program, gender-specific programming for females, and a commitment to delivering services in a way that is culturally competent. While the coverage here of North Carolina's emerging model of secure facilities for juveniles is not exhaustive, the central point should be clear: the YDC staff commits on a daily basis to reduce the risk factors in a child's life and to build on the protective factors that will keep that child crime-free for the long-term.

III. Juvenile Offending and Mental Health

A second major leverage point is to acknowledge the important nexus between juvenile offending and mental health and substance abuse issues. Researchers have documented that between 40 and 90% of children and adolescents involved in the juvenile justice system also suffer from a mental illness compared to 18–22% of the general youth population.[19] Additionally, as many as 50% of offending children have co-occurring substance use problems.[20] One study indicated that two-thirds of juvenile detainees in the baseline sample had one or more alcohol, drug, and/or mental disorders.[21] In fact, the vast majority of youth in the juvenile justice system have multiple mental health diagnoses—with one large multi-state, multi-system study reporting that 60% of youth had *three or more* co-occurring mental health diagnoses.[22] Given the astounding prevalence of mental health issues, it is likely that children's mental health and substance abuse problems play major roles in their offending behaviors.

In terms of specific mental health diagnoses, disruptive behavior disorders such as conduct disorders are often the first disorders to be diagnosed.[23] However, other more "hidden" disorders also are common. Cauffman and Grisso reported that while anxiety disorders impact 3–13% of the general youth population, they might impact about 6–41% of the juvenile justice population.[24] Other estimates indicate that 84–94% of juvenile offenders reported a history of trauma, with girls being more likely to meet criteria for post-traumatic stress disorder (PTSD) than boys.[25] A history of trauma increases the risk of arrest by 59% and of committing a violent crime by 30%.[26] The mental health consequences of trauma among girls may explain why the violent crime index has increased 25% for girls between 1992

19. *See* ALAN E. KAZDIN, PSYCHOTHERAPY FOR CHILDREN AND ADOLESCENTS 23, 29 (2000); Linda A. Teplin et al., *Psychiatric Disorders in Youth in Juvenile Detention*, 59 ARCHIVES GEN. PSYCHIATRY 1133, 1137 (2002); Linda A. Teplin, Assessing Alcohol, Drug, and Mental Disorders in Juvenile Detainees, ODJJP FACT SHEET (U.S. Dep't Justice, Wash., D.C.), Jan. 2001, *available at* http://www.ncjrs.gov/pdffiles1/ojjdp/fs200102.pdf.

20. Carol MacKinnon-Lewis, Martha Kauffman & James M. Frabutt, *Juvenile Justice and Mental Health: Youth and Families in the Middle*, 7 AGGRESSION & VIOLENT BEHAV. 353, 354 (2002).

21. *See* David Huizinga et al., *Co-occurrence of Delinquency and Other Problem Behaviors*, ODJJP JUV. JUST. BULLETIN (U.S. Dep't of Justice, Wash. D.C.), Nov. 2000, at tbl. 1.

22. KATHLEEN R. SKOWYRA & JOSEPH J. COCOZZA, NAT'L CTR. FOR MENTAL HEALTH & JUVENILE JUSTICE, BLUEPRINT FOR CHANGE 3 (2007).

23. *See id.* at 128.

24. Elizabeth Cauffman & Thomas Grisso, *Mental Health Issues Among Minority Offenders in the Juvenile Justice System*, *in* OUR CHILDREN, THEIR CHILDREN 390, 398 (Darnell F. Hawkins & Kimberly Kempf-Leonard eds., 2005).

25. Karen A. Abram et al., *Posttraumatic Stress Disorder and Trauma in Youth in Juvenile Detention*, 61 ARCHIVES GEN. PSYCHIATRY 403, 405–06, 408 (2004).

26. Cathy S. Widom, *Victims of Childhood Sexual Abuse—Later Criminal Consequences*, NAT'L INST. OF JUST.: RES. IN BRIEF, (U.S. Dep't of Justice, Wash. D.C.), Mar. 1997, at 5–7.

and 1996, although there were no increases for boys.[27] Exposure to trauma also increases the risk of substance use, which may explain the increase in arrests for drug abuse violations among adolescent females.[28] With these gender differences and the unique precursors to violence among girls,[29] juvenile justice programs should be cognizant that trauma-sensitive and gender-specific treatment models are needed to prevent future offending behaviors.

According to the National Mental Health Association, few of the youth entering the juvenile justice system receive adequate screening, assessment, or treatment.[30] Unfortunately, despite the substantially higher rates of mental health disorders among these youth, services and approaches are fraught with barriers including inadequate assessment, fragmentation, and deficit-based intervention.[31] To address this issue, professionals are charged with conducting comprehensive and strengths-based assessments that include mental health symptoms.[32] Strengths-based assessments are important because, historically, youth-serving agencies have utilized a deficit-based model, where attention was largely devoted to the deficits and problems regarding the child and family. However, Barnard posited that using such paradigms results in a failure to capitalize on available resources that can be considered tools for change.[33] That is, if a deficit-based paradigm is utilized, deficits will be the highlight of both assessment and treatment, preventing the recognition and utilization of strengths. In contrast, strengths-based paradigms shift the focus away from deficits by devoting attention to the strengths and resources within the child and family, and then incorporate those strengths into treatment planning.

Within strengths-based assessment, it is important to espouse an ecological approach to obtain a comprehensive picture of youth and their surroundings. These ecological factors can

---

27. Kimberly J. Budnick & Ellen Shields-Fletcher, *What About Girls?*, OJJDP FACT SHEET 1 (U.S. Dep't of Justice, Wash., D.C.), Sept. 1998, *available at* http://www.ncjrs.gov/pdffiles/fs-9884.pdf.

28. *Id.*

29. *See generally* Kelly N. Graves, *Not Always Sugar and Spice: Expanding Theoretical and Functional Explanations for Why Females Aggress*, 12 AGGRESSION & VIOLENT BEHAV. 131 (2007) (explaining why certain risk and protective factors appear to be stronger predictors of female violence than male violence).

30. *See* Nat'l Mental Health Ass'n, Justice for Juveniles, http://www1.nmha.org/children/justjuv/execsum.cfm (last visited Feb. 27, 2008).

31. *See* MacKinnon-Lewis et al., *supra* note 20, at 353.

32. *See* RONALD J. STERNBERG, PSYCHOLOGY 101 ½, at 83–87 (2004).

33. *See* Charles P. Barnard, *Resiliency: A Shift in Our Perception*, 22 AM. J. FAM. THERAPY 135, 143 (1994).

include person-level factors (e.g., anxiety, depression, inattention, trauma history), family-level factors (e.g., caregiver strain, history of parental violence), and school-level factors (e.g., attendance, academic performance, extracurricular activities).[34] Given that serious offenders often have complex needs, it is imperative that professionals understand youth behavior in context rather than as isolated incidents if we are to successfully intervene. Failure to do so raises the question: Are we incarcerating youth not because of their crimes, but because of our failure to address the possible mental health antecedents of their offending behavior?

During ethnographic interviews completed in North Carolina, one mother confided that she committed her child to the juvenile justice system so that she could get the appropriate mental health services for him.[35] Others have noted this "back door" approach to receiving necessary mental health treatment: "In states where mental health services are scarce, youth who need treatment may enter the juvenile justice system because that is the only place they can receive treatment."[36] In many cases, some parents are forced to give up their parental rights to allow their troubled children to receive mental health services.[37] Data from the "Pathways to Desistance" study conducted through the MacArthur Network on Adolescent Development and Juvenile Justice have supported this claim, with those who were institutionalized in state-run facilities being more likely to receive services than youth who were based in the community and receiving services from contracted residential providers.[38] Clearly, there is a need for greater identification and provision of mental

34. For a full review of these factors, see Kelly N. Graves, James M. Frabutt & Terri L. Shelton, *Factors Associated with Mental Health and Juvenile Justice Involvement Among Children with Severe Emotional Disturbance*, 5 YOUTH VIOLENCE & JUV. JUST. 147 (2007).

35. James M. Frabutt, Carol MacKinnon-Lewis & Brad S. Moorefield, *The Social Context of Delinquency: An Ethnographic Perspective of Court-Adjudicated Youth* (Apr. 2002) (unpublished poster presented at the Ninth Biennial Meeting of the Society for Research on Adolescence, New Orleans, L.A., on file with author).

36. FED. ADVISORY COMM. ON JUVENILE JUSTICE, ANNUAL REPORT 2007, at 10 (2007) [hereinafter ANNUAL REPORT 2007].

37. PRESIDENT'S NEW FREEDOM COMM'N ON MENTAL HEALTH, ACHIEVING THE PROMISE: TRANSFORMING MENTAL HEALTH CARE IN AMERICA 33 (2003), *available at* http://www.mentalhealthcommission.gov/reports/reports.htm (follow "Download Report in PDF Format" hyperlink) [hereinafter ACHIEVING THE PROMISE].

38. Edward P. Mulvey et al., *Theory and Research on Desistance from Antisocial Activity Among Serious Adolescent Offenders*, 2 YOUTH VIOLENCE & JUV. JUST. 213 (2004).

health services, as well as greater system-wide collaboration. Such efforts are in line with recent recommendations advocating for cross-system service planning in which juvenile justice personnel can participate in mental-health treatment planning through the creation of child and family teams, and mental-health staff can be housed within juvenile justice facilities.[39]

IV. Addressing the Process of Offender Reentry

The third major leverage point is to address the critical transition phase known as offender reentry. "Reentry refers to the process and experience of reentering society after a term of incarceration."[40] It is the term given to the facility-to-community transition experiences of offenders. The federal government recently responded to the scope and importance of the reentry issue by providing nearly $100 million to states through the Serious and Violent Offender Reentry Initiative.[41] But why is reentry such a critical juncture in the cycle of offending? Reentry is a serious public health issue because the return of high-risk offenders to the community has been a significant source of violent crime in the U.S.[42]

In 2006, over 650,000 prisoners were released to home communities across the country. Over twelve million adults were released from local jails. The majority of adults released are not on any formal supervision, leaving them on their own to navigate a successful transition back into a community that is often not equipped to meet their needs.[43] These adults are faced with multiple barriers including limited access to housing, education, job training, employment, mental health and substance abuse treatment, and family and social support networks. They often reenter society in a vulnerable state—concerned about how they will negotiate a daily routine in normal society and in fear of fail-

39. Achieving the Promise, *supra* note 37, at 35–37, 43.

40. Daniel P. Mears & Jeremy Travis, *Youth Development and Reentry*, 2 Youth Violence & Juv. Just. 3, 5 (2004).

41. For information on and evaluation of the Serious and Violent Offender Reentry Initiative, see the website, Serious and Violent Offender Reentry Initiative Multi-Site Evaluation, https://www.svori-evaluation.org (last visited Mar. 6, 2008).

42. *See* Timothy A. Hughes, Doris J. Wilson & Allen J. Beck, U.S. Dep't of Justice, Trends in State Parole, 1990–2000, at 8 (2001), *available at* http://www.ojp.usdoj.gov/bjs/pub/pdf/tsp00.pdf ("A majority of released State prisoners had been in prison before and were returned to prison for new offenses or parole violations.").

43. *See* Nancy G. La Vigne et al., Prisoner Reentry and Community Policing 3–4 (2006), *available at* http://www.urban.org/UploadedPDF/411061_COPS_reentry_monograph.pdf.

ure.[44] Roughly two-thirds of released offenders are rearrested and one-half are re-incarcerated within three years of release from prison.[45]

The impact on children and families is severe. One-and-a-half million children have a parent in prison.[46] In addition to practical stresses on the family and issues of post-traumatic stress that are often unrecognized and/or untreated, children whose parents have been incarcerated are also more likely to have longer and more serious histories of delinquency than children with parents who have not been incarcerated.[47] Moreover, there is little conflict within criminology research that criminal history is one of the biggest indicators of recidivism. The rate of offending is known to rise as youthful offenders age, then level off, and eventually decline into older age. Therefore, the earlier youth become involved in criminal activity, the more likely they are to follow a pattern of increased criminal activity and increased severity of criminal activity until they reach the "age-crime curve" plateau.[48]

In 2004, there were roughly 200,000 juveniles and young adults (under the age of twenty-four) returning home from juvenile correctional facilities and state or federal prisons. Their needs are much more severe than those of adults because they are compounded by multiple issues. Few of these youth and young adults receive adequate treatment and support during incarceration. Like adults, many have substance abuse, mental health, or physical health problems; several of them have children of their own. Many will return to communities that are marked by high rates of crime, poverty, unemployment, homelessness, and substance abuse. Most return to dysfunctional homes that are similarly blighted.[49]

---

44. *See generally* CHRISTY A. VISHER & SHANNON M.E. COURTNEY, URBAN INST. JUSTICE POL'Y CTR., ONE YEAR OUT (2007), *available at* http://www.urban.org/UploadedPDF/311445_One_Year.pdf (studying the experiences of released prisoners in the Cleveland, Ohio area).

45. PATRICK A. LANGAN & DAVID J. LEVIN, U.S. DEP'T OF JUSTICE, RECIDIVISM OF PRISONERS RELEASED IN 1994, at 1 (2002), *available at* http://www.ojp.usdoj.gov/bjs/pub/pdf/rpr94.pdf.

46. *See* VISHER & COURTNEY, *supra* note 44, at 4.

47. Anne M. Dannerbeck, *Differences in Parenting Attributes, Experiences, and Behaviors of Delinquent Youth with and without a Parental History of Incarceration*, 3 J. YOUTH VIOLENCE & JUV. JUST. 199, 209 (2005).

48. AVINASH S. BHATI, URBAN INST. JUSTICE POL'Y CTR., STUDYING THE EFFECTS OF INCARCERATION ON OFFENDING TRAJECTORIES, at ix (2006), *available at* http://www.urban.org/UploadedPDF/411427_Effects_of_Incarceration.pdf.

49. *See* DANIEL P. MEARS & JEREMY TRAVIS, URBAN INST. JUSTICE POL'Y CTR., THE DIMENSIONS, PATHWAYS, AND CONSEQUENCES OF YOUTH REENTRY 10 (2004), *available at* http://www.urban.org/uploadedpdf/410927_youth_reentry.pdf

The impact of prison-like settings on these youth presents challenges and barriers that differ from those on adults because of the developmental physical, emotional, and mental changes associated with their young age; these youth are also often undergoing transitions in the social expectations that correspond with aging from adolescence to adulthood. Many are undereducated and drop out of high school. Most have no independent living experience or life skill training and little or no job experience. These barriers are known to not only hinder successful transition into the community and society but also are known to contribute to the likelihood of continued criminal activity.[50] As U.S. Department of Justice Information Analyst Daryl Fox noted, reducing juvenile recidivism by 4% would prevent 131 assaults, four rapes, and ten murders by juveniles nationwide over a five-year period.[51]

Policy-makers, academics, and practitioners have recommended that juvenile reentry efforts include elevation of the issue of reentry within the juvenile and criminal justice systems, development of reentry programming that takes into account the needs of reentering juveniles and young adults that differ according to their ages, gender, and race/ethnicity, incorporation of community and family based support networks, continued research, and community awareness and education. Community-based comprehensive reentry approaches have been determined as critical to the success of the transition process.

In North Carolina, juveniles released from YDCs recidivate at alarming rates. According to the state-mandated 2001 recidivism study, nearly three-and-a-half years after release from the juvenile system, 88.5% of juveniles received subsequent adult criminal charges.[52] Clearly, any marked reductions in recidivism represent significant efforts toward injury prevention and control. So how does a justice system address the reentry process? North Carolina has addressed the issue by shifting to the notion of a "seamless" transition process. A reentry enhancement pilot program, named CORE, was developed to enhance participants' transitions from YDCs back into their home communities. It was designed to include services such as employment training and placement, education, medical care, housing assistance, and intensive case management. A staff person referred to as a Com-

("[O]ver half of all committed juvenile offenders have at least one family member who served a jail or prison sentence.").

50. *See id.* at 10.

51. Bill Alexander, *Turbulent Reentry*, YOUTH TODAY, June 1, 2003, at 1.

52. STEVENS H. CLARKE, CRIMINAL RECIDIVISM AFTER COMMITMENT FOR JUVENILE DELINQUENCY 2, 6–7 (2001).

munity Support Coordinator (CSC) assumes a case manager role as youth exit the YDC and continues to engage the family and community in support of that youth. The CSC maintains contact with youth and families for up to two years, assisting youth and families in connecting with the community resources they need to support successful transitions for youthful offenders.

The process of continued case management that exceeds the period of mandated supervision and closely ties together the networks of community support for these youth and families is promising.[53] Preliminary recidivism findings over a three year period indicated that of the forty-four youth who participated in the CORE program, the recidivism rate for all participating youth across the juvenile and adult systems was 36%. An interesting trend was noticeable with regard to the severity of recidivating offenses. Although recidivating youth were charged with multiple recidivating offenses, the nature of their initial recidivating offenses was almost always less severe than that of their commitment offenses. Additionally, the decrease in weapons-related recidivating offenses was notable. The severity of recidivating offenses tended to increase, however, with further offenses over time, indicating the importance of a constant monitoring of these youth that allows for immediate response to any criminal behavior.

Recommendations for replication and future implementation that resulted from the evaluation process included implementing appropriate training for CSCs, standardizing documentation for tracking, formalizing community partner roles and obligations, and implementing clear organizational management of the collaborative partnerships. With these recommendations at the forefront of developing juvenile reentry support programming, successful impacts are attainable, cost-effective, and often require coordination of community-based efforts that are already underway.

V. The Power of Prevention

The fourth major leverage point is not a new theme, but it is one that often gets lost in the reactionary, quick-fix mentality that sometimes governs the juvenile justice system: never losing sight of the power of prevention. Unfortunately, "[p]olicymakers typically respond once problems have been identified as needing

53. *See generally* Kristen L. Di Luca et al., Collaborative for Offender Reentry Enhancement (CORE): Implementation, Process, and Outcome Evaluation, 2003–2006 (2007) (providing a comprehensive review of the CORE program performance).

fixing, [and] program developers and service providers typically focus on addressing the deficits of a particular population experiencing problems . . . ."[54] That response pattern among social scientists, practitioners, and policymakers must change—truly embracing a prevention oriented philosophy requires a proactive stance, rather than a reactive one.

Juvenile justice systems must commit to maintaining legislative and fiscal support for a continuum of community-based prevention and intervention efforts. Maintaining a system of graduated sanctions ensures that the course of treatment is appropriate to the offense.[55] By design, graduated sanctions progress from the least restrictive environments (e.g., community-based mentoring programs) to the most restrictive environments (e.g., secure confinement for serious, violent, chronic offenders).[56] In the vast majority of juvenile delinquency cases, alternatives to incarceration—family counseling, restitution, mentoring, structured day programs—should take place in the home community of the youth. One way to ensure a broad, community-based continuum of services and placements is to allow prevention and intervention decisions to be made at the local level, but with fiscal support from the state.

North Carolina requires—by statute—that each of its 100 counties creates a Juvenile Crime Prevention Council (JCPC).[57]

54. Andrea L. Solarz et al., *A Blueprint for the Future*, *in* INVESTING IN CHILDREN, YOUTH, FAMILIES, AND COMMUNITIES 343, 344 (Kenneth I. Maton et al. eds., 2004).

55. Sweat, *supra* note 14.

56. *See* OFFICE OF JUVENILE JUSTICE & DELINQENCY PREVENTION, U.S. DEP'T OF JUSTICE, COMPREHENSIVE STRATEGY FOR SERIOUS, VIOLENT, AND CHRONIC JUVENILE OFFENDERS 18–19 (1993); OFFICE OF JUVENILE JUSTICE & DELINQENCY PREVENTION, U.S. DEP'T OF JUSTICE, GUIDE FOR IMPLEMENTING THE COMPREHENSIVE STRATEGY FOR SERIOUS, VIOLENT, AND CHRONIC JUVENILE OFFENDERS 11–12 (James C. Howell ed., 1995); *see also* JAMES C. HOWELL, PREVENTING & REDUCING JUVENILE DELINQUENCY (2003) (providing a comprehensive examination of the process and punishment of the juvenile justice system).

57. The statute reads:

> It is the intent of the General Assembly to prevent juveniles who are at risk from becoming delinquent. The primary intent of this Part is to develop community-based alternatives to youth development centers and to provide community-based delinquency and substance abuse prevention strategies and programs. Additionally, it is the intent of the General Assembly to provide noninstitutional dispositional alternatives that will protect the community and the juveniles.
>
> These programs and services shall be planned and organized at the community level and developed in partnership with the State. These planning efforts shall include appropriate representation from local government, local public and private agencies serving juveniles and their families, local business leaders, citizens with an interest in

The purpose of each JCPC is to galvanize local community support and input for creating a range of dispositional alternatives for at-risk and court-involved youth. JCPC membership, appointed by the county Board of Commissioners, must include local law enforcement leaders, judges, child attorneys, faith community members, juvenile court staff, service providers, and interested citizens.[58] Those representatives are charged with the following responsibilities: a) conducting an annual assessment of juvenile risks and needs as well as available community resources; b) determining the scope and array of prevention and intervention services needed; c) developing a written solicitation for providers of those services; d) funding programs and ensuring adherence to program guidelines; and e) evaluating program performance.[59]

---

youth problems, youth representatives, and others as may be appropriate in a particular community. The planning bodies at the local level shall be the Juvenile Crime Prevention Councils.

N.C. GEN. STAT § 143B-543 (2007).

58. As outlined in the statute:

The County Council shall consist of not more than 26 members and should include, if possible, the following:

(1) The local school superintendent, or that person's designee;
(2) A chief of police in the county;
(3) The local sheriff, or that person's designee;
(4) The district attorney, or that person's designee;
(5) The chief court counselor, or that person's designee;
(6) The director of the area mental health, developmental disabilities, and substance abuse authority, or that person's designee;
(7) The director of the county department of social services, or consolidated human services agency, or that person's designee;
(8) The county manager, or that person's designee;
(9) A substance abuse professional;
(10) A member of the faith community;
(11) A county commissioner;
(12) Two persons under the age of 18 years, one of whom is a member of the State Youth Council;
(13) A juvenile defense attorney;
(14) The chief district court judge, or a judge designated by the chief district court judge;
(15) A member of the business community;
(16) The local health director, or that person's designee;
(17) A representative from the United Way or other nonprofit agency;
(18) A representative of a local parks and recreation program; and
(19) Up to seven members of the public to be appointed by the board of commissioners of a county.

N.C. GEN. STAT § 143B-544.

59. *See* N.C. GEN. STAT §§ 143B-549 to -550.

In addition to those tasks, the JCPCs should "work to increase public awareness of the causes of delinquency and of strategies to reduce the problem; develop strategies to intervene and appropriately respond to and treat the needs of juveniles at risk of delinquency; and provide funds for services for treatment, counseling, or rehabilitation for juveniles and their families."[60] Although the amount varies from year to year, the state allocation to JCPCs totals approximately $20–$30 million. Those funds are distributed to each JCPC, which then disperses funds directly to each respective service provider. The broad, general categories of programming funded by JCPCs are: a) assessment programs (e.g., clinical evaluation and psychological assessment programs); b) clinical treatment programs (e.g., sex offender assessment and counseling, home-based family counseling, individual counseling programs; c) community day programs (e.g., juvenile structured day programs); d) residential programs; e) restorative programs (e.g., mediation/conflict resolution, restitution, and teen court); and f) structured activities programs (e.g., skill building and mentoring programs).

The structure and function of JCPCs in North Carolina exemplify an institutional model that embraces community-based, holistic prevention. The legislative directive given to JCPCs fundamentally places a focus on creating prevention and intervention opportunities for youth. Moreover, through JCPCs' mandated membership, a level of community involvement and buy-in is fostered, which reinforces the notion that court-involved youth are not "somebody else's" children—these are youth from the local community.

Creating provisions to support innovative prevention and intervention programming is a necessary first step. However, it is critical to note that not all programs and intervention methodologies are equally effective. Fortunately, there is a wide and growing investment of effort into discerning what works.[61] The federal Office of Juvenile Justice and Delinquency Prevention has

60. N.C. Dep't of Juvenile Justice & Delinqency Prevention, *Juvenile Crime Prevention Councils: General Statute*, http://www.juvjus.state.nc.us/jcpc/general_statutes.html (last visited Feb. 20, 2008) (discussing the intent and requirements of North Carolina's JCPC statute).

61. *See* Howell, *supra* note 56, at 173–223 (assessing effective prevention and rehabilitative techniques); Mark W. Lipsey & David B. Wilson, *Effective Intervention for Serious Juvenile Offenders: A Synthesis of Longitudinal Research*, *in* Serious & Violent Juvenile Offenders, *supra* note 13, at 86 (exploring the benefit of meta-analytic procedures in identifying at-risk youths and incorporating preventive intervention).

developed an internet-based Model Programs Guide,[62] which directs users to scientifically proven programs that match the user's criteria. The database includes an array of programs that span the continuum from prevention to reentry. Entire professional organizations, like the Society for Prevention Research, are devoted to advancing empirical research on prevention programs and policies. University-based academic centers, such as the Center for the Study and Prevention of Violence at the University of Colorado at Boulder advance the understanding of effective program selection, implementation, and evaluation. Through their Blueprints Project, the Center identifies and supports model and promising violence prevention programming that has met a rigorous standard of program effectiveness.

Finally, effective, evidence-based prevention programming is not only important and imperative from a human development standpoint. It potentially represents the best use of resources now, rather than exorbitant resources later. For example, consider the cost of a preventative investment in Multisystemic Therapy[63] versus the dramatically higher costs of secure confinement. Therefore, an important consideration whenever communities begin to discuss prevention and intervention programs is the need to use cost-benefit methodologies. As noted by the Juvenile Justice Evaluation Center, "[c]ost-benefit information can assist decisionmakers [sic] in more efficiently allocating scarce public resources among competing demands."[64] Cost-benefit analyses move beyond standard program evaluation, which is directed at the question of program efficacy and impact. "A good cost-benefit analysis, on the other hand, should be able to take the answer to this question one step further: Given what was found in the program evaluation, does the dollar value of a program's demonstrated level of success exceed the cost of the program?"[65] Economic cost-benefit analyses conducted by the Washington State Institute of Public Policy show that states should put most of their prevention portfolio into proven programs.[66] For example, the

62. Office of Juvenile Justice & Delinqency Prevention, Model Programs Guide, http://www.dsgonline.com/mpg2.5/mpg_index.htm (last visited Feb. 20, 2008).

63. *See generally* SCOTT W. HENGGELER ET AL., MULTISYSTEMIC TREATMENT OF ANTISOCIAL BEHAVIOR IN CHILDREN AND ADOLESCENTS (1998) (concluding that Multisystemic Therapy is validated by research).

64. STEVE AOS, OFFICE OF JUVENILE JUSTICE & DELINQENCY PREVENTION, COST-BENEFIT ANALYSIS FOR JUVENILE JUSTICE PROGRAMS 6 (2002), *available at* http://www.ojp.usdoj.gov/ccdo/programs/I_d.pdf.

65. *Id.* at 7.

66. *See* STEVE AOS ET AL., WASH. STATE INST. FOR PUB. POL'Y, BENEFITS AND COSTS OF PREVENTION AND EARLY INTERVENTION PROGRAMS FOR YOUTH 1, 8

per-child cost of Functional Family Therapy is about $2100; the per-child benefit—quantified as reduced crime, reduced grade retention, and increased graduation rates—is estimated at about $16,500. For every dollar invested, nearly eight dollars of benefit are realized. It is simply prudent fiscal policy to invest in evidence-based prevention programs.

Summary

Invariably in the field of juvenile justice, when issues such as comprehensive prevention programming, attentiveness to offenders' needs, and holistic therapeutic approaches are brought to the fore, there is a vocal contingent that intones the mantra that we are being "soft on crime." We reject the soft-on-crime versus hard-on-crime dichotomy in favor of the astute call from the Federal Advisory Committee on Juvenile Justice that it is time to get smart on crime, not soft, not tough: "Being smart on juvenile delinquency requires assessing the factors and influences that put youth at risk of delinquency, determining available resources, and establishing prevention programs to either reduce risk factors or provide protective factors that buffer juveniles from the impact of risk factors."[67]

In sum, promising practices in the juvenile justice system are out there. Embracing a therapeutic approach, addressing juvenile offenders' mental health needs, supporting the process of reentry, and never losing sight of the power of prevention are key elements of a juvenile justice system that ultimately supports positive youth development. Juvenile offenders are some of the most challenging and most difficult youth with whom to deal; but from our perspective, this challenge is an opportunity to impact recidivism so that youthful offenders of today do not become the adult offenders of tomorrow. Given their age, stopping the cycle of offending is best achieved through rehabilitation and treatment, and we should build a philosophy and systems committed to that goal.

(2004), *available at* http://www.wsipp.wa.gov/rptfiles/04-07-3901.pdf; *see also* Elizabeth Drake, Wash. State Inst. for Pub. Pol'y, Evidence-Based Juvenile Offender Programs (2007), *available at* http://www.wsipp.wa.gov/rptfiles/07-06-1201.pdf (identifying costs and benefits of designated evidence-based juvenile offender programs).

67. Annual Report 2007, *supra* note 36, at 4.

[7]

CRUEL AND UNUSUAL PUNISHMENT: MANDATORY SENTENCING OF JUVENILES TRIED AS ADULTS WITHOUT THE POSSIBILITY OF YOUTH AS A MITIGATING FACTOR

*Alison Powers**

It was once said that the moral test of government is how that government treats those that are in the dawn of life, the children . . . .

Hubert H. Humphrey[1]

I. INTRODUCTION

On November 28, 2001, twelve-year-old Christopher Pittman was not deemed old enough to vote,[2] to drink alcohol,[3] to operate a motor vehicle,[4] to serve as a juror,[5] to form a binding contract,[6] or

* Managing Editor, *Rutgers Law Review*; 2010 J.D. Candidate, Rutgers University School of Law – Newark; Master of Fine Arts, Brooklyn College; Bachelor of Arts, Binghamton University. I would like to thank my parents, Maureen and Tom Powers, for encouraging me to fly and for being there to catch me when I fall; my fiancé, Edward Herman, for holding my hand during the law school journey and loving me anyway; my grandmother, Grace Leddy, for reminding me that laughter makes everything better; my uncle, Daniel D. Leddy, Jr., for being the attorney (and person) that I aspire to be; and the Editors and Staff of the *Rutgers Law Review* for their excellent work and friendship. I dedicate this Note to the loving memory of my grandfather, Daniel Leddy, the wisest and kindest man I've ever known, who taught me all I really need to know in life while playing school when I was five.

1. THE YALE BOOK OF QUOTATIONS 376 (Fred R. Shapiro ed., 2006). Hubert H. Humphrey (1911-1978), "untiring champion" of the Civil Rights Movement, arms control, health care, and public education, served as Vice President of the United States under Lyndon B. Johnson from 1965 to 1969 and, as nominee of the Democratic Party in 1968, lost the presidential election to Richard Nixon. HUBERT H. HUMPHREY, THE EDUCATION OF A PUBLIC MAN: MY LIFE AND POLITICS (Norman Sherman ed., Univ. of Minn. Press 1991) (1976).

2. *See* U.S. CONST. amend. XXVI, § 1 (standardizing the voting age in the United States to eighteen).

3. *See* National Minimum Drinking Age Act of 1984, 23 U.S.C. § 158 (2006) (withholding federal highway funds from states which do not set a minimum age of twenty-one to purchase or possess alcoholic beverages).

4. *See* South Carolina Department of Motor Vehicles, Initial Driver License, http://www.scdmvonline.com/dmvnew/default.aspx?n=initial_driver_license (last visited Nov. 13, 2009) (allowing eligibility for a "regular driver license" to those at least seventeen years of age).

5. *See* Jury Act, 28 U.S.C. § 1865 (2006) (setting eighteen as the age qualification for jury service).

6. *See* RESTATEMENT (SECOND) OF CONTRACTS § 14 (1979) (stating that an

even to watch a PG-13 movie.[7] However, Christopher Pittman was held responsible as an adult for his actions on that day, and the resultant loss of freedom will see Christopher incarcerated in an adult-offender prison, without possibility of parole, until 2031.[8]

Despite being a "troubled child from an unhappy home,"[9] Christopher Pittman has been described as an "extremely well-mannered"[10] child and a "normal kid."[11] Abandoned by his mother shortly after birth, Christopher spent most of his young life in Florida with his father, a "strict disciplinarian" who struggled to raise his two children through an overseas tour in the Army during the Persian Gulf War and multiple failed marriages.[12] During the summer of Christopher's twelfth year, his life was "thrust . . . into emotional turmoil" when his mother abruptly returned to his life only to subsequently abandon the child for a second time.[13] The "shy, gentle, and loving" boy lashed out at his father, attempted to run away, and ultimately was prescribed antidepressants after threatening to harm himself.[14] Christopher was "rescued" when Joe and Joy Pittman, paternal grandparents with whom he enjoyed an "extremely close, loving, and devoted" relationship, convinced the father that the child would be better off living with them in South Carolina.[15]

Soon thereafter, on November 28, 2001, Christopher was dismissed from school early for disciplinary problems on the school bus the day before and was "beat . . . with a belt as punishment" by his grandfather and sent to bed.[16] That evening, the ninety-six-

individual "has the capacity to incur only voidable contractual duties until the beginning of the day before the person's eighteenth birthday").

7. *See* Motion Picture Association of America Film Rating System, http://www.mpaa.org/FlmRat_Ratings.asp (last visited Jan. 7, 2010) (describing how a PG-13 rating strongly cautions parents of the strong content in films that may be unsuitable for children under the age of thirteen).

8. Sarah Obeid, *Pardoning Pittman*, OPEDNEWS, Oct. 16, 2008, http://www.opednews.com/articles/Pardoning-Pittman-by-salah-obeid-081015-803.html (last visited Nov. 13, 2009) (explaining that without a pardon, Christopher will be in his mid-forties when released from incarceration).

9. Jim Polk, *Teen Gets 30 Years in Zoloft Case*, CNN.COM, Feb. 16, 2005, http:www.cnn.com/2005/LAW/02/15/zoloft.trial/index.html.

10. Erin Moriarty, *Prescription for Murder?*, CBS NEWS, Apr. 17, 2005, http://www.cbsnews.com/stories/2005/04/13/48hours/main687855.shtml.

11. Amended Initial Brief of Appellant at 1, State v. Pittman, 373 S.C. 527 (2007) (Nos. 2004-GS-12-00571 and 2004-GS-12-00572), http://www.justiceseekers.com/html/Appealbrief.pdf.

12. *Id.*

13. *Id.* at 2.

14. *Id.* at 2-3.

15. *Id.* at 1, 3.

16. Bill Mears, *Supreme Court Turns Down Boy Killer's Appeal*, CNN.COM, Apr.

pound child loaded the .410 gauge shotgun his father had given him as a gift and shot his "Pop Pop" and "Nana" to death in their bed.[17]

While the family court had original jurisdiction over Christopher's case, South Carolina has no minimum age at which to transfer a child accused of murder.[18] The State requested a waiver to the court of general sessions to try the child as an adult,[19] thereby perpetuating the "preposterous, albeit popular notion that little kids magically become mature adults when they do bad things."[20] With transfer findings focused solely on the seriousness of the offense and likelihood that Christopher would be found guilty, "[t]he only mention of [Christopher's] youth in the transfer order [was] the recitation of [his] birth date, current age, and age at the time of the offense."[21]

During the twenty-one-plus months that Christopher remained incarcerated before trial, he grew from a "scrawny little kid"[22] to a six-foot, one-inch young man.[23] The defense attorneys unsuccessfully attempted to persuade the jury that the twelve-year-old's age rendered him unable to form the requisite criminal intent to commit murder.[24] On February 15, 2005, more than three years after Christopher pulled the trigger, the jury ultimately decided that the now grown young man before them was able to discern right from wrong when he took the lives of the people he once called "Pop Pop" and "Nana."[25]

14, 2008, http://www.cnn.com/2008/CRIME/04/14/juvenile.killer/index.html?iref =mpstoryview.

17. Amended Initial Brief of Appellant, *supra* note 11, at 1, 6-9; *see also* Polk, *supra* note 9.

18. Patrick Griffin, National Center for Juvenile Justice, *State Juvenile Justice Profiles: South Carolina Transfer Provisions* (2008), http://www.ncjj.org/stateprofiles/asp/transfer.asp?topic=Transfer&state=SC06.asp&print=no# (last visited Nov. 13, 2009). As of 2007, twenty-three states have at least one provision for juvenile transfer with no explicit minimum age requirement. *See* Patrick Griffin, National Center of Juvenile Justice, *State Juvenile Justice Profiles: National Overviews* (2008), http://www.ncjj.org/stateprofiles/overviews/transfer5.asp (last visited Nov. 13, 2009).

19. Petition for Writ of Certiorari at 6, *Pittman*, 128 S. Ct. 1872 (Apr. 14, 2008).

20. Daniel Leddy, *Compounding Tragedy: Legal Victimization*, STATEN ISLAND ADVANCE, Feb. 14, 2005, at B2.

21. Petition for Writ of Certiorari, *supra* note 19, at 6-7.

22. John Springer, *Prosecutors End Rebuttal Against Teenage Killer, Closings Set for Monday*, COURT TV, Feb. 11, 2005, http://news.findlaw.com/court_tv/s/20050211/11feb2005174210.html (last visited Nov. 13, 2009).

23. Amended Initial Brief of Appellant, *supra* note 11, at 9.

24. John Springer, *Jurors Deliberate Fate of Teen Accused of Gunning Down His Grandparents*, COURT TV, Feb. 14, 2005, http://prawl.sartorelli.gen.nz/news/16.htm (last visited Nov. 13, 2009).

25. Polk, *supra* note 9; *see also* Amended Initial Brief of Appellant, *supra* note 11, at 1.

With a conviction of two counts of murder, the sentencing judge had extremely limited options.[26] Judge Pieper sentenced Christopher to the shortest sentence permitted under South Carolina law: imprisonment for thirty years without possibility of parole.[27] Prevented by law from considering Christopher's age in his sentence, Pieper noted the tragedy of the situation and stated that "[t]his case has called attention to the very core values of this society about the treatment of juveniles and punishment."[28]

Was Christopher a troubled child under the influence of antidepressants, unable to discern right from wrong, and in need of rehabilitation? Or was he "as malicious a . . . murderer as you're ever going to get"[29] and deserving of punishment? In the words of the Pittman family's pastor, "[w]e have been left with a question we must resign ourselves that we will never have the answer to, of how this could happen and why."[30] But Christopher's story raises strong questions about a justice system that, in essence, rejects the possibility of a child's rehabilitation, once the cornerstone of the juvenile justice movement, and substitutes the "informed and individualized" decision of the judge, with the "legislature's generalized judgments about an entire category of youth offenders."[31]

In practice, "[m]andatory sentencing schemes eliminate statutory provisions allowing a judge to exercise discretion because of a child offender's age, background, the legal interpretations of facts established at trial, or any other factor provided for by statute that might make another sentence more appropriate."[32] Such inflexible mandates in juvenile sentencing hold inevitable potential for Eighth Amendment violation as excessive or cruel and unusual punishment, especially in light of the Supreme Court's reasoning in *Roper v.*

---

26. *See* S.C. CODE ANN. § 16-3-20(A) (2007) ("A person who is convicted of or pleads guilty to murder must be punished by death, by imprisonment for life, or by a mandatory minimum term of imprisonment for thirty years.").

27. *Id.*

28. Obeid, *supra* note 8. Defense attorney Andy Vickery advocated that Pieper rule the mandatory minimum sentence unconstitutional considering Christopher's youth by stating that "[y]ou have a legislative mandate that says you shall not give him less than 30 years but you have a constitutional imperative . . . that the sentence must be in light of the full circumstances, including his age." John Springer, *Jurors Find Teenager Guilty of Murdering His Grandparents*, COURT TV, Feb. 16, 2005, http://www.courttv.com/trials/pittman/021505_verdict_ctv.html (last visited Nov. 13, 2009).

29. Moriarty, *supra* note 10 (relating Prosecutor Barney Giese's description of Christopher from the closing argument).

30. *Id.*

31. AMNESTY INTERNATIONAL HUMAN RIGHTS WATCH, THE REST OF THEIR LIVES: LIFE WITHOUT PAROLE FOR CHILD OFFENDERS IN THE UNITED STATES 90-91 (2005), http://www.amnestyusa.org/countries/usa/clwop/report.pdf.

32. *Id.*

Simmons.[33] The scary reality is that despite neurological and psychological studies of juvenile development,[34] judges lamenting the injustice resulting from their inability to use discretion in the individualized case,[35] and the "evolving standards of decency regarding the diminished capacity of children,"[36] approximately seventy-three people are serving life sentences for offenses committed while thirteen or fourteen years of age,[37] and hundreds more, like Christopher Pittman, are incarcerated from a sentence imposed by a judge whose hands were tied by mandatory sentencing schemes.[38]

This Note explores the constitutionality of mandatory sentences imposed upon juveniles tried in the adult criminal system without judicial discretion to consider youth as a mitigating factor. Part II traces the history and goals of juvenile justice policy in the United States, from the instatement of the juvenile justice system and emphasis on child rehabilitation to the establishment of transfer and waiver laws and the shift toward punishment and retribution. Part III explores how this evolution in juvenile justice policy impacts the

---

33. Roper v. Simmons, 543 U.S. 551 (2005) (abolished the death penalty for offenders under eighteen years of age).

34. See *infra* Part IV for a discussion of neurological and psychological discoveries regarding juvenile development and culpability.

35. *See* AMNESTY INTERNATIONAL HUMAN RIGHTS WATCH, *supra* note 31, at 90-92. The Honorable David Scott DeWitt "reflected on his own lack of discretion" in sentencing a fifteen-year-old to life imprisonment without parole and stated:

> [T]he sentence that I must impose is mandated by law. I don't have any choice in the matter. I'm not at all comfortable with this case, not because the Defendant didn't receive a fair trial. I think that he did. . . .
>
> One is always tempted in a case like this to search for some way to lessen the severity of the law because of the fact that the Defendant is only fifteen years old. The Motion for New Trial presented a certain amount of temptation to ignore the law and do something to fit the circumstances. I have sworn duty to follow the law, and think in the long run the performance of duty to follow the law is in the best interests of not only this community but the whole state.
>
> . . . It's obvious to me that we can't, as a society, say that fifteen-year-old children should be held to the same standards as adults. Our law provides this. I think the law is wrong.

Id. at 91 (quoting Sentencing Transcript, People v. Lashuay (1984) (on file with Human Rights Watch)).

36. Petition for Writ of Certiorari, *supra* note 19, at 8.

37. EQUAL JUSTICE INITIATIVE, CRUEL AND UNUSUAL: SENTENCING 13- AND 14-YEAR-OLD CHILDREN TO DIE IN PRISON 20 (2007), http://www.eji.org/eji/files/20071017 cruelandunusual.pdf (reporting data compiled "[b]y reviewing court decisions, searching media reports, and collecting information from state departments of corrections and from prisoners directly").

38. *See generally* AMNESTY INTERNATIONAL HUMAN RIGHTS WATCH, *supra* note 31.

sentencing of youths today, specifically addressing mandatory minimum sentences as applied to juveniles tried in the adult criminal system and proposing that such ultimate treatment violates the Eighth Amendment's prohibition on excessive and cruel and unusual punishment. Part IV discusses the 2005 United States Supreme Court decision, *Roper v. Simmons*, as an affirmative acknowledgment of the discounted culpability and maturity of the developing juvenile, and applies the Court's reasoning to abolish the death penalty for offenders under eighteen, in conjunction with modern scientific and psychological studies, to mandatory sentencing of juveniles. Part V explores the Supreme Court's interpretation of the Eighth Amendment leading up to *Roper*, applies the "gross proportionality" comparison standard, and concludes that the mandatory sentencing of juveniles without the possibility of consideration of youth as a mitigating factor clearly constitutes cruel and unusual punishment and thereby violates the Eighth Amendment.

II. THE HISTORY AND GOALS OF JUVENILE JUSTICE POLICY: WHERE HAVE WE GONE WRONG?

In eighteenth century America, no distinction was made between adult and juvenile defendants.[39] Children considered above the "age of reason," traditionally seven years of age or older, were deemed capable of criminal intent, and therefore were tried in the same courts and subjected to the same punishment as adult defendants.[40] The Progressive Era ushered in social reform[41] and a shifted perception of juveniles from "miniature adults" to "persons with less than fully developed moral and cognitive capacities."[42] Specialized facilities were established to focus on tending to the individualized

39. Janet Tobias & Michel Martin, *Frontline: Juvenile Justice* (PBS television broadcast Jan. 30, 2001), http://www.pbs.org/wgbh/pages/frontline/shows/juvenile/stats/childadult.html (last visited Nov. 13, 2009) (discussing the evolving view of juvenile culpability).

40. HOWARD N. SNYDER & MELISSA SICKMUND, JUVENILE OFFENDERS AND VICTIMS: 2006 NATIONAL REPORT 94 (2006), http://ojjdp.ncjrs.org/ojstatbb/nr2006/downloads/chapter4.pdf (noting that the child, who was over seven years of age, could be sentenced to life imprisonment or death if found guilty).

41. During the Progressive Era (1900-1918), America "saw the growth of the women's suffrage movement, the campaign against child labor, the fight for the eight-hour workday, and the uses of journalism and cartooning to expose 'big business' corruption." History of America's Juvenile Justice System, http://www.lawyershop.com/practice-areas/criminal-law/juvenile-law/history/ (last visited Nov. 13, 2009).

42. SNYDER & SICKMUND, *supra* note 40, at 94. Children were viewed as "passive and innocent beings incapable of possessing criminal intent." Joseph F. Yeckel, *Violent Juvenile Offenders: Rethinking Federal Intervention in Juvenile Justice*, 51 WASH. U. J. URB. & CONTEMP. L. 331, 334 (1997).

needs and rehabilitation of the child, culminating in the establishment of the first juvenile court in Cook County, Illinois in 1899.[43]

The juvenile courts were instituted under the *parens patriae*[44] legal doctrine, where the role of the state was "not only to protect the public interest," but also to primarily "serve as the guardian" of the juvenile's interests.[45] As children were considered more amenable to change and reformation than their adult counterparts, the juvenile court was "designed to be flexible, informal and to tailor to a juvenile's individual needs, with the ultimate goal of rehabilitation."[46] In the words of Judge Julian Mack, one of the first judges to preside over a juvenile court,

> [t]he child who must be brought into the court should, of course, be made to know that he is face to face with the power of the state, but he should at the same time, and more emphatically, be made to feel that he is the object of its care and solicitude. The ordinary trappings of the court-room are out of place in such hearings. The judge on a bench, looking down upon the boy standing at the bar, can never evoke a proper sympathetic spirit. Seated at a desk, with the child at his side, where he can on occasion put his arm around his shoulder and draw the lad to him, the judge, while losing none of his judicial dignity, will gain immensely in the effectiveness of his work.[47]

This benevolent mission of protecting and treating the child through a non-adversarial, rehabilitation model led to procedural and substantive differences in the juvenile and adult criminal systems.[48] The judge presiding in the juvenile court, a "concerned father" figure, was "free to consider all relevant information without regard for rules of evidence . . . . [which were deemed] too limiting in an endeavor where everyone was acting in the best interest of the child."[49] Additionally, because the goal of the juvenile justice system was protective rather than punitive in nature, "no due process

43. ABA DIV. FOR PUB. EDUC., THE HISTORY OF JUVENILE JUSTICE: DIALOGUE ON YOUTH AND JUSTICE 5 (2007), http://www.abanet.org/publiced/features/DYJpart1.pdf.

44. A Latin term for "parent of the country," *parens patriae* refers to the legal doctrine which gives the state the power to serve as parent or guardian to a juvenile with legal issues. *Id.*

45. Tobias & Martin, *supra* note 39.

46. *Id.* In stark contrast to the adult criminal system, the juvenile system "focused on the offender rather than the offense and emphasized rehabilitation over punishment." Yeckel, *supra* note 42, at 335.

47. ABA DIV. FOR PUB. EDUC., *supra* note 43, at 5 (quoting Julian Mack, *The Juvenile Court*, 23 HARV. L. REV. 104, 120 (1909)).

48. SNYDER & SICKMUND, *supra* note 40, at 94.

49. Marygold S. Melli, *Symposium: Juvenile Justice Reform: Introduction: Juvenile Justice Reform in Context*, 1996 WIS. L. REV. 375, 378-79 (1996) (discussing the characteristics of the separate juvenile system).

protections" applied.[50]

The 1960s brought great change to juvenile justice, beginning a trend toward "[b]lurring the [l]ines [b]etween [j]uvenile and [c]riminal [j]ustice."[51] With *Kent v. United States*,[52] the Supreme Court heard the first of many "cases that would profoundly change proceedings in the juvenile courts" and start the pendulum swinging in the direction of punishment and formal, adversarial proceedings.[53] In *Kent*, the Court held that juveniles are constitutionally entitled to the "essentials of due process and fair treatment" in ruling that Kent was entitled to a waiver hearing and explanation of the juvenile court's waiver decision.[54] One year later, the Supreme Court continued its extension of constitutional due process rights to juveniles in *In re Gault*.[55] The Court explicitly rejected the concept of *parens patriae*[56] and replaced individualized assessment and discretion with the juvenile's right to notice of the charges against him or her,[57] to legal counsel,[58] to privilege against self-incrimination,[59] and to confront and cross examine witnesses.[60] Noting the intended distinction between juvenile proceedings and criminal trials,[61] Justice Stewart warned in his dissent that by requiring the same due process guarantees, "the Court's opinion . . .

---

50. Tobias & Martin, *supra* note 39.

51. ABA DIV. FOR PUB. EDUC., *supra* note 43, at 7.

52. Kent v. United States, 383 U.S. 541 (1966).

53. ABA DIV. FOR PUB. EDUC., *supra* note 43, at 6.

54. *Kent*, 383 U.S. at 562.

55. *In re* Gault, 387 U.S. 1 (1967).

56. *See id.* at 17 ("The constitutional and theoretical basis for this peculiar system is—to say the least—debatable.").

> The early conception of the Juvenile Court proceeding was one in which a fatherly judge touched the heart and conscience of the erring youth by talking over his problems, by paternal advice and admonition, and in which, in extreme situations, benevolent and wise institutions of the State provided guidance and help "to save him from a downward career." . . . But recent studies have, with surprising unanimity, entered sharp dissent as to the validity of this gentle conception. They suggest that the appearance as well as the actuality of fairness, impartiality and orderliness—in short, the essentials of due process—may be a more impressive and more therapeutic attitude so far as the juvenile is concerned.

Id. at 25-26 (footnote omitted).

57. *Id.* at 33.

58. *Id.* at 41.

59. *Id.* at 55.

60. *Id.* at 56-57.

61. *See id.* at 79 (Stewart, J., dissenting) ("[A] juvenile proceeding's whole purpose and mission is the very opposite of the mission and purpose of a prosecution in a criminal court. The object of the one is correction of a condition. The object of the other is conviction and punishment for a criminal act.").

serves to convert a juvenile proceeding into a criminal prosecution."[62]

In the years that followed, the Court continued to "erod[e] the difference[] between juvenile courts and traditional criminal courts,"[63] in requiring the reasonable doubt standard in juvenile delinquency proceedings[64] and applying the double jeopardy protections of the Fifth Amendment to juveniles.[65] Dissenters continued to protest the transformation of juvenile justice[66] as "[t]he once rehabilitative ideal of the juvenile justice system gave way to aggressive implementation of transfer policies and procedures, representing a new retributive focus."[67]

Additional evidence of the juvenile justice pendulum's continued swing from benevolent, individualized assessment and rehabilitative goals toward prosecution and retributive goals can be seen in the increased transfer of juveniles to adult courts.[68] While mechanisms to transfer juveniles to criminal court are not new,[69] the 1980s and 1990s ushered in an era of "substantial misperception regarding increases in juvenile crime,"[70] and many states reacted by passing laws intended to increase incidence of juveniles handled as adults in criminal courts.[71] Between 1992 and 1997, forty-five states modified

---

62. *Id.*

63. *In re* Winship, 397 U.S. 358, 376 (1970) (Burger, C.J., dissenting). The Court only expressly denied juveniles the constitutional protection of right to trial by jury. *See* McKeiver v. Pennsylvania, 403 U.S. 528, 545 (1971) (holding that juveniles are not entitled to trial by jury in a juvenile court).

64. *In re Winship*, 397 U.S. at 368 (holding that proof beyond a reasonable doubt is required during the adjudicatory stage when a juvenile is charged with an act which "renders him liable to confinement for as long as six years").

65. Breed v. Jones, 421 U.S. 519, 541 (1975) (holding that the double jeopardy clause bars waiver of a juvenile to criminal court following adjudication in juvenile court).

66. *See In re Winship*, 397 U.S. at 376 (Burger, C.J., dissenting) ("What the juvenile court system needs is not more but less of the trappings of legal procedure and judicial formalism; the juvenile court system requires breathing room and flexibility in order to survive, if it can survive the repeated assaults from this Court.").

67. Enrico Pagnanelli, *Children as Adults: The Transfer of Juveniles to Adult Courts and the Potential Impact of* Roper v. Simmons, 44 AM. CRIM. L. REV. 175, 178 (2007).

68. *See* Bree Langemo, *Serious Consequences for Serious Juvenile Offenders: Do Juveniles Belong in Adult Court?*, 30 OHIO N.U. L. REV. 141, 141 (2004) (discussing how "the recent trend has been to restore the pre-reformation view of treating juvenile offenders as adults in order to punish and deter juvenile crime" by trying juveniles as adults).

69. SNYDER & SICKMUND, *supra* note 40, at 110.

70. *Id.* at 96.

71. *See id.* ("[O]ffenders charged with certain offenses now are excluded from juvenile court jurisdiction or face mandatory or automatic waiver to criminal court. In several states, concurrent jurisdiction provisions give prosecutors the discretion to file certain juvenile cases directly in criminal court rather than juvenile court. In some

transfer provisions, "ma[king] it easier to transfer juvenile offenders from the juvenile justice system to the criminal justice system."[72]

In addition, the past several decades have seen great modification in the transfer statutes of many states in order to "streamline" the transfer process and facilitate easier prosecution of juveniles in criminal court.[73] Methods implemented by the states to achieve this goal include:

> (1) expanding the types of cases and offenders judges can transfer for adult trials after a hearing; (2) lowering the age of criminal jurisdiction; (3) shifting the transfer decision from judges to prosecutors; and (4) increasing the number of offenses and types of offenders that are automatically tried in criminal courts as mandated by legislatures.[74]

"[A]s of the end of the 2007 legislative session [a]ll state[s] allow adult criminal prosecution and sentencing of juveniles under some

---

states, certain adjudicated juvenile offenders face mandatory sentences.").

72. *Id.* Transfer laws vary by state and are generally constricted by both the offender's age and the offense charged. Three categories of transfer provisions have alternate defining terms depending on the state: (1) judicial waiver, "certification, remand, or bind over;" (2) concurrent jurisdiction, "prosecutorial waiver, prosecutor discretion, or direct file;" and (3) statutory exclusion or legislative exclusion. *Id.* at 110. The mechanisms differ regarding where the decision responsibility for transfer exists:

> Waiver provisions leave transfer decisionmaking to the State's juvenile courts: juveniles may not be prosecuted as if they were adult criminals pursuant to a waiver provision until a juvenile court judge has ordered it. Waiver provisions differ from one another in the degree of decisionmaking flexibility they allow the courts. Some make the waiver decision entirely discretionary. Others set up a presumption in favor of waiver. And still others specify circumstances under which waiver is mandatory. . . .
>
> Direct File provisions leave it up to the prosecutor to determine whether to initiate a case against a minor in juvenile court or in criminal (adult) court.
>
> Statutory Exclusion provisions grant criminal courts original jurisdiction over a whole class of cases involving juveniles. Under statutory exclusion, a State legislature is essentially predetermining the question of criminal prosecution for itself and taking the decision out of both the prosecutor's and the court's hands.

PATRICK GRIFFIN, PATRICIA TORBET & LINDA SZYMANSKI, NAT'L CTR. FOR JUVENILE JUSTICE, TRYING JUVENILES AS ADULTS IN CRIMINAL COURT: AN ANALYSIS OF STATE TRANSFER PROVISIONS 1 (1998), http://www.ncjrs.gov/pdffiles/172836.pdf (emphasis omitted).

73. *See* Donna M. Bishop, *Juvenile Offenders in the Adult Criminal Justice System*, 27 CRIME & JUST. 81, 84 (2000) (discussing the "quick and dramatic" transformation of transfer policy in the 1990s as legislatures in forty-four states and the District of Columbia enacted provisions to facilitate transfer through "offense-based, categorical, and absolute alternatives to individualized, offender-oriented waiver proceedings").

74. Langemo, *supra* note 68, at 141.

circumstances."[75] Unfortunately, this "zeal for retribution,"[76] which has replaced the desire to reform the individual child, ignores both the interests of the child and ultimately the interests of the country. Simultaneously, it loses sight of the innate developmental differences between adult and child, and fails both in refusing to accommodate those distinctions.

III. MANDATORY MINIMUM SENTENCES: UNIFORMITY IN SENTENCING OR LOSS OF INDIVIDUALIZED ASSESSMENTS?

Prior to the enactment of the Sentencing Reform Act of 1984,[77] federal judges had great discretion in sentencing offenders.[78] Because most statutes provided only maximum sentences, judges were free to impose a broad range of punishments that reflected both their personal views of justice and the purposes of sentencing, and an individualized assessment of the specific circumstances of the offender and the offense.[79] While such discretion allowed judges to customize a punishment to match the crime,[80] critics noted the unpredictability and disparity of sentences.[81] As a result, as part of the Comprehensive Crime Control Act,[82] Congress instated the Sentencing Reform Act of 1984,[83] "the most sweeping and dramatic reform of federal sentencing," in order to "reduce unwarranted disparity, increase certainty and uniformity, and correct past patterns of undue leniency for certain categories of serious

75. Patrick Griffin, National Center of Juvenile Justice, *National Overviews: State Juvenile Justice Profiles*, http://www.ncjj.org/stateprofiles/overviews/transfer_state_overview.asp. It must be noted that without state transfer mechanisms, juveniles would never be subjected to the mandatory minimum sentences of the adult criminal court. However, analysis of transfer policy is beyond the scope of this note. See generally Bishop, *supra* note 73, Langemo, *supra* note 68, Pagnanelli, *supra* note 67, and Richard E. Redding, *Juveniles Transferred to Criminal Court: Legal Reform Proposals Based on Social Science Research*, 1997 UTAH L. REV. 709 (1997) for a discussion of this topic.

76. Bishop, *supra* note 73, at 85.

77. Sentencing Reform Act, 18 U.S.C. § 3551 (1984).

78. SANFORD H. KADISH, STEPHEN J. SCHULHOFER & CAROL S. STEIKER, CRIMINAL LAW AND ITS PROCESSES, CASES AND MATERIALS 105 (8th ed. 2007).

79. *Id.* at 105-06, 109-10.

80. *See* David Risley, Drug Watch International, Mandatory Minimum Sentences: An Overview, http://www.drugwatch.org/Mandatory%20Minimum%20Sentences.htm (last visited Nov. 13, 2009) (noting that judges had "unbridled discretion to impose whatever sentences they deemed appropriate, in their personal view, up to the statutory maximum").

81. *See* U.S. SENTENCING COMM'N, SPECIAL REPORT TO CONGRESS, MANDATORY MINIMUM PENALTIES IN THE FEDERAL CRIMINAL JUSTICE SYSTEM 47-54 (1991), http://www.ussc.gov/manmin/manmin51.htm.

82. Comprehensive Crime Control Act of 1984, 5 U.S.C. §§ 5314, 5315 (1984).

83. Sentencing Reform Act, 18 U.S.C. § 3551 (1984).

offenses."[84]

While the initial intention of this reform movement was to maintain discretion for the judiciary, it shifted in its development "toward a model of sharply limited discretion."[85] In 1986, Congress enacted mandatory minimum sentencing laws which force judges to impose fixed sentences on offenders, regardless of mitigating circumstances,[86] and by 1994 all states had enacted at least one mandatory minimum sentence law.[87] Premised on the goals of "deterrence and incapacitation," mandatory minimum sentencing allows "legislators [to] convey the message that certain crimes are deemed especially grave and that people who commit them deserve, and may expect, harsh sanctions."[88] However, mandatory minimums exclusively further retributive and deterrent goals of punishment without providing a possibility for sentencing judges to consider the individual offender or the circumstances surrounding the offense.[89] Mandatory minimums as applied to juveniles tried in the adult criminal justice system, therefore, showcase the extreme opposite considerations which founded the juvenile justice movement in the

84. U.S. SENTENCING COMM'N, *supra* note 81, at 7. The United States Sentencing Commission was thereby established as:

> [A]n independent commission in the judicial branch of the United States . . . which shall consist of seven voting members and one nonvoting member. . . . The purposes of the United States Sentencing Commission are to (1) establish sentencing policies and practices for the Federal criminal justice system that (A) assure the meeting of the purposes of sentencing as set forth in section 3553(a)(2) of title 18, United States Code; (B) provide certainty and fairness in meeting the purposes of sentencing, avoiding unwarranted sentencing disparities among defendants with similar records who have been found guilty of similar criminal conduct . . . and (C) reflect, to the extent practicable, advancement in knowledge of human behavior as it relates to the criminal justice process . . . .

28 U.S.C. § 991 (2006). The adoption of the United States Sentencing Guidelines, effective November 1987, resulted from this Commission and provided a resource for courts to determine a narrow sentencing range based on the severity of the offense and the extent of the offenders' criminal history. Risley, *supra* note 80; *see* 2005 FEDERAL SENTENCING GUIDELINES, SENTENCING TABLE, http://www.ussc.gov/2005guid/5a.htm.

85. PAUL J. HOFER, CHARLES LOEFFLER, KEVIN BLACKWELL & PATRICIA VALENTINO, U.S. SENTENCING COMM'N, FIFTEEN YEARS OF GUIDELINES SENTENCING: AN ASSESSMENT OF HOW WELL THE FEDERAL CRIMINAL JUSTICE SYSTEM IS ACHIEVING THE GOALS OF SENTENCING REFORM 7 (2004), http://www.ussc.gov/15_year/chap1.pdf.

86. Drug Policy Alliance Network, What's Wrong with the War on Drugs: Mandatory Minimum Sentences (2009), http://www.drugpolicy.org/drugwar/mandatorymin/ (last visited Nov. 13, 2009).

87. DALE PARENT, TERENCE DUNWORTH, DOUGLAS MCDONALD & WILLIAM RHODES, NAT'L INST. OF JUSTICE RESEARCH IN ACTION, KEY LEGISLATIVE ISSUES IN CRIMINAL JUSTICE: MANDATORY SENTENCING (Jan. 1997), http://www.ncjrs.gov/txtfiles/161839.txt.

88. *Id.*

89. U.S. SENTENCING COMM'N, *supra* note 81, at 8.

first place.[90] Instead of protecting the juvenile and working as a father figure determined to meet the child's best interest through rehabilitation,[91] these judges' hands are tied, forced to impose "harsh, automatic prison terms."[92]

Mandatory minimums provide potential for injustice in part because "[a] nuanced assessment of similarity across cases is not only a uniquely judicial function, but one that is best carried out by a judge immersed in the facts of the individual case."[93] The Supreme Court has recognized the importance of individualized assessment in holding the sentencing guidelines system instituted by the United States Sentencing Commission to be merely advisory, rather than mandatory.[94] Greater potential for just, individualized sentences seems to lie with an advisory sentencing guideline, rather than a mandatory minimum sentencing structure.[95] While sentencing guidelines "differentiate[] defendants convicted of the same offense by a variety of aggravating and mitigating factors, the consideration of which is meant to provide just punishment and proportional sentences, the structure of mandatory minimums lacks these distinguishing characteristics."[96] Therefore, mandatory minimums clearly disserve the best interests of juveniles tried as adults in failing to consider the distinct needs and developmental level of each child offender, while providing questionable benefits, if any,[97] to the

---

90. See *supra* text and accompanying notes 44 to 50 for a discussion of the principles supporting the juvenile justice movement which established the first juvenile courts.

91. Tobias & Martin, *supra* note 39.

92. Families Against Mandatory Minimums, What are Mandatory Minimums?, http://www.famm.org/UnderstandSentencing/WhatAreMandatoryMinimums.aspx (last visited Nov. 13, 2009) (noting that "judge[s] cannot lower a mandatory sentence because of the circumstances of the case or a person's role, motivation, or likelihood of repeating the crime"). Furthermore, in addition to the likelihood for unjust sentences due to lack of discretion, mandatory minimums have been found ineffective for a multitude of reasons, including its failure to deter crime and its impact on prison overcrowding. *See* Drug Policy Alliance Network, *supra* note 86 (noting that the Sentencing Commission and Department of Justice determined that deterrence has not been realized by mandatory minimums, which have "contributed greatly toward prison overcrowding").

93. Eric Citron, *Sentencing Review: Judgment, Justice, and the Judiciary*, YALE L.J. POCKET PART 150, 152 (2006), http://yalelawjournal.org/images/pdfs/3.pdf.

94. *See* Gall v. United States, 552 U.S. 38, 45-46 (2007) (rejecting the requirement of "extraordinary" circumstances to justify punishments outside of the Sentencing Guidelines specified range).

95. U.S. SENTENCING COMM'N, *supra* note 81, at 7 (quoting Pub. L. No. 91-513, 84 Stat. 1236 (1970)) (noting that mandatory minimum sentencing prevents "the judge from us[ing] his discretion in individual cases").

96. *Id.*

97. *See* Drug Policy Alliance Network, *supra* note 86 (noting that the Sentencing Commission and Department of Justice determined that deterrence has not been

country as a whole.

IV. THE REASONING OF *ROPER*: WHAT SHOULD THE ACKNOWLEDGEMENT OF JUVENILES' DIMINISHED CULPABILITY MEAN FOR JUVENILES SENTENCED AS ADULTS WITH MANDATORY MINIMUMS?

While juvenile jurisprudence has delineated a very clear transition in focus from rehabilitation to retribution and deterrence,[98] it is less clear what the future holds for offending juveniles. The Supreme Court in *Roper v. Simmons* "adopt[ed] a groundbreaking understanding of juvenile development, and the rationale undergirding its holding may have extreme implications" for the future of juvenile justice.[99] Throughout American history, the treatment of juveniles by the justice system has coincided with the attitude of society regarding the capability and culpability of children and adolescents as influenced by our evolving understanding of human development and maturity.[100] The Court's bold statement in *Roper*, that the Eighth Amendment's proscription against cruel and unusual punishment prohibited imposition of the death penalty for crimes committed when offenders were under the age of eighteen in part because "society views juveniles . . . as 'categorically less culpable than the average criminal,'" clearly indicates the Court's acknowledgement of the importance of youth and development in the sentencing of juveniles.[101] As such, *Roper* opens the door to the conclusion that mandatory minimum sentences imposed upon offenders under eighteen without the possibility of youth as a mitigating factor are equally afoul of the Eighth Amendment.[102]

A. *The Court's Acknowledgement of the Decreased Culpability of Children under Eighteen in* Roper v. Simmons *and the Science Behind the Reasoning*

In *Roper*, a seventeen-year-old boy was sentenced to death in

realized by mandatory minimums, which have "contributed greatly toward prison overcrowding").

98. See *supra* Part II for a discussion of the history of the juvenile justice system.

99. Pagnanelli, *supra* note 67, at 175.

100. Hillary J. Massey, Note, *Disposing of Children: The Eighth Amendment and Juvenile Life Without Parole after* Roper, 47 B.C. L. REV. 1083, 1083 (2006).

101. Roper v. Simmons, 543 U.S. 551, 567 (2005) (quoting Atkins v. Virginia, 536 U.S. 304, 316 (2002)).

102. *See id.* at 569-71 (holding that minors' "lack of maturity" and "underdeveloped sense of responsibility," as well as "vulnerab[ility] . . . to negative influences and outside pressures" and "transitory" personality traits, make the imposition of the death penalty a cruel and unusual punishment).

Missouri after planning and executing a vicious murder.[103] The Court affirmed the Missouri Supreme Court's decision to set aside the capital punishment and held the death penalty to be cruel and unusual punishment for all juveniles under the age of eighteen.[104] The Court acknowledged the Eighth Amendment guarantee against excessive punishment which "flows from the basic 'precept of justice that punishment for crime should be graduated and proportioned to [the] offense.'"[105] The Court continued on to note that the determination of whether a sentence is "so disproportionate as to be cruel and unusual" punishment[106] must be assessed by "referring to 'the evolving standards of decency that mark the progress of a maturing society.'"[107] Relying on *Atkins v. Virginia*,[108] the Court identified a nation-wide consensus that juveniles are "categorically less culpable than the average criminal."[109]

The Court identified three main differences between children under eighteen and adults which "demonstrate that juvenile offenders cannot with reliability be classified among the worst offenders."[110] First, the Court noted that "'[a] lack of maturity and an underdeveloped sense of responsibility are found in youth more often than in adults and are more understandable among the young. These qualities often result in impetuous and ill-considered actions and decisions.'"[111] Second, the Court pointed to the high level of vulnerability and lack of control of juveniles in identifying youth as "'a time and condition of life when a person may be most susceptible to influence and to psychological damage.'"[112] Third, the Court stated that "the character of a juvenile is not as well formed as that of an adult."[113] These distinct, albeit general, differences between juveniles and adults led the Court to hold that "[t]he Eighth and Fourteenth Amendments forbid imposition of the death penalty on

103. *Id.* at 556-58. Christopher Simmons, "[i]n chilling, callous terms," discussed his murder plan, entered his victim's home, tied her up, threw her off a bridge, and bragged about the murder to his friends. *Id.* at 556-57.

104. *Id.* at 560.

105. *Id.* (quoting *Atkins*, 536 U.S. at 311).

106. *Id.* at 561.

107. *Id.* (quoting Trop v. Dulles, 356 U.S. 86, 100-01 (1958) (plurality opinion)).

108. *Atkins*, 536 U.S. at 316 (holding the death penalty to be cruel and unusual punishment with respect to mentally retarded individuals).

109. *Roper*, 543 U.S. at 567 (quoting *Atkins*, 536 U.S. at 316). Evidence of the consensus includes, "the rejection of the juvenile death penalty in the majority of States; the infrequency of its use even where it remains on the books; and the consistency in the trend toward abolition of the practice." *Id.*

110. *Id.* at 569.

111. *Id.* (quoting Johnson v. Texas, 509 U.S. 350, 367 (1993)).

112. *Id.* (quoting Eddings v. Oklahoma, 455 U.S. 104, 115 (1982)).

113. *Id.* at 570.

offenders who were under the age of 18 when their crimes were committed."[114]

Although such general observations of differences between adolescents and adults seem "intuitively obvious,"[115] the Court presents little specific evidence in its opinion of the diminished culpability of juveniles despite the "substantial research"[116] presented to it in the sixteen amicus briefs submitted on behalf of the Respondent.[117] The juvenile's diminished culpability as a result of underdevelopment and immaturity is scientifically documented to a greater extent than the *Roper* Court explicitly discussed.[118] In 2006, the Coalition for Juvenile Justice held a national conference to illuminate current research on brain development and its implications on the criminal culpability of juveniles.[119] The research confirms and elaborates on that which is generally stated by the *Roper* Court: "[T]he distinction between youth and adults is not simply one of age, but one of motivation, impulse control, judgment, culpability and physiological maturation."[120]

1. The Immaturity, Irresponsibility, and Recklessness of Adolescents

In recognizing the diminished culpability of juveniles, the *Roper* Court acknowledged the immaturity, irresponsibility, and

114. *Id.* at 578.

115. Barry C. Feld, *Unmitigated Punishment: Adolescent Criminal Responsibility and LWOP Sentences*, 10 J.L. & FAM. STUD. 11, 45 n.191 (2007). Feld notes the Court's use of the phrase "as any parent knows" in its discussion of juveniles' immaturity and irresponsibility. *Id.* (quoting *Roper*, 543 U.S. at 569).

116. *Id.* at 45.

117. The Court broadly accepts and relies on "the scientific and sociological studies respondent and his amici cite" without clarifying the specific research which had impact on the Court's decision, thereby making it difficult to determine precisely what developmental research may be relied upon going forward. *See Roper*, 543 U.S. at 569; *see also* Deborah W. Denno, *The Mind of a Child: The Relationship between Brain Development, Cognitive Functioning, and Accountability under the Law: The Scientific Shortcomings of* Roper v. Simmons, 3 OHIO ST. J. CRIM. L. 379, 384-85 (2006) ("The *Roper* Court makes a strong move toward accepting the reliability and validity of social science research . . . . However, the Court never adequately explains how any of the research illuminates its conclusions. Likewise, the Court does not differentiate among the studies discussed in the sixteen amicus briefs to clarify which had the most impact on its decision making. . . . The Court's broadness could . . . suggest that these different kinds of research studies are comparably eligible for later use in case law. . . . On the other hand, there is some frustration in not knowing how *Roper* can be used more precisely as precedent since the Court is coy about these important details.").

118. *See generally* COAL. FOR JUVENILE JUSTICE, EMERGING CONCEPTS BRIEF: WHAT ARE THE IMPLICATIONS OF ADOLESCENT BRAIN DEVELOPMENT FOR JUVENILE JUSTICE? 2 (2006), http://juvjustice.org/media/resources/resource_134.pdf.

119. *Id.*

120. *Id.*

recklessness of adolescents and noted that they are "overrepresented statistically in virtually every category of reckless behavior" due to their indulgence in "impetuous and ill-considered" activity that is "understandable [for] the young."[121] More precisely, this behavior exists in adolescents because the prefrontal cortex, the part of the brain which controls the "executive functions" of reasoning, is the last section of the brain to mature, a process which concludes in approximately the human brain's twenty-fifth year.[122] As a result, adolescents are generally forced to rely on the emotional centers of the brain rather than the underdeveloped frontal regions, thereby functioning more so on impulse than on strategic decision-making.[123] Additionally, adolescents tend to participate in elevated risk-taking behavior because of fluctuating dopamine levels and other "changes in the brain's neurotransmitters . . . which influence memory, concentration, problem-solving and other mental functions."[124] Risk-taking behavior is further increased due to changes in the limbic system, a portion of the brain responsible for processing and regulation of emotion, which "stimulate[s] adolescents to seek higher levels of novelty."[125]

Because the adolescent brain is in a constant flux of development and formation, "[i]t's sort of unfair to expect [adolescents] to have adult levels of organizational skills or decision making before their brain is finished being built."[126] Therefore, while the *Roper* Court does not explicitly disclose the aforementioned developmental discoveries, its observation of the diminished culpability that accompanies youth because of "immaturity" and "irresponsibility" is

---

121. *Roper*, 543 U.S. at 569.

122. COAL. FOR JUVENILE JUSTICE, *supra* note 118, at 3 (citing Beatrice Luna, *Brain and Cognitive Processes Underlying Cognitive Control of Behavior in Adolescence* (Univ. of Pittsburgh Oct. 2005) and Paul Thompson, *Time-Lapse Imaging Tracks Brain Maturation from Ages 5 to 20* (Nat'l Inst. of Mental Health and the Univ. of Cal., L.A. May 2004)). "Executive functions" of reasoning include advanced thought and impulse control. *Id.*

123. Adam Ortiz, Am. Bar Ass'n, Juvenile Justice Center, *Cruel and Unusual Punishment: The Juvenile Death Penalty: Adolescence, Brain Development and Legal Culpability* 2 (2004), http://www.abanet.org/crimjust/juvjust/Adolescence.pdf (noting that a result of relying on the emotional centers of the brain is that "teenagers seem to . . . respond more strongly with gut response than they do with evaluating the consequences of what they're doing") (quoting PBS Frontline, *Inside the Teen Brain: Interview with Yurgelon-Todel*, www.pbs.org/wgbh/pages/frontline/shows/teenbrain/ (last visited Nov. 13, 2009)).

124. *See id.* (citing Linda Patia Spear, *Neurodevelopment During Adolescence, in* NEURODEVELOPMENTAL MECHANISMS IN PSYCHOPATHOLOGY 62 (Dante Cicchetti ed., 2003)) (noting that during adolescence dopamine is "not yet at its most effective level").

125. Elizabeth S. Scott & Laurence Steinberg, *Blaming Youth*, 81 TEX. L. REV. 799, 816 (2003).

126. Ortiz, *supra* note 123, at 2.

clearly well-documented in recent scientific analysis.[127]

2. The Vulnerability to Peer Pressure and Negative Influences of Adolescents

In addition to acknowledging the immaturity, irresponsibility, and recklessness of adolescents, the *Roper* Court cited the "vulnerab[ility] or susceptib[ility] to negative influences and outside pressures, including peer pressure," that young adults endure as further support for their diminished culpability.[128] While the Court broadly regards youth as "a time and condition of life when a person may be most susceptible to influence,"[129] substantial research supports the proposition that adolescents are influenced by peers to a greater extent than adults.[130] Susceptibility to peer pressures climaxes at age fourteen and embarks on a slow decline thereafter,[131] not nearing adult level of ability to resist negative influences until the early-twenties.[132] During this time, adolescent judgment is impacted by a desire for peer approval and a belief that adhering to examples set by peers will assist in achieving goals.[133]

The Court also notes that individuals under eighteen have little power over their own environment.[134] Financial dependency and legal restrictions on freedom impede adolescents from controlling their surroundings and removing themselves from outside pressures that may exist in the home, school, or community.[135] Through the

127. *See* Roper v. Simmons, 543 U.S. 551, 569 (2005) (discussing the "lack of maturity and . . . underdeveloped sense of responsibility . . . found in youth"); *see also supra* notes 122-25 and accompanying text.

128. *Roper*, 543 U.S. at 569.

129. *Id.* (quoting Eddings v. Oklahoma, 455 U.S. 104, 115 (1982)).

130. Scott & Steinberg, *supra* note 125, at 813.

131. *Id.* (citing Laurence Steinberg & Susan B. Silverberg, *The Vicissitudes of Autonomy in Early Adolescence*, 57 CHILD DEV. 841, 848 (1986)).

132. Feld, *supra* note 115, at 56.

133. Scott & Steinberg, *supra* note 125, at 813; *see* Christine S. Scott-Hayward, *Explaining Juvenile False Confessions: Adolescent Development and Police Interrogation*, 31 LAW & PSYCHOL. REV. 53, 62 (2007) (discussing the "heightened vulnerability [of adolescents] to coercive circumstances . . . [which forces them to] 'respond adversely to external pressures that adults are able to resist'") (quoting Thomas Grisso et al., *Juveniles' Competence to Stand Trial: A Comparison of Adolescents' and Adults' Capacities as Trial Defendants*, 27 LAW & HUM. BEHAV. 333, 357 (2003); *see also* MICHAEL A. CORRIERO, JUDGING CHILDREN AS CHILDREN: A PROPOSAL FOR A JUVENILE JUSTICE SYSTEM 30 (2006) ("The consequence of 'saying "no" to negative peer pressure is not just withstanding the "heat" of the moment,' but it is also coping with a sense of exclusion as others engage in the behavior and leave the adolescent increasingly alone . . . . This feeling of loneliness then becomes persuasive and carries an easy solution. Go along with the crowd.").

134. *Roper*, 543 U.S. at 569 ("[J]uveniles have less control, or less experience with control, over their own environment.").

135. *See* Scott & Steinberg, *supra* note 125, at 818 ("Because adolescents lack legal

Roper Court's broad acknowledgment of the adolescent's vulnerability to surrounding influences[136] and the scientific world's recognition of human beings as more resistant to outside pressure as age increases,[137] a consensus has formed that "youths who fail to resist [such pressures] are not as responsible for their behavior as we expect adults to be."[138]

3. The Underdeveloped Character and Transient Identity of Adolescents

The third difference between individuals under eighteen and adults relied on by the Court in *Roper* as reason for diminished culpability is the transient, un-formed personality that accompanies the adolescent stage of life.[139] While the Court does not delve into a great deal of scientific support,[140] studies of developmental psychologists show that two processes exist in this period of transition from child to adult: "individuation" and "identity development."[141] Individuation is "the process of establishing autonomy from one's parents" and identity development is "the process of creating a coherent and integrated sense of self."[142] These processes delineate the transition from pleasing and "parroting" influential adults' beliefs to establishing a unique identity and often involve "risky behavior reflecting rebellion."[143]

According to developmental theory, the process of identity

---

and practical autonomy, they are in a real sense trapped in whatever social setting they occupy and are more restricted in their capacity to avoid coercive criminogenic influences than are adults.").

136. *Roper*, 543 U.S. at 569.

137. *See* MACARTHUR FOUND. RESEARCH NETWORK ON ADOLESCENT DEV. AND JUVENILE JUSTICE, DEVELOPMENT AND CRIMINAL BLAMEWORTHINESS, http://www.adjj.org/downloads/3030PPT-%20Adolescent%20Development%20and%20 Criminal%20Blameworthiness.pdf (charting the decline of susceptibility to influences with increased age); *see also* MACARTHUR FOUND. RESEARCH NETWORK ON ADOLESCENT DEV. AND JUVENILE JUSTICE, LESS GUILTY BY REASON OF ADOLESCENCE, http://www.adjj.org/downloads/6093issue_brief_3.pdf (chronicling recent research illuminating a decline in vulnerability to peer pressure with age and connecting adolescent risk-taking to the presence of peers).

138. Feld, *supra* note 115, at 56.

139. *Roper*, 543 U.S. at 570 ("The personality traits of juveniles are more transitory, less fixed.").

140. *See id.* (dedicating two short sentences to this difference); *see also* Denno, *supra* note 117, at 389-96 (questioning the Court's lone use of general support in Erikson's book).

141. Scott & Steinberg, *supra* note 125, at 819 (citing Peter Blos, *The Second Individuation Process of Adolescence*, 22 THE PSYCHOANALYTIC STUDY OF THE CHILD 162-68 (1967)).

142. *Id.*

143. *Id.*

> development is a lengthy one that involves considerable exploration and experimentation with different behaviors and identity "elements." These elements include both superficial characteristics, such as style of dress, appearance, or manner of speaking, and deeper phenomena, such as personality traits, attitudes, values, and beliefs. As the individual experiments, she gauges the reactions of others as well as her own satisfaction, and through a process of trial and error, over time selects and integrates the identity elements of a realized self. Not surprisingly, given adolescent risk preferences (perhaps combined with rebellion against parental values in the course of individuation), identity experimentation often involves risky, illegal, or dangerous activities – alcohol use, drug use, unsafe sex, delinquent conduct, and the like. For most teens, this experimentation is fleeting; it ceases with maturity as identity becomes settled.[144]

Therefore, because the coherent "self" does not generally form until early adulthood,[145] an adolescent is clearly less blameworthy for his or her actions than a fully formed adult and, as noted by the *Roper* Court, more likely to reform upon maturation.[146]

B. *The* Roper *Court's Assessment that the Justifications for the Death Penalty are Inadequate When Applied to Juveniles*

The Court rationalized that "[o]nce the diminished culpability of juveniles is recognized, it is evident that the penological justifications for the death penalty apply to them with lesser force than to adults."[147] Neither retribution nor deterrence can satisfactorily justify the capital sentencing of children who are broadly distinct from adults in development, maturity, and vulnerability.[148] Considering retribution, the Court noted that "[w]hether viewed as an attempt to express the community's moral outrage or as an attempt to right the balance for the wrong to the victim, the case for retribution is not as strong with a minor as with an adult."[149] Considering deterrence, the Court acknowledged the lack of evidence of deterrent impact and concluded that "the same characteristics that render juveniles less culpable than adults suggest as well that

144. *Id.*

145. *Id.* at 820.

146. *See* Roper v. Simmons, 543 U.S. 551, 570 (2005) ("The reality that juveniles still struggle to define their identity means it is less supportable to conclude that even a heinous crime committed by a juvenile is evidence of irretrievably depraved character.").

147. *Id.* at 571.

148. *Id.* at 569-72; *see supra* text and accompanying notes in Part III(A).

149. *See Roper*, 543 U.S. at 571 ("Retribution is not proportional if the law's most severe penalty is imposed on one whose culpability or blameworthiness is diminished, to a substantial degree, by reason of youth and immaturity.").

juveniles will be less susceptible to deterrence."[150] Therefore, the Court clearly determined that the death penalty was inappropriate for even the worst juvenile offenders not only because children under eighteen have diminished culpability, but also because the overall purposes of the punishment, in this case retribution and deterrence, were ineffective.[151]

C. Roper*'s Reasoning Applied to Mandatory Minimum Sentences for Juveniles Tried as Adults*

Because the Court in *Roper* acknowledged a diminished culpability of juveniles under eighteen due to underdevelopment, immaturity, and vulnerability,[152] it is logical to transfer that same reasoning to juveniles subjected to mandatory minimum sentencing. As discussed in Part III of this Note, mandatory minimum sentencing schemes "are aimed at deterring known and potentially violent offenders and incapacitating convicted criminals through long-term incarceration."[153] Not only are such justifications ineffective in punishment for juveniles, but they also fail to consider the individualized need of each specific, distinct child for an equally individualized rehabilitative punishment. The Court in *Roper* stated:

> The reality that juveniles still struggle to define their identity means it is less supportable to conclude that even a heinous crime committed by a juvenile is evidence of irretrievably depraved character. From a moral standpoint it would be misguided to equate the failings of a minor with those of an adult, for a greater possibility exists that a minor's character deficiencies will be reformed. Indeed, "[t]he relevance of youth as a mitigating factor derives from the fact that the signature qualities of youth are transient; as individuals mature, the impetuousness and recklessness that may dominate in younger years can subside."[154]

The Court clearly indicates a shift in trajectory for juvenile justice back toward the rehabilitative thrust which motivated the

150. *Id.* The Court quoted *Thompson v. Oklahoma* and noted "[t]he likelihood that the teenage offender has made the kind of cost-benefit analysis that attaches any weight to the possibility of execution is so remote as to be virtually nonexistent." *Id.* at 572 (quoting Thompson v. Oklahoma, 487 U.S. 815, 837 (1988)).

151. *Id.*

152. *Id.* at 569-70.

153. PARENT ET AL., *supra* note 87.

154. *Roper*, 543 U.S. at 570 (quoting Johnson v. Texas, 509 U.S. 350, 368 (1993)). "For most teens, [risky or antisocial] behaviors are fleeting; they cease with maturity as individual identity becomes settled. Only a relatively small proportion of adolescents who experiment in risky or illegal activities develop entrenched patterns of problem behavior that persist to adulthood." *Id.* (quoting Laurence Steinberg & Elizabeth S. Scott, *Less Guilty by Reason of Adolescence, Developmental Immaturity, Diminished Responsibility, and the Juvenile Death Penalty*, 58 AM. PSYCHOLOGIST 1009, 1014 (2003)).

establishment of the juvenile justice system to begin with. By recognizing the diminished culpability of juveniles and admitting the failure of retributive and deterrent justifications for punishment, the Court "denounces the shift towards retributive stance on violent juvenile offenders and advocates a return to a focus on rehabilitation."[155]

The Court, therefore, impliedly rejects the basic foundation of mandatory minimum sentences when applied to individuals under the age of eighteen because mandatory minimums are aimed to deter crime and punish offenders through incarceration.[156] Developmental psychologists have noted that "juvenile decisions, as opposed to adult decisions, are influenced more heavily by the potential rewards of their choices rather than by the potential risks involved, as well as the short-term, rather than long-term, consequences of their actions."[157] In *Roper*, the Court clearly recognized the failure to deter juveniles because of this skewed reward/risk balancing ability,[158] and as such, it follows that if juveniles would not be deterred by the potential of a death sentence as punishment for their actions, then certainly the expectation of a mandatory minimum term of incarceration cannot be expected to impact their underdeveloped decision-making methods.[159]

V. THE EIGHTH AMENDMENT: WHERE HAVE THE STANDARDS OF DECENCY EVOLVED TO NOW AND WHAT SHOULD IT MEAN FOR MANDATORY MINIMUM SENTENCES FOR JUVENILES?

A. *The Evolution of Eighth Amendment Interpretation by the Supreme Court*

The prohibition against cruel and unusual punishment specified in the Eighth Amendment has been evoked and analyzed in a variety of ways. While proportionality principles have traditionally been based on a retributive theory which compares the offense to the punishment imposed on the offender,[160] the culpability of the

155. Pagnanelli, *supra* note 67, at 191.

156. PARENT ET AL., *supra* note 87.

157. Benjamin Steiner & Emily Wright, *Assessing the Relative Effects of State Direct File Waiver Laws on Violent Juvenile Crime: Deterrence or Irrelevance?*, 96 J. CRIM. L. & CRIMINOLOGY 1451, 1469 (2006) (citing Steinberg & Scott, *supra* note 154, at 1011-13.)

158. Roper v. Simmons, 543 U.S. 551, 570-72 (2005).

159. *See* Steiner & Wright, *supra* note 157, at 1469 (applying this same reasoning to conclude that juveniles would not be deterred by the potential of being transferred to an adult criminal court).

160. *See* Harmelin v. Michigan, 501 U.S. 957, 1005 (1991) (Kennedy, J., concurring) (discussing the "threshold comparison of the crime committed and the sentence imposed [which] leads to an inference of gross disproportionality").

offender is a natural consideration which should, and at times has, been a factor in the analysis.[161] While the Court has narrowed the proportionality analysis away from culpability concerns and toward a more objective inquiry into the comparison of sentence to crime, the Justices have spoken out on a variety of occasions through this less-than-smooth Eighth Amendment jurisprudence to call for an individualized evaluation of culpability in the proportionality assessment.[162]

The proportionality analysis of the Eighth Amendment was first pronounced by the Court as a three-factor test in *Solem v. Helm*:

> When sentences are reviewed under the Eighth Amendment, courts should be guided by objective factors that our cases have recognized. First, we look to the gravity of the offense and the harshness of the penalty. . . .
>
> Second, it may be helpful to compare the sentences imposed on other criminals in the same jurisdiction. If more serious crimes are subject to the same penalty, or to less serious penalties, that is some indication that the punishment at issue may be excessive. . . .
>
> Third, courts may find it useful to compare the sentences imposed for commission of the same crime in other jurisdictions.[163]

However, eight years later, in *Harmelin v. Michigan*,[164] the Court retreated from the proportionality factors enunciated in *Solem* and held that for noncapital sentences "intrajurisdictional and interjurisdictional analyses are appropriate only in the rare case in which a threshold comparison of the crime committed and the sentence imposed leads to an inference of gross disproportionality."[165] Delivering the opinion of a fractured Court, Justice Scalia rejected Harmelin's contention that his life without parole ("LWOP") sentence

161. *See* Wayne A. Logan, *Proportionality and Punishment: Imposing Life Without Parole on Juveniles*, 33 WAKE FOREST L. REV. 681, 701-02 (1998) (noting that the Court has been mindful of the culpability of the offender in its assessment of punishment and "acted in a manner consistent with a basic precept of Anglo-American law: that proportionality bars punishment in excess of the moral blame of the offender").

162. *See, e.g.*, Stanford v. Kentucky, 492 U.S. 361, 394 (1989) (Brennan, J., dissenting) ("Proportionality analysis requires that we compare 'the gravity of the offense,' understood to include not only the injury caused, but also the defendant's culpability, with 'the harshness of the penalty.'") (quoting Solem v. Helm, 463 U.S. 277, 292 (1983)); Thompson v. Oklahoma, 487 U.S. 815, 853 (1988) (O'Connor, J., concurring) ("'[P]roportionality requires a nexus between the punishment imposed and the defendant's blameworthiness.'") (quoting Enmund v. Florida, 458 U.S. 782, 825 (1982) (O'Connor, J., dissenting)).

163. *Solem*, 463 U.S. at 290-92 (holding that a sentence of LWOP was cruel and unusual and disproportionate to the crime committed).

164. 501 U.S. 957 (1991).

165. *Id.* at 1005 (Kennedy, J., concurring). The Court sustained a mandatory LWOP sentence for drug possession. *Id.* at 994-95.

was contrary to the Eighth Amendment because it is cruel and unusual to impose a mandatory sentence without consideration of mitigating factors.[166] Scalia noted that "[s]evere, mandatory penalties may be cruel, but they are not unusual in the constitutional sense, having been employed in various forms throughout our nation's history."[167]

Joined by Chief Justice Rehnquist, Scalia additionally concluded that "the Eighth Amendment contains no proportionality guarantee"[168] and that proportionality review should not be extended beyond capital cases because "death is different" and therefore requires "protections that the Constitution nowhere else provides."[169] In contrast, in separate concurring and dissenting opinions, all seven other Justices concluded that a proportionality analysis applies to both capital and noncapital cases.[170] Since *Harmelin*, the modified view of the *Solem* proportionality factors enunciated in Justice Kennedy's concurrence has "emerged as the operative test for proportionality."[171] Therefore, in analyzing an Eighth Amendment claim of cruel and unusual punishment, the Court must determine whether a "threshold comparison of the crime committed and the sentence imposed leads to an inference of gross proportionality."[172] Such comparison requires a consideration of the "gravity of the offense" and the "harshness of the penalty."[173] However, exactly what factors should be considered and weighted in this comparison is unclear; therefore, because of the diminished culpability of juveniles, it may be argued that youth should be considered in the "gravity of the offense" evaluation and that the impact of severe sentences on

166. *Id.*

167. *Id.* In addition, Scalia noted that "here can be no serious contention . . . that a sentence which is not otherwise cruel and unusual becomes so simply because it is 'mandatory.'" *Id.* at 995.

168. *Id.* at 965.

169. *Id.* at 994.

170. In his concurring opinion, Justice Kennedy, joined by Justice O'Connor and Justice Souter, while recognizing that the "proportionality decisions have not been clear," *id.* at 996 (Kennedy, J., concurring), acknowledged the existence of a "narrow proportionality principle" that applies to both capital and noncapital sentences, *id.* at 997. In separate dissenting opinions, Justice White (joined by Justices Blackmun and Stevens), Justice Marshall, and Justice Stevens (joined by Justice Blackmun) all acknowledged a proportionality requirement in the Eighth Amendment. *Id.* at 1009-29 (White, J., dissenting; Marshall, J., dissenting; Stevens, J., dissenting).

171. Logan, *supra* note 161, at 699. Logan notes that the majority of the *Harmelin* Court refused to overrule *Solem*. *Id.* at 699 n.96 ("Although some doubt has been expressed as to the continued validity of *Solem* in the wake of *Harmelin*, the great majority of courts have concluded that *Solem*'s three-part test remains intact, although in the modified form enunciated by Justice Kennedy.").

172. *Harmelin*, 501 U.S. at 1005 (Kennedy, J., concurring).

173. *Id.* at 1004 (quoting Solem v. Helm, 463 U.S. 227, 290-91 (1983)).

juveniles should be considered in the "harshness of the penalty" evaluation.[174]

B. *Juveniles and the Eighth Amendment: Looking Beyond Capital Punishment and* Roper *to the Unconstitutional Nature of Mandatory Minimum Sentences*

In holding that "[t]he Eighth and Fourteenth Amendments forbid imposition of the death penalty on offenders who were under the age of 18 when their crimes were committed,"[175] the *Roper* Court looked to its own judgment regarding the culpability of juveniles,[176] as well as confirmed its conclusions through analysis of national consensus and world opinion,[177] in an effort to coincide with the "evolving standards of decency."[178] As Justice O'Connor noted:

> It is by now beyond serious dispute that the Eighth Amendment's prohibition of 'cruel and unusual punishments' is not a static command. Its mandate would be little more than a dead letter today if it barred only those sanctions—like the execution of children under the age of seven—that civilized society had already repudiated in 1791.[179]

As time progresses, the scientific world advances, moral consensus shifts, and accepted beliefs and norms modify; such evolution significantly impacts the interpretation of the Eighth Amendment.[180] Groundbreaking studies have illuminated physiological and psychological realities of the unique developmental period in human maturity that exists prior to full adulthood.[181] The acknowledgement of the diminished culpability of juveniles under the age of eighteen by the *Roper* Court cannot be ignored in future Eighth Amendment analysis. Despite the *Harmelin* Court's refusal

---

174. See *infra* Part V(B) for an application of this proposal and ultimate conclusion that mandatory minimum sentences without the opportunity to consider youth as a mitigating factor violate the Eighth Amendment as grossly disproportionate sentences.

175. Roper v. Simmons, 543 U.S. 551, 578 (2005).

176. See *supra* Part IV for a discussion of diminished culpability.

177. *Roper*, 543 U.S. at 578.

178. *See id.* at 560-61 ("The prohibition against 'cruel and unusual punishments' . . . must be interpreted according to its text, by considering history, tradition, and precedent, and with due regard for its purpose and function in the constitutional design. To implement this framework we have established the propriety and affirmed the necessity of referring to 'the evolving standards of decency that mark the progress of a maturing society' to determine which punishments are so disproportionate as to be cruel and unusual.") (quoting Trop v. Dulles, 356 U.S. 86, 100-01 (1958)).

179. *Id.* at 589 (O'Connor, J., dissenting).

180. *See, e.g.*, Stanford v. Kentucky, 492 U.S. 361, 368 (1989), overruled by *Roper*, 543 U.S. 551).

181. See *supra* Part IV(A) for a discussion of the science behind the reasoning of *Roper*.

to consider mandatory sentences a per se violation of the Eighth Amendment, the now-recognized developmental differences between juveniles and adults, as discussed in *Roper*, mandate that the Court distinguish its *Harmelin* holding.

Culpability and developmental considerations severely impact the Eighth Amendment comparison of the "gravity of the offense" and the "harshness of the penalty," and ultimately reveal that mandatory minimum sentences imposed on minors without allowing sentencing judges the opportunity to consider youth as a mitigating factor create an inference of "gross disproportionality."[182] When discussing the evaluation of the "gravity of the offense," the Court in *Solem* stated that "[c]omparisons can be made in light of the harm caused or threatened to the victim or society, and the *culpability of the offender*."[183] Therefore, in light of the Court's holding in *Roper*, the future of Eighth Amendment proportionality analysis should include a consideration of youth and the developmental position of the child offender.

The second factor in the proportionality comparison, "harshness of the penalty," should also be impacted by *Roper*'s groundbreaking developmental understanding of adolescents. Children are impacted to a greater extent than adults by punishment.[184] To conclude that a fourteen-year-old is affected by a mandatory thirty-year imprisonment sentence in the same way that a fully-developed adult is affected, would be to strip adolescence of its developmental significance. Realistically speaking, "[t]he years child offenders spend in prison are the most formative ones, in which typical adolescents finish their education, form relationships, start families, and gain employment."[185] Therefore, any penalty is clearly harsher when applied to an individual at the fragile developmental period of life known as adolescence.

VI. CONCLUSION

Imposing mandatory minimum sentences on juveniles under the age of eighteen violates the Eighth Amendment as cruel and unusual punishment. Mandatory sentences eliminate the opportunity for a

182. *See* Massey, *supra* note 100, at 1109-13 (concluding that juvenile LWOP sentences are a constitutional violation).

183. Solem v. Helm, 463 U.S. 277, 292 (1983) (emphasis added); *see also Stanford*, 492 U.S. at 394 (Brennan, J., dissenting) ("[T]he gravity of the offense [is] understood to include not only the injury caused, but also the defendant's culpability . . . .") (internal quotation omitted).

184. *See* EQUAL JUSTICE INITIATIVE, *supra* note 37, at 11 ("A sentence of imprisonment until death is a different and harsher punishment when inflicted on a young child.").

185. Massey, *supra* note 100, at 1111.

judge to "exercise discretion because of a child offender's age, background, the legal interpretations of facts established at trial, or any other factor . . . that might make another sentence more appropriate"[186] or more suitable to the rehabilitative needs of the child. The Court's acknowledgement in *Roper v. Simmons* of both the diminished culpability of juveniles and the resultant ineffectiveness of retributive and deterrent justifications of punishment clearly signal a long due shift away from blind application of punitive punishments to children.[187] Hopefully this shift will continue its trajectory toward proportional punishment for juveniles in light of their newly-recognized diminished culpability, developmental state, and rehabilitative potential.

The Court will have the opportunity to continue this ideological shift toward proportional punishment for juveniles in *Sullivan v. Florida*[188] and *Graham v. Florida*.[189] The Supreme Court granted certiorari in the two Florida cases on May 4, 2009, thereby agreeing to consider the constitutionality of life without parole sentences for juveniles.[190] While neither case specifically involves the imposition of a mandatory sentence, and neither case deals with the loss of a life from the minor's actions,[191] at the very least the review of these cases should allow the Court to clarify the scope of the *Roper v. Simmons* decision.[192] While it is certainly possible that the Court will narrowly focus its decision to the specific facts of these cases and "leave for another day . . . the question of how murders committed by juveniles may be punished"[193] or the question of whether juveniles should be blindly subjected to mandatory punishments, it is the great hope of this author that the Supreme Court will seize the opportunity to take *Roper's* reasoning beyond the narrow scope of the death penalty and embrace a broad acknowledgment that minors are simply

186. AMNESTY INTERNATIONAL HUMAN RIGHTS WATCH, *supra* note 31, at 91.

187. *See* Roper v. Simmons, 543 U.S. 551, 569-72 (2005).

188. Sullivan v. Florida, 129 S. Ct. 2157 (2009).

189. Graham v. Florida, 129 S. Ct. 2157 (2009); Adam Liptak, *Justices Agree to Take Up Sentencing for Young Offenders*, N.Y. TIMES, May 4, 2009, http://www.nytimes.com/2009/05/05/us/05scotus.html.

190. Liptak, *supra* note 189.

191. Larry A. Wojcik, ABA Criminal Justice Section. *Supreme Court Grants Certiorari in Juvenile Life Without Parole Cases*, June 2009, http://www.abanet.org/crimjust/juvjust/newsletterjune09/june09/lwop.htm.

192. Equal Justice Initiative, Death in Prison Sentences for 13- and 14-Year-Old Kids, http://eji.org/eji/childrenprison/deathinprison/sullivan.graham (last visited Nov. 13, 2009). In both *Sullivan v. Florida* and *Graham v. Florida*, the Court is asked to "address whether the differences between children and adults that led the Court to strike down the death penalty for children also make permanent imprisonment a constitutionally impermissible punishment for a child." *Id.*

193. Liptak, *supra* note 189.

developmentally different than adults, and therefore less culpable than adults, more receptive to rehabilitation, and more severely damaged by punishments that fail to consider their individuality and unique developmental state.

[8]

Pre-sentence reports, magisterial discourse and agency in the Youth Courts in England and Wales

Jo Phoenix
Durham University, UK

Abstract

This article draws on interviews with Youth Court magistrates to examine if and how discourses, strategies and technologies of risk governance have affected Youth Court magistrates in England and Wales. The aim of the article is to detail the complex relationship between magisterial agency in decision making and youth justice policies which focus on risk control and management. The article demonstrates that, contrary to what might be assumed from the youth and risk governance theoretical literature, Youth Offending Team risk assessments form only one part of the information used by magistrates to explain young people's presence in courts. This article concludes that magisterial decision making is framed not by formal, expert assessments of risk, but by magistrates' claims that they are 'knowing outsiders', who through judicious use of information presented to them and their own life experiences are able to make objective judgements about both the risk assessments authored by Youth Offending Teams and the young lawbreakers before them.

Keywords

magistrates' discourse, risk, sentence decision making, youth governance, youth justice

Introduction

Since the introduction of the Crime and Disorder Act 1998, critical scholarship in the field of youth justice in England and Wales has tended to focus on the way that risk thinking and risk governance have dominated youth justice policy and practice. What have been highlighted are the institutional arrangements of governance between the Youth Justice Board (YJB),[1] multi-agency Youth Offending

Teams (YOTs)[2] and Youth Courts and the impact this has had on practice. Shortly after its inception the YJB advocated the adoption by YOTs of evidence-based practice based on the risk factor prevention paradigm, and the principles of risk, need and responsivity which would provide targeted work capable of having some 'real' effects, that is, measurable reductions in the risk of young people's offending (Chapman and Hough, 1998). Central to this new way of working was a set of standardized tools of assessment[3] that would ensure consistent practice and, most importantly, would provide an evidential foundation for sentencing and interventions. A decade later, the YJB explicitly tied assessments of riskiness to new Youth Rehabilitation Orders and the interventions that make them up (YJB, 2009). Hence, at least at the level of policy, risk-assessment, risk thinking and risk governance form a central strategy in youth justice; with the standardized tools of assessment and the pre-sentence reports to the court providing the basis upon which all decisions are, at least in principle, made.

To date, empirical studies of this 'new' youth justice in England and Wales have tended to focus on youth justice workers, rather than Youth Court magistrates, and have examined issues such as: risk-assessment tools (ASSET) and their use; the ability of YOT workers to use professional discretion; the degree to which there has been the predicted standardization of practice across the country; or, how and in what ways some type of unified occupational culture has or has not been created. Since 1998 there has been no research focusing on Youth Court magistrates, and the influence of the wider institutional and policy context on their decision making. This article is an attempt to fill that gap.

The research question this article addresses is whether risk thinking influences or shapes English Youth Court magisterial decision making, and if it does, in what ways. This article draws upon, but is critical of, youth and risk governance theoretical literature. It argues that although risk dominates the policies of youth justice, magisterial discourse disrupts any pervasive impact of risk thinking in the courts. To put it another way, the criteria by which magistrates make decisions are not determined by the policy context they inhabit. At an empirical level, this article shows how a small group of Youth Court magistrates in a semi-rural local authority in England ($N = 13$) talked about their roles as lay magistrates, about the role that their own experiences played in how they made decisions and about how they were influenced, or otherwise, by the assessments of risk in Pre-Sentence Reports (PSRs) they received from YOTs. In doing so, this article demonstrates that, contrary to what is assumed in YJB policy and in risk governance theoretical literature, magistrates based their decisions on 'common sense' and their experience of life and young people.

The article is broken into four main sections. The first two sections provide a methodological and an analytical note regarding a wider research project[4] from which the data used in this article were drawn. The third section provides a description of the youth and risk governance theoretical literature and describes the theoretical model used for analysing the magistrates' interviews. The final section provides an analysis of the data.

Methodology

This article provides an analysis of interviews with an entire bench of Youth Court lay magistrates ($N = 13$) in a small semi-rural local authority in England (given the pseudonym 'Haverset'). These interviews formed one of the data sets acquired for a much larger Economic and Social Research Council funded project on assessments of 'risk' and 'need' in youth justice. From the outset, key gatekeepers in Haverset were contacted, and the research proposal was discussed with them. The key gatekeepers included the local Chair of the Youth Court Bench, the Chief Superintendent of Haverset Police, the Director of Haverset Social Services and the Haverset YOT Manager. Once funding had been obtained, each gatekeeper provided an opportunity for the research proposal to be presented to key personnel within their area. The purpose of these presentations was two-fold: first, to refine further the aims and objectives of the overall research project; and second, to negotiate access. In the case of the Youth Court Bench, the research proposal was presented at a meeting when all 13 Youth Court magistrates were present. During that meeting questions of ethics and anonymity were addressed and final access arrangements made. Access to the retiring room was denied, as was the request to be able to ask about actual cases and specific decisions made. Despite the fact that prior approval of the research project had been sought and obtained from the Department of Constitutional Affairs, the Haverset magistrates felt that retiring room discussions were too confidential to be included in the research project. Similarly, they were concerned about the issue of maintaining confidentiality if they were asked about specific cases and decisions. Instead, it was agreed that: (1) each magistrate would be interviewed separately at a time and place of mutual convenience; (2) all magisterial interviews would be conducted by the author and would be taped and later transcribed; and (3) each magistrate was free to withdraw consent at any stage in the process. No magistrates withdrew from the research process and many were keen to talk about their work as magistrates. This seemingly easy rapport and relationship was, no doubt, helped by the fact that there was magisterial and youth justice practitioner input in the research design itself. It is important to note, however, that the District Judge serving the Haverset Youth Court declined to take part in the research.

The interviews were semi-structured. The schedule of topics was constructed in such a way as to elicit from the respondents the various ways in which they understood and acted upon the issue of 'risk' and 'need' in the context of their work as magistrates in the Youth Court. Specific questions were asked about PSRs and the assessments of risk contained therein.

For the purposes of addressing the empirical and theoretical questions of this article, three themes were extracted from the data set for further analysis. These were: the ways that the magistrates perceived the Youth Court and their role within it; the ways that they discussed PSRs in relation to their role; and, the criteria on which they based their own assessments of the young people in front of them. The data were then subjected to theoretical coding (Glaser, 1998). The theoretical proposition applied to these data was that magistrates *did not* make sense of their work, organize the information presented to them and understand the cases in front of them according to an actuarial risk-assessment and management frame of reference. This proposition was derived from the youth and risk governance literature. As I argue below, a pre-occupation within that literature is the question of the extent to which actuarialism, risk thinking and risk governance determine (or not) the practices of social actors. The theoretical model developed in order to analyse the magisterial interviews drew on arguments developed within the risk and youth governance literature which highlighted the ways in which social actions in youth justice are not over-determined by the policy context, but are volatile, contested and contingent.

Situating Youth Court magistrates' decision making

While this article focuses on questions of decision making in the context of youth justice, it is not a sociological study of decision making in a Youth Court, per se. It does borrow, albeit loosely, from some of the key organizing assumptions within socio-legal studies and sociological literature in order to examine the influence risk governance has on the way magistrates make decisions (see Hawkins, 2002). Put another way, this article provides some thoughts on the relative weight and merit in magisterial thinking of the broader social and political context and organizational setting (i.e. that encapsulated under the concept of 'risk governance').

It is possible to make three analytical distinctions when thinking about legal decision making (Hawkins, 2002).[5] The wider social, political, economic and ideological context shaping youth justice (or 'the surround') can be distinguished from the narrower institutional and organizational setting and relationships that comprise what might be called a 'youth justice system' (or 'the field'). Both 'the surround' and 'the field' can be distinguished from the criteria by which those charged with decision making organize information, knowledge, experiences and their understandings of the world to make particular decisions about particular cases (or the 'interpretive frame') (Hawkins, 2002). Although these different spheres can be analytically distinguished, Hawkins (2002) claims that each one shapes the other in complex and unpredictable ways. The analytical distinctions between the wider social context (i.e. 'the surround'), the youth justice context (i.e. 'the field) and the symbolic frame of reference (i.e. the 'interpretive frame') are used in this article as organizational tools in the interrogation of both the theoretical literature that follows and the empirical analysis at the end of this article.

Risk governance: Theorizing the surround and the field of youth justice in england and wales

It is not particularly contentious to observe that the context and the setting of youth justice in England and Wales is focused on risk-assessment and management and shaped by a broader audit culture (see Kempf-Leonard and Peterson, 2000 for a fuller discussion, see also Smith, 2006). Witness the publication of *Youth justice: The scaled approach* (YJB, 2009). This approach placed risk 'work' at the very centre of youth justice and Youth Court practice by prioritizing the match between the intensity of interventions and the assessment of risk of the young person. In short, through a package of new targets for practitioners, new guidelines for practice and a set of new sentences for the court, *The scaled approach* highlighted the crucial role played by risk-assessment in the management and reduction of youthful crime – and in informing court reports.

The most clearly articulated theorization of the links between 'risk' and youth justice is the 'youth governance thesis' which runs like this: the reforms introduced to youth justice in England and Wales with the Crime and Disorder Act 1998 were little more than 'institutionalized intolerance' of young people (Muncie, 1999). In the name of managing and controlling the risk of re-offending, they represented a significant extension of punitive, rather than welfare-based, social controls (Goldson, 1999, 2000, 2002, 2005), which in turn reflected broader shifts towards punitiveness across criminal justice (Pratt et al., 2005). These shifts were achieved by the rise to dominance of a 'new penology' which privileges risk control and management in dealing with crime and organizes criminal justice according to the principles of managerialism and audit (Feeley and Simon, 1992; Carlen, 2009). In terms of youth justice, increased levels of punitiveness occur within a wider ideological context in which 'the young' are demonized by both the mass media and the Government. Taken together, these shifts in the context and setting of youth justice are seen as shaping the decision making of politicians, policy-makers and youth justice practitioners and professionals. Hence, just as the policies and context become more punitive and more focused on controlling and managing riskiness, so too the actions and decisions of those working in youth justice become dominated by risk thinking. By making such an assumption, critical scholars have been able to explain the 'dematerialization' of youth justice, that is, the seeming irrelevance of young lawbreakers' experiences of poverty, vulnerability, abuse and neglect, educational exclusion and so on (see also Scraton and Haydon, 2002; Scraton, 2004). In many senses, this version of the youth governance thesis differs little from the various ways in which researchers have thought about the changes to adult criminal justice brought about by neo-liberalism more generally (Rose, 1996; Miller and Rose, 2008). As far as adult criminal justice is concerned, other critical scholars are claiming that the sort of shifts outlined above and encapsulated by the term 'risk-crazed governance' have meant that there is now little or no space for sentencers or justice workers to resist or subvert policy (see especially Carlen, 2009; Tombs, 2009). The logical extension of this set of arguments is that the frame of reference in which lay Youth Court magistrates make decisions about young offenders is one that should be increasingly permeated, dominated or inflected by risk and audit thinking. It follows, therefore, that it should be possible to trace the ways in which risk thinking forms a significant point of reference in Youth Court magisterial decision making in England and Wales. However, as will be demonstrated in the final section of this article, this was not the case in regards to Haverset Youth Court magistrates.

There is another understanding of the relationship between youth justice policy and practice in England and Wales in which risk thinking is seen as having some influence, albeit as yet unspecified, on decision making, but is not seen as determining social action. This approach to thinking about youth governance highlights the deeply contradictory and increasingly hybridized rationalities governing young lawbreakers in England and Wales (Armstrong, 2004; Goldson, 2005; Goldson and Muncie, 2006; Fergusson, 2007) and emphasizes that there is no clear, coherent, single trajectory of policy that shapes social action. Instead, what might be called the 'surround' and the 'field' of youth justice is seen as being particularly volatile and contingent. Risk thinking and actuarialism operate to constrain, but not determine, the social practices of practitioners and professionals (including lay magistrates) working to deliver youth justice.

Thinking about the extent to which practice is determined by policy is not new or exclusively related to risk and audit governance literature. For instance, Lipsky (1980) explored the question of unintended consequences of policy when he observed that the ways in which front-line workers in public services made sense of their roles, and the strategies that they employed to resist management control of their work, had the effect of determining policy outcomes. In the context of Scottish courts, Halliday et al. (2009) extended the work of Lipsky by examining the inter-professional relationships and specifically the mechanisms used by social workers writing court reports to deal with their uncertainty of status in the courts. They found that the various coping mechanisms adopted by social workers operated to undermine the policy objectives of PSRs (Halliday et al., 2009). More recently, literature focusing on a range of public welfare policy areas is emerging. Within this literature, a conceptualization of 'governmentality' is used, derived largely from the work of Miller and Rose (2008), and similar to that underpinning risk governance in criminal justice literature. So, for instance, Prior (2009) conceptualizes what is referred to in this article as the policy 'field' as the transmission of discourse which has an attendant set of strategies and technologies associated with it, but which also requires some practical instrument for its administration. In other words, rationalities of governance necessarily incorporate a set of strategies and techniques for achieving the aims of policy. In this conceptual terrain, *practice* is understood as being a practical instrument by which social actors implement policies. Prior (2009) argues that there is no a priori justification for privileging the policy context or setting over practice. In relation to youth governance theories, the argument Prior (2009) is making is a significant point of departure. Specifically, regardless of the extent to which policy is seen as determining practice, the policy field itself is given a privileged analytical status as the unquestioned 'background' against which questions of practice are brought to the fore. In contrast, Prior (2009: 21) is claiming that in any sphere of public policy, competing strategies and technologies, as well as the possibility of competing rationalities, exist, but that importantly '[o]fficials are human actors and as such bring their own agency to bear on the policy/practice dynamic when faced with the myriad choices involved in deciding what to do and how to do it in any particular situation'. This point was made, explicitly, by Cheliotis (2006) in a critique of another variation of risk governance – Simon's and Feeley's thesis on the new penology. Cheliotis (2006) argued that no matter how seductive this thesis might be in evoking something of the spirit of the time, the thesis is based on a number of assumptions that cannot be sustained in the face of empirical evidence. Key to Cheliotis' (2006) critique is the argument that professionals within criminal justice can, do and are able to bring individual and personal values and meanings to their decisions and in so doing are able to generate and sustain organizational change. In other words, human agency is not eclipsed, or indeed over-determined, by processes of governance.

There are other examples of writers questioning the assumption that modes of risk governance determine justice workers' agency in practice and/or decision making. Kemshall (2003) claimed that many of the unintended consequences of adult justice policy were caused because practitioners *mediate* the policies during the process of implementing them. Kemshall (2003) argued that operational managers and practitioners interpret and put into action policy changes in the face of limited resources, pre-existing or well-established professional ideologies, local partnership arrangements and so on, although the manner in which they do this is fundamentally shaped by the setting that they inhabit (see also Kemshall, 2008; McNeill et al., 2009). In the field of youth justice, a recent study of resistance to the introduction of a Bail Support Scheme (BSS) in the Youth Courts identified that the abilities of youth justice practitioners to influence decision making was limited by the relative power of the magistracy. Hughes (2009) argued that youth justice workers were able to subvert the explicit aims of the Bail Support Scheme through a process of reinterpreting the statutory aims and, in some places, even reversing the priorities. He also noted that magistrates were able to override both the Bail Scheme workers' subverted aims, and the official explicit governmental aims of the BSS, in order to meet their own objective of a well-ordered, smooth-running Youth Court. He concluded that in practice, Bail Support Scheme workers needed to work in ways which accommodated the concerns of the magistracy, as well as their own informal priorities. Studies like this confirm what Kemshall (2003, 2008), Muncie (2006) and Prior (2009) have all indicated: the relationship between policy and practice is not closed. The relationship is contested, volatile, unstable, contingent and unpredictable (see, for instance, Eadie and Canton, 2002; Baker, 2005; Field, 2007; Souhami, 2007; Hughes, 2009; Westmarland and Clarke, 2009). It is this less deterministic approach to understanding youth and risk governance that provided the foundation for the analysis of the empirical data described below.

Magistrates' discourse

The rest of this article focuses on what Haverset magistrates had to say. It describes the way they talked about what made them qualified to make decisions and on what they based their decisions. Before detailing the criteria by which magistrates said they made decisions, it is helpful to show that, on one level, Haverset Youth Court magistrates claimed that they were not able to make any real decisions. Following on from this, I detail the basis upon which Haverset Youth Court magistrates claimed that they were able to make decisions; namely a combination of their 'common sense' and their experience of young people and of life. From there, I demonstrate how such claims enabled Haverset Youth Court magistrates to assert that they were able better to understand young lawbreakers through the process of engaging with them in the court, were able to be more objective than YOT workers in assessing the young people before them and were thereby able to extract useful information from young people and the court reports in the process of making decisions.

Magisterial (lack of) choice

The interviews with magistrates were wide-ranging and covered topics such as how they came to the sorts of decisions that they did, what they would change about the Youth Court, how they read, understood and used the PSRs, whether they found the risk-assessments useful and in what ways, if there were factors other than the information contained in the PSRs that helped them make their decisions. Before exploring some of the interview material, it may be useful to provide a sense of how the magistrates in Haverset Youth Court made sense, more generally, of the task of sentencing. There was a consensus that there was little or no choice in decision making in sentencing – that as magistrates, they merely followed procedures and guidelines as set out by the Magistrates' Association and contained in the *Youth Court Bench book* (Sentencing Guidelines Council, 2005):

> We just follow procedures. You've got the offence. You've got the entry point. You've then got the aggravating and mitigating factors as far as the offence is concerned and then you've got the aggravating and mitigating factors as far as the offender is concerned. So, you've got that logical process. There's no real decisions to make. (Magistrate 2)

What Magistrate 2 was describing is what others have called 'structured decision making' (see, for instance, Rumgay, 1995). For some of the interviewees 'structured decision making' felt like a curtailment of flexibility and a limit to their discretion:

> We're made to believe that in the Youth Court we have a more flexible sentencing – but we don't actually. If fact, they're not flexible at all... You can't give them a supervision order unless they've done something first, rather than giving them an action plan order. (Magistrate 5)

> Magistrates have a lot less discretion now than they did up to about 15 years ago. Essentially, the whole time that I have been sitting as a magistrate I have been limited by what is in the guidelines and policy. (Magistrate 9)

These quotations echo other studies of Adult Court magistrate and Scottish sheriff decision making (see Millie et al., 2007; Tombs, 2009). However, regardless of the way that Haverset's Youth Court magistrates positioned themselves as having little choice, or as occupying a field in which their ability to make choices about sentencing is curtailed, they nevertheless make decisions in the process of sentencing; and in particular, decisions about how much weight to give to the risk-assessment and information contained in the PSRs and how to weigh up *all* the different pieces of information presented to them (i.e. the defence provided by the young person's solicitor, any comments made by the young person or the court clerk, the case put forward by the Crown Prosecution Service and so on). In what follows I trace the ways in which Haverset's Youth Court magistrates talked about themselves as being qualified to adjudicate *young* offenders, and ordered the various pieces of information presented to them in order to come to a sentencing decision.

Common sense, experience and Youth Court magistrates as 'knowing outsiders'

A lay magistrates' court is not the administration of justice by legally qualified experts. It is an amateur court, although lay magistrates do have at their disposal the assessments of risk and recommendations made by qualified experts, that is, the YOTs, solicitors, court clerks and so on. As Parker et al. (1989), Worrall (1990) and Brown (1991) all argued, a key component to magisterial discourse is an appeal to 'common sense'. It is through this appeal to 'common sense' that magistrates are able to make the case that sentencing and other decisions can be arrived at through 'intuition', 'gut feelings', 'instinct' and so forth, rather than by other, more 'expert' means. For Worrall (1990), however, there is much more about the use of 'common sense' than the possession of 'a good instinct'.

For magistrates, the appeal to common sense functions as a procedural device, a technology, which allows the individual to create a plausible story from information which has no fixed or *essential* meaning. Magistrates will therefore construct their own narrative explaining the young person's presence in court by treating the various pieces of information presented to them *as though* that information has a deeper truth to it (i.e. it is 'common sense' that children from poor single parent households will be more prone to getting into trouble with the law). Common sense also functions to create a 'reciprocity of perspectives' (Cicourel cited in Worrall, 1990: 18). In the case of magistrates' justice, this appeal to common sense is also a claim to informal, anecdotal knowledge based on the assumption that most 'ordinary people' would come to the same conclusions as they, if presented with the same information. At the heart of the appeal of common sense, then, is the presumption of a common universe of meanings, a set of shared values and understandings (see also Parker et al., 1989). This presumption is often little more than a thin veil drawn over what might be called stereotypes or dominant discourses of particular 'types' of subjects. Worrall (1990) also argued that common sense is 'sense' because it is derived from the intuitive and the instinctive, from some notion of lived experience which can then be applied to others. In this way, Worrall was able to constitute the decision making by magistrates in an Adult Court as based on (1) the exclusion of expert knowledge and (2) the elevation of their own lived experiences to the level of universally applicable knowledge, and, by extension, the construction of that which was outside their experience as being not knowable, not understandable and thereby not relevant.

Analysis of the Haverset magistrates' interviews would suggest that something more complex than this is happening in the Youth Courts. One of the key differences between sitting on the Adult Court Bench and sitting on the Youth Court Bench is that the Youth Court is a court with *special, albeit common sense, knowledge* in dealing with a particular constituency – young people. To sit on the Youth Court Bench requires extra training in comparison to that required by the Adult Court Bench. The Youth Court magistracy must demonstrate that they are not simply a panel of 'peers' who are able to administer justice, but that they are qualified amateurs, enthusiasts, *knowing* outsiders with a special set of skills or expertise in understanding young people and assessing information presented by and about young lawbreakers.

As the interviews show, the Haverset Youth Court magistrates claimed their ability to administer youth justice was not just based on their training in Youth Court policies, procedures and processes. When probed about the basis of their 'lay expertise', the Haverset Youth Court magistrates said that their own experiences of working with young people or having a family gave them the specialist knowledge on which they could make assessments of the young lawbreakers in court:

> I used to teach a bit and I'd teach at the borstal institutions, it was called then, in the south of England. And one of our neighbours was a Chairman of the Bench or something in Weymouth, and she was quite keen to get me involved in the magistracy and Youth Court in particular because of my knowledge. (Magistrate 5)

> I would have always chosen the youth one, because I have an interest in youth ... I've been involved in things like rugby clubs going through to coaching rugby and various others. (Magistrate 10)

In a similar fashion, just under half of the Haverset magistrates claimed that because they had a particular set of experiences of life (rather than of young people) they were able to adjudicate and judge young people:

> I still look at them and think, well I had, if not the same, as bad an upbringing as they've got. My parents never knew where I was from dusk' till dawn, didn't care, as long as I didn't have a policeman come to the door, they didn't worry. I had a free licence, and I think up to a point I'm okay. I know what their lives are like. (Magistrate 12)

Using their experience and common sense – assessment through engagement

Youth Courts are designed to be more informal than Adult Courts, and magistrates are enjoined to engage with the offending young person (i.e. speak to them directly). Within the Adult Court, the exchange of information between the bench and the offending adult is channelled through, and is mediated by, the offending adult's legal expert (Tata, this issue). In the Youth Court, magistrates address questions directly to the young people and listen to what they have to say at key stages in the process, in particular just before the magistrates retire to make a decision.

From the perspective of the magistrate, this process of participation enabled them to assess the 'real' young person and to bring to bear their own privileged knowledge and experiences when interpreting the information presented to them – including, importantly, the pre-sentence or specific sentence reports. The policy of engagement in the Youth Court further acted to enable that privileging of experiential knowledge by creating a process in which magistrates are encouraged to 'read' the specific young person in front of them. Engagement is important because it provided a means by which these Youth Court magistrates claimed they were able to balance or assess the risk-assessments and recommendations in the pre- or specific sentence reports made by the YOT against their own evaluation of the young person:

> I'm pleased that we had this engagement because I've always wanted to talk to the young people. They open their mouths and sometimes you get completely a different picture. I mean you can be watching this youth and then their defence lawyers are talking about them, and the YOT is talking about them. That's fine, but you never get the picture and I always wanted to. Even just a sentence. And just the way in which the sentence is delivered you can tell something about that young person... and also the sort of young person's standing, sitting there, you know, to me it enlightens me, as soon as I hear their voices. It really does help me. (Magistrate 3)

> You're trying to get through to them to find out what it is they're thinking, and on the basis of that, you get some idea, or basically you hope to get some idea of how they're going to react to different sentences. And occasionally, you know, you're just not engaging with them at all. That may be my fault, it may be their fault, but I mean I have to assume that it's their fault, you know. So if you had a young person who says just these words, I'm not going to put any inflection in them, 'What I did was wrong. I'm sorry.' How do you know that they are? By looking in their eyes and looking at their body language. ... But I think if they're genuinely sorry, and then you can perhaps engage a bit further and say 'Well, what can we do? Do you have a problem with, it may be alcohol, it may be drugs, or you may be having a problem with anger, and so on.' ... So I think you get some sense of whether the thing [i.e. the sentence] has got a chance of working. (Magistrate 4)

Experience, common sense and the disqualification of 'expert' risk assessments

Haverset Youth Court magistrates recognized the good work of Haverset's YOT, while at the same time raising questions about the nature of the knowledge the YOT produced. They were concerned that the claims made by the YOT workers were biased because of the way policy structured an ambiguous relationship between the YOT workers and the offending young people. Put another way, the magistrates called into question the 'objectivity' of YOT workers – not because they did not have faith in them, but rather because they recognized that in order for the YOT workers to do their job, to make the assessments which informed the PSRs, YOT workers needed to form a relationship with the young person. In some cases, a few of the magistrates interviewed felt that this relationship was too close and/or too sympathetic, and that their own opinion of the young person, based on their own common sense and their interaction with the young person, was more relevant (see also Tata et al., 2008; Beyens and Scheirs, this issue):

> On the whole they do a good job, the YOT, for what they're doing. They can from time to time get too emotionally involved with the defendant. Some of the views [i.e. of the magistrates] sometimes is [*sic*] that the YOTs have had the wool pulled over their eyes. . . . sometimes their conclusions [i.e. recommendations] are way short of the mark really. (Magistrate 9)

> They're there to administer community punishment, but they're also there to provide reports for the court, and I think sometimes they forget that they are servants of the court. (Magistrate 4)

The above quotations highlight some of the ways that Haverset magistrates made sense of the recommendations made in the reports, as well as the 'authority' of the report writers. Indeed the concern that the recommendations made by the Haverset YOT were not 'in line' with the magistrates' own views demonstrates the degree to which they were able to interpret selectively the report by privileging their own ability to understand and know the young person above the YOT workers' abilities. Importantly though, the magistrates did not entirely dismiss the YOTs' views. Some commented that this close relationship enabled the YOT workers to get really good quality information (as opposed to a good assessment) that they, the magistrates, could use when forming their own explanations about the young person's lawbreaking and prospects for the future (see also Tata, this issue).

Five Haverset magistrates claimed that not only were their own assessments of young lawbreakers more objective than those contained within the court reports authored by the YOT, but also YOT assessments of risk of re-offending were not that relevant to the task of sentencing:

> Of course, they've introduced this risk-assessment which is a real pain in the backside quite frankly, because we don't want to know about that. We want to know about the background to the offending, a bit more about the personal circumstances. (Magistrate 7)

> For me personally I'm more interested in the facts surrounding the background, the offences, why it was caused and the attitude towards the victim. Whether he's going to re-offend... is not really that important to me. And my view is that it's something that's just clogging up the system because the facts of the matter – that's what are interesting. And we make the judgment on the facts. (Magistrate 8)

Notwithstanding the above, none of the magistrates rejected the *logic* of risk-assessment, per se. Most simply supplanted the YOT assessments with assessments of their own:

> Sometimes they [i.e. the YOT] come with a medium risk and you think... if somebody is taking drugs and then someone [i.e. the YOT] tries to tell us they're low risk, that's very difficult to come to terms with. I mean [for] me that's one of the triggers, drugs or alcohol. If they're really having this or dossing around with friends you'd feel... there's more of a likelihood that they're going to re-offend and like they've also got lots of friends who are re-offending all the time. (Magistrate 2)

In forming their own assessments, Haverset magistrates focused on the young person's history of offending and any suspected links to drug use:

> Well, the problems about [the assessment of the] risks of re-offending is that it's done by a computer program... which is slightly irritating because we see these people who we know are going to re-offend, but then [in the PSR they are] entered as low risk, and it's really because of [the] level of offending. You know, multiple low level shoplifts, lifting to feed a drug habit, [but the] drug habit is not made explicit. But you know if you've had them back for shoplifting again and again that they probably have got a drug habit and it's not there, which in my mind makes them a higher risk. (Magistrate 5)

> I make decisions from knowing about their [offending young people's] background and also their history of offending, the type of offences as well. Is it the sort of thing that is a one-off? Or if you've got a sort of 15-year-old who doesn't go to school any more and spends all his day drinking, goes out and commits shoplifting to get money to buy more drink or drugs or whatever. That's how I decide. (Magistrate 8)

What is clear from the preceding quotations is that Haverset magistrates made decisions about young people that were not necessarily based on the risk-assessments in the reports or provided to them by the report writers in court. Instead they drew on their own ability to explain or make sense of the young people's offending. Indeed, as the quotations demonstrate, what took precedence in these magistrates' decisions were the ways in which *they* (rather than the report writers) put together the pieces of information about the backgrounds and circumstances of the young people in accordance with their own 'folk' explanations of youth offending. In this respect the reports functioned as an efficient way to get that information:

> You've got all these headings [in the PSR] and you can identify what you want to see there. Whereas before it was waffle, waffle, waffle. Not that they are much better or more precise [it's just that] you can pick out the things you need. (Magistrate 3)

As two magistrates commented the reports functioned as a yardstick by which they could measure their own explanations and decisions:

> I compare as I go through and I see if what I think coincides with what they think. (Magistrate 4)

> What the YOT says is helpful because well, it's like you think: 'Hang on a minute, I don't agree with that!' Or, 'I don't want to know that.' I think it [i.e. the report] just gives you a fuller picture. (Magistrate 10)

What the above sections demonstrate is that how these magistrates read and used the PSR was different than might be presumed from the literature on risk and youth governance. The magistrates used the PSRs to extract information in order to come up with their own stories explaining the young person's presence in the court. They used the PSRs as a way to gauge their decision making. They were able to do this because they recognized the merit and quality of the *information* presented to them in the reports. But as far as the status of the PSR or the merit of the risk-assessment was concerned, by disqualifying actuarial YOT *knowledge* these magistrates were able to substitute their own assessments in place of the YOT assessments.

Conclusion

There are a number of inter-related conclusions that can be drawn from the above analysis. Haverset's magistrates talked about the various ways that they displaced, or rendered less-than-relevant, some of the technocratic instruments and strategies of risk governance, that is, risk-assessment and the recommendations for sentencing based on risk-assessment. They selectively interpreted, used, ignored or questioned both the contents of the reports and the authority of the report writers in ways which enabled them to author their own magisterial stories of youth offending (see also Tata et al., 2008; Field and Nelken, this issue). It was not the case that

Haverset magistrates disregarded the expert knowledge of court report writers in any simple fashion. Rather, and as argued above, magisterial discourse (and indeed legitimacy) in the Youth Court is based in part on an appeal to common sense and being a 'knowing outsider' - and importantly it is also based on privileging their *experiential* knowledge above expert knowledge, including that of the authors of court reports. More than this, however, Haverset magistrates positioned themselves, relative to the court report authors as untainted by the biasing 'effect' of having a relationship with the young lawbreaker. In common with the magistrates in Parker et al.'s (1989) research, Haverset magistrates 'took each case on its merits' and sought to 'understand' the young person, their actions and their context using all the information presented to them. In privileging their own experiences and their magisterial expertise in knowing young people (and young offenders), Haverset magistrates thereby constructed narratives about how young people should or should not act in any given situation. In this sense, these magistrates were eloquent in discussing and talking through the choices that they could and did make in how they ordered the information presented to them in the reports. Although Haverset's magistrates authored an explicit narrative about having little or no choice in sentencing, it was clear that they operated within an interpretive frame that allowed them to bring to bear other (i.e. non-actuarial, non-risk) knowledge when making decisions and when weighing up the relative merits of PSRs in their decision-making processes – and ultimately their sentences. The importance of this observation is this: in making choices about how to order information and thereby transform it into knowledgeable accounts/explanations of young people's offending, these magistrates actively demonstrated that the policy obsession with risk control and management did not shape their frames of reference for decision making. This article demonstrates that even though there may be a policy drive towards risk management and risk governance of young people, the rationales and understanding of their 'lay expertise' allowed them to remain relatively isolated from the effects of that policy drive. So, although 'risk-crazed' governance may well act in ways to delimit (and 'govern') judicial discretion and decision making (see, for instance, Tombs, 2009), the analysis herein indicates that it has had a less constraining, delimiting or determining effect on the logics that shape magisterial decisions. That said, it is not possible to generalize from the specific empirical details of the preceding analysis. The Youth Court Bench in Haverset was a very small Youth Court in a location that did not identify itself as having any real 'problem' with youth crime. The court was not a busy one and the young people who cycled through that court were often the same young people seen by the same magistrates time and time again. For these reasons, the main conclusions to be drawn from the analysis cannot be about the specific explanations that the magistracy did eventually author to explain youth offending but rather about the ways in which magisterial discourse and knowledge functioned to override more 'expert' (i.e. YOT) assessments of risk and to subvert the determining effects of policy. In the final analysis, it is arguable that Youth Court magistrates may be relatively impervious to any thorough-going, pervading penetration of risk governance – regardless of the inability of magistrates to resist policies which limit their use of discretion and which, through a culture of audit and managerialism seek to bring them into control. The fundamental basis which shapes Youth Court magisterial decision making is the privileging of 'common sense' and their own experiences of young people over and above those of any risk experts. Indeed, it is their experiences of reading the expert risk recommendations and balancing these recommendations against their knowledge of young people and their 'folk' explanations of youthful offending that provides the foundation for treating risk reports and risk expertise with scepticism.

Notes

1. The YJB oversees the youth justice system in England and Wales, advising its Secretary of State for Justice.
2. There is a YOT in every local authority of England and Wales. YOTs are multi-agencies teams that comprise representatives from police, social services, education, health and youth justice, but not the judiciary.
3. ASSET, ONSET, etc.
4. The study, entitled 'Doing justice: Analysing "risk" and "need" assessment in Youth Justice' was funded by the Economic and Social Research Council (RES-000–23–0515). The aims were: (1) to investigate and analyse the social, political and ideological conditions in which youth justice practitioners, including lay magistrates, YOT workers, police and solicitors assessed the risks and needs of and made decisions or recommendations about young lawbreakers and; (2) to describe and analyse the engagement (or not) of young people in those processes. Please see http://www.esrcsocietytoday.ac.uk/ESRCInfoCentre/ViewAwardPage.aspx?awardnumber=RES-000–23–0515 for a discussion of the findings of that larger study and for a discussion on methodological issues. The protocols for analysis that were followed in this research project were adopted, loosely, from a discourse analytical perspective. In practical terms, each dataset was subjected to theoretical coding (Glaser, 1998).
5. This theoretical framework is one explicitly developed by Hawkins (2002). However, theoretically informed, empirical analyses of legal decision making have long since used similar frameworks to analyse decision making from a more social or naturalistic perspective (see Hawkins for a discussion of this perspective). In this way, researchers have highlighted, inter alia, how organizational contexts, inter-personal factors, cultural, gender and/or ethnic stereotypes and broader social patterns of inequality affect legal decision making and indeed, that 'law' is only one factor in the process (see, for instance, McBarnet, 1981; Carlen, 1983; Worrall, 1990; Dixon, 1995; Heddernan and Gelsthorpe, 1997; Sanders and Young, 2000).

References

Armstrong D. A risky business? Research, policy and governmentality and youth offending. *Youth Justice* 2004; 4(2): 100–16.

Baker K. Assessment in youth justice: Professional discretion and the use of asset. *Youth Justice* 2005; 2(5): 106–22.

Brown S. *Magistrates at Work*. Buckinghamshire: Open University Press, 1991.

Carlen P. *Women's Imprisonment*. London: RKP, 1983.

Carlen P (ed.) *Imaginary Penalities*. Devon: Willan Publishing, 2009.

Chapman T, Hough M. *Evidence Based Practice: A Guide to Effective Practice*. London: Home Office, 1998.

Cheliotis L. How iron is the iron cage of the new penology. *Punishment & Society* 2006; 8(3): 313–40.

Dixon J. The organisation context of criminal sentencing. *American Journal of Sociology* 1995; 100(5): 1157–98.

Eadie T, Canton R. Practising in a context of ambivalence: The challenge for youth justice workers. *Youth Justice* 2002; 1(2): 14–26.

Feeley M, Simon J. The new penology: Notes on the emerging strategy of corrections and its implications. *Criminology* 1992; 30(4): 449–74.

Fergusson R. Making sense of the melting pot: Multiple discourses in youth justice policy. *Youth Justice* 2007; 7(3): 179–94.

Field S. Practice cultures and the "new" youth justice in (England and) Wales. *British Journal of Criminology* 2007; 47(2): 311–30.

Glaser B. *Doing Grounded Theory: Issues and Discussion*. Mill Valley, CA: Sociology Press, 1998.

Goldson B. Youth (in)justice: Contemporary developments in policy and practice. In: Barry G (ed.) *Youth Justice: Contemporary Policy and Practice*. Aldershot: Ashgate, 1999, p.1–18.

Goldson B. "Children in need" or "young offenders"? Hardening ideology, organisational change and new challenges for social work with children in trouble. *Child and Family Social Work* 2000; 5(3): 255–65.

Goldson B. New labour, social justice and children: Political calculation and the deserving–undeserving schism. *British Journal of Social Work* 2002; 32(6): 683–95.

Goldson B. Taking liberties: Policy and the punitive turn. In: Hendrick H (ed.) *Children and Social Policy: An Essential Reader*. Bristol: Policy Press, 2005, p.255–68.

Goldson B, Muncie J (eds) *Youth Crime and Justice: Critical Issues*. London: SAGE, 2006.

Halliday S, Burns N, Hutton N, McNeill F, Tata C. Street-level bureaucracy, interprofessional relations and coping mechanisms: A study of criminal justice social workers in the sentencing process. *Law & Policy* 2009; 31(4): 405–28.

Hawkins K. *Law as Last Resort*. Oxford: Oxford University Press, 2002.

Heddernan C, Gelsthorpe L (eds) *Understanding the Sentencing of Women*. HORS 170 London: The Stationery Office, 1997.

Hughes N. Managerialism subverted? Exploring the activity of youth justice practitioners. In: Michael B, Prior D (eds) *Subversive Citizens: Power, Agency and Resistance in Public Services*. Bristol: Policy Press, 2009, p.155–70.

Kempf-Leonard K, Peterson E. Expanding realms of the new penology: The advent of actuarial justice for juveniles. *Punishment & Society* 2000; 2(1): 66–97.

Kemshall H. *Understanding Risk in Criminal Justice*. Buckingham: Open University Press, 2003.

Kemshall H. Risks, rights and justice: Understanding and responding to youth risk. *Youth Justice* 2008; 8(1): 21–37.

Lipsky M. *Street Level Bureaucracy: Dilemmas of the Individual in Public Services*. New York: Russell Sage Foundation, 1980.

McBarnet D. *Conviction: Law, the State and the Construction of Justice*. London: Macmillan, 1981.

McNeill F, Burns N, Halliday S, Hutton N, Tata C. Risk, responsibility and reconfiguration: Penal adaptation and misadaptation. *Punishment & Society* 2009; 11(4): 419–42.

Miller P, Rose N. *Governing the Present*. Cambridge: Polity, 2008.

Millie A, Tombs J, Hough M. Borderline sentencing: A comparison of sentencers' decision-making in England and Wales and Scotland. *Criminology and Criminal Justice* 2007; 7(3): 242–67.

Muncie J. Youth justice: Institutionalized intolerance: Youth Justice and the 1998 Criminal Justice Act. *Critical Social Policy* 1999; 19(2): 147–75.

Muncie J. Governing young people: Coherence and contradiction in contemporary youth justice. *Critical Social Policy* 2006; 26(4): 770–93.

Parker H, Sumner M, Jarvis G. *Unmasking the Magistrates*. Milton Keynes: Open University Press, 1989.

Pratt J, Brown D, Hallsworth S, Brown M, Morrison W (eds) *The New Punitiveness: Trends, Theories, Perspectives*. Cullompton: Willan Publishing, 2005.

Prior D. Policy power and the potential for counter-agency. In: Michael B, Prior D (eds) *Subversive Citizens: Power, Agency and Resistance in Public Services*. Bristol: Policy Press, 2009, p.17–32.

Rose N. The death of the social? Refiguring the territory of government. *Economy and Society* 1996; 25(3): 327–56.

Rumgay J. Custodial decision making in a magistrates' court. *British Journal of Criminology* 1995; 35(2): 201–17.

Sanders A, Young R. *Criminal Justice*. London: Butterworth, 2000.

Scraton P. Streets of terror: Marginalization and criminalization, and authoritarian renewal. *Social Justice* 2004; 31(1–2): 130–57.

Scraton P, Haydon D. Challenging the criminalization of children and young people: Securing a rights based agenda. In: Muncie J, Hughes G, McLaughlin E (eds) *Youth Justice: Critical Readings*. London: SAGE, 2002, p.311–28.

Sentencing Guidelines Council. *Youth Court Bench Book*. http://www.jsboard.co.uk/magistrates/ycbb/index.htm London: Judicial Studies Board, 2005.

Smith R. Actuarialism and early intervention in contemporary youth justice. In: Barry G, Muncie J (eds) *Youth Crime and Justice: Critical Issues*. London: SAGE, 2006, p.78–91.

Souhami A. *Transforming Youth Justice: Occupational Identity and Cultural Change*. Cullompton: Willan Publishing, 2007.

Tata C, Burns N, Halliday S, Hutton N, McNeill F. Assisting and advising the sentencing process: The pursuit of "quality" in pre-sentence reports. *British Journal of Criminology* 2008; 48(6): 835–55.

Tombs J. Telling sentencing stories. In: Carlen P (ed.) *Imaginary Penalities*. Devon: Willan Publishing, 2009, p.84–112.

Westmarland L, Clarke J. Awkward customers? Policing in a consumer age. In: Michael B, Prior D (eds) *Subversive Citizens: Power, Agency and Resistance in Public Services*. Bristol: Policy Press, 2009, p.171–90.

Worrall A. *Offending Women: Female Lawbreakers and the Criminal Justice System*. London: Routledge, 1990.

Youth Justice Board (YJB). *Youth Justice: The Scaled Approach*. London: YJB, 2009.

Jo Phoenix is Reader in Criminology and Co-Convenor of the Crime, Violence and Abuse Research Group in the School of Applied Social Sciences, Durham University.

Part IV
Youth Offenders and Restorative Justice

[9]

Restorative Justice – Is More Better? The Experience of Police-led Restorative Cautioning Pilots in Northern Ireland

DAVID O'MAHONY and JONATHAN DOAK

David O'Mahony is Senior Lecturer, School of Law, Queen's University, Belfast; Jonathan Doak is Lecturer in Law, Department of Law, University of Sheffield

Abstract: In recent years there has been a considerable growth in the use of restorative justice schemes, particularly for young offenders. This article describes how two police-led restorative cautioning pilots for juveniles operated in Northern Ireland. The pilots were found to offer a number of distinct advantages over the traditional cautioning practice and helped secure some of the values of restorative justice. However, they were not without fault and the research found evidence of 'net-widening', whereby some offenders appeared to have been drawn into the schemes unnecessarily. It was also evident that the schemes required significant resources in order to involve participants (particularly victims) and to operate effectively. In light of the government's intention to greatly expand restorative practice in Northern Ireland generally, this article argues for the need to do so with care, if the quality of restorative justice is not to be compromised.

In recent years, restorative justice has been catapulted onto the international platform, with many criminal justice schemes adopting various restorative processes in order to address some of the traditional concerns voiced over the effectiveness of orthodox criminal procedure.[1] Most of these practices are based around John Braithwaite's (1989) theory of reintegrative shaming which involves encouraging offenders to experience shame for their actions whilst allowing them to maintain their dignity. It endeavours to repair the relationship through a healing process designed to meet the needs of victims, whilst also reintegrating the offender into society.

Proponents of restorative schemes have argued that the conventional criminal justice system has been overly focused on 'public interest', which effectively amounted to the State subsuming the interests of the other stakeholders. Restorative processes, on the other hand, which aim to address the victim's material, emotional and psychological needs, seem to be perceived as procedurally fairer, with victims in particular emerging from the process with more respect for the police and criminal justice system than those whose cases were processed by the formal courts (Sherman and Barnes 1997).

One model of restorative justice which is growing in popularity is that of police-based conferencing. Common in Australia, New Zealand, and parts of the USA and UK, police-based conferences are designed as an alternative to formal prosecution. They provide a forum for the police to bring together young offenders and their victims, with their respective families and supporters. The conferences are generally organised, managed and facilitated by a police officer, and examine ways of providing redress to the victim and reintegrating the offender, although solutions are never imposed by the facilitator. The goals of police-conferencing are to encourage young offenders to achieve empathy towards their victim and assume responsibility for their actions, to allow victims to move towards forgiveness and healing, and to empower citizens to address their own problems (McCold 1996; Moore and O'Connell 1994; Young and Goold 1999).

This article gives an insight into the effectiveness of police-led juvenile conferencing pilots in Northern Ireland.[2] Following a major review of criminal justice and the publication of the Criminal Justice Review in March 2000,[3] the police instigated two pilot schemes: one was based in Ballymena, County Antrim and the other in Mountpottinger, Belfast. Both schemes adopted a restorative approach for dealing with juveniles (under 17 years of age) who committed an offence, but were diverted away from prosecution by way of a formal caution, delivered using a restorative framework.

This research is of interest for two main reasons. Firstly, it adds to the body of empirical studies evaluating various restorative justice schemes. Secondly, the research could inform the growth of emerging restorative practices for juveniles; in particular the growth of such practices in Northern Ireland that form part of the package of measures which the government implemented in response to the Criminal Justice Review.[4] These measures will lead to a considerable growth in restorative work with juvenile offenders, beyond police-led conferencing. It will be asked, in light of the present findings which highlight a number of implications, both positive and negative, whether in the context of restorative justice 'more' is always better.

The Research

The fieldwork for this research study covered a period from September 2000 to April 2001, in which all case files dealt with by the juvenile liaison officers in two areas over the duration of the pilots were reviewed. The review explored the types of cases that came to the attention of the juvenile liaison officers and how cases were disposed of, using 'no further police action', 'advice and warning', 'caution' or 'prosecution'.

The researchers examined a total of 1,861 juvenile liaison referrals made between May 1999 and September 2000, including 969 cases from Mountpottinger and 892 from Ballymena. Information gathered included the nature of the incident and the outcome of the case. The team also collected more detailed information about the backgrounds of individuals and any previous contacts they had with the police from a random sample of 265 case files, including all cases dealt with by way of restorative caution or conference (n = 70).[5] The researchers observed a total of 29 restorative sessions during the period of the fieldwork, and conducted telephone interviews or sent out questionnaires to all past participants, to shed further light on the process from a 'consumer' viewpoint.

File Review: Profile and Outcome of Cases Referred to Juvenile Liaison

Of the 1,861 police case files opened, it emerged that the majority of young people referred to the juvenile liaison officers were boys (77%), mostly between 13 and 15 years of age (see *Table 1*). Typically the cases referred involved relatively minor criminal incidents, such as shoplifting or criminal damage and 95% of the cases related to a single incident or offence. However, just under a third (29%) were referred for non-criminal incidents, such as a missing persons report, or 'general misbehaviour' (see *Table 2*).[6]

Over half of the young people had not come to the attention of the police previously. Of those who had, most had been dealt with by 'advice and warning' or by 'no further police action' (60%). Only 15% had a criminal record. The most common outcome for a referral was 'advice and warning' or 'no further police action' (79%). Only 13% of cases resulted in prosecution and about 7%[7] resulted in some form of official caution, including 4% that were dealt with by restorative caution or conference (see *Table 3*).

'Orthodox' case disposals

It was evident that the police tended to classify offences in certain ways. Disposals such as 'no further police action' and 'informal advice and warning' were used for very minor offences, and many could not even be classed as criminal (such as a report of a missing person or for 'general

TABLE 1

Age and Sex of Juvenile Liaison Referrals – May 1999 to September 2000

	Mountpottinger	Ballymena
Age (years)		
5–9	6%	5%
10–13	36%	36%
14–16	58%	59%
Sex		
Male	78%	77%
Female	22%	23%
N	969	892

TABLE 2
Grounds for Referral to Juvenile Liaison – May 1999 to September 2000

	Mountpottinger	Ballymena
Violence	12%	12%
Sexual offences	1%	2%
Burglary	3%	4%
Robbery	*	0%
Theft	19%	15%
Fraud/Forgery	1%	*
Criminal damage	13%	15%
Drugs	*	2%
Motoring offences	4%	3%
Disorderly behaviour	6%	7%
Taking and driving away	2%	3%
Harassment	1%	*
Under-age drinking	2%	6%
Other criminal	4%	5%
Missing person**	5%	6%
General misbehaviour**	27%	20%
N	969	892

(*Notes:* *less than 1%; **i.e. non-criminal matters – see note 6)

TABLE 3
Juvenile Liaison Outcomes – May 1999 to September 2000

	Mountpottinger	Ballymena
No further police action	17%	21%
Advice and warning	67%	53%
Caution	2%	6%
Restorative caution	4%	*
Restorative conference	*	3%
Prosecution	10%	17%
N**	946	783

(*Notes:* *less than 1%; **Total number is lower as 132 cases had no outcome recorded – these were pending a decision or outcome)

misbehaviour'). These cases tended to involve very young juveniles (10 to 14 years), few of whom had been previously cautioned or prosecuted. By contrast, those given traditional cautions were generally older, with the majority (70%) being between 14 and 16 years of age. They were all dealt with for criminal matters and unlike those above, two-thirds had been dealt with by the police previously.

Those prosecuted generally had committed more serious offences, such as burglary, violent offences, theft and criminal damage. Most of these juveniles had been previously cautioned (66%) or prosecuted (67%) and

89% had been dealt with by the police previously. Overall therefore, it was evident that disposal decisions were made appropriately, taking into account factors such as the seriousness of the incident, age of the young person and the number and nature of previous contacts with the police.

Restorative cases: general profile

On examination of cases that were dealt with using a restorative model it was found that there were clear differences in practice between the two pilot areas. In Mountpottinger where the restorative scheme evolved from traditional cautioning practice,[8] the sessions appeared to be used as an alternative to the traditional caution. Here, 39 of the 42 restorative cases were dealt with by way of a restorative caution (without the presence of the victim), and only three were dealt with by a restorative conference (including a victim). In Ballymena, however, the scheme had been developed from a local 'retail theft initiative', and generally only dealt with shoplifting cases. Here, 25 of the 28 cases resulted in a restorative conference, though these mostly used a surrogate victim who was drawn from a volunteer panel of local retailers and only three cases were dealt with by way of a restorative caution.[9]

It was evident from the cases we examined that the majority of conferences were not being used as an alternative to prosecution. Instead, they were used mostly for less serious cases involving young juveniles (12 to 14 years) that previously would not have resulted in formal action. For instance, over 90% of the restorative conference cases were for minor thefts, and 80% of these involved goods with values under £15. In over half the cases, goods were worth less than £5. Indeed, the profile of those given restorative cautions and conferences was more similar to those given 'advice and warning' than those cautioned previously and was not at all similar to those referred for prosecution. This suggests a degree of net-widening was taking place which will be discussed in more depth below.

Restorative cases: process and delivery

The restorative sessions were usually facilitated by a trained police officer. While the majority of the restorative cautions took place in a police station, most of the conferences (primarily in Ballymena) took place elsewhere.[10] Levels of victim participation were low. The actual victim attended only 20% of the conferences and in the Ballymena area (where most conferences took place), they invariably used a surrogate victim. The young person and their parent(s) usually attended, and occasionally a social worker or a teacher was also in attendance. The majority (over 90%) of the restorative sessions resulted in a written or verbal apology to the victim and in only 8% of the cases did the young person refuse to apologise. Few of the sessions resulted in any compensation or reparation, though the majority of cases in both locations involved retail theft, where goods were normally recovered immediately.

The restorative sessions were found to be resource-intensive. Although the restorative cautions generally took about a quarter of an hour to administer and the conferences usually lasted between half an hour and an hour, they took considerable time to set up and arrange. The research team concluded that a relatively conservative estimate of the time commitment for the police was on average about four hours for a restorative caution and about $4\frac{1}{2}$ to five hours for a conference.

These findings raise important issues that have implications with regard to 'best practice'. They show a number of particularly poignant problems including: the lack of meaningful involvement of the victim; the choice of a 'neutral' venue; possible 'net-widening', that is drawing petty, first time offenders into the criminal justice system; and the use of a very resource intensive process to deal with relatively low-level offending. Before exploring these issues it is worth looking beyond the files to how the restorative sessions were handled in practice and what participants thought of the process.

Observational Research

The researchers observed 29 restorative sessions, ten of which were restorative cautions and 19 were restorative conferences. What follows is a description of how the restorative work was carried out in practice and the reactions and interplay between the participants.

Restorative cautions

All of the restorative cautions that were observed were held in a police station. The offences varied considerably, and included five cases of criminal damage, motoring offences, arson and theft. The offences had taken place from one month to nine months prior to the caution. Most of the cautions took between ten and 15 minutes to administer. The police officers wore plain clothes and were friendly, informal and well prepared. The facilities were comfortable and proceedings ran on time. The officers made clear opening statements, introducing everyone and explaining that they were not there to judge whether the young person was 'good' or 'bad' and respect was shown for all parties involved. The officers did not always clarify the voluntary nature of the process, however, and its legal implications. At the end of the process, several parents and young people were still unclear about whether they would have to go to court and whether they would have a criminal record.

After introducing everyone the police officer would invite the young person to say in their own words what they had done. This was usually followed up by a question about what the young person was thinking when they committed the offence. The facilitator would then inquire about the actual and potential consequences of the act. In some cases the young person said very little and in such cases the facilitator sometimes seemed at a loss as to how to enable the young person to take responsibility for their behaviour and to acknowledge the harm it had caused, particularly to the victim. The effect on the victim (not present) and the young person's family would then be probed. In one case of stone throwing, the victim was actually an off-duty police officer. While in this case it did not seem to damage the process, the representation of the victim's views by the facilitator would risk placing in jeopardy the perceived neutrality of the process, given that the facilitator was himself a police officer.

Facilitators often found it difficult to engage the young person in the process. Dialogue worked best where officers moved proceedings along at a relatively easy pace and tried to maintain a natural conversational style. Some officers had the 'script' with them but left it on their lap only to be used if they got stuck. This enabled a more personal style to emerge and this generally encouraged the young person to speak up more. Some officers did not feel comfortable with some of the language in the script and changed it to suit the language, maturity and culture of the young people. One officer had created a shortened script that only included the key questions and issues, which seemed a positive compromise between following the script rigidly and developing one's own personal style. On occasions however, the reluctance of juveniles to communicate seemed to exacerbate officers' own anxiety and lack of experience, which only contributed to making the atmosphere even more uncomfortable. For example, some officers tended to go through the process too quickly, often filling silences or prompting the young person with appropriate responses, and sometimes providing the young person with virtually all the answers. Furthermore, once the officers lost confidence they tended to lead rather than facilitate, thus effectively ceasing to be neutral facilitators.

Since the restorative cautions that were observed did not involve a victim (even in a surrogate capacity), the facilitator would often try to inject a 'victim perspective' into proceedings, through perhaps reading a letter or recounting a conversation with the victim. This approach had an impact in that the young person and parent had to respond to another perspective. However, since the victim's view was not informed by an encounter with the offender, the value of this process was obviously limited by lack of interaction and exchange.

The restorative cautioning agreements that were observed included:

- Simple cautions, such as in road traffic cases in which there was no actual victim
- Expressions of remorse without any gesture towards the victim
- Agreements to pay for damage; sometimes coupled with written or verbal apologies
- Agreements such as: to avoid certain people who use drugs; to clean the house; or to make up for the distress caused to the offender's parents

The formalities of the cautioning process were conducted with clarity, brevity and respect. After the relevant forms were completed, the facilitator summed up usually along the lines of how the young person had made a bad choice, but now, through agreeing to apologise, had made a good choice. This is regarded as an important element of the reintegration process (Braithwaite 1989; Umbreit 2000), although at times it did appear to get lost in the confusion of filling in forms.

Restorative conferences

The 17 restorative conferences that we observed were all held in Ballymena. The offences were all theft (shoplifting) except for one of criminal damage. Most of the conferences lasted between 35 and 45 minutes.

In contrast to Mountpottinger, the conferences usually took place in a private room at the local shopping centre. This helped to emphasise the victims' stake in the process and avoided the stigma of them having to enter a police station. Only two cases in Ballymena were not held at the shopping centre,[11] but the organisation of these particular sessions gave rise to a number of serious concerns.

The facilitator was about ten minutes late for both the sessions, which led to some confusion. At the police station, the surrogate victim and the young person and his father had to wait in the same room for the facilitator to arrive. In one case, the parties did their best to have a friendly chat while waiting, but in the other the atmosphere was somewhat tense. Obviously this situation could have become even more difficult if the 'real victim' had been present.

As with the restorative cautions in Mountpottinger, the young people in the conferences held at Ballymena were also generally reluctant to communicate. In some cases the facilitator or parent had to prompt the young person to respond to the questions, and would often suggest answers in the process. On a few occasions, this was done even before the young person had the opportunity to speak.

In another case a 15-year-old girl spent most of the conference crying. This meant that it was difficult to see whether she was taking any responsibility for her actions and their consequences. Significantly, when the facilitator and mother suggested that she should go to the shop and apologise, she became animated and said that she would not do that because the shopkeeper was 'ignorant'. She then lapsed back into silence only to communicate as the apology was being negotiated, but without entering into any further dialogue. This suggests that young people's silence may not just be due to immaturity, shame or shyness but may sometimes be used as a tactic when feeling threatened by a process led by adults.

The presence of a surrogate victim at the Ballymena conferences appeared to have more impact on the offender and family than a letter or a report from the facilitator of the victim's experience (as used at Mountpottinger). The surrogate tended to describe the typical effects of theft for a retailer. Although this did enable the young person to appreciate the consequences of their behaviour, it nevertheless lacked emotional impact. Some retailers merely made their views known while others attempted to engage in a dialogue. This seemed to arouse more interest in the young person and presumably had a greater impact, although in two cases the victim representative tended to dominate the process.

Most conferences ended in an agreement to apologise to the victim either through a letter or face-to-face. Occasionally it seemed that the facilitator was only aiming for an apology, which meant that the offender was not asked to consider any other way of making amends. This may have been because of low expectations of the young person's motivation, or because the young people were generally petty offenders and an apology was considered sufficient. Once an agreement had been made the facilitator asked the young person and parent to sign the relevant forms. These needed to be explained and this was generally accomplished effectively.

Interviews with Participants

During the period of the fieldwork, the team conducted separate face-to-face interviews with the participants immediately after the 29 sessions which were observed. In addition, we also interviewed over the telephone 30 families who had participated in restorative sessions prior to the beginning of the fieldwork.[12]

Attitudes of the parents

Almost all of the parents felt they had been kept informed about the arrangements of the conference, and around half praised the police for their flexibility in relation to organisation, and the timing of the conference. Satisfaction with the police was generally high. The parents were positive in relation to the way in which facilitators handled their role at the conference, over 90% of respondents using positive phrases such as 'helpful', 'supportive', 'understanding', 'fair' and 'sympathetic'.

Most parents described the conference as 'informal', 'relaxed' or 'friendly': three-quarters of interviewees described this as the 'best part' of the process, although most of those who were interviewed in person immediately after the sessions just seemed relieved that it was over. Only three respondents described it negatively – one saying that he felt 'tense and uneasy, and just wanted to get it over with'. Just under half said that they had felt tense and nervous to begin with, but that the facilitator had made an effort to make everyone feel at ease. Just over half of the parents identified the *reintegrative shaming* aspect of the process as its best feature (Braithwaite 1989). One parent stated in relation to her daughter that it had 'shamed her into admitting that she'd done wrong'. Notably, none of the respondents felt that their son or daughter was stigmatised as a 'bad' person, although there were mixed impressions as to whether the process was worthwhile. Two parents mentioned that they felt that the level of shame experienced during the conference was unjustified, but another parent interviewed in person said that he felt an 'old fashioned telling off' would have been better. Indeed, in more than one case the parents actually expressed a preference for the imposition of more punitive measures.

The team asked the telephone interviewees about the effect of the conference on the young person. About two-thirds of the parents agreed that the session helped the offender to understand the impact of the offence upon the victim. A clear majority were particularly impressed by the degree of regret shown by their son/daughter after the conference. One parent said:

> [My son] was really reflective afterwards and I think he felt really ashamed of himself for a while. From a parent's point of view, it was a bit uncomfortable to know

> that he was feeling bad, but from the conference, I knew that this was part of the process and was very necessary.

Nonetheless, it was evident that while parents were, on the whole, supportive of the initiative, many also had reservations. One criticism of the Mountpottinger cases was that conferences were held at a neighbouring police station, Willowfield. While most respondents felt happy enough about this venue, three people from Belfast mentioned that they were unhappy with the stigma of going to a police station, and four respondents expressed relief that their conferences were held in a neutral venue.

One of the most important concerns of three parents, all from the Ballymena sub-division, was that their children had been unfairly dragged into the criminal justice system for committing very petty offences. One concerned father complained:

> [T]he theft was relatively minor as far as the value of the goods was concerned. He was very humiliated when he was brought in and fingerprinted and when they took a DNA sample and stuff . . .

The mother of one girl, who was apprehended for shoplifting, commented:

> I think overall she was treated fairly, but I was just a bit surprised they told me she would have to go through all this for lifting sweets.

Another notable reservation raised by three interviewees was the fear that the sympathetic attitudes displayed by the facilitator in the conference would not be matched by police attitudes on the ground. One parent felt that the police were out to 'bully children and will lift them for anything' and one said: 'they're out to get everyone on our estate, no matter what age they are'. One juvenile's father expressly mentioned the fact that police harassment of young people could '. . . undermine the good work he [the facilitator] did in the conference'.

Attitudes of offenders

The four offenders to whom we spoke on the telephone were reluctant to respond substantially to open-ended questions. All agreed that the process had been handled fairly and most spoke highly of the facilitator. They all agreed that the conference had helped them to understand the impact of their actions, and two said it would make them less likely to get into trouble again. The juveniles we interviewed in person were slightly more forthcoming. Most were positive about the way the conference had been handled and felt they had been treated fairly, and were adamant that they would not reoffend.

Attitudes of victims

The surrogate victims who attended conferences expressed a high degree of satisfaction and seemed to appreciate the remorse shown. However, the one 'true' victim who was interviewed was very dissatisfied with the conference, as the individual offender was not prepared to apologise or admit responsibility. This illustrates the importance of the facilitator making a home visit prior to the conference, in order to assess the young person's level of remorse and whether he or she demonstrates a willingness to apologise. There is a clear onus on the facilitator to ensure that the victim is given a clear understanding of the risks as well as the potential benefits in attending a conference (Hoyle 2002). As this one case has shown, a conference with an offender who is not prepared to admit liability can result in a form of secondary victimisation.

Police officers

The police officers we interviewed who facilitated the process were convinced of its value in comparison with the former cautioning practice, expressing a belief that it avoids the tendency to write young people off. They believed it was a fairer and more human and emotional process. The officers felt they had received adequate training and that the programme was being properly supported and resourced. There was no evidence that the legitimacy deficit traditionally suffered by the police in certain areas of Northern Ireland had hindered their work. Indeed, there was a strong belief among officers that the schemes had the potential to assist community policing and build better relationships with families living in socially deprived areas.

Discussion

It is often argued that, to avoid being marginalised, restorative justice practices must be placed firmly within the formal criminal justice system (Shapland 2003; Dignan 2003). It was clear that this was the case in the pilots, as the police retained close control over the management of the schemes, and were keen to see them develop successfully. All stakeholders valued the philosophy behind the schemes and thought highly of the way they had been managed. There were, nonetheless, a number of major concerns arising from the research. It was found that, on a number of fronts, the practices of the police service did not reflect internationally accepted standards of best practice.[13] These standards reach beyond superficial perceptions and act as benchmarks against which schemes can be evaluated. If the rights and interests of all parties involved in the process are to be respected, and if broken relationships are to be mended, those responsible for managing and implementing restorative programmes are under an onus to take active steps to ensure that principles of best practice are always observed.

There were two major areas which gave the research team cause for concern. These were the apparently high risk of net-widening and the lack of real victim participation in the schemes. A number of other issues were also identified as falling short of best practice. While these are perhaps less serious, action is nonetheless needed if the Northern Ireland system is to operate effectively and take advantage of the potential of restorative practices.

Net-Widening

There has always been a danger that when informal alternatives are introduced into the criminal justice system they may serve to supplement rather than substitute for existing procedures (Davis, Boucherat and Watson 1989; Dignan 1992; O'Mahony and Deazley 2000). Since one of the aims behind most restorative programmes is to divert young people from court, prosecution, and the criminal process generally, it is crucial that new restorative schemes do not extend beyond the bounds of the previous system by drawing new cases into the system.

One of the greatest concerns arising from the pilots was that they appeared to draw in some very young and petty offenders who consequently experienced a very demanding process of accountability that, in our opinion, was disproportionate to the harm caused. Some 80% of cases that we examined were for offences concerning property worth less than £15. It was not uncommon to come across cases where a considerable amount of police time had been invested in arranging a full conference for the theft of a chocolate bar or a can of soft drink.

These findings all pertain to the question of whether it is appropriate to use restorative conferences, which are obviously costly and time-consuming, for mainly first-time offenders involved in very petty offences. It could be argued that a better course of action might be to deal with such cases by way of 'advice and warning', particularly where the value of goods involved is under £15 to £20; the young person has had no previous contact with the police; and he or she shows remorse.

While the use of restorative conferences for such minor incidents may have a beneficial effect, in that it may help a young person realise the harm they cause and the impact on victims, such decisions place the young person higher up the criminal justice tariff. This is because they result in a formal caution, which is a police record that can be cited in court as part of a criminal record.[14] This thereby raises the prospect of prosecution, should the juvenile come to the attention of the police in the future. As such, there is a real risk that these practices may lead to net-widening by drawing less serious offenders further into the criminal justice system.

It is possible that this could merely be a teething problem with these schemes. The police may have been overly enthusiastic to appear successful in implementing the new scheme widely across the board. There was, however, an assumption among stakeholders that a conference is less punitive than a prosecution and thus should generally be reserved for first or second time offenders. As the scheme develops and officers become more familiar with principles of good practice, the danger of net-widening may well address itself over time through effective gate-keeping.

Considering that the restorative sessions were very labour intensive, it might be better if they were targeted towards more 'at risk' and 'in need' offenders. Indeed, Maxwell and Morris (2001) have argued that because effective restorative work is so resource intensive, it should be directed towards more serious offenders and not at first time offenders who have committed minor offences. Such a change would result in a full restorative conference being put on a more equal footing with a prosecution, rather than being seen as the equivalent of (at most) a caution.[15] In this way the restorative justice philosophy would be seen as a real alternative to prosecution, rather than as a less serious response to offending. There are strong arguments in favour of making the restorative process at least as taxing as whatever sentence a court would impose, particularly on a first conviction, but it should *never* be more onerous in terms of what is demanded from the offender (Braithwaite 1994; Davis, Boucherat and Watson 1989; Dignan 1992).

Victim Participation

The low level of victim participation highlighted by our findings suggests a greater effort needs to be made to encourage victim participation. Though the lack of direct victim participation in the schemes was disappointing, it perhaps was unsurprising given that other evaluations of similar schemes in the UK have produced similar findings. Crawford and Newburn (2003) noted that victims attended youth offender panel meetings in only 13% of cases. Similarly Hoyle, Young and Hill (2002) found that just 16% participated in their evaluation of the Thames Valley scheme. In contrast, extremely high rates of victim participation have been reported from some Australian projects, notably the Canberra RISE experiment, and also the Wagga Wagga conferencing evaluation where recorded rates of victim participation were as high as 90% (Moore and O'Connell 1994).

It is difficult to pinpoint the precise reasons for this difference, although the fact that the UK schemes are comparatively new may indicate that they are still experiencing teething problems. Non-participation is unlikely to be attributable to the lack of effort on the part of the juvenile liaison officers in Northern Ireland, who seemed extremely enthusiastic about the schemes. Hill (2002) has suggested that while any sort of coercion to attend would obviously be undesirable, there was a risk in Thames Valley that the police had become so over-sensitised to the need not to apply pressure, that they did not take the opportunity to explain fully the potential benefits of the process to victims. Similarly, Hoyle (2002) noted that many of the Thames Valley facilitators gave victims a misleading idea of restorative justice: for example, in many cases victims were not told that they could bring along a supporter. As such, victims may have been inadvertently dissuaded from attending. It is not possible to gauge whether this may also have been the case in these two projects, since interviews were not conducted with non-participating victims. It should be stressed, however, that given the fact that non-participation is a major problem for more police-led schemes, it is probable that there are deeper issues at play, including a lack of understanding of the nature of restorative processes (Hill 2002; Daly 2003); fear of retaliation (Hoyle, Young and Hill 2002; Crawford and Newburn 2003); and/or simply not being able to attend (Hoyle, Young and Hill 2002).

Given that the UK schemes are still in comparative infancy in comparison to their Australasian counterparts, it could be that increased rates of victim participation will follow if current practices are fine-tuned and further developed. For example, greater emphasis could be placed on taking time to explain the various options to the victim, the different processes, their advantages and disadvantages, as well as developing their capacity to participate. Capacity building may include transport and child-care arrangements, as well as arranging suitable dates, times and venues for conferences. Another clear issue of concern to many of the parents we interviewed was their unhappiness about police stations being used as venues for the conferences. As a basic point of good practice, the venue should be a neutral, comfortable setting for all parties involved. Obviously the use of the police station as a venue could make both victims and offenders feel uncomfortable, particularly if they have had previous involvement with the police (Zehr 1990). This also raises questions as to whether victims should be better prepared for the conferences so that they have a good idea of what to expect. There might be, for example, a further role for volunteers from Victim Support in effecting this end.

If implemented, such measures could undoubtedly go some way to addressing the problems which may discourage both victims and offenders from participating in conferences. While it would be entirely contrary to good practice to suggest that any sort of pressure be applied to either victims or offenders (Hill 2002), taking active steps designed to encourage and facilitate participation would add a great deal to the provisions already in place.

Another interesting issue in relation to victim participation was the use of surrogate victims. In Ballymena, the practice of using surrogate victims was developed from an earlier retail theft initiative which used a panel of volunteer shopkeepers to impress upon young shoplifters the impact of their actions on local businesses, the livelihoods of shopkeepers and their staff. The panel was incorporated into the new restorative conferencing scheme, and panel members were used to represent the views of the victim, if the actual shopkeeper declined to participate. Since the vast majority of cases that were dealt with by conferencing in Ballymena involved shoplifting, the scheme appeared to work well. It addressed a problem whereby it was difficult to get shopkeepers to attend conferences, especially when the value of the goods was generally low, and these had usually been recovered immediately when the young person was apprehended. So the surrogate victims offered the advantage of at least being able to get someone from a victim's perspective to participate in the conference.

It was clear there were a number of advantages of involving surrogate victims in the conference process. The surrogates brought a strong victim's perspective into the process and appeared to have had more of an impact on the young people than the facilitator simply reading a letter from a victim, or recounting something the victim had said about the offence. But using surrogate victims also had a number of distinct disadvantages, especially over using the real victim. For instance, it was probable that the impact of the restorative process on the offender was diminished by them not being confronted and having to explain their actions to the real victim at the conference. Using a surrogate also obviously detracted from the restorative goals of conferencing, where there should be a process of empowerment, dialogue, negotiation and agreement between *all* the parties. And from the victim's perspective there were obvious disadvantages as the victim does not get the opportunity to confront the offender, to have the offender explain their actions, and importantly to understand circumstances and reasons behind the offence (as well as negotiate compensation or restitution), all of which are central to the conferencing process. Furthermore, there may be a danger of routinely using surrogates when they are easily available, rather than embarking on the difficult process of trying to get the real victims involved in the process. Though we found no evidence of this practice in the pilots, this would obviously be counter-productive towards achieving the restorative goals of conferencing. However, having said this, given the reality of low levels of victim participation in many police-led conferencing schemes, surrogates offer another useful way of injecting the victim's perspective into conferencing proceedings, and other programmes may wish to consider this approach in suitable situations.

More fundamental questions arise, as it is questionable whether a justice system in which victims rarely participate can be said to be truly 'restorative' (Daly 2003). Schemes can still be 'restorative' without the participation of the victim, although most commentators are in agreement that best outcomes are achieved when victims and offenders are brought together in a face-to-face meeting (Hoyle 2002). In theory, victims should be able to 'enjoy the benefits of the restorative process even if they choose not to attend a meeting with the offender' (Hoyle 2002, p.102). However, as in Hoyle, Young and Hill's (2002) evaluation of the Thames Valley scheme, there were very few occasions where an immediate, direct apology could be given and accepted. Financial restitution was very rare, and it is not clear how often offenders followed through with their promises to apologise to the victim. It is therefore doubtful whether the pilots can be described as *de facto* 'restorative', both in terms of process and outcome. However, as Roach (2000) argues, popular ideas in criminal justice will, by definition, mean different things to different people. Therefore labelling a scheme as 'restorative' or 'unrestorative' is perhaps unhelpful, given the policy objective behind the pilots was to deliver cautions using a restorative 'framework'.

Other Concerns

Other important aspects of these pilots also fell short of good practice. These included the lack of a holistic approach, problems regarding effective facilitation, and the absence of any follow-up process or monitoring of the agreements.

The lack of a holistic approach

An effective working partnership is also required to realise the full potential of restorative solutions. There are limits on the ability of the police to organise and facilitate conferences without effective links with the statutory, voluntary and private sectors. Without such partnerships, there is little chance of a holistic picture being drawn up of the offender and his background circumstances, and underlying reasons as to why he may have committed the offence may remain hidden. The uncovering of such information can be effective in producing increasingly satisfying results at conference stage (Umbreit 2000), although effective partnership is largely dependent upon skilled management, commitment and the investment of resources (Marshall 1999). As far as possible, other statutory and community bodies should be involved in the process. (Pavlich 2001; Van Ness 2003).

Unfortunately, in the two pilot areas there were very few outside the police who were trained as facilitators: during the course of our observations we observed only one such case. There is nothing to suggest that the police discouraged outsiders to contribute, but the problem would instead seem to stem from the reluctance of other agencies to provide facilitators due to staffing or resourcing issues.[16] Undoubtedly increased participation by other agencies and community workers should nevertheless be encouraged, as it could enhance the reintegrative potential of the process.

Problems regarding effective facilitation

It is worth noting that the suitability of a police officer to undertake effectively the role of a conference facilitator has been questioned by a number of commentators (Braithwaite 1994; Umbreit and Zehr 1996; Dignan 1999). Concerns have included suggestions that the police may be more prone to coercion and less sensitive to the needs of the parties than lay persons; that young offenders may be intimidated in front of police officers; and that there remains a risk of authoritarian behaviour. However, empirical evidence discussed by McCold (1998) refutes many of these concerns, and he also outlines a number of potential advantages to police-based models. These include the arguments that conferencing led by the police is perceived as being more 'serious' and part of the mainstream criminal process; that the police are more likely to be successful in ensuring that undertakings are carried out; that victims feel safer with the police as facilitators; and that many of the skills required for facilitation are already developed in many officers who are involved in community policing. Braithwaite (1994) seems to share this view and argues that police can be trained to be 'competent, empowering, facilitators'. Indeed, data from previous evaluations would seem to suggest that both victims and offenders trust the police to organise a fair and non-authoritarian conference (McCold and Wachtel 1998; Hoyle, Young and Hill 2002), and with a lack of empirical evidence to the contrary, it would appear that police-facilitation is consistent with restorative justice principles.

Our research found that each of the facilitators in the pilot areas seemed to be enthusiastic and sincerely committed to the restorative process. They had been well trained in the use of the script. In most cases they created safe and comfortable settings and atmospheres, sometimes in spite of the facilities. From time to time however, poor practice did seem to creep in: for example, there was generally too much use of suggestion, and most facilitators encountered difficulties in engaging the young person in the dialogue.

One of the main problems in relation to the facilitation was the apparent reluctance of many facilitators to encourage reparation. In one case, the juvenile's offer to compensate the victim was actually turned down. In cases where the young person is struggling or is reluctant to offer a means of repairing the harm, consideration should be given to allowing private planning time for the family and young person to draw up an action plan. This would reduce the anxiety and tension among all the parties, which may be inhibiting creative problem solving. This action plan may include a request for services for both the young person and the family.

The absence of follow-up

A follow-up process is essential to encourage all parties to keep agreements which are not enforceable at law and to keep everyone informed (Claassen 1996; Umbreit 2000). Crawford and Newburn (2003) and Hoyle, Young and Hill (2002) also noted that follow-up was deficient in terms of the quality of feedback delivered to victims. The facilitator should obtain regular updates from the offender, keep the victim informed and schedule additional sessions if required.[17] The conference agreements observed were adequately geared towards problem-solving, and sought to provide a pathway for the offender to reintegrate into the community. However, it was regrettable that in many of the cases in this study, follow-up work was not undertaken to ensure that undertakings given by the young person in the agreement were being met. Indeed, seven of the parents whom we interviewed cited this as the worst aspect of the process. Whilst infractions in individual cases may appear to be minor, a failure to address these would undoubtedly set a poor precedent and potentially could lead to future problems in receiving co-operation from individuals and local businesses. A system of monitoring should be put in place that assesses satisfaction with the process following all restorative sessions, and post-session monitoring needs to be completed to see whether agreements have been carried out to the satisfaction of all parties.[18]

Conclusions

This study of two restorative justice pilot projects provides a useful insight into the practical, procedural and operational aspects of delivering a police-led restorative cautioning process for juveniles. The schemes were successful to some extent in securing the traditional aims of restorative programmes in that reintegration was achieved through avoidance of prosecution and through a process which emphasised that the young person was not 'bad'. It highlighted the impact of their offending on the victim and may even have helped foster better police community relations. In these respects the pilot projects represented a substantive improvement in quality on previous cautioning practice.

However, as noted in the discussion above there were drawbacks, not least of which was the fact that the process led to a degree of net-widening. This was evidenced by the fact that some of the people dealt with under the scheme were very young, had no previous police contact, committed trivial offences and previously would have been dealt with through informal means (such as 'No Further Police Action' or informal 'Advice and

Warning'). There also appeared to be a tendency to include some offenders because it was seen as new, effective and a 'good thing' – something young people could learn from. Though intentions may have been admirable, the restorative sessions were part of the cautioning scheme, which meant that these young people ended up with a formal caution at the end of the process. Since cautions are recorded by the police and cited in court, they could have negative impacts in any subsequent proceedings. The restorative sessions were also shown to be very resource-demanding. They took a lot of time and effort to organise and run, in order to be done properly. Despite this there was relatively little actual victim participation. This obviously limited their restorative potential in terms of reparation, reconciliation and getting young people to understand the real impact of their actions on their victims, or for victims to benefit by being involved in the process.

Even in spite of the low level of victim participation, however, the schemes have the potential to contribute to the spirit of transition in a 'post-conflict' society such as Northern Ireland. McEvoy and Mika (2002) have illustrated the significant potential that community-led schemes hold in this regard. In Northern Ireland where criminal justice processes and institutions have suffered traditionally from a legitimacy deficit,[19] restorative practices hold tremendous potential to introduce new values into the criminal justice system (Dignan and Lowey 2000). Indeed, they also hold the potential to transform not only criminal justice systems, but also legal systems and even culture and politics (Bayley 2001; Braithwaite 2002). It could be said that police-led restorative justice could also aid the transitional process in Northern Ireland by helping foster improvements in strained police / community relations in many areas, even since the end of the conflict. Pollard (2001) has suggested that a shift has already taken place in policing in the Thamas Valley towards a more problem-orientated, community-based paradigm. It was clear from the interviews we conducted that the parents of the young people involved placed a high degree of trust in juvenile liaison officers and there was no evidence that either the parents or the young people felt that they were being 'picked on' because of their religious beliefs or political opinions. If the police are perceived as upholding restorative values, this may well help strengthen police / community relations which in turn may contribute to the broader social transitional process as we move towards a truly 'post conflict' society.

Since our evaluation, the police have changed and improved their practice and formalised their cautioning policy so that all juvenile cautions in Northern Ireland are now delivered using a restorative framework. The government is also greatly extending the use of restorative practices for juveniles throughout the criminal justice system in Northern Ireland under the Justice (Northern Ireland) Act 2002, which came into effect in the Winter of 2003. In Part 4 of the legislation, Sections 53 to 57 allow for 'youth conferencing' – which can either be of a diversionary nature, in which case the Director of Public Prosecutions will decide whether or not to refer the juvenile to youth conferencing, or they can be ordered by a court as a means of disposal subject to the conditions laid down in Section

56 of the Act. Such changes will have profound implications for the operation of youth justice in Northern Ireland, as the vast majority of juvenile criminal cases brought for prosecution will now be dealt with through conferences.

A 'conference plan' will seek to facilitate reparation to the victim, as well as providing a process by which reintegration of the young person back into society can occur. While such plans are subject to the agreement of all parties involved, and thereafter to the approval of the DPP, the Northern Ireland Human Rights Commission has recently expressed some concerns. These have included the possibility of the proportionality of conference plans being undermined, in that there is no linkage between the diversionary plan and the severity of the offence, and that some children may run the risk of being pressurised into agreeing to overly burdensome reparative tasks. Furthermore, the Human Rights Commission have expressed concerns that conference plans are not subject to any independent scrutiny.[20]

It is a matter of some concern that these types of issues have not been fully addressed in the legislation and this remains an issue to which the government may have to return in future years. As such, it has become even more important that principles of best practice are given due regard by the criminal justice agencies when formulating internal protocols, policies and practices surrounding the use of youth conferences.

Our research has shown that if conferences are to be effective they will need to be mindful of avoiding net-widening, so that less serious offenders are not needlessly drawn into the criminal justice system simply because it is seen as a 'better' approach. They will need to ensure that requirements imposed on young people are not disproportionate to the seriousness of their offence. Youth conferences will require significant resources, as this study has shown that facilitation takes considerable time and effort to arrange and run. If they are to be effective the organisers will have to invest considerable effort in ensuring that victims actually participate in the process. The process should allow for meaningful victim/offender dialogue and reparation to occur if they are to achieve their restorative potential. Therefore, while it may be appealing to expand the use of restorative cautioning in principle, given the heavy resource demands of doing it properly, the obvious limited financial resources available and the dangers of net-widening, 'more' in this context does not necessarily mean better. Rather, we would suggest, based on the findings of this research, that it may be advisable to concentrate on delivering a higher quality restorative process with fewer, more serious cases.

Notes

1 Such concerns often focus on the fact that victims tend to feel excluded from the process (Shapland, Willmore and Duff 1985; Elias 1986); that the offender does not seriously participate (Dignan and Lowey 2000); and that outcomes are frequently unsatisfactory for both victims and offenders alike (McCold 1996).

2 The police in Northern Ireland have operated specialist juvenile liaison schemes to deal with juveniles since 1975. These were aimed at diverting young offenders away

from prosecution through an extension of the system of cautioning, and specialist officers are used to review cases and decide how they are best dealt with. The liaison schemes have largely been successful, in that the majority (over 90%) of juveniles referred to them are usually dealt with by means short of prosecution, such as by 'advice and warning', 'no further action' or by caution (O'Mahony and Deazley 2000).

3 The Review Group was established as a result of the Belfast Agreement of April 1998, as part of the attempts to ensure widespread participation in and acceptance of criminal justice institutions and processes in the province.

4 In particular, Part 4 of the Justice (Northern Ireland) Act 2002 greatly expands the use of restorative practices throughout the criminal justice system for juveniles by way of 'youth conferencing' (see conclusions below for more details).

5 Restorative cautions did not directly involve a victim, while restorative conferences generally involved input from a victim.

6 'General misbehaviour' was used as a catch-all for any non-criminal act construed as a nuisance, and included things like hanging about making noise, breaking bottles, causing a disturbance etc.

7 Three per cent were given cautions, 2% given restorative cautions and 2% given restorative conferences.

8 The 'traditional' caution was usually administered by a senior police office at the station with the young person and their parents. It usually involved the young person being given a stern warning about the consequences of any further offending. See Hoyle, Young and Hill (2002) for a good description of traditional cautioning practice.

9 The distinction between restorative caution – not involving a victim, and restorative conference – involving a victim, was later removed by the police, with all restorative work being referred to as restorative conferencing.

10 Usually at a private room in a local shopping centre.

11 One of these conferences was held in a police station, and the other at the local office of a community organisation.

12 Unfortunately only four juveniles were willing to speak on the telephone, and they were generally unresponsive, especially to some of the open-ended questions.

13 See, generally, Umbreit 2000; Marshall 1999; Braithwaite 1994; Dignan 1992.

14 Whilst not strictly a 'criminal record' under the Rehabilitation of Offenders (NI) Order 1978, such police cautions can, and often are, cited in court as part of an individual's criminal record. Previous cautions are also taken into account by the police when deciding how to respond to any subsequent offending.

15 Some police officers suggested that magistrates should be given the power and encouraged to adjourn more serious cases for restorative conferences, thus avoiding convictions even when the police felt a prosecution was necessary.

16 Representatives of agencies we spoke to, such as social services, were very supportive of the approach but were over-committed with other work.

17 For example, Umbreit (2000) points out that brief phone calls can reinforce the facilitator's role as a continuing source of information and referral for a period of up to six months after the conference.

18 Even if this monitoring process is not enforceable.

19 O'Mahony *et al.* 2000 note from their findings of Northern Ireland Communities Crime Survey, that criminal justice agencies such as the police have experienced a significant legitimacy deficit especially in communities which are either strongly republican or loyalist.

20 Submission by the Northern Ireland Human Rights Commission to members of the House of Commons, 27 February 2002 (available on-line at *www.nihrc.org/files/justice_ni_bill_27_feb_2002.htm*).

References

Bayley, D. (2001) 'Security and justice for all', in: H. Strang and J. Braithwaite (Eds.), *Restorative Justice and Civil Society*, Cambridge: Cambridge University Press.

Braithwaite, J. (1989) *Crime, Shame and Reintegration*, Cambridge: Cambridge University Press.

Braithwaite, J. (1994) 'Thinking harder about democratising social control', in: C. Alder and J. Wundersitz (Eds.), *Family Conferencing and Juvenile Justice: The Way Forward or Misplaced Optimism?*, Canberra, Australia: Australian Institute of Criminology.

Braithwaite, J. (2002) *Restorative Justice and Responsive Regulation*, Oxford: Oxford University Press.

Claassen, R. (1996) *Restorative Justice: Primary Focus on People not Procedures* (available on-line at *www.fresno.edu/dept/pacs/docs/rjprinc2.html*).

Crawford, A. and Newburn, T. (2003) *Youth Offending and Restorative Justice: Implementing Reform in Youth Justice*, Cullompton: Willan.

Daly, K. (2003) 'Mind the gap: restorative justice in theory and in practice', in: A. von Hirsch, J. Roberts, A. Bottoms, K. Roach and M. Schiff (Eds.), *Restorative Justice and Criminal Justice*, Oxford: Hart.

Davis, G., Boucherat, J. and Watson, G. (1989) 'Pre-court decision making in juvenile justice', *British Journal of Criminology*, *29*, 219–35.

Dignan, J. (1992) 'Repairing the damage: can reparation be made to work in the service of diversion?', *British Journal of Criminology*, *32*, 453–72.

Dignan, J. (1999) 'The Crime and Disorder Act and the prospects for restorative justice', *Criminal Law Review*, 48–60.

Dignan, J. (2003) 'Towards a systemic model of restorative justice', in: A. von Hirsh, J. Roberts, A. Bottoms, K. Roach and M. Schiff (Eds.), *Restorative Justice and Criminal Justice*, Oxford: Hart.

Dignan, J. and Lowey, K. (2000) *Restorative Justice Options for Northern Ireland: A Comparative Review*, Belfast: Criminal Justice Review Group, HMSO.

Elias, R. (1986) *The Politics of Victimization: Victims, Victimology, and Human Rights*, New York: Oxford University Press.

Hill, R. (2002) 'Restorative justice and the absent victim: new data from the Thames Valley', *International Review of Victimology*, *9*, 273–88.

Hoyle, C. (2002) 'Securing restorative justice for the non-participating victim', in: C. Hoyle and R. Young (Eds.), *New Visions of Crime Victims*, Oxford: Hart.

Hoyle, C., Young, R. and Hill, R. (2002) *Proceed with Caution: An Evaluation of the Thames Valley Police Initiative in Restorative Cautioning*, York: Joseph Rowntree Foundation.

Marshall, T.F. (1999) *Restorative Justice: An Overview*, London: HMSO.

Maxwell, G.A. and Morris, A. (2001) 'Family group conferences and re-offending', in: A. Morris and G. Maxwell (Eds.), *Restorative Justice for Juveniles: Conferencing, Mediation and Circles*, Oxford: Hart.

McCold, P. (1996) 'Restorative justice: the role of the community', in: B. Galaway and J. Hudson (Eds.), *Restorative Justice: International Perspectives*, Monsey, NY.: Criminal Justice Press.

McCold, P. (1998) *Police-facilitated Restorative Conferencing: What the Data Show* (paper presented to the Second Annual International Conference on Restorative Justice for Juveniles, Florida Atlantic University, and the International Network for Research on Restorative Justice for Juveniles, Fort Lauderdale, Florida, 7-9, available on-line at *fp.enter.net/restorativepractices/policeconferencing.pdf*).

McCold, P. and Wachtel, B. (1998) *Restorative Policing Experiment: The Bethlehem, Pennsylvania, Police Family Group Conferencing Project*, Pipersville, PA.: Community Service Foundation.

McEvoy, K. and Mika, H. (2002) 'Restorative justice and the critique of informalism in Northern Ireland', *British Journal of Criminology*, *43*, 534–630.

Moore, D.B. and O'Connell, T. (1994) 'Family conferencing in Wagga-Wagga: a communitarian model of justice', in: C. Adler and J. Wundersitz (Eds.), *Family Conferencing and Juvenile Justice: The Way Forward or Misplaced Optimism?*, Canberra, Australia: Australian Institute of Criminology.

O'Mahony, D., Geary, R., McEvoy, K. and Morison, J. (2000) *Crime, Community and Locale: The Northern Ireland Communities Crime Survey*, Aldershot: Ashgate.

O'Mahony, D. and Deazley, R. (2000) *Juvenile Crime and Justice: Review of the Criminal Justice System in Northern Ireland*, Belfast: Criminal Justice Review Group, HMSO.

Pavlich, G. (2001) 'The force of community', in: H. Strang and J. Braithwaite (Eds.), *Restorative Justice and Civil Society*, Cambridge: Cambridge University Press.

Pollard, C. (2001) 'If your only tool is a hammer, all your problems will look like nails', in: H. Strang and J. Braithwaite (Eds.), *Restorative Justice and Civil Society*, Cambridge: Cambridge University Press.

Roach, K. (2000) 'Changing punishment and restorative justice', *Canadian Journal of Criminology and Criminal Justice*, *42*(3), 249–80.

Shapland, J. (2003) 'Restorative justice and criminal justice: just responses to crime?', in: A. von Hirsch, J. Roberts, A. Bottoms, K. Roach and M. Schiff (Eds.), *Restorative Justice and Criminal Justice*, Oxford: Hart.

Shapland, J., Willmore, J. and Duff, P. (1985) *Victims in the Criminal Justice System*, Aldershot: Gower.

Sherman, L. and Barnes, G.C. (1997) *Restorative Justice and Offenders' Respect for the Law* (RISE Working Paper No.3), Canberra, Australia: Australian National University (available on-line at *www.aic.gov.au/links/risepap3.html*).

Umbreit, M. (2000) *Victim Offender Mediation and Dialogue: Guidelines for Victim Sensitive Practice*, Washington, DC.: US Department of Justice, Office for Victims of Crime.

Umbreit, M. and Zehr, H. (1996) 'Family group conferences: a challenge to victim offender mediation?', *Victim Offenders Mediation Association Quarterly*, 7(1), 4–8.

van Ness, D. (2003) 'Proposed basic principles on restorative justice: recognising the aims and limits of restorative justice', in: A. von Hirsch, J. Roberts, A. Bottoms, K. Roach and M. Schiff (Eds.), *Restorative Justice and Criminal Justice*, Oxford: Hart.

Young, R. and Goold, B. (1999) 'Restorative police cautioning in Aylesbury: from degrading to reintegrative shaming ceremonies?', *Criminal Law Review*, 126–38.

Zehr, H. (1990) *Changing Lenses: A New Focus for Criminal Justice*, Scottdale, PA.: Herald Press.

[10]

JUVENILE VICTIMS IN RESTORATIVE JUSTICE

Findings from the Reintegrative Shaming Experiments

Tali Gal* and Shomron Moyal**

Using a randomized experimental design the Reintegrative Shaming Experiments (RISE) showed that restorative justice (RJ) is significantly more satisfying than court for both victims and offenders. It did not, however, explore the effect of victims' age and baseline differences in the level of harm caused to victims of different crimes on outcome variables. The current study uses a two-factor ANCOVA to address these questions. Main findings suggest that whereas RJ made adults more satisfied than courts (Cohen's d = 0.50), conference juvenile victims were less satisfied than court juvenile victims (Cohen's d = –0.28). Moreover, more serious harm is associated with decreased process satisfaction for all victims. A complementary qualitative analysis identifies adult domination and insensitivity to youth's special needs as recurring themes.

Keywords: young victims, juvenile victims, restorative justice, RISE, ANCOVA

Introduction

Restorative Justice (RJ) offers a 'new lens' to look at crime and reactions to it. According to the restorative lens, 'Crime is a violation of people and relationships. It creates obligations to make things right. Justice involves the victim, the offender, and the community in a search for solutions which promote repair, reconciliation, and reassurance' (Zehr 1990: 181). In their ideal form, RJ processes involve a safe and respectful encounter between the parties, in which they discuss the crime and its effects and together reach an agreement regarding ways of repairing the harm, to the extent possible, and preventing further harm.

Being a relatively new approach to justice, RJ necessitates empirical evidence for its success in achieving its own goals (repairing harm, preventing future harm) as well as the goals set by the retributive justice approach. Therefore, the central questions researchers have been asking are whether RJ reduces crime; whether it leads to agreed-upon plans; whether these plans are eventually followed; whether stakeholders are satisfied with the process; and, finally, whether RJ actually helps victims (for comprehensive reviews of research and meta analyses, see Umbreit *et al.* 2001;Bonta *et al.* 2002; 2006; Latimer *et al.* 2005; Sherman and Strang 2007).

RJ researchers have made particularly significant achievements in the development of theory and applied research focusing on offenders. Notable theories explaining the effectiveness of RJ in reducing reoffending are procedural fairness (Tyler 1990; Sherman and Barnes 1997; Tyler *et al.* 2007), reintegrative shaming (Braithwaite 1989) and shame management (Ahmed *et al.* 2001; Morrison 2007). Evaluative and experimental studies

* PhD, Institute of Criminology, Faculty of Law, The Hebrew University, Mount Scopus, Jerusalem, 91905, Israel; tali.gal.04@gmail.com.

**Institute of Criminology, Faculty of Law, The Hebrew University, Mount Scopus, Jerusalem, 91905, Israel.

have also explored the success of specific RJ programmes, either in comparison with court processes (Strang 2002; Sherman and Strang 2007; Shapland *et al.* 2008) or with respect to conditions for their success within the programme (Maxwell and Morris 2001). Consequently, there exists by now a significant body of knowledge explaining whether, why and under what conditions RJ is effective with regard to offenders.

Much less, however, has been done in the development of theory regarding victims and RJ (Sherman *et al.* 2005). Although RJ literature has identified what victims want (Zehr 1990; Strang 2002) and although it has been shown consistently that RJ is more satisfying for victims than court (see, e.g. Strang 2002; Shapland *et al.* 2007; Sherman and Strang 2007), RJ theory still lags behind in the provision of sound explanations as to why, to whom and under what conditions RJ can address the needs and wishes of crime victims and enhance their rehabilitation.[1]

Child victims (the UN Convention on the Rights of the Child defines all people under the age of 18 as 'children'. Since children's involvement in RJ, however, is typically limited to those over a certain age, we also use 'young', 'youth' or 'juvenile' victims interchangeably in this paper) have been particularly neglected in applied and theoretical research of RJ, although they do hold distinct characteristics in terms of victimization risk, effects and reactions to formal criminal processes (Morgan and Zedner 1992; Gal 2006; Finkelhor 2008). Nor has there been an attempt to find theoretical explanations for the success of RJ for young victims or the specific challenges it creates, considering the differences between juveniles and adults.

In practice, however, juvenile victims have been involved in RJ processes in many parts of the world, including New Zealand, Australia, the United States, Canada and the United Kingdom. Although young victims have not been the focus of evaluation studies in these programmes, still the existing data reveal that they can participate in such processes, their satisfaction can be very high and their well-being promoted through the process (see, e.g. Daly *et al.* 2003 for South Australia, and Pennell and Burford 1995 and 2000 for Newfoundland and Labrador Province in Canada). Restorative justice, however, can also harm young victims (Cossins 2008), presumably because they are more vulnerable to power imbalances, manipulation and victim blaming. The 'special case' of juvenile victims in RJ calls, then, for a closer look at what happens in existing programmes, what makes young victims benefit from RJ and what hinders their participation and even causes further harm.

Aiming to contribute in this direction, this study examines whether young victims were as satisfied with RJ processes conducted in Canberra, Australia, following their victimization as were adult victims involved in similar processes. Our theoretical framework is based on literature pertaining to the importance of procedural justice and sense of control as promoting process satisfaction for victims in general and young victims in particular.

Following a review of the theoretical background, the paper presents the Reintegrative Shaming Experiments (RISE) conducted in Canberra, Australia, between 1995 and 2000, and the data collected from them. It then describes the current quantitative analysis, where the satisfaction of juvenile victims participating in either court or conferences is compared with the satisfaction level of adult victims who participated in RISE. The relatively lower satisfaction of young victims who participated in conferences is further

[1]Two prominent exceptions are Angel's (2005) study on post-trauma symptoms and RJ, and Collins's (2004) analysis of RJ as a form of Interaction Ritual. See also Strang et al. (2006).

explored through a qualitative analysis that uncovers some distinct child–adult dynamics. The findings are then discussed and recommendations for further research and practice are suggested.

Children as Victims: Theoretical Background

Childhood presents an increased risk for becoming a victim of crime (Finkelhor 2008: Chapter 1). Furthermore, a victimized child is more likely to experience other victimizations as well, resulting in 'poly-victimization' (Finkelhor 2008: 35). Yet, the knowledge base on what helps victimized children as well as what creates further pain and frustration to them during the legal process that follows their victimization has not yet been developed. While there are numerous studies on child sexual and physical abuse, on its effects on children and on what happens to victims of such crimes in the criminal process (see, e.g. Goodman *et al.* 1998; Wade 2002; Whitcomb 2003), these questions have not been adequately studied with regards to child victims of other crimes. Furthermore, very little use has been made of findings from psychological and sociological studies regarding the needs, justice perceptions and wishes of juvenile victims. The following paragraphs synthesize psychosocial findings illuminating two central dimensions of process satisfaction that are arguably important to young victims: control and procedural justice. Although these concepts are well established with regard to adults, only rarely has there been any acknowledgment of their importance for young victims.

Procedural justice

Victimologists have found that crime victims want to feel that they are treated fairly, namely that they are given opportunities to express their views and being treated with respect (Strang 2002: 13–15). People care more about how they are treated in decision-making processes than they do about the outcome (Thibaut and Walker 1975; Tyler 1988). Procedural justice is particularly important for those who feel excluded or marginalized (Gonzales and Tyler 2008). Perhaps more importantly, procedural *injustice* is connected with feelings of anger and dissatisfaction (Folger 1977; Greenberg 1987) even when the outcome is considered positive (Koper *et al.* 1993).

Children and adolescents perceive procedural justice as no less important. Melton and Limber (1992: 180) found strong preference for an adversarial procedure where due process rights are protected (especially through participation) among both Norwegian and American children. Graham and Fitzgerald (2006) interviewed children of separating parents and asked them about their participation in matters regarding their residences. Children were clear about their wishes to be listened to and be taken seriously. Like adults (Tyler 1988), adolescents consider their representation by a lawyer as important, as well as judges making an effort to be fair, impartial, polite and calm, and the process to be confidential (Hicks and Lawrence 1993).

Empowerment and control

Victimology studies show that victims want to take part in the process that follows their victimization, to be listened to and to be informed about its progress (Strang 2002: 8–13). Why is being involved in the legal process so important for crime victims?

One possible explanation is the notion of control—a central term in psychological literature on stress and trauma. Control is associated with coping, rehabilitation and positive appraisals (Lazarus and Folkman 1984). At the same time, asserting control might induce feelings of anger, dissatisfaction and frustration, particularly when exerted in uncontrollable situations. Having control means being able to influence or change events (Brickman *et al.* 1982: 369). Therefore, being able to participate in a process that follows one's victimization—and, more so, feeling that, by participating, one is able to affect the outcomes—generates a sense of control, which, in turn, arguably promotes satisfaction and empowerment.

But only a certain type of control enhances victims' satisfaction and helps them cope with the aftermath of crime: a sense of control in the process itself. Attributing control for the crime, that is, blaming the victim, might lead to opposite reactions. The differentiation between attributed responsibility for the crime (blame) and attributed responsibility for the solution (control) has been typologized by Brickman *et al.* (1982): people may be blamed for the situation *and* regarded responsible for the solution (the *moral model*); or they can be held responsible for neither the problem nor the solution (*medical model*), in which case, they are expected to be passive and receive the help of others in resolving their problem. People may also be considered responsible for the problem but unable to solve it by themselves (the *enlightenment model*) or, lastly, they may not be blamed for their situation but regarded responsible for the solution (the *compensatory model*), in which case, help is provided through encouragement to take control and make the necessary steps to solve the problem themselves. The compensatory model is the only one that allows people to maintain a sense of control without being blamed for their situation (Brickman *et al.* 1982: 377). The criminal and restorative processes differ in the alternating messages of guilt, responsibility and accountability that are communicated during these encounters. The criminal justice process often treats victimized children according to the medical model. While they are typically not blamed for their victimization, children are also excluded from taking part in the solution. Conversely, RJ processes ideally absolve victims from blame over their victimization while inviting them to control the way the solution is shaped.

Children and control

Having a sense of control is an important coping mechanism for children as well. Children use control in three different models of coping (Rothbaum *et al.* 1982). *Primary control* means changing the stressful environment in order to make it more comfortable for the individual. *Secondary control* means changing oneself to fit the environment. *Relinquishing control* means, simply, giving up. As children age, they use more active methods of coping, believing that they can address and change existing challenges (primary control strategies) [see, e.g. LaMontagne *et al.*'s (1996) study of children undergoing surgery]. Most children engage in 'layered coping'—a mix of secondary and primary control (Thurber and Weisz 1997). When children manage to switch from primary to secondary coping and back according to the controllability of the situation, they can reduce stress and cope more effectively. Conversely, children who assert primary control in relatively uncontrollable situations experience more negative feelings (see Thurber and Weisz 1997: 516 for children coping with homesickness and Langer *et al.* 2005 for children undergoing medical treatment).

In sum, the literature on procedural justice and control as applied to children and youths suggests that young victims who experience the legal processes that follow their victimization as fair and who feel that they have been able to assert some level of control in them would be satisfied with these processes. Conversely, young victims can feel unsatisfied, bitter and frustrated when they think the process was unjust or that they had no control on its progress or outcomes.

Restorative justice is indeed experienced as more just and more controllable (by both victims and offenders) than the court process (Strang 2002; Shapland *et al.* 2007). This is not surprising, since, by definition, the decision-making power in RJ processes is at the hands of the direct stakeholders. None of these assumptions, however, has been tested empirically with RJ involving *young* victims. While the RISE experiment did not focus on the juvenile victims who participated in it, its data can tell us about their experiences and be linked with these conclusions.

The effectiveness of RJ in different types of crime

The accumulation of findings from different studies has led researchers to conclude that RJ is generally more effective in reducing recidivism in violent crimes and in crimes that have induced significant emotional harm to victims (Sherman and Strang 2007: 68). From offenders' perspectives, having an intense face-to-face encounter with a significantly affected victim induces real change and hence has the potential of reducing recidivism. When the victim has not been emotionally affected by the crime, in contrast, RJ may be experienced as an 'easy way out' and loses much of its transformative power.

From victims' perspectives, studies consistently show the greater benefits of RJ compared with court (Sherman and Strang 2007). However, there are still no conclusive data as to differences in victim satisfaction with the process or its success in reducing harm to victims across different types of crimes. It is possible to assume that, when the emotional effects of the crime are salient, the opportunities provided in RJ to discuss the harm, receive answers, express feelings and receive reparation are most beneficial. Conversely, when the crime effects are insignificant, those opportunities are less meaningful. At the same time, it is also plausible that the more emotionally charged the crime is, the more vulnerable would victims be when things go wrong at a conference (Strang 2002: 208). In the RISE study, victims' satisfaction levels were consistently higher among conference victims for both violent and property crimes, but property victims were slightly more pleased with their conferences than violence victims (Sherman and Strang 2007: 63). Without clearer evidence, it is impossible to conclude in what types of crime (and at what level of emotional harm) RJ is more beneficial for victims. The current analysis, however, provides a good opportunity to further examine the association between the effects of crime and the level of victim satisfaction. In RISE, 86 per cent of all juveniles were victims of *violent crimes*, compared with only 25 per cent of adult victims. To overcome this baseline difference, we constructed a *crime-effects* index and included it as a covariate in our two-way ANCOVA model.

RISE on Victims as a Semi-Experimental Trial

Heavily influenced by John Braithwaite's (1989) Reintegrative Shaming Theory, the Reintegrative Shaming Experiments (RISE) used a stratified randomized experimental design to compare outcomes of court and conference cases held in Canberra, Australia, in 1995–2000 (Strang 2002). Drink-driving, shoplifting, property crimes and violent crimes were randomly assigned within each crime to either RJ conferences or traditional courts by a computer program.[2]

The study on victims, however, focused on victims of property and violent crimes only. RISE design on victims has been described in detail elsewhere (Strang 2002). Crimes eligible for randomization were property crimes involving individual victims and committed by admitting offenders under the age of 18 and violent crimes committed by admitting offenders aged up to 29 years. Only *middle-range* crimes were included (Strang 2002: 67). That is, serious offences, sexual and domestic violence offences were excluded. Cases referred into the experiment did not necessarily represent the total population of eligible offences known to the police during the course of the study. It was in the judgment of the apprehending police officer to decide whether or not to refer cases to RISE. 'Despite very close contact and co-operation between the researchers and police at every level throughout the study, RISE missed many ostensibly eligible cases' (Strang 2002: 69).

Ninety-seven per cent of the court victims went through the assigned court process, compared with 77 per cent of the assigned conference victims. After all cases were disposed, 260 victims were identified for post-trial interviews, resulting from 175 property offences and 100 violent offences. In few of the offences, individual victims could not be identified, since the victims were the public at large or an institution such as a school or bus company. Whenever multiple victims were involved in one case, only one was interviewed, keeping the outcomes measured independent of each other.[3] Out of the 260 victims approached, 232 (89 per cent) agreed to be interviewed, divided in a 1:1 ratio between conferences (N = 116) and courts (N = 116). Response rates for post-treatment interviews were similar for property and violence victims and for conference and court victims.

Despite the design limitations, as expected in a randomized controlled trial, conference and court victims *within* each experiment (property/violence) did not differ in known baseline characteristics or in the level of material, physical and emotional harm they had experienced as a result of the offence. Among key outcome criterions were victims' satisfaction with the process, perceptions of procedural justice and protection of rights. Most of the analyses were performed on an 'intention-to-treat' basis (bearing in mind that some assigned cases were not eventually adjudicated as planned). The findings suggested that, *overall*, conferences 'worked' better for victims (Strang 2002: 154).

The Current Study: Research Hypothesis and Model Specification

We use the RISE data to examine whether conferences are equally beneficial for juvenile and adult victims. That is, we ask whether the effect of conferencing on victims' overall satisfaction depends on the age group of the victims, so that, as our research hypothesis suggests, juveniles will be less satisfied than adults from conferences that are not

[2]It was suggested that stratifying 'the sample of eligible cases by the type of the offence has the benefit of distinguishing different effects of conferencing under different circumstances' reducing variance of the outcome variables within each of the four experiments and increasing the overall statistical power of the study (Strang 2002: 65).

[3]Interviewing multiple victims of the same crime could violate the *independence of errors* assumption (see Cochran 1947).

specifically designed to address their special needs. The model we specified includes *level of satisfaction* as a continuous outcome variable, *process assignment* (conference/court) as treatments variable, *victim's age group* (juveniles/adults) as a grouping factor, *treatments* by *age group* interaction and *crime effects* as a continuous covariate. The table in the Appendix shows the statistical coding and description of all variables included.

The outcome variable: overall satisfaction

Overall level of satisfaction as the *outcome variable* is indicated by eight items (N valid = 209, $\alpha = 0.866$), each measured on a five-point Likert-type scale. For all victims, a *summated* satisfaction scale was constructed ranging from 0, *least* satisfied, to 32, *most* satisfied. The scale is normally distributed with a mean of 19.24 (SD = 5.99, Skewness = –0.74). The eight items used to compose the satisfaction scale are listed in Table 1.

Fixed factors

Our model includes two fixed factors. The first is *assigned treatments* with victims whose cases were randomly assigned to conferences as the experimental condition (N = 116) and victims involved in cases assigned to court as the comparison group (N = 116). The second factor, *age group*, was of secondary importance to the original study. To examine whether prior conclusions on victims' benefits from conferences are equally valid for both juveniles and adults, we divided the sample by the age group of victims.

Table 2 shows that the randomization process in RISE resulted in proportional number of adults and juveniles assigned to either RJ conferences or traditional courts. For adults, 98 cases were assigned to conferences and 98 to court. Similarly, cases involving 18 out of the 36 juveniles were assigned to conferences.[4] Yet, our two-way ANCOVA model is *unbalanced*, since the number of adults (196) is approximately five times larger than the number of juveniles (36).

Crime effects as covariate

The type of crime was identified prior to randomization as a baseline stratification factor. The study on victims focused on property and violent crimes. Adult and young victims differed in the distribution of crimes within each group: among young victims, only five were of property crime and 31 of violent crimes, while three-quarters of the adult victims were of property crime. We therefore constructed a 'crime-effects' index (N valid = 231, $\alpha = 0.804$, nine items), in order to control for possible variation on victims' level of satisfaction depending on the level of harm caused by different crimes. The index captures the *severity of physical and psychological harm* caused by the offence. For each victim, a *summated* scale was constructed ranging from 0, *least* affected by the offence, to 9, *most* affected by the offence (M = 2.30, SD = 2.32, $\alpha = 0.804$). Since the scale is positively skewed (skewness = 1.17), we normalized its distribution by taking the square root of the values and reached a range of 0, least affected, to 3, most affected

[4]The mean age of juvenile victims in our sample is 15.88 (SD = 1.95, Range: 10–18), with a mean age of 15.22 for court victims and 16.55 for conference victims. Twenty-four of all juvenile victims (67 per cent) are at the age of 16 and above. See Table 4 for mean ages of conference and court victims of the full sample.

TABLE 1 *Overall satisfaction scale*

Item	Scale	Mean	SD
Satisfied with way case was dealt with by justice system?	0 = Strongly disagree 4 = Strongly agree	2.33	1.21
The way case was dealt with made you feel angry?	0 = Strongly agree 4 = Strongly disagree	2.48	1.14
You feel bitter about the way you were treated in case?	0 = Strongly agree 4 = Strongly disagree	2.77	1.12
Pleased your case dealt with this way rather than other?	0 = Strongly disagree 4 = Strongly agree	2.55	1.08
As a result of way case handled, has respect for police?	0 = Gone down a lot 4 = Gone up a lot	2.30	0.99
You felt you could trust the police during your case?	0 = Strongly disagree 4 = Strongly agree	2.97	0.89
As result of experience with case, has respect for justice system?	0 = Gone down a lot 4 = Gone up a lot	2.03	0.90
As result of experience with case, has respect for the law?	0 = Gone down a lot 4 = Gone up a lot	2.06	0.77

TABLE 2 *Model specification: a 2x2 factor ANCOVA (unbalanced orthogonal design)*

	Conference	Court	Total
Adults	98	98	196
Juvenile	18	18	36
Total	116	116	232

(M = 1.24, SD = 0.866, skewness = 0.023). The nine items used to compose the index are listed in Table 3.

Findings

Initial analyses

Table 4 describes the sample of victims and shows that there are no statistically significant differences between conference and court victims on selected demographics and offence-related variables ($p \geq 0.155$).[5]

The correlation matrix in Table 5 shows that victims assigned to conferences are significantly more satisfied than victims assigned to courts ($r_{(230)} = -0.16$, $p = 0.017$). We also see that the perceived physical and psychological harm caused by the offence (i.e. crime effects) is negatively correlated with satisfaction. As victims are more harmed by the crime, they are less satisfied with both court and conference processes ($r_{(230)} = -0.20$, $p = 0.003$). When we regressed (using OLS regression) satisfaction on crime effects within the group of conference and court victims separately (not shown in Table 5), we found that, as the effects of crime are more severe, victims' satisfaction from the process is likewise to decrease within both the group of conference victims ($B = -0.147$, $t(114) = -2.24$, $p = 0.027$) and the group of court victims ($B = -0.147$, $t(114) = -2.48$, $p = 0.014$).

[5]Given random assignment, group means or frequencies on any baseline, pre-treatment characteristic should not differ between treatment and control groups except by chance.

TABLE 3 *Crime-effects index*

Item	Agreed %
The offence made you feel you were unworthy of respect	19.05
You suffered a loss of dignity as a result of offence	43.29
You suffered loss of self-respect as a result of offence	24.24
Have you suffered because of offence—loss of confidence?	21.21
Have you suffered because of offence—loss of self-esteem?	14.29
Have you suffered because of offence—suspicion/distrust?	58.87
Have you suffered because of offence—fear of being alone?	17.32
Have you suffered because of offence—sleeplessness?	15.58
Have you suffered because of offence—headaches, symptoms?	17.32

Note: the first three items were originally measured on a five-point Likert-type scale, ranging from strongly disagree to strongly agree. The remaining items are measured on a yes (coded 1) and no (coded 0) scale. We first recoded the Likert-type items into dichotomous scale (*agree* and *strongly agree* = 1, *neither, disagree* and *strongly disagree* = 0) and then checked for the reliability of the crime-effects index.

TABLE 4 *Selected baseline characteristics of conference and court victims*

	Conference victims (N = 116)	Court victims (N = 116)	P
Demographics			
Age (range, 10–68)	32.20 (12.94)	34.51 (14.71)	0.205
Juveniles	18 (50.0%)	18 (50.0%)	1.00
Females	46 (51.6%)	43 (48.4%)	0.685
Born outside Australia	26 (49.0%)	27 (51.0%)	0.876
Aboriginals or Torres Strait	4 (50.0%)	4 (50.0%)	1.00
Did not complete high school	46 (49.4%)	47 (51.6%)	0.893
Level of religiosity (ordinal, 0–6)	2.50 (1.56)	2.72 (1.66)	0.324
Offence-related			
Violent crimes	45 (55.6%)	36 (44.4%)	0.215
Crime-effects index (standardized, 0–3 scale)	1.32 (0.891)	1.16 (0.835)	0.155

Note: data of continuous variables are presented as means with standard deviations in brackets, and associated P-values of t-test for mean differences. For binary variables, absolute numbers are followed by percentages (%), with associated P-values of χ^2-test.

We also see that the perceived harm caused by the offence is uncorrelated with conferencing ($r_{(230)} = 0.09$, $p = 0.155$). That is, conference and court victims did not differ in the level of physical and psychological harm they had experienced as a result of the offence. Interestingly, juveniles are significantly more associated with being a victim of violent crimes ($r_{(230)} = 0.46$, $p < 0.0001$) and reasonably are more affected than adults by the crime ($r_{(230)} = 0.23$, $p = 0.0003$).

Statistical model

We use a two-factor *analysis of covariance* (ANCOVA), in order to adjust for differences in level of satisfaction that may result from baseline imbalances in the level of harm (the covariate) caused to victims of different crimes. Analyses were conduced on SPSS 18, using the GLM procedure. We employ the *Type III method* for calculating the

TABLE 5 *Inter-correlations, means and standard deviations (N = 232)*

	1	2	3	4	5
Level of satisfaction	1				
Conferencing	0.16*	1			
Juveniles	0.07	0.001	1		
Violent crimes	−0.10	0.08	0.46***	1	
Crime effects (*Normalized*)	−0.20**	0.09	0.23***	0.41***	1
Mean	19.24	0.50	0.16	0.35	1.24
SD	5.99	0.501	0.36	0.478	0.866
Range	0–31	0–1	0–1	0–1	0–3

* $p < 0.05$; ** $p < 0.01$; *** $p < 0.001$.
Note: *Conferencing*, *Juveniles* and *Violent Crimes* (all coded 1) are binary variables and their means indicate the proportion of the named category.

sum-of-squares, which is considered appropriate for *unbalanced* two-way ANOVA/ ANCOVA designs with interaction term.[6]

ANCOVA is a combination of analysis of variance and regression analysis (Cochran 1957: 261). As sources of variability on the outcome variable, it accounts for both the *mean differences* on each factor and the *correlation* between the covariate (crime effects) and the outcome variable (satisfaction). If basic statistical assumptions of ANCOVA are met,[7] then covariate adjustment reduces the error variance resulting in increased statistical power and greater precision in the estimation of treatments effect (Cochran 1957; Miller and Chapman 2001).

Results

Table 6 shows the results of hierarchical ANCOVA. In model 1, the treatment variable (*conferencing*) is shown to have a significant effect on victims' overall satisfaction ($F_{(1,230)} = 5.83$, $p = 0.017$), yet the size of the effect is relatively small (Cohen's $d = 0.32$). The mean differences on satisfaction indicate that conference victims (N = 98, M = 20.18, SD = 6.37) were significantly more satisfied than court victims (N = 98, M = 18.30, SD = 5.44). Moving to model 2, the beneficial effect of conferences is shown to be stronger when we adjust for crime effects in comparing the mean levels of satisfaction (Cohen's $d = 0.37$). In fact, adding crime effects into the model reduced by nearly three times the probability of making a type-I error in concluding that conferences 'work' ($p = 0.006$ for the adjusted treatment effect compared with $p = 0.017$ for the

[6]There are four methods for computing the sums-of-squares and testing hypotheses in factorial ANOVA, called Types I–IV. In unbalanced two-way ANOVA/ANCOVA, the debate revolves on whether to use Type II or Type III method; both do not depend on the order of entering the variables into the model. Overall, it is recommended by the statistical literature to use Type III method (default option in SPSS, GLM) with unbalanced two-way ANOVA with interaction for two main reasons: (1) it is the only technique that uses the rationale of an ordinary OLS regression, in which the effect of each factor/variable is evaluated controlling for *all* other factors in the model (including the interaction term); (2) it is the only method that uses *unweighted* means analysis where the row and column means are found by taking the simple average of the two cells' means in each row or column, ignoring any differences in cell sizes. The method is thus independent of the cell sample sizes and 'can be thought of as testing variables in unbalanced datasets as if those data sets were actually balanced and orthogonal' (Hector *et al.* 2010: 312; Shaw and Mitchell-Olds 1993).

[7]The assumptions central to ANCOVA are: (1) randomization, (2) correlation of the covariate and the outcome variable, (3) statistical independence of the covariate and treatment variable, and (4) homogeneity of regression slopes. We conducted a preliminary analysis, available upon request from the authors, and found that these assumptions are generally supported by the data. In addition to the assumptions central to ANCOVA, the usual ANOVA assumptions—homogeneity of variance, normality and independence of scores—apply for ANCOVA as well.

TABLE 6 *Hierarchical two-way ANCOVA*

	Model 1: unadjusted			Model 2: adjusted			Model 3: adjusted			Model 4: adjusted + interaction		
	F	P	*d*	F	P	*d*	F	P	*d*	F	P	*d*
Sources of variation												
Conferencing	5.83	0.017	0.32	7.66	0.006	0.37[a]	7.97	0.005	0.34	0.38	0.537	0.08
Age group							3.53	0.061	0.35	3.60	0.059	0.35
Crime effects				11.06	0.001		13.62	<0.001		13.91	<0.001	
Conferencing*age										4.42	0.037	
Model summary [b]												
R^2	0.025			0.070			0.084			0.101		
F statistic	$F_{(1,230)} = 5.83$*			$F_{(1,229)} = 8.57$***			$F_{(3,228)} = 6.96$***			$F_{(4,227)} = 6.40$***		
R^2 change				0.045**			0.014(p = 0.061)			0.018*		
Levine's test	$F_{(1,230)} = 2.11$			$F_{(1,230)} = 2.90$			$F_{(3,228)} = 1.32$			$F_{(3,228)} = 1.96$		

* $p < 0.05$; ** $p < 0.01$; *** $p < 0.001$.
[a]On models 2–4, Cohen's *d* is based on comparing the marginal mean differences and standard deviations that are adjusted for crime effects as covariate.
[b]The R^2 change and its significance were computed using conventional OLS regressions (SPSS program, version 18), which enables us to customize *hierarchical* regression models. The OLS regressions produced on each step (i.e. model) R squares and F statistics that are *completely identical* to those reported here based on the *univariate* GLM procedure (SPSS program).

unadjusted effect). The age-group factor, added in model 3, did not alter the results. The effect of conferencing remained stable in its size and significance ($F_{(1,230)} = 7.97$, $p = 0.005$, Cohen's $d = 0.34$), and so did the significant association between crime effects and satisfaction ($F_{(1, 231)} = 13.62$, $p < 0.001$). Finally, in model 4, the main effect of conferencing loses its significance ($F_{(1,230)} = 0.38$, $p = 0.537$); the effect sizes of age group and crime effects are almost identical to those observed in model 3; and the conferencing*age group interaction is significant ($F_{(1,228)} = 4.42$, $p = 0.037$). Our findings therefore indicate that the effect of RJ conferences on victims' level of satisfaction varies by the age group of the victim.

We also conducted a simple effects analysis (adjusted for crime effects as covariate) in order to learn more about the nature of conferencing by age-group interaction. Within each group, we entered into the model the conferencing variable as a fixed factor and crime effects as covariate. Table 7 shows that, for the full sample of victims, conferencing had a significant beneficial effect (Cohen's $d = 0.36$, $p = 0.006$). Within the group of adults, the beneficial effect of conferencing is higher and medium in its size (Cohen's $d = 0.50$, $p = 0.001$). Within juveniles, however, conferences made victims slightly, and insignificantly, *less* satisfied compared with courts (Cohen's $d = -0.28$, $p = 0.406$).

In sum, our hypothesis is generally supported by the data: as practised in the RISE experiments, juvenile victims benefited less from RJ conferences compared with adults. The interaction effect is illustrated visually in Figure 1.

A Qualitative Analysis: The Experiences of Young Victims in RJ

To further understand the differences in satisfaction levels between adult and juvenile victims of conference cases, it was important to explore the lived experiences of young victims who participated in diversionary conferences in RISE.

TABLE 7 *Simple effects analysis*

	RJ conferences	Traditional courts	Cohen's *d*	F
All samples (N = 116 in each condition)	20.30 (0.540)	18.18 (0.540)	0.36	7.66 (p = 0.006)
Within adults (N = 98 in each condition)	20.50 (0.577)	17.64 (0.577)	0.50	12.18 (p = 0.001)
Within juveniles (N = 18 in each condition)	19.37 (1.39)	20.99 (1.39)	–0.28	0.707 (p = 0.406)

* The reported means and standard errors (in brackets) of overall satisfaction are adjusted for 'crime effects' as covariate.

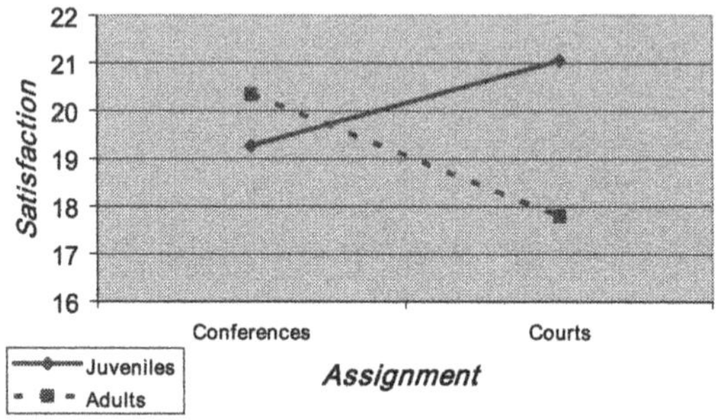

FIG. 1 Court assignment by age group: interaction effect

Because of the time that has passed since the actual conferences (10–15 years) and due to geographical distances, it was unrealistic to locate and interview those victims. The richness of the original dataset, however, provided valuable information to explore the dynamics at each process, which can perhaps shed light on the relative lower satisfaction of victimized youth with the conferences they were involved in. The qualitative analysis was based on repeated readings of each young victim's file. The materials in the files included the first and second-wave interviews (including some answers to open-ended questions), police reports and RISE observers' reports of some conferences. While most young victims were satisfied with the way in which their cases were handled, seven appeared having negative views of the process and its outcomes. Focusing first on the unsatisfying conferences, we identified the following distinct themes that are interesting from a child-inclusive perspective.

A. Parents deciding for their children. When the victim is under the age of 18, most jurisdictions require parents' consent for their participation in legal processes, as was the case in Canberra. Consequently, and in contrast to adult victims, young victims depend on their parents in this important matter. Considering the importance of having a sense of control, it is reasonable to assume that the freedom to choose whether or not to take part in a face-to-face encounter with the perpetrator is crucial for young victims' sense of satisfaction with the process. Indeed, some young conference victims whose parents made that decision for them were very unsatisfied, bitter and did not benefit from the process. For instance, Michael,[8] a 13-year-old victim, joined his parents to

[8]All names have been changed.

a conference following a theft of his push bike, because, as he stated, 'Dad said I had to go'. When asked about the conference shortly afterwards, Michael and his mother felt quite differently about it. Michael was unsatisfied and regretted that his case was dealt with through a conference. His mother, however, was satisfied with both the referral and the process itself. During the conference, Michael felt he had no control and that he was pushed into things he did not agree with, while his mother felt she had control, and was not intimidated, pushed or pressured in any way. Summing up, Michael thought the conference was unhelpful for him and said he would not choose this option again. His mother felt it was helpful and said she would prefer the conference option rather than the court.

B. Parents 'taking over' at the conference. A related issue similarly unique to juvenile victims is the domination of young victims by their own parents during the process. While it is natural for parents to talk on behalf of their children, it is also possible to imagine situations in which the parent's participation contradicts the young victim's wishes or interests. Moreover, since children need more explanations and encouragement to participate than adults (Melton and Limber 1992), facilitators might find it easier to speak directly with the parents during and before conferences. Parents may also volunteer their opinions more easily than their children. Yet, the literature on the importance of control and fairness suggests that turning to the parent instead of the juvenile might reduce the victim's sense of inclusion and overall satisfaction with the process.

Seventeen-year-old Nigel, for instance, had been punched in the jaw by his teenaged neighbour. Nigel was consequently hospitalized, operated and had two plates and eight pins in his jaw. The observer's notes portray a positive conference, but commented that the victim's mother did most of the talking. Towards the end of the conference, the offender's supporters suggested that the two shake hands—a gesture with which Nigel passively cooperated. At the interview, Nigel reported feeling dissatisfied, angry and suffering various physical harms, such as sleeplessness and headaches, which the conference did little to repair. He felt the conference had been 'somewhat fair' and that he could influence its outcomes, but, at the same time, said he felt awkward during the conference, regretted not being repaid and was dissatisfied with the outcome.

C. Sensitivity to 'the other'. People with disabilities and non-English speakers are only two examples of people of all ages who challenge RJ to address their special needs in order to make the process accessible and respectful for them. Leonard, a 17-year-old mentally disabled young man, had been punched in his head outside the nightclub he was attending. The observer commented that the conference was very poorly conducted and that the facilitator did not manage to support Leonard's participation, although it seems that, in a better setting, he could have managed well. As part of the restoration plan, the offender was expected to invite Leonard for a meal at McDonald's—despite the victim's fear of him. At the following interview, Leonard expressed his dissatisfaction with the processes. He reported that he had not understood the process, that his views were not respected and that he was pushed to the decision that was made. He further stated that the conference was very unfair and he was not treated with respect. According to Leonard, meeting the offender at the conference was 'a major upset, I would never do it again'. Following the conference, the observer reported that the McDonald's meeting never took place; apparently, there was never any intention on the part of Leonard—or his mother—that this would happen, but they chose not to argue about it in the conference. They evidently felt so disempowered by the time of the outcome agreement that they just wanted the conference to end.[9]

Another conference was held after 16-year-old Martin had been punched twice in his face by a 24-year-old man, an uncle of an 11-year-old boy known to Martin, whom he had previously pushed. The retaliating assault resulted in some serious injury in Martin's nose and he was later hospitalized for surgery.[10] All parties had to wait outside the conference room together before its commencement—a situation that made Martin feel very uncomfortable. During the conference, the offender's family did not speak much English and spoke Cambodian to each other. The offender did not show any remorse and kept arguing that Martin was as responsible as he was for what had happened. In the subsequent interview, Martin stated that the conference was only somewhat fair and respected his rights 'a little'. He was very unsatisfied, very angry and bitter, regretted his case was assigned to a conference and would not choose to attend a RJ conference again.

D. Bad facilitation. The correlation between inadequate facilitation and the low 'restorativeness' of the process and hence participants' dissatisfaction has been argued before (see, e.g. Maxwell *et al.* 2004: 302). 'Bad facilitation' was probably one of the causes for the victims' negative experiences in several of the cases involving youth. The following provides an example: 17-year-old Dylan had been assaulted by another youth and attended the resultant conference with his parents. The facilitator did not manage to move the discussion toward a denunciation of the crime and allowed it to continue despite the fact that the offender's parents were not there, only five of his friends. Dylan's mother reported being very dissatisfied, explaining that there was no denouncing of the offence. Dylan himself reported that he felt too intimidated to speak freely at the conference, had no control over the way things went and could not correct any mistakes if there were any made at the conference. Dylan also said he felt awkward during the conference and that the process did not take any account of the effects of the incident on him.

The positive experiences of young victims in RISE

Notwithstanding the importance of exploring the themes emerging from the unsuccessful conferences, it is similarly important to learn from the positive experiences of young victims. Unfortunately, however, the information on the successful conferences was much less detailed. Typically, young victims stated that they were satisfied with the way their cases were handled, felt they had enough control over the process and were treated fairly, and stated that the process was helpful for them.

The following is a deeper examination of one conference that actually delivered the promise of a respectful, safe and fruitful restorative process. Gina was 17 years old when she was assaulted at school by Betty, a classmate and former friend. The assault left Gina physically and emotionally scarred and she consequently placed a restraining order on Betty, fearing she would assault her again. Both girls came to the conference with many supporters, including two friends supporting each. The conference was strikingly

[9] Communication with Heather Strang, 28 April 2003.

[10] The conference was apparently so badly organized that it was one of the original study's examples of failed conferences, described in detail (Strang 2002: 146–8).

youth-led. Much of the discussion was about the rumours that led to the fractured friendship between the two girls. The participants also talked about the restraining order and how it affected everyone. Gina explained that it made her feel safe and, reacting to Betty's attempts to apologize, she stated 'I don't accept it'. At a certain point at which Betty repeatedly asked for her forgiveness and expressed her will to 'move on', Gina became very upset, left the conference room and was crying outside. Upon her return, the facilitator reiterated Betty's unacceptable action and Gina's hurt as a result. The conversation returned to the origin of the conflict and the name of a male, whom they were both friends with, came to light as the one who fuelled the rumours and amplified the tension between the girls. This was the turning point at which Gina finally made eye contact with Betty, body language became open and there was a noticeable drop in the tension. Both Gina and Betty agreed on the need to speak with that person and to tell him to stop making lies and gossiping. There were some jokes at this point and the atmosphere became humorous and friendly. Betty personally apologized to Gina, who accepted the apology, and the participants moved to constructing a restoration plan. The conference concluded with all parties happy with its outcomes.

Discussion

The data examined in this study were collected by Heather Strang and Lawrence Sherman from the Australian National University in 1995–2000. The RISE study showed that conferences were significantly more satisfying than court for both victims and offenders. The original study, however, did not explore the distinct results for victims of various ages and, accordingly, did not compare the experiences of adult and young victims involved in the study. The current analysis returned to the RISE data to address this question.

Our two-factor ANCOVA showed, first, that, for all victims, conferences were significantly more satisfying than courts, echoing Strang's (2002) conclusion. When we added crime effects into the model, we found that the covariate adjustment resulted in increased statistical power in the estimation of the effect of conferencing, and also that higher levels of harm caused by the offence are associated with lower levels of satisfaction with both courts and conferences (see also the inter-correlations in Table 5). These findings did not change when we added the age factor (juveniles/adults) into the model. Yet, in our forth and final model, we found that the effect of conferencing on victims' satisfaction varies by the victims' age group (i.e. statistically significant interaction effect) and that the main effect of conferencing becomes marginal and insignificant.

Explaining the conferencing*age group interaction, it is probable that, since crime effects were more noticeable among young victims, and since crime effects decreased victim satisfaction, young victims were less satisfied than adult victims with conferences. Indeed, in the simple effects analysis we conducted (Table 6), while conference adult victims were significantly more satisfied than court adult victims (Cohen's $d = 0.50$, $p = 0.001$), *young* victims assigned to conferences were slightly, and insignificantly (Cohen's $d = -0.28$, $p = 0.406$), less satisfied compared with young court victims.

Our findings regarding the negative correlation between the level of crime effects and level of satisfaction for all victims (both conferences and court) are somewhat surprising and call for further research. One possible explanation is that those who were seriously harmed would be less satisfied with any process following their victimization, simply by the nature of their condition. On the other hand, one would expect that, since RJ offers symbolic reparation for victims, its benefits would be most appreciated by those who mostly need it. But perhaps those mostly harmed by crime are most vulnerable to anything that might go wrong in either court or conference, and therefore would be (very) satisfied only when conferences are practised in their ideal form. It would be interesting to further explore the relationship between the level of harm and level of satisfaction in other studies, focusing on different crimes, age groups and processes.

The main finding of our analysis, however, is that the effect of RJ conferences facilitated by the Australian Federal Police (AFP) on victims' satisfaction varied by the victim's age group. The difference was so substantial that the overall satisfaction level of young victims from conferences was a little lower than that of court young victims. In other words, the substantial benefits of RJ for victims documented in the RISE study and in many other studies did not materialize into higher levels of satisfaction for young victims and in fact made conferences a little less desirable than court for those victims. But the specific young victims' sub-group participating in RISE was mainly harmed by violence, while the adult victims' sub-group was mainly harmed through property crimes. This baseline difference led to variance in the *crime effects* covariate, which, in turn, was strongly correlated with decreased satisfaction with the process. One explanation, then, for the lower satisfaction score conferences received from young victims is the type of crime they have been victimized by. Perhaps the conferences led by AFP were more suitable for property victims than for violence victims. We cannot reach such conclusions because juvenile victims might be more severely affected by all crimes. Again, further research is needed to explore the correlation between the level of psychological and physical harm caused by different crimes and the satisfaction of both adult and young victims with RJ conferences.

In any case, beyond the crime effects differences, the qualitative analysis provides additional possible explanations for the lower scores given by young victims to conferences. After all, the seven cases that were marked here as the less successful cases involving juvenile victims undoubtedly shaped the statistics described earlier, given the small sample size.

Perhaps the most important observation that the qualitative analysis offers is the one relating to control, or the sense of lacking control, that surfaced in the unsuccessful conferences. In processes that follow victimization, having some degree of control over the procedure and its outcomes may provide a powerful coping tool for victims in their healing, and this is true for child victims as well. Teenagers in particular prefer primary control strategies—trying to affect the situation (LaMontagne *et al.* 1996). At the same time, low controllability makes coping more difficult for young victims; asserting control in relatively uncontrollable situations is worse still (Thurber and Weisz 1997: 516; Langer *et al.* 2005). The problem that young victims often face, however, is that, because of their limited experience in group discussion, adult–children power imbalances and their still evolving capacities, asserting a sense of control during the process becomes almost impossible. If a restorative process is in fact uncontrollable (e.g. when one of the participants dominates the discussion), then victims might be worse off, either because their efforts to assert some (primary) control are futile or because they perceive the process as uncontrollable in the first place. Whether it was the victim's own parents that dominated the discussion (Nigel's case) or made decisions for them (Michael's case), or other adults such as the conference facilitator (Leonard's case) or the offender's supporters (Dylan's case), clearly, in at least some of the unsuccessful conferences, victims felt that they could not meaningfully influence the course of the conferences they participated in, and this might explain their dissatisfaction with the process.

Procedural fairness and respect for rights are also important for young victims and the qualitative analysis highlighted this assertion. This is no surprise considering that disempowered populations are more sensitive to having their procedural rights met (Gonzales and Tyler 2008). Leonard's anger and bitterness about his conference and his feeling that it was very unfair and that he was not treated with respect provide an anecdotal reminder that victims with special needs deserve and expect a fair process. Martin's case demonstrates how a failure to make specific arrangements such as the provision of a translator may be perceived as a procedural right violation. To treat victims with special needs (such as Leonard) or victims who do not speak the language of their offenders (such as Martin) with respect and fairness, conferences need to provide them with the extra help they need to overcome their difficulties and have an equal status in the discussion.

Finally, special attention should be given to support people coming along with young victims to conferences. The presence and active participation of support people can enhance young victims' ability to participate and might negate power imbalances (although supporters may unintentionally do just the opposite). The active participation of both Gina's and Betty's youth supporters helped Gina feel comfortable enough to insist on her needs until a genuine reconciliation occurred. Conversely, in Dylan's case, the absence of the offender's parents and the presence of five of his peers prevented any denunciation of the crime and made Dylan and his parents feel dissatisfied and angry about the process.

Conclusion

One of the major difficulties we faced in this analysis was the small number of young victims involved in the RISE study (only 36) and the unbalanced comparison group of adult victims (196). Another challenge was the higher rate of violent crimes experienced by young victims compared with the adult sample, which consisted mostly of property crimes. Using the two-factor analysis of covariance (ANCOVA) tool, however, made it possible to overcome the relatively small sample-size challenge and examine the effect of conferencing (compared with traditional courts), age group (being a juvenile or an adult victim) and conferencing by age-group interaction, on victims' level of satisfaction, adjusting for the effects of crime as covariate. Our analyses showed clearly that the effect of RJ conferencing on victims' level of satisfaction varies by the age group of the victim. That is, whereas RJ conferences made adults more satisfied than traditional courts (Cohen's $d = 0.50$), juveniles assigned to conferences experienced lower levels of satisfaction compared with juveniles assigned to courts (Cohen's $d = -0.28$). This means that, considering the substantial accumulated knowledge regarding the benefits of RJ (Latimer *et al.* 2005; Bonta *et al.* 2006; Sherman and Strang 2007), there is much to learn about how to make RJ more sensitive to juvenile victims' needs, vulnerabilities and wishes. In their ideal, RJ processes provide space for an egalitarian discussion in which all parties can speak freely and affect the outcomes. This indeed happened in most of the conferences in the RISE project. But, when conferences are not accommodated to address the specific needs and wishes of disempowered victims, then they may result in feelings of disappointment, unfairness and lack of control—as was the case in some of the conferences described here, which resulted in very low levels of satisfaction. Considering the higher levels of physical and emotional harm that young victims in this sample endured resulting from the crimes committed against them, it is not surprising that they were particularly vulnerable to any unfair or dominating experience.

Many obstacles stand in the way of young victims who feel there is something wrong at a conference. Shyness, respect for adults, difficulty in finding the right words or simple inexperience in speaking up at a group discussion may all prevent young victims from raising an objection or insisting on their viewpoint. The stories emerging from the qualitative analysis illustrate that, when juvenile victims are involved, it might be helpful to invite a large number of young participants. It might also be helpful to sensitize all adult participants for the need to empower the young participants to speak up and express their views freely, even when their views are different from those of their supporters.

It is important to note that the current findings are based on a single study with particular characteristics. Conferences in Canberra were facilitated by police officers who varied in their level of training, views of RJ and facilitation capacities. In particular, the programme did not pay special attention to juvenile victims' unique needs, wishes and vulnerabilities, and the results are noticeable in the findings. Accordingly, this study provides a valid instrument to warn against 'standard' practice of RJ when young victims are involved. From the picture emerging, it is fair to conclude that, at a minimum, when young victims are involved, special measures should be taken to meet their special needs, in accordance with their age and wishes, and based on theoretical knowledge on child victims.

Acknowledgements

We thank Heather Strang from the Centre for Restorative Justice, Regulatory Institutions Network at the Australian National University for her ongoing and significant assistance throughout this project and for providing us with full access to the RISE dataset. David Weisburd from the Institute of Criminology at the Hebrew University contributed helpful comments on an earlier draft and we are thankful for his assistance as well. The theoretical background and the qualitative component in this paper draw largely on the first author's PhD thesis (Gal 2006)

References

Ahmed, E., Harris, N., Braithwaite, J. and Braithwaite, V. (2001), *Shame Management through Reintegration.* Cambridge: Cambridge University Press.

Angel, C. M. (2005), Crime Victims Meet their Offenders: Testing the Impact of Restorative Justice Conferences on Victims Post-Traumatic Stress Symptoms, dissertations available online at http://repository.upenn.edu/dissertations/AAI3165634.

Bonta, J., Jesseman, R., Rugge, T. and Cormier, R. (2006), 'Restorative Justice and Recidivism: Promises Made, Promises Kept?', in D. Sullivan and L. Tifft, eds, *Handbook of Restorative Justice: A Global Perspective.* New York, NY: Routledge.

BONTA, J., WALLACE-CAPRETTA, S., ROONEY, J. and MCANOY, K. (2002), 'An Outcome Evaluation of a Restorative Justice Alternative to Incarceration', *Contemporary Justice Review*, 5: 319–38.

BRAITHWAITE, J. (1989), *Crime, Shame and Reintegration*. Cambridge: Cambridge University Press.

BRICKMAN, P., RABINOWITZ, V. C., KARUZA, J. JR, COATES, D., COHN, E. and KIDDER, L. 'Models of Helping and Coping', *American Psychologist*, 37: 368–84.

COCHRAN, W. G. (1947), 'Some Consequences when the Assumptions for the Analysis of Variance are Not Met', *Biometrics*, 3: 22–38.

——— (1957), 'Analysis of Covariance: Its Nature and Uses', *Biometrics*, 13: 261–81.

COLLINS, R. (2004), *Interaction Ritual Chains*. Princeton and Oxford: Princeton University Press.

COSSINS, A. (2008), 'Restorative Justice and Child Sex Offences', *British Journal of Criminology*, 48: 359–78.

DALY, K., CURTIS-FAWLEY, S. and BOUHOURS, B. (2003), *Sexual Offence Cases Finalized in Court, by Conference, and by Formal Caution in South Australia for Young Offenders, 1995–2001*, technical report, School of Criminology and Criminal Justice. Griffith University.

FINKELHOR, D. (2008), *Childhood Victimization: Violence, Crime and Abuse in the Lives of Young People*. New York: Oxford University Press.

FOLGER, R. (1977), 'Distributive and Procedural Justice: Combined Impact of "Voice" and Improvement on Experienced Inequity', *Journal of Personality and Social Psychology*, 35: 108–19.

GAL, T. (2006), *Victims to Partners: Child Victims and Restorative Justice*. Canberra, Australia Australian National University, available online at http://hdl.handle.net/1885/47077.

GONZALES, C. M. and TYLER, T. R. (2008), 'The Psychology of Enfranchisement: Engaging and Fostering Inclusion of Members through Voting and Decision-Making Procedures', *Journal of Social Issues*, 64: 447–66.

GOODMAN, G. S., TOBEY, A. E., BATTERMAN-FAUNCE, J. M., ORCUTT, H., THOMAS, S., SHAPIRO, C. and SACHSENMAIER, T. (1998), 'Face-to-Face Confrontation: Effects of Closed-Circuit Technology on Children's Eyewitness Testimony and Jurors' Decisions', *Law and Human Behavior*, 22: 165–203.

GRAHAM, A. and FITZGERALD, R. (2006), 'Taking Account of the "To and Fro" of Children's Experiences in Family Law', *Children Australia*, 31: 30–6.

GREENBERG, J. (1987), 'Using Diaries to Promote Procedural Justice in Performance Appraisals', *Social Justice Research*, 1: 219–34.

HAYES, H. and DALY, K. (2003), 'Youth Justice Conferencing and Reoffending', *Justice Quarterly*, 20: 725–64.

HECTOR, A., VON FELTEN, S. and SCHMID, B. (2010), 'Analysis of Variance with Unbalanced Data: An Update for Ecology and Evolution', *Journal of Animal Ecology*, 79: 308–16.

HICKS, A. J. and LAWRENCE, J. A. (1993), 'Children's Criteria for Procedural Justice: Developing a Young People's Procedural Justice Scale', *Social Justice Research*, 6: 163–82.

KOPER, G., VAN KNIPPENBERG, D., BOUHUIJS, F., VERMUNT, R. and WILKE, H. (1993), 'Procedural Fairness and Self-Esteem', *European Journal of Social Psychology*, 23: 313–25.

LAMONTAGNE, L. L., HEPWORTH, J. T., JOHNSON, B. D. and COHEN, F. (1996), 'Children's Perspective Coping and Its Effects on Postoperative Anxiety and Return to Normal Activity', *Nursing Research*, 45: 141–7.

LANGER, D. A., CHEN, E. and LUHMANN, J. (2005), 'Attributions and Coping in Children's Pain Experiences', *Journal of Pediatric Psychology,* 30: 615–22.

LATIMER, J., DOWDEN, C. and MUISE, D. (2005), 'The Effectiveness of Restorative Justice Practices: A Meta-Analysis',, *The Prison Journal,* 85: 127–44.

LAZARUS, R. S. and FOLKMAN, S. (1984), *Stress, Appraisal and Coping.* New York: Springer Publishing Company.

MAXWELL, G. and MORRIS, A. (2001), 'Putting Restorative Justice into Practice for Adult Offenders', *The Howard Journal of Criminal Justice,* 40: 55–69.

MAXWELL, G., KINGI, V., ROBERTSON, J., MORRIS, A. and CUNNINGHAM, C. (2004), Achieving Effective Outcomes in Youth Justice: Final Report. Ministry of Social Development, New Zealand.

MELTON, G. B. and LIMBER, S. P. (1992), 'What Children's Rights Mean to Children: Children's Own Views', in M. Freeman and P. Veerman, eds, *The Ideologies of Children's Rights.* Dordrecht: Kluwer Academic Publishers.

MILLER, G. A. and CHAPMAN, J. P. (2001), 'Misunderstanding Analysis of Covariance', *Journal of Abnormal Psychology,* 110: 40–8.

MORGAN, J. and ZEDNER, L. (1992), *Child Victims: Crime, Impact and Criminal Justice..* Oxford: Clarendon Press.

MORRISON, B. (2007), *Restoring Safe School Communities: A Whole School Response to Bullying, Violence and Alienation.* Sydney: Federation Press.

PENNELL, J. and BURFORD, G. (1995), *Family Group Decision-Making: New Roles for 'Old' Partners in Resolving Family Violence: Implementation Report.* Technical Report 1. Memorial University of Newfoundland.

——— (2000), 'Family Group Decision-Making: Protecting Children and Women', *Child Welfare,* 79: 131–58.

ROTHBAUM, F. M., WEISZ, J. R. and SNYDER, S. S. (1982), 'Changing the World and Changing the Self: A Two Process Model of Perceived Control', *Journal of Personality and Social Psychology,* 42: 5–37.

SHAPLAND, J., ATKINSON, A., ATKINSON, H., CHAPMAN, B., DIGNAN, J., HOWES, M., JOHNSTONE, J., ROBINSON, G. and SORSBY, A. (2007), *Restorative Justice: The Views of Victims and Offenders. The Third Report from the Evaluation of Three Schemes,* Ministry of Justice Research Series 10/08, Crown Copyright.

SHAPLAND, J., ATKINSON, A., ATKINSON, H., DIGNAN, J., EDWARDS, L., HIBBERT, J., HOWES, M., JOHNSTONE, J., ROBINSON, G. and SORSBY, A. (2008), *Does Restorative Justice Affect Reconviction? The Fourth Report from the Evaluation of Three Schemes,* Ministry of Justice Research Series 10/08, Crown Copyright.

SHAW, R. G. and MITCHELL-OLDS, T. (1993), 'Anova for Unbalanced Data: An Overview', *Ecology,* 74: 1638–45.

SHERMAN, L. and STRANG, H. (2007), *Restorative Justice: The Evidence.* London: The Smith Institute.

SHERMAN, L., STRANG, H., ANGEL, C., WOODS, D., BARNES, G. C., BENNETT, S., INPKEN, N. and ROSSNER, M. (2005), 'Effects of Face-to-Face Restorative Justice on Victims of Crime in Four Randomized, Controlled Trials', *Journal of Experimental Criminology,* 1: 367–95.

SHERMAN, L. W. and BARNES, G. ((1997)), 'Restorative Justice and Offenders' Respect for the Law', RISE Working Paper No. 3, Research School of Social Sciences, The Australian National University.

STRANG, H. (2002), *Repair or Revenge: Victims and Restorative Justice.* Oxford: Clarendon Press.

STRANG, H., SHERMAN, L., ANGEL, C., DANIEL, W., BENNETT, S., NEWBURY-BIRCH, D. and INKPEN, N. (2006), 'Victim Evaluations of Face-to-Face Restorative Justice Conferences: A Quasi-Experimental Analysis', *Journal of Social Issues,* 62: 281–306.

THIBAUT, J. and WALKER, L. (1975), *Procedural Justice: A Psychological Analysis..* Hillsdale: Erlbaum.

THURBER, C. A. and WEISZ, J. R. (1997), '"You Can Try or You Can Just Give Up": The Impact of Perceived Control and Coping Style on Childhood Homesickness', *Developmental Psychology,* 33: 508–17.

TYLER, T. R. (1988), 'What Is Procedural Justice: Criteria Used by Citizens to Assess the Fairness of Legal Procedures', *Law and Society Review,* 22: 103–35.

——— (1990), *Why People Obey the Law.* New Haven: Yale University Press.

TYLER, T. R., SHERMAN, L., STRANG, H., BARNES, G. C. and WOODS, D. (2007), 'Reintegrative Shaming, Procedural Justice, and Recidivism: The Engagement of Offenders' Psychological Mechanisms in the Canberra RISE Drinking-and-Driving Experiment', *Law & Society Review,* 41: 553–86.

UMBREIT, M., COATS, R. B. and VOSS, B. (2001), 'The Impact of Victim–Offender Mediation: Two Decades of Research', *Federal Probation,* 65: 29–35.

WADE, A. (2002), 'New Measures and New Challenges: Children's Experiences of the Court Process', in H. L. Westcott et al, ed, *Children's Testimony: A Handbook of Psychological Research and Forensic Practice.* Chichester, West Sussex: John Wiley and Sons.

WHITCOMB, D. (2003), 'Legal Interventions for Child Victims', *Journal of Traumatic Stress,* 16: 149–57.

ZEHR, H. (1990), *Changing Lenses: A New Focus for Crime and Justice.* Scottdale, PA: Herald Press.

Appendix

Appendix: A Statistical Coding and Description of Variables

Variables	Coding	Description
Outcome		
Level of satisfaction	0 = Least satisfied 31 = Most satisfied	Outcome variable. Composite scale representing victims' level of satisfaction of the process, indicated by eight Likert-type items (alpha reliability = 0.866)
Predictors		
Court assignment	1 = Conference 0 = Court	Treatments. Binary variable coded 1 for victims whose cases were assigned to conferences (treatment) and 0 for court victims (comparison group)
Age group	1 = Juveniles 0 = Adults	Grouping factor. Binary variable coded 1 for juveniles (below the age of 18) and 0 for adults (aged 18 and above)
Court x Age	1 = Adults—court 2 = Adults—conference 3 = Juveniles—court 4 = Juveniles—conference	Interaction variable. Represents each of the four groups crated by the 2x2 factorial design
Crime effects	0 = Least affected 3 = Most affected	Covariate. Continuous, normalized scale that indicates the level of perceived physical and psychological harm caused by the offence (nine yes/no items, alpha reliability = 0.804)

[11]

RESTORATIVE JUSTICE AND YOUTH JUSTICE IN ENGLAND AND WALES: ONE STEP FORWARD, TWO STEPS BACK

*DAVID O'MAHONY**

This article analyses the emergence and impact of restorative justice within youth justice in England and Wales. It critically examines progress that has been made, highlighting how restorative initiatives have been largely targeted towards 'diversionary' applications, low level offending, or first time offenders. It contrasts developments and research evidence from other jurisdictions, which have incorporated restorative justice within youth justice and applied it as a mainstreamed approach to sentencing. The benefits and difficulties of delivering restorative justice within criminal justice are considered, as well as factors which appear to have impeded its development within youth justice England and Wales. Broader implications for the development of restorative programmes in other jurisdictions are considered, in the light of the experience of England and Wales.

INTRODUCTION

Restorative justice is a broad concept encompassing many different practices and used in diverse ways by state and non-state actors seeking 'justice'.[1] This diversity is particularly evident in the field of youth justice, where a wide variety of schemes and practices are labelled as 'restorative'. Some restorative schemes are based in statute and require that offenders are dealt with through a strict framework, while others are practice led, 'voluntary' and may be much more informal. The young person may be referred to restorative schemes at different stages in the criminal justice system, with some programmes taking referrals as diversionary interventions, or as a form of police caution, while others may be referred by the prosecutor or by the courts as an official form of disposal. Programmes can be led by different agencies, such as the police, an independent conferencing service, or even local community organisations. Programmes also differ according to the level of victim involvement, with some using face-to-face meetings, or mediation schemes, while others rarely use direct victim input. Similarly, the extent to which the victim is allowed to participate in decision making regarding how the offence is be dealt with differs. Some schemes actively engage the victim in the process of arriving at an agreed outcome, to address the harm caused. Others use the victim as a way of bringing home the impact of the crime on the offender. Victim input may be limited, in some cases to letters or statements, read out to the offender. Even the nature of the offence and type of offender differ, with some schemes only open to first time offenders who have committed relatively minor offences, while others deal with a wide range of offences and individuals who have previously offended.

*David O'Mahony is Reader in Law at Durham Law School, Durham University.

[1] There are a whole range of differing restorative practices including programmes in areas diverse as corporate crime, see J. Braithwaite, 'Responsive Regulation', *Restorative Justice and Responsive Regulation* (2002, Oxford University Press); to programmes in prisons see E. Elliott, 'Security, Without Care: Challenges for Restorative Values in Prison', *Contemporary Justice Review* (2007) 10, 2, 193–208; and schools, see Morrison, 'Restorative Justice in Schools', in E. Elliott and R. M. Gordon (eds.), *New Directions in Restorative Justice: Issues, Practice, Evaluation* (2005, Willan). Some restorative schemes focus on particular types of offences such as more serious violent crime or domestic violence, see J. Stubbs, 'Beyond Apology? Domestic Violence and Critical Questions for Restorative Justice', *Criminology and Criminal Justice* (2007) 7, 2, 169–87; it has even been used as a form of conflict resolution in relation to broader political conflicts such as in South Africa, to deal with the aftermath of the apartheid regime, see A. Skelton, "Africa" in G. Johnstone and D. Van Ness (eds.), *Handbook of Restorative Justice* (2007, Routledge); or in Northern Ireland as an alternative to punishment beatings and political violence, see H. Mika and K. McEvoy, *Restorative Justice in Conflict: Paramilitarism, Community, and the Construction of Legitimacy in Northern Ireland*(2001) 4 Contemporary Justice Review 291–319.

Because of the wide variety of restorative practices, there are obviously differences in the extent to which they can embrace the principles of restorative justice. Taking Marshall's definition of restorative justice, as 'a process whereby all the parties with a stake in a particular offence come together to resolve collectively how to deal with the aftermath of the offence and its implications for the future', it is clear that many schemes only offer elements of this ideal.[2] Wilcox and Hoyle make important distinctions in the extent to which schemes are restorative.[3] For example, some schemes only provide compensation or reparation for damage caused, which may be direct or indirect, with little input from the victim. Some simply offer victim awareness to offenders, whereby they seek to confront offenders with the consequences of their actions. Such schemes can only be described as 'partly restorative'.[4] Others offer mediation, which provides victims with the opportunity to meet the offender, in a safe environment with a trained mediator, which can be described as 'mostly restorative'. Some allow for a full interaction between the victim and offender, allowing the parties to deal with the offence and decide collectively how it should be resolved; these can be described as 'fully restorative'. Thus, a distinction can be made between 'restorative justice' and 'restorative practices'. Restorative justice requires the incorporation of all the core elements of what is defined as restorative justice. Practices which fall short of this, being either 'partly restorative' or 'mostly restorative' should only be described as being 'restorative practices'.[5]

This article will argue that the development of restorative justice in youth justice England and Wales has been largely confined to restorative practices. These have been generally restricted to first time offenders, limited to minor offences and have provided little engagement with victims of crime. Though the government has made commitments to place restorative justice heart of the youth justice system,[6] in reality this has simply not materialised. Furthermore, while there has been a clear agenda of promoting victim rights and the advantages of restorative justice, in reality there has been only limited development of restorative justice in youth justice. It appears the lack of restorative justice is largely due to a lack of commitment to fully embrace the core principles of restorative justice. In advancing this argument, the article will firstly examine how restorative justice has developed in England and Wales. It will then consider examples of successful restorative justice programmes in other jurisdictions, before reflecting on reasons why restorative justice in England and Wales has failed to properly materialise, despite the significant support it has received.

DEVELOPMENTS IN RESTORATIVE JUSTICE AND YOUTH JUSTICE IN ENGLAND AND WALES

Restorative programmes first began to emerge within youth justice in England and Wales with the development of victim-offender mediation schemes, piloted in the 1980s. This led to the emergence of a range of police-led restorative cautioning practices. Further developments occurred with the introduction of reparation orders and referral

2 See T. Marshall *Restorative Justice: An Overview*, (1999, Home Office).

3 A. Wilcox and C. Hoyle *National Evaluation of the Youth Justice Board's Restorative Justice Projects*, Youth Justice Board, (2004).

4 *Ibid.*

5 This is not to suggest that restorative practices cannot deliver some of the aims of restorative justice, such as raising awareness of the impact of the crime, or seeking forgiveness and restitution.

6 See Youth Justice Board *Developing Restorative Justice: An Action Plan* (2006, Youth Justice Board); also Home Office *Rebalancing the Criminal Justice System*(2006, The Home Office,).

orders which were designed to incorporate the needs of victims within the process of criminal justice and to extend restorative justice principles within these measures. Most recently, a new restorative justice disposal has been piloted, which allows police officers to use restorative justice principles to deal with young people who have committed offences. The following sections examine how restorative practices have emerged within youth justice in England and Wales before going on to consider practices in other jurisdictions and the extent to which they embrace the principles of restorative justice.

1. Victim-offender mediation

Most victim-offender mediation programmes within the criminal justice sphere have their roots in programmes that were developed in the mid-1970s, in Ontario Canada. They were promoted by the Christian Mennonite movement with an emphasis on the values of personal reconciliation between victims and offenders. Howard Zehr's writings have been highly influential for restorative justice and he has been one of its major supporters, popularising and advocating such practices.[7]

Victim-offender mediation involves bringing together victims and offenders with a facilitator or mediator, who is usually professionally trained. The aim of mediation is to give victims and offenders a safe environment in which they are able to discuss the crime, its impact and the harm it may have caused, and to allow an opportunity to put right the harm caused. Some forms of victim-offender mediation have limited the role of the offender and others have used shuttle type interactions or go-betweens, limiting the victim's contact with the offender. But more commonly, the mediation takes place on a face-to face basis between victim and offender, with the mediator acting as a neutral facilitator.

Victim-offender mediation has proved very popular and is currently the most common form of restorative practice used across the United States.[8] It has also developed into more general forms of dispute resolution and mediation services which can include neighbourhood disputes, especially where there has been a history of conflict between the parties that has not been resolved by other forms of intervention. It has also gained in popularity across many parts of Europe where it is currently one of the most dominant forms of restorative justice practice.[9]

In the United Kingdom there have been numerous victim-offender mediation projects, which have developed largely on an ad-hoc basis. Generally, they have been relatively small scale and are often local initiatives, rather than national projects. This has largely been the result of a lack of any statutory authorisation or long-term national funding, which has impeded their development.[10] Those that exist have usually been developed through good working partnerships between criminal justice agencies such as probation, the police and social services. But there have also been considerable difficulties over which agency should support and fund such schemes and where referrals come from, which has made their development and operation problematic.[11]

While there has been official government support for victim-offender mediation in the England and Wales, financial support for such schemes has been limited. A range of schemes were supported in the mid-1980s when the Home Office funded the

[7] See H. Zehr *Changing Lenses: A New Focus for Crime and Justice* (1990, Herald Press) and H. Zehr and H.Mika 'Fundamental Conceptsof Restorative Justice', (1997). *Contemporary Justice Review*, 1: 47.

[8] J. Dignan, 'Evaluating Restorative Justice from a Victim Perspective: Empirical Evidence', *Understanding Victims and Restorative Justice* (2005, Open University Press).

[9] D. Miers *An International Review of Restorative Justice* (2001, HMSO).

[10] See J. Dignan and K. Lowey*Restorative Justice Options for Northern Ireland: A Comparative Review*, Criminal Justice Review Research Report No 10 (2000, HMSO).

[11] T. Marshall and S. Merry *Crime and Accountability: Victim/offender mediation in practice* (1990, HMSO).

development of pilot projects in England and Wales, however this funding was discontinued.[12] More recently, a range of mediation projects were supported by the Youth Justice Board and various victim support organisations. In 2004 Wilcox and Hoyle evaluated 46 restorative justice projects, including mediation projects that were funded by the Home Office.[13] While noting a range of differing practices across these programmes, the research was generally positive about their operation and impact, demonstrating that 83% of projects were successfully completed and many had high levels of satisfaction reported by participants. The data provided by local evaluators also demonstrated that most victims and offenders found the process of mediation to be fair and they were well prepared and supported through the process. They believed that the intervention had helped the offender to take responsibility for their offence and helped them understand how it affected victims. However, the research was critical of how such projects relied on short-term funding and lacked independent evaluation from the outset. Particular concern centred on the wide range of projects funded under the umbrella of restorative justice and the poor focus on what they were supposed to deliver.

Further mediation and restorative projects have been funded by the Home Office, the largest of which provides services to adult offenders. These have been subject to an intense evaluation which has demonstrated encouraging results.[14] Thus, a patchwork of mediation programmes continues to exist in England and Wales, some of which deliver excellent services. However, most programmes are still dependent on short term funding grants and have limited capacity to provide services in the longer term. The lack of long term core funding available at a national level has hampered the successful development of mediation programmes and has undermined the development of a consistent practice necessary in the delivery of such programmes.[15]

2. Police-led Restorative Cautioning

Police-led restorative cautioning schemes have their roots in Australia where they were developed in the early 1990s, mostly as an alternative approach to traditional formal police cautioning. The approach proved popular and was taken up and used in various forms in New Zealand and America, particularly in Minnesota and Pennsylvania in the mid 1990s.[16] It then spread considerably and the North American programmes have promoted the approach and trained many facilitators worldwide.[17]

During the 1990s, police-led restorative cautioning schemes also expanded considerably in England and Wales. The process was championed by the Thames Valley Chief Constable Charles Pollard, who committed himself to incorporating restorative cautioning for young offenders. This also included a broader programme to train police officers and implement a variety of restorative-based processes, including a complaints system and a comprehensive monitoring / evaluation package.

[12] See G.Davis, J.Boucherat and D. Watson 'Pre-Court Decision Making in Juvenile Justice', (1989) *British Journal of Criminology*, 29: 219.

[13] A.Wilcox and C. Hoyle *The National Evaluation of the Youth Justice Board's Restorative Justice Projects* (2004, Youth Justice Board).

[14] J.Shapland, A. Atkinson, E. Colledge, J. Dignan, M. Howes, J. Johnstone, R. Pennant, G. Robinson and A. Sorsby *Implementing Restorative Justice Schemes (Crime Reduction Programme): A Report on the First Year,* Home Office Online Report 32/04. (2004, Home Office).

[15] Even in relation to providing services through the Reparation Order, only a small proportion of the cases dealt with have resulted in any form of mediation between victims and offenders. See S. Holdaway, N. Davidson, J. Dignan, R. Hammersley, J. Hine and .P Marsh *New strategies to address youth offending – the national evaluation of the pilot youth offending teams* (2001, RDS Occasional Paper No 69, Home Office).

[16] P.McCold 'The Role of the Community in Restorative Justice' in B. Galaway & J. Hudson (eds) *Restorative Justice: International Perspectives* (1996, Criminal Justice Press) .

[17] P. McCold and B. Watchell *Restorative Policing Experiment: The Bethlehem Pennsylvania Police Family Group Conferencing Project* (1998, Community Service Foundation,).

The process of 'reintegrative shaming', which is central to the restorative cautioning approach, attempts to deliver the police caution in a way that is not degrading but performs a 'reintegrative ceremony'.[18] This is achieved by firstly attempting to get the young person to realise the harm caused by their actions to the victim, their family and themselves. The focus is placed on the wrongfulness of the action or behaviour rather than the wrongfulness of the individual. The process then attempts to reintegrate the young person, after they have admitted what they did was wrong, by focusing on how they can put the incident behind them, for example by repairing the harm caused through reparation and apology. Thus, it allows the young person to move forward and reintegrate back into their community and family. The whole process is usually facilitated by a trained police officer and often involves the use of a script or agenda that is followed. The victim is encouraged to play a part in the process, particularly to reinforce upon the young person the impact of the offence on them. However, as Dignan notes, restorative cautioning schemes have (at least initially) placed a greater emphasis on the offender and issues of crime control, than on their ability to meet the needs of victims.[19]

The Thames Valley scheme was subject to an intense evaluation from 1998–2001.[20] During this period, 1,915 restorative conferences took place at which victims were present. In a further 12,065 restorative cautions, victims were not present, but the cautioning officer attempted to input some form of victim perspective into the proceedings. In the evaluation, the researchers reported that offenders, victims and their supporters were generally satisfied and felt they had been treated fairly. However, a minority of victims and offenders felt they had not been adequately prepared for the process, or felt they had been pressured into participating. Nonetheless, both victims and offenders generally believed that the encounter helped offenders to understand the effects of the offence and induced a sense of shame in them, which is a particularly important goal of a restorative intervention. Over half of the participants reported gaining a sense of closure and felt better because of the restorative session, and four-fifths saw holding the meeting as a good idea. Indeed, almost a third of offenders entered into a formal written reparation agreement at the restorative caution. Within a year, the vast majority of these had been fulfilled.

The researchers found that the implementation of the restorative cautioning model in individual cautions was sometimes deficient, with facilitators occasionally excluding certain participants or asking inappropriate questions (eg, relating to prior offending or attempts to gather criminal intelligence). Some two-fifths of offenders reported feeling stigmatised as a 'bad person' and some officers appeared to pressurise offenders into apologising or making reparation. More generally it was found that some officers tended to dominate discussions and did not allow other participants to freely express themselves. However, the researchers noted that practice improved considerably towards the end of the research period. Overall, their view was that restorative cautioning represented a significant improvement over traditional cautioning, and was more effective in terms of reducing recidivism.[21] The research also found the police to be enthusiastic and sincerely committed to the restorative process. They had been generally well trained and it was clear from the interviews with the young people and

[18] J .Braithwaite *Restorative Justice and Responsive Regulation*, (2002, Oxford University Press).

[19] J. Dignan, 'Evaluating Restorative Justice from a Victim Perspective: Empirical Evidence', *Understanding Victims and Restorative Justice* (2005, Open University Press).

[20] C. Hoyle, R. Young and R. Hill *Proceed with Caution: An Evaluation of the Thames Valley Police Initiative in Restorative Cautioning*, (2002, Joseph Rowntree Foundation).

[21] *Ibid.*

their parents involved in the process that they had a high degree of confidence and support for the scheme. There was also some evidence that it had other beneficial effects especially in terms of helping improve police/community relations.

In England and Wales the use of restorative principles to shape and guide police cautioning and final warnings for young offenders became standard practice with the introduction of the Crime and Disorder Act 1998.[22] The Act followed the Government White Paper 'No More Excuses – A New Approach to Tackling Youth Crime in England and Wales' published in 1997. One of the core aims was to toughen up the approach to dealing with young offenders by limiting the number of times individuals could be cautioned by the police. The Act saw the introduction of a new final warning scheme which replaced the police caution. Importantly, the guidance issued to the police emphasised that final warnings should be carried out using a restorative framework.[23] Police officers administering final warnings were thus advised to organise a restorative final warning for all young offenders that would have been formerly dealt with by way of a traditional caution. Those affected by the offence, including the offender, victim and any relevant supporter / family member could be invited to attend the final warning and police officers received training to facilitate a restorative-based structured discussion about the harm caused by the offence and how it might be repaired.

Restorative-based interventions by the police expanded further with the introduction of the Youth Restorative Disposal in 2008.[24] This new disposal allows police officers to deal with minor offences by young people by way of a summary disposal, similar to a reprimand or final warning. It seeks to challenge inappropriate behaviour by using restorative justice principles and is supposed to provide the police with another tool to handle young offenders who have committed low level offences. The disposal is aimed at allowing the victim to take a role in the process. It also enables the early identification of young people by referring cases to the Youth Offending Team where the young person lives. The disposal has been designed to offer police officers more discretion with a quick and effective alternative means of dealing with anti-social and nuisance offending. As such, it is designed to deliver a swift response and reduce the amount of time that police officers spend completing paperwork and attending court.

A recent evaluation[25] of the Youth Restorative Disposal has shown it to be effective in delivering a swift response to minor offending by young people, mostly involving shoplifting, assault and criminal damage. It has been shown to be popular with officers, not just because it was perceived to save time, but because they felt that it offered a proportionate response, which was perceived to have a positive impact on young offenders and for victims. In practice the majority of Youth Restorative Disposals are given on the spot, by police officers (usually on the street), with the consent of the offender and victim. The research reveals that the disposal normally entailed not much more than a simple verbal apology to the victim at the scene of the incident and few cases are actually referred to Youth Offending Teams or involve any further intervention. As such, despite being called restorative disposals, there is little to suggest

[22] The Crime and Disorder Act 1998 also introduced the Reparation Order.

[23] R. Young 'Just Cops Doing 'Shameful' Business? Police-led Restorative Justice and the Lessons of the Research' in A. Morris and G. Maxwell (eds), *Restorative Justice for Juveniles: Conferencing, Mediation and Circles*, (2001, Hart).

[24] The Restorative Justice Disposal was launched by the Home Office in a number of pilot areas in England and Wales, see Ministry of Justice web pages: http://www.justice.gov.uk/guidance/youth-justice/courts-and-orders/disposals/youth-restorative-disposal-pilot-scheme.htm (accessed Dec 2011).

[25] A. Rix, K. Skidmore, R. Self, T. Holt and S. Raybould *Youth Restorative Disposal Process Evaluation*. (Youth Justice Board, 2011) see http://yjbpublications.justice.gov.uk/Scripts/prodView.asp?idproduct=500&eP=(accessed Dec 2011).

that they involve any significant restorative intervention or process. In many respects, the disposal simply provides the police with another mechanism to informally deal with minor offending, on the spot, by way of an immediate warning that includes an apology.

Other developments have included the introduction of the Youth Conditional Caution, on a pilot basis from 2010, to extend the use of conditional cautions to young people aged 10–17.[26] The Government agreed during the enactment of the Criminal Justice and Immigration Act 2008 that the Youth Conditional Caution would be introduced in stages, beginning with 16–17 year olds. The youth conditional caution aims to reduce the number of young people being taken to court for a low-level offence. The disposal is available for use by the Police and the Crown Prosecution Service if the offender has not previously been convicted of an offence, admits guilt and consents to the caution. The caution can have conditions attached to it that include restorative provisions supporting rehabilitation and effecting reparation. It can also include a fine and/or an attendance requirement. It can be offered to those aged 16 and 17 at the time of the offence (for the duration of the pilots) where there is sufficient evidence to charge with an offence and the young person has admitted guilt. The decision to administer a youth conditional caution has the effect of suspending any criminal proceedings while the young person is given an opportunity to comply with the agreed conditions. The offender can accept or refuse the conditional caution and if the latter option is selected the offender will be placed before the court. Where the conditions attached to the caution are complied with, the case will be discharged and no further prosecution and/or proceedings for the offence(s) will be commenced. However, where there is no reasonable excuse for non-compliance, the caution offer can be withdrawn and criminal proceedings commenced for the original offence(s).

Youth conditional cautions will initially be implemented for 16 and 17-year-olds before being extended to 10–15 year olds. They are intended to provide an additional out-of-court option to deal with offending. They will be used where the offender has either committed an offence which is not suitable to be dealt with by way of a reprimand or final warning, or where the offender has already been subject to the reprimand or final warning scheme.

3. Reparation Orders and Referral Orders

A third area where restorative justice is used within youth justice in England and Wales relates to the use of reparation orders and referral orders for young people brought before the courts. The reparation order is available for 10 to 17 year olds who have been convicted of an offence. It is designed to take into account the feelings and wishes of victims of crime and to help prevent the young offender from committing further offences by confronting them with the consequences of their criminal behaviour. The order requires the young offender to make specific reparation either to the individual victim of his crime, where the victim desires this, or to the community which they have harmed.[27] Research looking at the operation of reparation orders has found that in practice there has been less focus on involving victims directly in the process than originally envisaged in the legislation. Reparation orders largely focus on indirect reparation for the benefit of the community, which is not dependent on consent or

[26] Section 48 of The Criminal Justice and Immigration Act 2008 was amended to include 10–17 year olds.

[27] S. Holdaway, N. Davidson, J. Dignan, R. Hammersley, J. Hine and P. Marsh *New strategies to address youth offending – the national evaluation of the pilot youth offending teams* (2001, RDS Occasional Paper No 69, Home Office).

participation from actual victims. Thus, the practical operation of the reparation order shows it to have limited restorative impact because the individual needs of victims and their wishes are often not taken into account in its delivery.[28]

In relation to referral orders the Youth Justice and Criminal Evidence Act (1999) extended the use of restorative justice to young offenders.[29] The referral order is available to the Youth Courts as a primary disposal for offenders if they have not previously been convicted by a court.[30] The order is overseen by youth offender panels, which are made up of two community panel members and a member of the local youth offending team. They deal with young offenders referred to them by the courts (on referral orders) and are supposed to address the young person's offending behaviour and decide what form of action should be taken, providing a restorative justice approach. The panels are designed to operate on the restorative justice principles of responsibility, reparation and reintegration. Restorative justice in this context helps enable offenders to become aware of and take responsibility for the consequences of their offending and to have an opportunity to make reparation to victims and the wider community. Victims have the opportunity, if they wish, to say how they have been affected by the offence, ask questions, receive an explanation and/or an apology and discuss how the offender can make practical reparation for the harm that has been caused.[31]

When a young person is referred by the court to a youth offender panel, the panel decides how the offending should be dealt with and what form of action is necessary. If the victim wishes they may attend the panel meeting and describe how the offence affected them. Parents are required to attend panel meetings (if the young person is under the age of 16) and meetings are usually held in community venues. The Government guidelines state that young people should not have legal representation at panel meetings, as this may hinder their full involvement in the process, but if a solicitor is to attend they may do so as a 'supporter'.[32]

The panel has to decide on an agreed plan which can provide reparation to the victim or community and include interventions to address the young person's offending. This can include victim awareness, counselling, drug and alcohol interventions and forms of victim reparation. The amount of reparation and length of the plan has to be proportionate to the seriousness of the offence and the young person must agree to the plan. If the young person fails to agree to a plan, they will be referred back to the court for sentencing. Once a plan is agreed it is monitored by the Youth Offending Team and if the young person fails to comply with its terms they may be referred back to court for sentencing.

Research examining the operation of referral orders in 2000 and 2001 found that 'within a relatively short time youth offender panels have established themselves as constructive, deliberative and participatory forums in which to address young people's offending behaviour'.[33] The orders were rolled out across England and Wales in April

[28] *Ibid.*

[29] The Referral Order was revised under the Criminal Justice and Immigration Act 2008, which came into force on 27 April 2009. The updated guidance on the order is provided the Ministry of Justice, 'Referral Order Guidance (2009)' (2009, Ministry of Justice).

[30] The Courts also have discretion to use the Referral Order if a young person has been previously convicted by a court, but not given a Referral Order and exceptionally they may be used under the recommendation of a Youth Offending Team more than once, *Ministry of Justice, 'Referral Order Guidance'* (2009, Ministry of Justice).

[31] See '*Referral Order Guidance (2009)*' (2009, Ministry of Justice).

[32] Home Office *Referral Order, Guidance for Courts* (2009, Home Office).

[33] T. Newburn, A. Crawford, R. Earle, S. Goldie, C. Hale, A. Hallam, G. Masters, A. Netten, R. Saunders, K. Sharpe and S. Uglow '*The Introduction of Referral Orders into the Youth Justice System* (2002, Home Office Research Study 242).

2002.[34] The research concluded that the new orders were working well and many young people played an active role in their panel meetings and were happy with their experience.[35] It was found that 84% of the young people felt they were treated with respect and 86% said they were treated fairly. The research showed that 75% of the young people agreed that their plan or contract was 'useful' and 78% agreed that it should help them stay out of trouble.[36] Parents also appeared to be positive about the orders and, compared to the experience of the Youth Court, appeared to understand the referral order process better and felt it easier to participate.

Despite these positive findings, a number of concerns have been raised about referral orders. For instance, the discretion of magistrates was greatly curtailed in the legislation, whereby minor, first time offenders had to be referred to panels.[37] The research by Newburn et al confirms this point, as 45% of the magistrates interviewed felt that the lack of discretion in the legislation undermined their authority.[38] Crawford and Newburn also found that some panels had difficulty devising suitable plans because of a lack of local resources, and that panel members believed that adequate local facilities and resources were crucial to the success of panels.[39]

After the publication of this evaluation of the referral orders, further research was conducted to follow up issues that had arisen.[40] This resulted in key recommendations to improve the delivery of the orders, including ensuring consistent implementation of guidance on reprimands and final warnings, with a clear process for sending back to the police cases where there was a denial on arrest but a guilty plea at court. There was also a recommendation that referral orders should not be extended to young offenders convicted after a 'not guilty' plea and that in certain circumstances a referral order may be given to individuals with a previous conviction. Subsequently, the Government introduced changes to help address such concerns, contained under the Criminal Justice and Immigration Act 2008.

Research evaluating referral orders has yet to establish whether such orders are having net-widening effects, drawing minor offenders further into the criminal justice system. There are concerns as to whether such orders are proportionate and there are questions over their longer term impact on recidivism, especially by comparison to other disposals.[41] More fundamental problems with the referral order relate to the extent to which they actually embrace the principles of restorative justice. The fact that there is limited victim involvement in the process is a major cause for concern. In their research, Newburn et al, note that a victim attended in only 13% of cases where at least an initial panel meeting was held.[42] More recently, a joint inspection of youth offending teams in 2007 found that only 8% of referral orders included a victim at the panel

[34] *Youth Justice Board Annual Review* (2002, Youth Justice Board).

[35] T. Newburn, A. Crawford, R. Earle, S. Goldie, C. Hale, A. Hallam, G. Masters, A. Netten, R. Saunders, K. Sharpe and S. Uglow '*The Introduction of Referral Orders into the Youth Justice System* (2002, Home Office Research Study 242).

[36] *Ibid*

[37] C. Ball 'A Significant Move Towards Restorative Justice, or a Recipe for Unintended Consequences?' (2000) *Criminal Law Review* 211.

[38] T. Newburn, A. Crawford, R. Earle, S. Goldie, C. Hale, A. Hallam, G. Masters, A. Netten, R. Saunders, K. Sharpe and S. Uglow '*The Introduction of Referral Orders into the Youth Justice System* (2002, Home Office Research Study 242).

[39] A.Crawford and T. Newburn, *Youth Offending and Restorative Justice: Implementing Reform in Youth Justice* (2003, Willan Publishing).

[40] Youth Justice Board *Referral Orders: Research into the issues raised in 'The Introduction of the Referral Order into the Youth Justice System'* (2003, Youth Justice Board).

[41] S.Mullan and D.O'Mahony *A Review of Recent Youth Justice Reforms in England and Wales* (2003, Northern Ireland Office).

[42] T. Newburn, A. Crawford, R. Earle, S. Goldie, C. Hale, A. Hallam, G. Masters, A. Netten, R. Saunders, K. Sharpe and S. Uglow '*The Introduction of Referral Orders into the Youth Justice System* (2002, Home Office Research Study 242).

meeting.[43] Such low levels of victim participation obviously greatly limits any chance of 'encounter, reparation, reintegration and participation', supposedly central for restorative justice.[44] Moreover, given these orders are mandatory for the courts, the issue of consent for participants - a crucial element for restorative justice - is seriously undermined.

INTEGRATING RESTORATIVE JUSTICE INTO YOUTH JUSTICE

Reflecting on the development of restorative justice in youth justice in England and Wales it is clear that it has been limited in two broad respects. Firstly, the practice that has emerged has been largely diversionary, targeted towards first time offenders and those who have committed minor offences. Secondly, the measures available involve victims to a limited extent. As noted above, only a small minority of referral orders involve direct participation by victims in the process, despite the underlying importance of victim participation as a key aspect for the successful delivery of restorative justice. Moreover, there is little evidence that referral orders allow victims a meaningful role in deciding how the offence is dealt with. The limited involvement of victims obviously restricts their restorative potential and impact. Thus, while there have been many different initiatives to develop restorative justice across youth justice in England and Wales, these have only resulted in programmes that can be described as restorative practices. They have lacked a commitment to fully embrace the core principles of restorative justice and have only engaged with selective aspects of what is restorative justice. In effect, what has been delivered has only resulted in restorative practices, rather than restorative justice.

However, there are examples of restorative justice being used within youth justice systems elsewhere, which strongly embrace the core restorative justice principles. The following examines two of the most integrated restorative justice programmes, based in New Zealand and Northern Ireland. Both use restorative justice conferencing models that have been successful in involving a high proportion of victims. They deal with a wide range of offences, including very serious crimes. The methods used by both schemes also actively engage victims in the process of deciding how the offender is dealt with. As such, they are good examples of how restorative justice (rather than restorative practices) can be used to allow victims a role in 'deal[ing] with the aftermath of the offence and its implications for the future'.[45]

New Zealand

Perhaps the best known restorative justice conferencing scheme that has been integrated into a criminal justice system is the family group conferencing model developed in New Zealand under the Children, Young Persons and their Families Act 1989. The model was devised as part of a more general initiative which sought to address difficulties in the way young people, particularly minority group offenders such as the Maori and Pacific Island Polynesians, were being treated in the criminal justice and welfare systems in New Zealand.[46] The model sought to develop a more culturally sensitive approach to offending that emphasises inclusive participation and collective

[43] HM Inspectorate of Probation *Joint Inspection of Youth Offending Teams, 2006/07*. (2007, HM Inspectorate of Probation).

[44] D. Van Ness and K. Strong, *Restoring Justice* (1997, Anderson Publishing).

[45] T. Marshall *Restorative Justice: An Overview* (1999, Home Office) p5.

[46] G.Maxwell and A. Morris *Families, Victims and Culture: Youth Justice in New Zealand*. (1993, Social Policy Agency and Institute of Criminology, Victoria University of Wellington).

decision making, bringing together young people, their families and their communities to determine appropriate means of redress for victims.[47]

The family group conferencing scheme was brought into New Zealand under a reform agenda that emphasised diverting young people away from criminal justice interventions through police cautions or informal resolutions. The legislation made conferencing the main avenue of disposal for all but the most serious offences (such as murder and manslaughter). In effect, family group conferencing became the main statutory method of disposal for young offenders. Young people can only be prosecuted if they have been arrested and referred by the police through a family group conference. The courts are also required to send offenders for family group conferences, they have to consider the recommendations of the conference and they generally do not deal with cases until they have had a conference recommendation.[48]

Family group conferences are administered by the Department of Social Welfare using a youth justice co-ordinator and cases are referred either by the police following an admission of guilt or by the Youth Court for those pleading guilty or found guilty in court. The main aim of the conference is to agree a plan which should involve a process of dialogue between the offender (and his family) and the victim (and community representatives – where appropriate). In the conference the victim and offender participate in the decision about how best to deal with, and make amends for, the offending.[49] The process aims to meet victims' needs, including helping to make them feel better about what has happened to them, through the process of participation in the conference. It seeks to foster reconciliation between the parties leading to agreements that provide reparative outcomes and broader reconciliation for the offender and victim with their community.[50]

Research evaluating these family group conferences has been carried out over a number of years and has looked at various aspects of their operation, including the process and outcomes. Maxwell and Morris found that young people were able to play an active part in the conference process. Nearly half of young people felt involved in reaching the decision and in coming up with the recommendations.[51] The research found decisions in the conferencing process were very much driven by the young person and their family, rather than being imposed by the coordinator. It was apparent that families of the young people were involved in the conferences, as almost all conferences had family members present and about 40% had extended members of the family involved.

The research found that the young offenders usually felt they had a better understanding of the consequences of what they had done following the conference.[52] Following interviews with young people after conferences, most said they felt involved in the decision making process and were satisfied with the outcome. The majority of young people said they had the opportunity to say what they wanted and almost all said they understood the decisions that were made.[53]

[47] A Morris and G Maxwell 'Restorative Justice in New Zealand: Family Group Conferences as a Case Study' (1998)*Western Criminology Review* 1: 1.

[48] *Ibid.*

[49] A. Morris and G. Maxwell (eds) *Restorative Justice for Juveniles: Conferencing, Mediation and Circles* (2001, Hart Publishing).

[50] K. Daly 'Conferencing in Australia and New Zealand: Variations, Research Findings, and Prospects' in A. Morris & G. Maxwell (eds), *Restoring Justice for Juveniles: Conferencing, Mediations and Circles* (2001, Hart Publishing).

[51] G. Maxwell and A. Morris *Families, Victims and Culture: Youth Justice in New Zealand.* (1993, Social Policy Agency and Institute of Criminology, Victoria University of Wellington).

[52] G.Maxwell, V. Kingi, J. Robertson, A. Morris and C. Cunningham*Achieving Effective Outcomes: Youth Justice in New Zealand* (2004, Ministry of Social Development).

[53] G. Maxwell and A. Morris *Families, Victims and Culture: Youth Justice in New Zealand.* (1993, Social Policy Agency and Institute of Criminology, Victoria University of Wellington,).

Not all young people felt so positively following their conference. Some complained that they did not feel fully involved and felt too intimidated to say what they wanted to. However as Maxwell et al note, the overall picture regarding involvement and participation in conferences was far more positive than for young people who appear in the courts.[54] Furthermore, there was little doubt that those participants who had experienced court and conferencing preferred the conference.

In relation to victims, the experience of family group conferencing has generally been shown to be positive and research has consistently illustrated that such conferences can more fully involve victims than conventional criminal justice. Importantly, the family group conferences give victims the right to be present in the process. Good preparation is important for victims, so they understand what they can realistically get from it and how it might help them. Victims were generally willing to meet the offender and wanted to be involved in the process. The research showed that only 6% of victims said they did not want to meet the offender.[55] Later research found that the most common reasons victims gave for not attending conferences were not wanting to meet the young person or their family, or that they wanted to attend but were unable to do so, underlining the importance of adequate victim preparation.[56]

Many victims involved in conferences found it to be a positive process and felt better as a result of participating. Subsequent research showed that those victims who attended conferences were able express their views and were given a chance to explain how the offence had impacted on them.[57] Indeed, about 60% of victims said they found the conference to be helpful, positive and rewarding. Aspects of the conference they found particularly rewarding included being given the opportunity tell the young person what they felt as a result of the crime and being able to contribute to the decision making process regarding what should happen to the young person.

Early research in New Zealand found that some victims reported feeing worse after attending their conference.[58] The most frequent reasons were because they thought the young person was not remorseful, or that they were unable to express themselves properly in the conference. Others felt their concerns were not properly addressed, or they had not been listened to. However, later research by Maxwell et al found only 5% of victims said they felt worse following the conference.[59] The later results may have been a reflection of improved practice in terms of preparing victims before conferences and supporting them after. This research highlights the importance of providing training for effective mediation and managing conferences, so victims' needs are properly met and they have realistic expectations of what can be achieved. This research revealed that many victims felt the conference had helped them put the incident behind them and 81% of victims said they felt better after the conference.

In terms of levels of satisfaction with conference outcomes, generally the research showed high levels of satisfaction, especially from young people and their families. For example, the research by Morris and Maxwell found that 84% of young people and

54 G. Maxwell, A. Morris and H. Hayes 'Conferencing and restorative justice' in D. Sullivan and L. Tifft (eds), *Handbook of Restorative Justice: A Global Perspective* (2006, Routledge,).

55 G. Maxwell and A. Morris *Families, Victims and Culture: Youth Justice in New Zealand.* (1993, Social Policy Agency and Institute of Criminology, Victoria University of Wellington,).

56 G. Maxwell, V. Kingi, J. Robertson, A. Morris and C. Cunningham *Achieving Effective Outcomes: Youth Justice in New Zealand* (2004, Ministry of Social Development,).by Maxwell et al (2004).

57 *Ibid.*

58 A. Morris and G. Maxwell 'Restorative Justice in New Zealand: Family Group Conferences as a Case Study' (1998)*Western Criminology Review* 1: 1.

59 G. Maxwell, V. Kingi, J. Robertson, A. Morris and C. Cunningham *Achieving Effective Outcomes: Youth Justice in New Zealand* (2004, Ministry of Social Development).

85% of their parents said they were satisfied with the outcomes of the family group conferences.[60] Only a small number of young persons (9%) and their parents (11%) said they were dissatisfied with the outcome. For parents, an issue that appeared to cause dissatisfaction was the perception that some kind of help or treatment they thought necessary was not offered. For offenders it was more often related to their perceptions of the outcome and whether they felt the penalty was too severe.

Overall the research from New Zealand has been encouraging with respect to family group conferencing. It shows that most victims are usually willing to participate in restorative justice processes and they are generally positive about their experience of the process and outcomes. Family group conferencing appears to be effective in holding offenders to account and it can help them realise the harm they have caused. It also gives offenders constructive opportunities to make amends to their victims by apologising, making reparation, or performing community work or services for victims.

Northern Ireland

In the United Kingdom the only jurisdiction to adopt a mainstreamed statutory-based restorative justice conferencing model for young offenders has been Northern Ireland.[61] The introduction and mainstreaming of restorative interventions into the youth justice system in Northern Ireland was a radical departure from previous responses to young offending. The measures provide for two types of disposal, diversionary and court-ordered conferences. Both types of conference take place with a view to a youth conference co-ordinator providing a plan to the prosecutor or court on how the young person should be dealt with for their offence.

Court-ordered conferences are referred for conferencing by the court; the young person must agree to the process and they must either admit guilt, or have been found guilty in court. An important feature of the legislation is that the courts *must* refer all young persons for youth conferences, except for offences carrying a mandatory life sentence. The court *may* refer cases that are triable by indictment only or scheduled offences under terrorism legislation. In effect, the legislation makes conferencing mandatory except for a small number of very serious offences.

The format of the Youth Conference itself bears much similarity to the general model used in New Zealand. It normally involves a meeting, chaired by an independent and trained youth conference facilitator (employed by the Youth Conferencing Service), where the young person will be provided with the opportunity to reflect upon their actions. The victim, who is encouraged to attend, is allowed to explain to the offender how the offence affected them, in theory giving the offender an understanding of their actions and allow the victim to separate the offender from the offence. Following a dialogue a 'youth conference plan' will be devised which should take into consideration the offence, the needs of the victim and the needs of the young person. The young person must consent to the plan, before it becomes actionable. Typically plans require the young offender to complete acts, such as reparation to the victim, requirements to address their offending and/or restrictions on the young person's conduct or whereabouts. The conference may even recommend the imposition of a custodial sentence to the court.

[60] G. Maxwell and A. Morris *Families, Victims and Culture: Youth Justice in New Zealand.* (1993, Social Policy Agency and Institute of Criminology, Victoria University of Wellington).

[61] For further information see D. O'Mahony and C. Campbell 'Mainstreaming Restorative Justice for Young Offenders through Youth Conferencing: The Experience of Northern Ireland' in *International Handbook of Youth Justice* J. Junger-tas and S. Decker (eds) (2006, Springer Academic Press) p 93–116.

The youth conferencing scheme was subject to a major evaluation in 2006.[62] The findings were generally very positive concerning the impact of the scheme on victims and offenders and it was found to operate with relative success. Importantly, the research showed that youth conferencing considerably increased levels of participation for both offenders and victims in the process of seeking a just response to offending. The scheme engaged a high proportion of victims in the process: over two-thirds of conferences (69%) had a victim in attendance, which is relatively high compared with other restorative-based programmes.[63]

Victims were willing to participate in youth conferencing and 79% said they were actually 'keen' to participate. Most (91%) said the decision to take part was their own and not a result of pressure to attend. Interestingly, over three quarters (79%) of victims said they attended 'to help the young person' and many victims said they wanted to hear what the young person had to say and their side of the story. It was apparent that victims' reasons for participating were based around seeking an understanding of why the offence had happened; they wanted to hear and understand the offender and to explain the impact of the offence to the offender. A lot of work was also put into preparing victims for conferencing and they were well prepared.

Youth conferencing was by no means the easy option and most offenders found it very challenging. Offenders found the prospect of coming face to face with their victim difficult. For instance, 71% of offenders displayed nervousness at the beginning of the conference. Despite their nervousness, observations of the conferences revealed that offenders were usually able to engage well in the conferencing process, with nearly all (98%) being able to talk about the offence and the overwhelming majority (97%) accepting responsibility for what they had done.

The direct involvement of offenders in conferencing and their ability to engage in dialogue contrasts with the conventional court process, where offenders are usually afforded a passive role - generally they do not speak other than to confirm their name, plea and understanding of the charges - and are normally represented and spoken for by legal counsel throughout their proceedings. Similarly, victims were able to actively participate in the conferencing process and many found the experience valuable in terms of understanding why the offence had been committed and in gaining some sort of apology and restitution. This too contrasts with the typical experience of victims in the conventional court process where they often find themselves excluded and even alienated, or simply used as witnesses for evidential purposes if the case is contested. A clear endorsement of victims' willingness to become involved in a process which directly deals with the individuals that have victimised them was evident in that 88% of victims said they would recommend conferencing to a person in a similar situation to themselves.

A recent qualitative study by Maruna et al (2007) of the longer-term impacts of youth conferencing process on young offenders in Northern Ireland has also found 'many of the post-conference outcomes were positive',[64] and a report produced by the Criminal Justice Inspectorate in 2008 has corroborated those findings.[65] This is not to

[62] C.Campbell, R. Devlin, D. O'Mahony, J. Doak, J. Jackson, T. Corrigan, and K. McEvoy *Evaluation of the Northern Ireland Youth Conference Service*, NIO Research and Statistics Series: Report No. 12. (2006, Belfast, Northern Ireland Office).

[63] See for example, T. Newburn, A. Crawford, R. Earle, S. Goldie, C. Hale, A. Hallam, G. Masters, A. Netten, R. Saunders, K. Sharpe and S. Uglow '*The Introduction of Referral Orders into the Youth Justice System* (2002, Home Office Research Study 242); D.O'Mahony and J. Doak 'Restorative Justice: Is more better?' (2004) *Howard Journal*, 43: 484.

[64] S.Maruna, S.Wright, J. Brown, F.Van Marle, R. Devlin and M. Liddle *Youth Conferencing as Shame Management: Results of a Long-term Follow-up Study* (2007, Northern Ireland Youth Justice Agency) p. 2.

[65] Criminal Justice Inspectorate, *Inspection of the Youth Conferencing Service* (2008, Northern Ireland, Criminal Justice Inspectorate).

suggest that the integration of restorative justice within criminal justice through youth conferencing works effectively all the time and in all cases. Some cases are not suitable for conferencing, such as where the young person is unwilling to actively participate, or where the evidence or facts are disputed. However, when used for suitable cases, the research evidence has been largely positive and there is now a considerable international body of research demonstrating advantages of integrating restorative justice within criminal justice for offenders, victims and the broader community.[66]

There is emerging research evidence that shows that the youth conferencing system in Northern Ireland is having positive impacts in terms of reducing reoffending rates. Figures that compare the re-offending rates of young people given a range of sentences in Northern Ireland demonstrate that those given restorative conferencing have a relatively low level of reoffending.[67] Much of the difference in reoffending rates across disposal types can largely be explained by differences in the characteristics of offenders and the types offences for which they are convicted. However, the research shows that those given court-ordered youth conferences have a lower level of reoffending (45%) than those given community based sentences (54%) or custodial sentences (68%).[68]

A number of studies have looked at the issue of reconviction and restorative interventions more generally. For example, in a wide review of international studies of differing criminal justice programmes it was found that restorative programmes produced a significant reduction in reoffending over a follow-up period.[69] Programmes which had clear restorative objectives, goals and principles appeared to deliver the strongest reductions in recidivism. Programmes which included more serious offences and violent offenders were also able to produce the most significant reductions in recidivism.[70]

Further recent research in England has shown that the way in which offenders experience restorative interventions is related to subsequent offending.[71] This research reveals that offenders who felt the restorative intervention had made them realise the harm they had caused and found the experience useful, as well as those who had wanted to meet the victim and were observed to be actively engaged in the conference, were significantly less likely to be reconvicted.[72] These findings support the broad theoretical work on effective practice, which emphasises the importance of the restorative elements, such as: bringing the parties together; working towards meeting needs; seeking to repair injuries caused, and thus restoring relationships.[73]

Other studies have looked in detail at the experiences of participants in restorative justice and how this is related to recidivism. These broadly confirm the importance of

[66] See for example: D. Miers *An International Review of Restorative Justice*(2001, Home Office); L. Sherman and H. Strang, *Restorative Justice: The Evidence* (2007, The Smith Institute); J. Shapland, G. Robinson and A. Sorsby, *Restorative Justice in Practice* (2011, Routledge). However, Goldson is critical of restorative youth conferencing, especially as a model for criminal justice reform as proposed by the Commission on Youth Crime and Antisocial Behaviour (2010) in England and Wales: B. Goldson, 'Time for a Fresh Start' (2011) *Youth Justice* 11(1), 3.

[67] D. Lyness 'Northern Ireland Youth Re-offending: Results from the 2005 Cohort' Statistics and Research Statistical Bulletin (2008, Northern Ireland Statistics and Research Agency).

[68] D. Lyness and S. Tate 'Northern Ireland Youth Re-offending: Results from the 2008 Cohort' Statistics and Research Statistical Bulletin (2011, Northern Ireland, Department of Justice).

[69] J. Bonta, T. Jesseman, T. Rugge and R. Cormier 'Restorative Justice and Recidivism: Promises Made, Promises Kept?' in D. Sullivan and L. Tifft (eds), *Handbook of Restorative Justice* (2008, Routledge).

[70] For an very complete review of the research evidence see L.Sherman and H. Strang *Restorative Justice: The Evidence* (2007, London, Smith Institute).

[71] J. Shapland, A. Atkinson, H. Atkinson, J. Dignan, L. Edwards, J. Hibbert, M. Howes, J. Johnstone, G Robinson and A Sorsby *Does restorative justice affect reconviction? The fourth report from the evaluation of three schemes* (2008, Ministry of Justice Research Series, 10/08).

[72] *Ibid.* p iv.

[73] R. Classen *Restorative Justice – Fundamental Principles* (1996, presented to the UN Alliance of NGO's Working Party on Restorative Justice).

the impact that the encounter between the victim and offender has in a conference, especially on the offender.[74] A large study in New Zealand found those who complete restorative conferences were less likely to reoffend when the conference was rated as inclusive, fair and forgiving.[75] It appears that allowing the young person to 'make up' for what they have done was important, as was avoiding stigmatising them as 'bad' individuals. Thus, the quality of the restorative conference and the experience of the young person is an important determinant of subsequent reoffending. In other words, conferences that succeed in achieving restorative justice goals are more likely to reduce the probability of reoffending.

Discussion

The restorative justice schemes developed in Northern Ireland and New Zealand use conferencing models that adhere closely to what can be described as 'restorative justice'. They are based on voluntary participation and consent. They seek to bring victims and offenders together to discuss the offence and actively involve the parties in deciding how the matter is dealt with. The schemes are set in legislation and require the courts to refer cases for conferencing. They are used for more serious offences, and repeat offenders. The conferencing process is integral to the sentencing process, rather than a diversionary measure. Both systems were brought about through major changes to their juvenile justice systems and they received significant financial investment and support when established. The schemes clearly show that restorative justice can be successfully implemented within youth justice and victims can play an integral part in the process. Furthermore, there is a growing body of evidence to show that schemes which fully embrace restorative principles and deliver restorative justice are effective in producing high levels of satisfaction for participants and reduced levels of reoffending.[76]

However, England and Wales has seen only limited development of restorative justice within youth justice over the last decade. The restorative programmes that have emerged have largely been used as diversionary tools, or as alternative ways of dealing with young people who offend (other than prosecution through the courts). This approach is evident across all of the disposals available, from mediation and final warnings to referral orders. For example, the final warning scheme allows young people who have offended to be given a formal restorative police warning, rather than being prosecuted. Similarly, the recent introduction of the youth restorative disposal gives the police a diversionary method of dealing with young offenders by way of a summary disposal, similar to a reprimand or final warning. It provides the police with a diversionary tool to handle young people who have committed offences, other than prosecution.

The restorative provisions currently available have also been largely directed towards minor offences and first time offenders. Many of the mediation programmes only deal with minor criminal acts or neighbourhood disputes, which are unlikely to be brought through the criminal justice system.[77] The final warning schemes were specifically designed to deal with young offenders who have not been cautioned or prosecuted

[74] L. Sherman and H. Strang, *Restorative Justice: The Evidence* (2007, The Smith Institute).

[75] G. Maxwell, V. Kingi, J. Robertson, A. Morris and C. Cunningham *Achieving Effective Outcomes: Youth Justice in New Zealand* (2004, Ministry of Social Development,).

[76] L. Sherman and H Strang, *Restorative Justice: The Evidence* (2007, The Smith Institute).

[77] There are also a range of mediation projects for adult offenders that deal with serious offences and offenders in custody, see J.Shapland, A. Atkinson, E. Colledge, J. Dignan, M. Howes, J. Johnstone, R. Pennant, G. Robinson and A. Sorsby *Implementing Restorative Justice Schemes (Crime Reduction Programme): A Report on the First Year*, Home Office Online Report 32/04. (2004, Home Office,).

previously and have not committed serious offences. Similarly, the referral order was established for young people brought before the courts for the first time. It allows cases to be dealt with through a youth offender panel, rather than the normal court process. Only recently has the referral order been slightly widened in scope, to include some young people with previous convictions, but this is restricted and the order remains primarily for those appearing before the courts for the first time.[78]

These programmes have also had limited success in involving victims. Though victim involvement is a core element of providing restorative justice, the experience of achieving this in practice in England and Wales has been poor. For example, only a very small minority of referral orders directly involve victims. Research shows only 8–13% of referral orders had a victim attend a panel meeting.[79] Such low levels of victim participation greatly limits their ability to provide a restorative process or outcomes. Similarly, for final warnings, although these are intended to be delivered restoratively, in reality few involve victims when they are delivered.[80]

Related to victim participation rates, is the extent to which victims are given an input in the restorative process and how the offence is dealt with. There is little evidence that any of the schemes in England and Wales provide a process in which the victim is given a meaningful say in how the offence is dealt with. Even the new youth restorative disposal, which has high levels of victim participation, only achieves very limited involvement of victims in its decision making process. The disposal provides a swift response to minor offending and is popular with police officers because it saves time and it delivers an apology to the victim. But there is little to suggest it involves any significant restorative intervention and few cases are referred on to youth offending teams for further interventions.[81] The disposal largely arms the police with another mechanism to informally deal with offending by way of an immediate warning that includes an apology, rather than providing any substantive restorative justice. Similarly, the referral order lacks a strong restorative justice element. As noted previously, few victims are involved in the process and there is little room for them to play a part in deciding how the offence is dealt with, as this is decided by the youth offending panel.[82] Victims, when involved, have largely been used to highlight the impact the offence, for the offender's benefit.[83] Furthermore, referral orders are mandatory order, which undermines consent, another crucial element needed for the delivery of restorative justice.

As noted previously, there is an important distinction between restorative justice, and what can be described as restorative practices. Restorative justice requires the incorporation of core restorative principles and for the victim to be able to play a part in collectively deciding how the offence is dealt with.[84] Restorative practices, on the other hand, only include elements of restorative justice. Some include limited victim input (so the offender may better understand the consequences of their actions),

[78] The scope of the referral order was widened by the Criminal Justice and Immigration Act 2008.

[79] T. Newburn, A. Crawford, R. Earle, S. Goldie, C. Hale, A. Hallam, G. Masters, A. Netten, R.Saunders, K. Sharpe and S. Uglow *The Introduction of Referral Orders into the Youth Justice System* (London, Home Office Research Study 242, 2002); HM Inspectorate of Probation *Joint Inspection of Youth Offending Teams, 2006/07* (2007, HM Inspectorate of Probation,).

[80] C. Hoyle 'Restorative Justice Policing in Thames Valley' (2009)*Journal of Police Studies, Cahiers Politiestudies* 2009–2.

[81] A. Rix, K. Skidmore, R. Self, T. Holt, and S. Raybould *Youth Restorative Disposal Process Evaluation* (2011, Youth Justice Board).

[82] T. Newburn, A. Crawford, R. Earle, S. Goldie, C. Hale, A. Hallam, G. Masters, A Netten, R. Saunders, K. Sharpe and S. Uglow '*The Introduction of Referral Orders into the Youth Justice System* (2002, Home Office Research Study 242).

[83] A. Newbury '"I Would Have Been Able to Hear What They Think": Tensions in Achieving Restorative Outcomes in The English Youth Justice System' (2011)*Youth Justice: An International Journal* Vol 11, 3.

[84] T. Marshall *Restorative Justice: An Overview* (1999, Home Office).

however, they often fall short of providing full restorative justice. In reality, the restorative measures currently available in England and Wales generally facilitate a level of participation that can only be described as partially restorative.

Yet, for over a decade there have been sustained calls to incorporate restorative justice in youth justice and criminal justice in England and Wales. The Crime and Disorder Act 1998 and the Youth Justice and Criminal Evidence Act 1999, were the first pieces of legislation that facilitated a 'restorative justice' approach to the delivery of final warnings and referral orders. Since then, the Home Office, Youth Justice Board, Association of Chief Probation Officers and the Crown Prosecution Office have jointly promoted the further involvement of victims and of using a 'restorative approach to make final warnings more effective and meaningful'.[85] They highlight the impact of a final warning on a young offender, which can be significantly enhanced by delivering it restoratively. In relation to the introduction of referral orders, the primary aim of the order sought to prevent young people from re-offending and to provide a restorative justice approach for dealing with young offenders. The order sought to emphasise 'responsibility, reparation and rehabilitation', enabling offenders to become aware of and take responsibility for the consequences of their offending and to have the opportunity to make reparation to victims and the wider community. The process was also designed to give victims the opportunity to say how they have been affected by the offence, ask questions, receive an explanation or apology and discuss how the offender can make practical reparation for the harm that has been caused.[86] As such, this restorative measure was introduced into the youth justice system with the aim of enabling young people to take responsibility for their offending through a system which helps them understand the impact and consequences of their actions on victims and the broader community. The measures were also designed to accommodate victim-offender mediation and to involve service providers (youth offending teams) in a process of restorative justice.

The importance of giving victims a greater role in the delivery of justice and in enabling restorative justice to play a part in criminal justice were specifically outlined by central Government in Home Office publications in 2006.[87] The Youth Justice Board stated its commitment to 'placing restorative justice at the heart of the youth justice system' and has noted how restorative justice can help reduce offending, better support victims of crime, and help build public confidence.[88] Thus the rhetoric used by Government and key service providers appears to show them strongly wedded to incorporating restorative justice within youth justice and endorsing it as a beneficial process, advancing the aims of delivering more effective criminal justice.

Similarly, service providers and other organisations have been active in promoting restorative justice within youth justice. The Prison Reform Trust in its publication 'Out of Trouble' in 2009, specifically supported the adoption of an integrated system of restorative justice, along the lines of the model developed in Northern Ireland. They suggest this could bring benefits to victims, offenders and the broad community.[89] The Prison Reform Trust also advocated the adoption of a system which properly integrates victims into a restorative process, to play an active part in how young people who offend are dealt with. Similarly, the Independent Commission on Youth Crime

85 Home Office *Delivering Simple, Speedy, Summary Justice* (2006, The Home Office,).

86 Ministry of Justice *Referral Order Guidance* (2009, Ministry of Justice).

87 Home Office *Rebalancing the Criminal Justice System*(2006, The Home Office)and Home Office *Delivering Simple, Speedy, Summary Justice* (2006, The Home Office).

88 Youth Justice Board *Developing Restorative Justice: An Action Plan* (2006,Youth Justice Board).

89 J. Jacobson and P. Gibbs *Out of Trouble* (2009, Prison Reform Trust).

published proposals in 2010 promoting the adoption of restorative justice within criminal justice and youth justice.[90] They see restorative justice as an approach in which those with a stake in an offence can collectively resolve how to deal with the offence and offender. Thus, offenders agree to discuss the consequences of their behaviour, its effects on the victim(s), and consider how to make amends. Victims are able to make the offender aware of the harm they have experienced and to discuss what remedies would be acceptable. The commission recommended that youth conferencing should become the centrepiece of responses to all but the most serious offences committed by children and young people in England and Wales. Similarly, the Criminal Justice Alliance in 2011, a coalition of organisations and criminal justice service providers, strongly encouraged the Government to place a 'duty on all criminal justice agencies to offer restorative justice' for victims of crime and offenders.[91]

The Government's Sentencing Green Paper 'Breaking the Cycle', published in 2010 as part of plans for fundamental changes to the criminal justice system, made clear its commitment to developing the use of restorative justice at all stages of the criminal justice system, for both young and adult offenders.[92] The paper proposed increasing the range and availability of restorative justice approaches to support reparation and, in appropriate cases, making it a fundamental part of the sentencing process. It suggested that this may be most appropriate as part of a broader approach to support victims and witnesses. In relation to youth justice, the paper broadly endorsed the use of restorative justice.[93] Specifically, it proposed strengthening the referral order, so it has a clearer restorative approach. It encouraged the use of restorative justice across the youth justice sentencing framework and recommended drawing from the experience of youth conferencing in Northern Ireland.

However, despite all of the public rhetoric and sustained calls for restorative justice to be incorporated within youth justice, the development and delivery of actual services that can be described as 'restorative justice' has simply not materialised. Making sense of the limited progress over the past decade is difficult to understand, particularly given the strong support. It appears one of the main obstacles that has hindered the emergence of restorative justice has arisen due to a lack of commitment to fully embrace the core principles of restorative justice in youth justice. Thus while the Government has been willing to espouse the importance of giving victims further rights, of providing a fairer system of justice and of supporting the development of restorative programmes within youth justice,[94] in reality its approach has been much more conservative and limited in scope. In effect, the Government seems willing to promote restorative practices, but it has not been willing to fully embrace what is restorative justice.

This approach is evident in the Government's response to the sentencing Green Paper 'Breaking the Cycle'.[95] While the paper strongly supports the development of restorative programmes and the broad rights of victims in youth justice, it provides little support for the development of full-blooded restorative justice. It sees restorative measures as only appropriate for low level offenders and suitable as an alternative to

[90] Independent Commission on Youth Crime *Time for a Fresh Start*, (2010, London).

[91] Criminal Justice Alliance (2011) *Restorative Justice: Time for Action*, See www.criminaljusticealliance.org (accessed Dec 2011).

[92] Ministry of Justice *Breaking the Cycle: Effective Punishment, Rehabilitation and Sentencing of Offenders* (2010, The Stationary Office).

[93] Ibid, see chapter 5 Youth Justice, p 67–76.

[94] Ibid, see especially chapter 1 Punishment and Payback and chapter 5 Youth Justice.

[95] Ministry of Justice *Breaking the Cycle: Government Response* (2011, The Stationary Office).

formal criminal justice action.[96] The proposals include giving victims a more central role in the criminal justice system, so they have the opportunity to explain the harm crime causes, and that sentences ensure offenders make amends, especially through the use of victim impact statements, which can be submitted prior to sentencing. While the response paper suggests the Government will improve restorative justice provision, this is limited to low-level offending and encourages its use for out-of-court and informal disposals. It calls for the development of minimum standards for youth offending teams using restorative justice and seeks to make the referral order a more restorative disposal for young offenders. This is to be achieved by increasing training given to referral order panel members and by removing some restrictions on when the order can be imposed. As such, the Government's approach to restorative justice appears strong on rhetoric but it is weak on commitments that actually deliver restorative justice.

The lack of commitment to deliver restorative justice has also been reflected in the way many programmes have been funded in the recent past. Poor financial provision has undermined the development of many restorative programmes. For example, restorative based mediation programmes that have been developed have experienced financial difficulties which have undermined their ability provide services. This has also resulted in some good mediation services being developed, but subsequently closed when funding has run out. Likewise, the referral order has been imposed on local youth offending teams, without significant additional financial support. Youth offending teams have to deliver a wide range of services to young offenders under very tight financial constraints. Yet, as the research from Northern Ireland and New Zealand demonstrates, properly engaging victims in a restorative process is a resource intensive and time consuming process, if it is to be conducted properly. Arguably, this has resulted in youth offending teams being unable to prioritise victim involvement, beyond their other statutory obligations.[97] The Government has also recognised that local agencies lack financial incentives and opportunities to develop effective alternatives to custody for young people.[98] Furthermore, there are strict time limits in which the referral order needs to be implemented. This makes it even more difficult for youth offending teams and offender panels to properly involve victims, whilst dealing with the needs of offenders and the prompt delivery of the order.

An important point that appears to have undermined the growth of restorative justice relates to the way the programmes in England and Wales have actually evolved. The emergence of new restorative programmes has been largely dependent on the successful implementation and evaluation of existing schemes. In particular, there has been a reluctance to consider new schemes, without clear evidence of success, like showing participants are satisfied with it and reducing re-offending rates.[99] But the research evidence relating to the effectiveness of restorative programmes shows them to be most effective with more serious offences, when victims have direct role in the process, and when they provide meaningful interactions between the participants, dealing with the offence and its aftermath.[100] However, as noted above, the restorative justice schemes in England and Wales have centred on programmes which have targeted low level offending, first time offenders and have provided limited engagement with victims. They have provided restorative practices, rather than restorative justice.

[96] Ibid, see especially sections 25 to 30 pages 8–11.

[97] See also L. Sherman and H,.Strang *Restorative Justice*, (2008, Youth Justice Board).

[98] Ministry of Justice *Breaking the Cycle: Effective Punishment, Rehabilitation and Sentencing of Offenders* (2010, The Stationary Office, p73); Ministry of Justice. *Breaking the Cycle: Government Response* (2011, The Stationary Office).

[99] Restorative Justice Council *A new way of doing justice: The response of the Restorative Justice Council to the Sentencing Green Paper – Breaking the Cycle* (2011, Restorative Justice Council).

[100] L. Sherman and H. Strang, *Restorative Justice: The Evidence* (2007, The Smith Institute).

These types of schemes are actually the least likely to provide significant positive results, thus it is probably unsurprising that progress has been so slow.

The continued reluctance to extend restorative justice to more serious offences and offenders may be related to a perception that restorative justice is a soft option.[101] However, evidence shows that restorative justice is a demanding process and offenders find it very challenging, especially when they have to explain their actions in front of their family and the victim in a conference.[102] The Government approach, which is clearly driven by a political agenda of being seen to be tough on crime, continues to emphasise using restorative interventions for low-level offending, despite it being better suited to dealing with serious offences.[103]

Reflecting on the developments in England and Wales, there are lessons that can be learnt for other jurisdictions considering the adoption of restorative justice. The research from New Zealand and Northern Ireland shows that it is a demanding process and it requires substantial change to be properly established. It requires a significant ongoing investment in terms of resources, time and effort, to be delivered properly. Restorative justice is a challenging process for offenders and victims, and research clearly shows it to be most suitable and effective with more serious types of offences and offenders.[104] Indeed, it has been argued that using restorative programmes to deal with minor offences, can potentially lead to net-widening – drawing young people, who have committed minor offences into demanding criminal justice interventions.[105] Thus, it is questionable whether the widespread use of restorative programmes for minor criminal offences is either desirable, cost efficient, or effective in terms of its impact on offenders or victims.[106]

There is now a strong body of research evidence showing the positive results of adopting restorative justice measures within criminal justice for suitable cases and in the right circumstances. This is not to suggest that restorative justice offers some kind of 'silver bullet' for all the problems of criminal justice. However, countries considering the adoption of restorative justice can learn much from the evidence available from jurisdictions which have implemented and utilised it effectively. Whilst restorative practices may be helpful in providing elements that are restorative, they are not the same as delivering restorative justice. The experience from England and Wales demonstrates that introducing restorative practices in small steps can actually lead to very little restorative justice being delivered.

[101] Ministry of Justice *Breaking the Cycle: Government Response* (2011, The Stationary Office).

[102] D. O'Mahony and C. Campbell 'Mainstreaming Restorative Justice for Young Offenders through Youth Conferencing: The Experience of Northern Ireland' in *International Handbook of Youth Justice* J Junger-tas and S Decker (eds) (2006, Springer Academic Press).

[103] L. Sherman and H. Strang, *Restorative Justice: The Evidence* (2007, The Smith Institute).

[104] *Ibid.*

[105] D.O'Mahony and J. Doak 'Restorative Justice: Is More Better?' (2004) *Howard Journal*, 43: 484.

[106] L. Sherman and H. Strang, *Restorative Justice: The Evidence* (2007, The Smith Institute) p. 57.

Name Index

In memory of my parents

Smt. Achamma and Sri Sidda Reddy

Contents